Interpretation and Revision of International Boundary Decisions

This book seeks to examine a legal theme which occurs typically with respect to judgments and awards given by international courts and tribunals in the matter of boundary disputes. The theme in question is predicated on the fact that, from time to time, litigating States will find difficulties with these awards and judgments and seek to delay implementation of the decision or modify the alignment determined by the tribunal. The reason why dissatisfaction features prominently in boundary and territorial decisions is because questions of title and territorial sovereignty nearly always go to the very core of statehood, creating situations of unease at best and conflict at worst. Thus, while disputing States may resort to adjudication and arbitration for the settlement of a boundary problem, that alone is no guarantee that the dispute will thereafter terminate. Indeed, the author shows convincingly that the history of arbitration, going as far back as ancient Greece, is closely intertwined with problems of territorial claims and frontier disputes. Two remedies frequently relied on by litigating States in this context are those of interpretation and revision. The author sheds light on how, when and in what circumstances a tribunal is able to interpret or revise either its own or another tribunal's decisions on boundary problems. By exploring these issues, the author seeks to provide a rigorous analysis in an area of law which has escaped the attention of many international lawyers.

KAIYAN HOMI KAIKOBAD is Reader in International Law, Department of Law at the University of Durham

---

CAMBRIDGE STUDIES IN INTERNATIONAL AND COMPARATIVE LAW

Established in 1946, this series produces high quality scholarship in the fields of public and private international law and comparative law. Although these are distinct legal sub-disciplines, developments since 1946 confirm their interrelation.

Comparative law is increasingly used as a tool in the making of law at national, regional and international levels. Private international law is now often affected by international conventions, and the issues faced by classical conflicts rules are frequently dealt with by substantive harmonisation of law under international auspices. Mixed international arbitrations, especially those involving state economic activity, raise mixed questions of public and private international law, while in many fields (such as the protection of human rights and democratic standards, investment guarantees and international criminal law) international and national systems interact. National constitutional arrangements relating to 'foreign affairs', and to the implementation of international norms, are a focus of attention.

The Board welcomes works of a theoretical or interdisciplinary character, and those focusing on the new approaches to international or comparative law or conflicts of law. Studies of particular institutions or problems are equally welcome, as are translations of the best work published in other languages.

A list of books in the series can be found at the end of this volume.

Interpretation and Revision of International Boundary Decisions

Kaiyan Homi Kaikobad
University of Durham

CAMBRIDGE
UNIVERSITY PRESS

CAMBRIDGE UNIVERSITY PRESS
Cambridge, New York, Melbourne, Madrid, Cape Town, Singapore, São Paulo

CAMBRIDGE UNIVERSITY PRESS
The Edinburgh Building, Cambridge CB2 8RU, UK

Published in the United States of America by Cambridge University Press, New York

www.cambridge.org
Information on this title: www.cambridge.org/9780521869126

First published 2007

Printed in the United Kingdom at the University Press, Cambridge

A catalogue record for this publication is available from the British Library

ISBN 978-0-521-86912-6

In memory of my sister

Every question in the judgment relating to the moneys and boundaries of Apollo I will decide as is true to the best of my belief, nor will I in any wise give false judgments for the sake of favour, friendship or enmity; and the sentence passed in accordance with the judgment I will enforce to the best of my power with all possible speed, and I will make just restoration to the god. Nor will I receive gifts, neither I myself nor any one else on my behalf, nor will I give aught of the common moneys to any one or receive it myself. These things I will thus do and if I swear truly may I have many blessings, but if I swear falsely may Themis and Pythian Apollo and Leto and Artemis and Hestia and eternal fire and all gods and goddesses take from me salvation by a most dreadful doom, may they permit me myself and my race to enjoy neither children nor crops nor fruits nor property, and may they cast me forth in my lifetime from the possessions which I now have, if I shall swear falsely.

Oath taken by the Delphian Amphictiones, 117 BC (M. N. Tod, *International Arbitration Among the Greeks*, Oxford, 1913, p. 116)

Contents

Maps

Preface

The genesis of this work started interestingly enough. I was invited by Scarborough College, then part of the University of Hull, to read a paper on the relation between geography and the international law of the sea. I began to research and write the paper, but noticed soon enough that far too much attention had been paid to just one aspect of the various issues identified for discussion and decided then to redress the matter and restore some balance to the project. The aspect in question dealt with the topic of dispute settlement, with particular emphasis on the difficulties attending the judicial and arbitral settlement of maritime delimitation disputes. The conference at Scarborough over, I went back to the work accumulated on dispute settlement and set upon re-examining the issues in greater detail, but once again realised that there were still a number of matters which warranted discussion at greater length, and that, importantly, these matters were not confined to maritime delimitation; indeed, they encompassed delimitation issues on land as well.

Nonetheless, I elected to focus on the problems attending the adjudication and arbitration of maritime delimitation disputes and went on to publish my work in the periodical *The Law and Practice of International Courts and Tribunals*, but the fact that there was still a significant gap in the literature on related matters proved to be a strong catalyst for further investigation. Eventually, after more writing and research, the decision was taken to provide a detailed account of just two important but relatively unexplored aspects of the powers generally exercised by international tribunals, namely, the powers of interpretation and revision of judgments and arbitral awards. This decision was prompted by two facts. In the first place, the interpretation and revision of decisions of such tribunals were, as between themselves, sufficiently related in juridical terms as to constitute a doctrinal unity. In the second place, and as against other areas of the law, these two categories were sufficiently discrete and self-contained to justify rigorous examination at length. It was convenient therefore to separate them from other aspects of the scrutiny already carried out with a view to producing a sustained monograph on the selected topics.

Certainly, in some ways, the scope of the subject-matter is narrow in that the powers of revision and interpretation examined in this study are limited to decisions adopted by international courts and arbitral tribunals with respect to boundary disputes. This, of course, reflects in part the original survey referred to above. It is evident that a piece of work, which has its genesis in a conference paper devoted to the geographical and legal aspects of the maritime territory of coastal States, would be limited by one underlying feature of this topic, namely, questions of title to territory.

The fact, however, is that, despite the limited scope of the subject-matter examined, there is a good amount of international law to be investigated, discussed and analysed within the area of territorial and boundary disputes. It is of interest that, on the one hand, as Felix Frankfurter and James M. Landis wrote in 1925 on the Compact Clause of the United States Constitution and interstate adjustments, boundary disputes are so obstinate to litigious treatment that the more complicated interstate controversies are less amenable to court control. On the other hand, territorial entities frequently opt for the settlement processes of arbitration and adjudication (indeed, as this work attempts to show, the history of arbitration is clearly entwined with such disputes). But it is also the case that, from time to time, States seek nevertheless to revisit matters decided by international tribunals, and, on occasion, seek even to claim that the award or judgment is null and void. The simple fact is that, given the enormity of the interests at stake, a theme constantly to be found in this area of law and politics is the perenniality not only of boundary and territorial problems but also of disputes with respect to settled disputes. This theme, importantly, exists not only at the national level between disputing provinces and the states of a federation or confederation but also at the international plane between sovereign nations. In a nutshell, boundary disputes and decisions provide a fertile ground for the study of the international tribunal's powers of revision and interpretation.

While it constitutes a significant reason for keeping the subject-matter within its narrow confines, this theme does not constitute the main argument for choosing this topic of international concern. The essence of the matter is that this book is not primarily dedicated to scrutinising the law and practice of international tribunals with specific reference to the powers of revision and interpretation. It is primarily intended to contribute to the body of learning in the law of title to territory. In an important sense, then, this book is an attempt to reflect upon issues of law relating to matters dealing with territory and international boundaries in the context of dispute settlement by way of adjudication and arbitration. It was this fact which informed the decision to exclude consideration of revision and interpretation on a universal basis, for that would have required examining the jurisprudence of all the global and regional international tribunals in the international legal system, including those dealing with matters of international trade, human rights and economic integration.

This, it is easy to see, would have altered fundamentally not only the character of the book but also its essential object and purpose as outlined above. It is for this reason that this study is prefaced by a legal account of some of the salient difficulties associated with the settlement of boundary and territorial disputes by way of treaties. The point of interest is that these difficulties, which include those arising from the succession of States to treaties and the unilateral denunciation and rejection of boundary treaties, judgments and awards, are treated separately from a discussion regarding the legal aspects of the dissatisfaction experienced by States in connection with the arbitration and adjudication of boundary and territorial disputes. A significant aspect of this relates to the discussion of the nullity of boundary awards and judgments.

The fundamental premise of this analysis is that a core area of the law of title to territory is comprised of the settlement of boundary and territorial disputes by way of adjudication and arbitration and accordingly that due attention must be paid to the powers of international tribunals to interpret and revise their judgments and awards. This approach is highlighted, *inter alia*, by the fact that these two judicial remedies are not always *incidental* to the main case and that therefore applications for the interpretation and revision of boundary treaties can, in some circumstances, be treated as the main case itself. There is, of course, no profit in pre-empting matters here beyond identifying another salient feature of this study. Thus, although the latter is concerned with the interpretation and revision of boundary decisions, the law regarding the purpose, scope, interpretation and application of these remedies is not confined to boundary or territorial issues, and it follows therefore that the law on the matter is of universal application.

Acknowledgments

It would not have been possible for me to write this book without the help of colleagues, friends and family members. I wish, therefore, to take advantage of these pages to record a few words of gratitude. In the Law Library on Palace Green in Durham, I have received enormous help, co-operation and indeed indulgence from a number of members of staff. Out of many, Miss Sheila Doyle, Mrs Anne Farrow, Ms Sally Hoddy, Ms Barbara Johnson and Ms Judy McKinnell have been particularly kind to and co-operative with me on every occasion. Patiently helping me with my queries and requests, the Law Library staff has been a great pillar of support. I am also grateful to Mr Shaun Hunter for his advice and help on a number of occasions. Despite having repeatedly to teach me how to work the microfilm machine, Mr Hunter seemed to embody the very notion of equanimity. Among the varied student staff, my sense of gratitude extends in particular to Miss Lucy Carey and Ms Fiona Tolan for their co-operation and assistance regarding book loans and returns over a number of years.

In the Main Library, Ms Jackie Knowles, Mrs Trixie Khoja and Ms Judith Walton have always been extremely kind to me and have on occasion gone out of the way to help. I am grateful to Mrs Khoja for, among other kindnesses, facilitating the loan of confined large-size atlases and to Ms Walton for managing efficiently my numerous requests for inter-library loans. To Mr Mamtimyn Sunuodola, the Area Studies Librarian, I extend my sincere gratitude for helping me obtain official documents issued by the Government of China by way of Chinese-language websites and for doing so with great skill and cheerful co-operation. One member of staff deserves special mention. Mr David Sowerbutts, the former Librarian, whose expertise in locating books and articles on every topic imaginable was a genuine asset to the Library, and I, for one, a regular consumer of his expertise. I sincerely thank him for all his help.

I must also mention several members of the Department of Law with a view to thanking them for their unstinted support, and I therefore express my gratitude to Miss Helen Hewitson, Mrs Sheila Jobling and Ms Claire Purdue for helping me in a variety of ways, including helping me with typing, photocopying, the ordering of books and general co-operation; and to Mr Rupert Prudom, the computer officer, for advice and assistance in information technology. For compiling the bibliography, I am very thankful to Miss Joanne Emerson, and, I must add, for her pointing out various eccentricities in several footnotes which her careful eye for detail was quick to notice.

For the cartography, my gratitude goes out to Mr David Hume and Mr Chris Orton in the Design and Imaging Unit of the Department of Geography. Their outstanding professionalism was matched by the enthusiasm and alacrity with which they drew the maps.

Several of my colleagues stand out for their graciousness. Professor Michael Bohlander was always at hand with words of advice, and both he and Professor Rosa Greaves, now Professor of European Law at the University of Glasgow, were happy to help with the translations of various French-language documents and articles. Mr Antonis Antoniadis willingly gave me his time on many occasions and never hesitated to help with advice on European Union/Community documentation. I am of course very grateful to all three of them. I also thank Dr Claire McIvor, now a lecturer at the University of Birmingham, for buoying me up from time to time with words of encouragement and support, and also to Professor Bob Sullivan, now Barber Professor of Jurisprudence at the University of Birmingham, a good friend and a great colleague. I do, however, reserve a special word of gratitude for Professor Colin Warbrick, now at the University of Birmingham, who, with his insightful comments and suggestions, has not only enhanced the strengths of this monograph but who, more generally, has been a beacon of inspiration for my teaching and research.

I must also thank staff members of the Cambridge University Press and especially Ms Finola O'Sullivan, Mrs Brenda Burke, Ms Jane O'Regan, Wendy Gater and Jodie Barnes for putting up with a large number of requests, queries and suggestions. The co-operation extended to me with respect to the late submission of the manuscript, and various aspects of editing, including the compilation of the table of cases, chapter organisation and footnote management has not been lost on me, and I want to record here my sense of gratitude to them and to the Press as a whole, not forgetting the copy-editorial manager and her team. A key figure in the whole process, Professor James Crawford, the Series Editor, provided useful suggestions and incisive comments for which I am extremely grateful. It is, however, important for me to add that, despite all the help received by me from various persons, including those mentioned above, I alone stand responsible for all the flaws and weaknesses present in this book.

It would be remiss of me not to express my thankfulness to several postgraduate students and research assistants, all of whom were courteously helpful in a large number of ways, including the photocopying of articles, securing print-outs of documents and articles, tracing books and instruments from electronic databases and for providing informal translations of documents. Here, I have to thank Dr Eleni Katselli, now lecturer at the University of Newcastle, and Mr Zeray Yihdego, Mr Francis Oni and Mr Jacques Hartman. Ms Sangeeta Shah, now at the University of Nottingham, deserves a special word of thanks for the meticulousness and conscientiousness with which she responded to all my requests and for twice helping me to procure a large set of documents after she had left the Law Department in Durham.

At home, the assistance given by our nephew, Master D. Murrell, cannot go unacknowledged. For the help he gave me by reading and dictating a good many long passages for verbatim insertion and verification, I thank him. Finally, and perhaps most importantly, I owe a debt of gratitude to my long-suffering wife for her abundant patience, cheerful encouragement and unwavering confidence in me, grounded, no doubt, in a deep sense of understanding of a profession which seems to absorb all hours of the working day and weekends. Without these assets, my work would have floundered a long time ago, and so I do thank her profusely indeed.

Durham
March, 2006.

Table of cases

International Court of Justice

Permanent Court of International Justice

Permanent Court of Arbitration

Arbitral decisions

European Court of Human Rights

Switzerland

United States

Abbreviations

AJIL	*American Journal of International Law*
BFSP	*British Foreign and State Papers*
Hazard	*Historical Collections; Consisting of State Papers, and Other Authentic Documents; Intended as Materials for an History of the United States of America*, Philadelphia, 1792, vol. 2
ICJ	International Court of Justice
ILM	*International Legal Materials*
ILR	*International Law Reports*
Moore	*History and Digest of the International Arbitrations to Which the United States Has Been a Party*, Washington DC, 1898, vols. 2 and 5
PCIJ	Permanent Court of International Justice
UNRIAA	*United Nations Reports of International Arbitral Awards*
Wetter	*The International Arbitral Process*, New York, 1979, vols. 1 and 2

PART I · INTRODUCTION

1 Introduction

I. Preliminary observations

Territoriality, it is well known, stands at the very heart of statehood.[1] Both in law and in fact, it is difficult, but not impossible, to conceptualise a State without territory. The Montevideo Convention on the Rights and Duties of States,[2] concluded in 1933, gave due weight to this when it recognised, in Article 1, that territory was one of the four component elements of an entity claiming statehood. It was this primacy which prompted Jennings to write: 'The whole course of modern history testifies to the central place of State territory in international relations.'[3] An important aspect of territoriality and of statehood is the fact that they are primarily notions of law. They do, of course, have a corresponding political and

1 Generally, on the notion of territory, territoriality and statehood, States, see De Visscher, *Theory and Reality in Public International Law*, trans. P. E. Corbett, Princeton, 1968, pp. 204–27; Verzijl, *International Law in Historical Perspective*, Part Three, *State Territory*, Leyden, 1970, pp. 1–13; Kelsen, *Principles of International Law*, 2nd edn, New York, 1966, pp. 177–82 and 307–20; Olivier, 'Aspects of the Establishment of Sovereignty and the Transfer of Authority', 14 (1988–9) *South African Yearbook of International Law* 85, especially pp. 112 *et seq.*; Jennings, *The Acquisition of Territory in International Law*, Manchester, 1963, Chapters I and V; Crawford, *The Creation of States in International Law*, Oxford, 1977, pp. 36–40; Shaw, *Title to Territory in Africa: International Legal Issues*, Oxford, 1986, Chapter 1, pp. 1–16, and Chapter 4, pp. 145–79; Brownlie, 'International Law at the Fiftieth Anniversary of the United Nations General Course of Public International Law', 255 (1995) *Hague Recueil* 9, Chapters IV, XI and XII; Schwarzenberger, *International Law*, vol. I, *International Law as Applied by International Courts and Tribunals*, London, 1957, pp. 289–309; Andrews, 'The Concept of Statehood and the Acquisition of Territory in the Nineteenth Century', 94 (1978) LQR 408; and Hill, *Claims to Territory in International Law and Relations*, Oxford (Westport Reprint), 1945. For a polemical essay, see Strydom, 'Self-Determination: Its Use and Abuse', 17 (1991–2) *South African Yearbook of International Law* 90.

2 165 LNTS 19; 137 BFSP 282.

3 Supra (note 1), p. 1. Generally, see Shaw, 'Territory in International Law', 13 (1982) NYIL 61.

factual reality, but from time to time a hiatus between law and reality can arise and create anomalies of various kinds. Thus, where a State is occupied by illegal armed force and is subsequently annexed by the occupying State, the State illegally occupied will continue in law to exist,[4] not unlike the situation of Kuwait when it was invaded, occupied and annexed by Iraq in August 1990.

Nonetheless, it cannot be doubted that the ideal of territorial sovereignty guides and informs the foreign relations of States at the most fundamental of levels. While even the slightest possibility of territorial loss or detriment is vigilantly monitored and, where necessary, opposed, no opportunity to gain or maximise territory by lawful means is passed over. It is this centrality of territory for States which helps to explain, for example, the rapid evolution of a simple municipal law declaration into a fully formed principle of customary international law. There is no doubt that the engaging prospect of gaining title to large tracts of submarine territory adjacent to the coast, once known exclusively to geographers as the continental shelf, was a catalytic agent, as it were, in the crystallisation of the 1945 United States Proclamation on the Subsoil and Seabed of the Continental Shelf[5] into a right sanctioned by international law.

In this politico-legal climate, then, a territorial or boundary dispute can almost never be welcome. Where States are unhappy with the location of a boundary line or dissatisfied with the territorial *status quo* because of its claims to territory on the other side of the alignment, the maintenance of a dispute is a necessary evil; and, for the opposing State, the existence of a claim to the whole or a part of its territory by way of a territorial or boundary dispute is an obvious source of tension. The *degree* of tension, however, is a different matter, for that is a function of several factors, including the nature and significance of the territory in dispute, and the overall cordiality of relations, or lack thereof, between the disputing States.

Although a good number are quite intractable and destined perhaps to simmer on, many disputes are relatively more manageable and at times even amenable to settlement by way of one or more of the recognised dispute resolution methods. Accordingly, it is not uncommon for disputing States to turn to adjudication or arbitration as a sensible way out of a troublesome diplomatic impasse. While the International Court of Justice has done its duty when called upon by States to resolve their territorial

[4] Cf. Oppenheim, *International Law*, 7th edn by H. Lauterpacht, London, 1955, p. 451; and, generally, see pp. 451–60. Further, see Lawrence, *The Principles of International Law*, 7th edn by P. H. Winfield, London, 1928, p. 136; and Shaw (note 3), p. 61. See also the text to note 21; and Chapter 2, section II.c.

[5] 10 Fed. Reg. 12303.

and boundary disputes, both land and maritime, some States have turned to the Permanent Court of Arbitration. Others have relied simply on *ad hoc* arbitral tribunals, not uncommonly designated by the disputing States simply as a 'Court of Arbitration' or 'Arbitral Tribunal'.

In most cases, especially where there are no controversies about consent to jurisdiction, the act of referring the matter to an international tribunal will come as a source of consolation to the litigating parties, a characteristic legitimate expectation of which is that the dispute is finally coming to an end. By agreeing to submit the dispute to an international tribunal, the disputing parties can rightly be optimistic that a period of unease, or indeed an era of tension, will disappear; and, where States are burdened by several territorial issues, a judgment by the International Court of Justice or an *ad hoc* arbitral tribunal will constitute an important step towards the ultimate narrowing of differences between them. The fact, however, is that, at times, a judgment or an award may prove to be less a source of comfort and more a basis for new or continuing conflict. Nor, indeed, can the longevity of such disputes be underestimated. The dispute between Canada and the United States regarding the Dixon Entrance is a direct result of conflicting interpretations of an award given over 100 years ago.

On many occasions, litigating parties, dissatisfied with the territorial outcome of the proceedings, may seek to challenge such unfavourable decisions in whole or in part. The dispute, thus, acquires a new layer of difficulties. The nature, extent and reasons for issuing a challenge to an arbitral or judicial decision will vary according to the law, facts and circumstances of the case, but the common thread uniting them is the fact that a serious challenge to a decision will almost always be based on law, even if it is a flawed or misconceived statement and application thereof. Indeed, one of the more enduring facts of international political life is that even the most fanciful or controversial of claims to territory are usually dressed up in the finest legal vestments. It stands to reason, then, that, because issues of territory are involved, States will not hesitate, whenever they reasonably can, to grasp at every opportunity to secure a more favourable judgment on title, or a judicial delimitation which gives them more territory, even if the territorial gains are relatively modest.

The claims States make with respect to decisions returned by tribunals are many and varied, and an account of some of these difficulties is presented in sections III.b.3, IV.c and IV.d of Chapter 2 below. It will suffice here to observe that one of the more common sources of dissatisfaction is the claim of jurisdictional *ultra vires*, that is, that the tribunal has managed to exceed the scope of its jurisdiction and that the award or judgment is therefore null and void. In other circumstances, States may choose to rely on another well-received rule of international law relating to judicial and arbitral settlement, namely, that a decision is without legal effect where an adequate statement of reasons is not provided. While the existence of serious or essential errors in the decision is also regarded as a ground for nullity of the decision to the extent of the essential error, it is the case that tribunals, upon request of the parties, may, without much ado, rectify minor clerical errors in their decisions. In any event, the precise remedy or remedies which litigating States seek to claim with respect to impugned decisions will, no doubt, depend on the law and facts of the case.

Thus, where the contention is *excès de pouvoir* or lack of a motivated decision, a State could be heard to argue that, because the entire decision is null and void, the tribunal is obliged to re-examine the case, and, by doing so, the objecting State will hope to secure a new, more favourable judgment. It may, for completeness, be added that unilateral allegations of nullity do not automatically make such decisions void, nor do they enable the objecting State to commence new proceedings. Where such allegations are resisted by the other State, it will be for an international tribunal, for which in general further consent would be needed, to examine the allegations of nullity; and until such time the decision will stand.

Be that as it may, not every plea with respect to a decision is predicated on allegations of nullity and the initiation of fresh proceedings before a different tribunal. The point here is that, at times, States will seek to contend that errors in the decisions be deleted in order to make the decision conform to the relevant principles of the law. Similarly, in certain circumstances, States may find some parts of the decision ambiguous or difficult to implement in practice; they may also find themselves unable to agree on the meaning to be attributed to certain passages therein.

Problems of this kind are known to originate in a variety of ways, including geographical uncertainties, as, for example, confusion or controversy over the location of natural features on the ground, including the source of a river or the contours of a watershed. It is evident that States are wont to dispute not only the salient *geographical effects* of a boundary award, but also some of the broader issues such as the status of the line. Discontentment for the objecting State could also be occasioned by the discovery of a new fact unknown to the tribunal at the time of the decision, leading it to request a reopening of the case with a view to a redrawing of the boundary consistent with the new fact. Thus, the discovery, say, of the 'real' source of a river, or the correct course thereof, or the determination of more precise or accurate termini of the boundary, may give a State the opportunity to request the tribunal to revise the judgment.

The common underlying theme of all these issues is that of a perceived need on the part of one State (or both States, for that matter) to secure a more favourable readjustment, for one legal reason or another, of the judgment on title to territory or the judgment boundary, and it is this fact which is of crucial significance to this study, for international law does accommodate the re-examination of judgments and awards, provided always that all the substantive and procedural criteria therefor are met. Eschewing the rules of law dealing with allegations of nullity and the existence of material or essential errors, this investigation is confined to the study of two kinds of judicial remedies, namely, the interpretation of judgments and awards and the revision of decisions on proof of discovery of a fact crucial to a decision. Firmly anchored in both customary international law and the Statute of the International Court of Justice, the remedies of interpretation and revision are ancillary modes of dispute settlement and, under the Statute, constitute part of the incidental jurisdiction of the Court. They are, therefore, available, in principle, in every kind of case before all tribunals, consent permitting. Indeed, the jurisprudence of both permanent international tribunals and *ad hoc* arbitral bodies is substantial enough to indicate that this is a rapidly developing body of law.

In order, however, to keep the study within manageable proportions, this investigation is confined to the interpretation and revision of judgments, arbitral awards and quasi-arbitral decisions[6] given by tribunals,

[6] For the purposes of this work, a quasi-arbitral decision is one which is akin to the Final Report of the Iraq–Kuwait Boundary Demarcation Commission issued in 1994, where the Commission was conscious of and took into consideration a variety of rules of international law in its decision-making process, the main object of which was to demarcate the border delimited by the Iraq–Kuwait Agreed Minutes of 1963, on which see the text to notes 24–7 below. Note, however, that the Decision of 28 July 1920 adopted by the Conference of Ambassadors regarding the Polish–Czech frontier was seen by the Permanent Court of International Justice in the *Jaworzina Boundary* advisory opinion as '[having] much in common with arbitration' insofar as the Supreme Council of the Conference of Ambassadors was 'guided by sentiments of justice and equity'. PCIJ Reports, Series B, No. 8 (1923), p. 6, at p. 29. Similarly, the *Mosul Boundary (Interpretation of Article 3, Paragraph 2 of the Treaty of Lausanne)* advisory opinion (PCIJ Reports, Series B, No. 12 (1925), p. 6) is relevant insofar as the Permanent Court of International Justice gave two alternative meanings to the term 'arbitration' and opted for the narrower interpretation 'if the intention were to convey a common and more limited conception of arbitration, namely, that which has for its object the settlement of differences between States by *judges* of their own choice and *on the basis of respect for law*'. See *ibid.*, p. 26 (emphasis in original). The Court noted that 'the arguments put forward on both sides before the Council [of the League of Nations], the settlement of the dispute in

some national but mostly international, in territorial and boundary disputes. The precise range of such decisions is described in section III below. Doctrinal extent, however, is not the only reason for limiting this work to such disputes. As indicated above, litigating parties frequently use these two judicial remedies as another chance, or as a 'last chance', to gain or regain the boundary or territory they believe they are 'entitled' to acquire or retain, as the case may be, but were unable so to do in the original proceedings; and, because a number of territorial and boundary disputes and decisions have been subject to such remedies, a body of case law relevant to interpretation and revision has emerged out of disputes involving problems of title to territory. The principles of interpretation and revision are typically applied in cases dealing with such problems.

The third reason for this relatively confined review is that it has afforded an opportunity to scrutinise certain cases which normally do not receive the same level of attention as do judgments and awards dealing directly with the merits of the case, that is, the substantive issues of title and location of the boundary. This is understandable as far as it goes, given the fact that the emphasis is usually on eliciting the finer points of law on these matters. Even so, it is believed that cases concerned with the interpretation and revision of judgments and awards can hardly be relegated to secondary status.

For one thing, issues going to or involving the merits of the dispute are not unknown in litigation generally, and are regarded as incidental to the main case, and the resolution of such issues can indeed provide valuable insights into the central problems confronting the disputant parties. At times, however, issues before the tribunal are presented as those of revision and interpretation of a judgment, but effectively constitute the main case itself, a matter discussed below. Where this is so, it is hardly appropriate to consider the decision only as an ancillary judgment, and as such deserving of greater attention. For another, this study has enabled the examination of certain cases from an altogether different perspective,

question depends, at all events for the most part, on considerations not of a legal character; moreover, it is impossible, properly speaking, to regard the Council, acting in its capacity of an organ of the League of Nations . . . as a tribunal of arbitrators'. See *ibid.* It went on to decide that the decision to be taken by the Council for the boundary between Iraq and Turkey was a definitive determination of the frontier (but not necessarily an arbitral award): p. 33. Where, therefore, law constitutes the basis for the decision it is arbitration, as for example the Decision of 13 April 2002 issued by the Eritrea–Ethiopia Boundary Commission in the matter of the *Eritrea–Ethiopia Border Delimitation* process.

occasioning a fresh look at the law. In short, a good range of legal issues has been thrown up for consideration by this study.

Finally, as far as the basis on which these two judicial remedies have been selected for scrutiny is concerned, the defining criterion is the fact that both interpretation and revision are predicated on a continuation of the judgment or award, whereas allegations of nullity are put forward as a legal escape from obligations arising from the impugned decision. Where consent can be secured, the latter category of claims serves as a basis for a rehearing *de novo* of the merits of the case, while the opposite is true for the two processes under consideration here. Certainly, it is true that claims of material errors also constitute a basis for interpretation and revision, as opposed to the wholesale negation of the boundary or territory awarded by the tribunal, and to that extent such issues cannot be ignored. In some cases, even essential errors can serve to provide a basis for continuing the judgment and where relevant these matters are investigated. By and large, however, it has been found necessary to exclude errors and mistakes from detailed consideration here.

It remains to point out that the fundamental premise of this work is grounded in the proposition that two essential vectors are at play in this sphere of international politics and that they pull in opposite directions. On the one hand, there is the basic need in both law and politics to eradicate or minimise tension and friction between States, and it is obvious therefore that one of the main sources of tension in international political life, namely, territorial and boundary disputes, needs vigorously to be discouraged as far as possible. One expression of this is the principle of stability, finality and continuity of boundary and territorial settlements, a principle which plays an axiomatic role in the international legal order.

On the other hand, there is also the need to provide relief and remedies to States which have *bona fide* grievances about a territorial or boundary disposition or location. This includes at times challenges to the very existence of a State or an international entity. The situation, therefore, becomes one in which the need for stability and finality requires States and the legal system itself to preserve the territorial *status quo* against a situation in which opposing States are loath to forego territory which they are convinced rightfully belongs to them. In short, while one vector reaches forward towards stability and continuity, the other reaches backwards in search of new, more just or more appropriate territorial or boundary arrangements.

While the doctrine of finality and continuity has been examined in other works and studies,[7] it is now appropriate to scrutinise some of the legal aspects of the difficulties and dissatisfaction attending the definitive closure to boundary and territorial disputes.[8] The examination of such issues below is predicated in the fact that the settlement of territorial and boundary disputes is inherently a difficult task not only in terms of seeking acceptable terms of compromise, especially where any gain for one party constitutes a corresponding loss for the other. The fact is that in many cases a fully satisfactory discontinuance of the dispute is difficult to achieve. This study attempts to investigate the role international law plays in situations where, despite the existence of arbitral awards and judicial decisions in the matter of territorial and boundary disputes, States seek to revisit the issues in one form or another, bringing, thus, the earlier settlements on the matter under scrutiny. It seeks, accordingly, to understand the way international law has approached these problems, and it does so by isolating and identifying the relevant rules of international law and by examining the precise remedies available to States.

The work is divided into four broad parts, the first of which is a study predicated in supplying essential legal perspectives to facilitate the examination of the central themes of this work. Accordingly, Part II is a brief examination of the salient legal aspects of and problems connected with territorial settlements emerging after the conclusion of armed conflict between States and their effect on the notion of self-determination. Reference is also made to difficulties which continue despite the peaceful settlement of disputes by way of boundary treaties and other kinds of legal methods and techniques, including internal administrative arrangements. Parts III and IV constitute the main focus of the enquiry: they deal sequentially with the law relative to the interpretation and revision of judgments and awards, as discussed above. While it is the case that the rules applicable to these two remedies are relatively well developed, it is also true that they have not been explored by writers to any great depth. Nor have they been isolated and scrutinised in the context of territorial

[7] See, generally, Cukwurah, *The Settlement of Boundary Disputes in International Law*, Manchester, 1967, Chapter V; Brownlie, *African Boundaries: A Legal and Diplomatic Encyclopaedia*, London, 1979, pp. 5–12; Shaw, 'Peoples, Territorialism and Boundaries', 3 (1997) EJIL 478; and Kaikobad, 'Some Observations on the Doctrine of Continuity and Finality of Boundaries', 54 (1984) BYIL 119. See also the text to note 225 below.

[8] See, generally, Shaw, 'The International Law of Territory: An Overview', in Shaw (ed.), *Title to Territory*, Dartmouth, 2005, p. xi, at pp. xxvi–xxix; and Anyangwe, 'African Border Disputes and Their Settlements by International Judicial Process', 28 (2003) *South African Yearbook of International Law* 29, at pp. 29–35.

and boundary disputes. It is important, however, to note that it is one thing to claim that well-developed rules of law exist on the matter; it is quite a different thing to show success in resolving such disputes by reference to such principles of the law. A study dealing with that aspect of the matter goes into a different plane of enquiry and cannot be investigated here. Part V rounds off the investigation, providing as it does some general themes of discussion ensuing from the legal issues examined.

II. Fundamental parameters and perspectives

The law relating to interpretation and revision is examined below, with the former taking the lead. The analysis is based on the view that there are two aspects to the interpretative process and, although there are many overlapping features, such a distinction is indeed useful. One of the more fundamental issues in interpretation is the requirement of consent, that is to say, the requirement that States must agree to submit the decision to an international tribunal for the purposes of interpretation. The significance of this is somewhat underestimated in the literature, as are the various ways in which consent can manifest itself. The role of the admissibility of pleas for the interpretation of judgments and awards is also a crucial issue meriting discussion, not least because it constitutes the doctrinal threshold for this judicial remedy. At the heart of the substantive aspects of interpretation lies a number of interesting questions, the most important of which is the role of the *res judicata* principle and its effect on the interpretation of decisions.

This matter is of importance because, wherever interpretation has the effect of modifying a judgment boundary, there arises the potential for conflict with the *res judicata* rule. Insofar as the need for interpretation of judgments has to be a *bona fide* one, international law must also provide effective guidance as to the circumstances in which it will permit a tribunal to re-examine by way of interpretation a decision, and, to that end, it is appropriate to take into account the tests for interpretation followed by reference to some interesting features thereof. Another salient aspect of the law on the matter, which also fails to feature conspicuously in the literature, is the body of rules of law governing the actual interpretation of decisions, and, although the case law here is not extensive, it is interesting to scrutinise the principles by which tribunals guide themselves for the purposes of interpreting their own or other tribunals' decisions. Their approach to the interpretation and application of one of the more essential doctrines of title to territory, namely, acquiescence and estoppel, is a matter worthy of note.

Revision is equally, if not more, complex. Questions of admissibility are also relevant here, but, as is often the case in international law, there is an intertwining of questions of admissibility with substantive issues of revision. It is an interesting fact that the Statute of the International Court of Justice provides for the making by the Court of a special preliminary finding with respect to admissibility, whereas a similar preliminary finding is not required for the purposes of the interpretative process. The problems of *res judicata* are more acute here, inasmuch as the very object and purpose of the application for revision is none other than the modification of the earlier judgment or award. These issues require careful analysis, one characterised by a need to reconcile conflicting principles of law, the harmonisation or reconciliation of which eschews the need to provide a hierarchical approach with respect to various norms of international law on the matter, not least because it is neither correct nor necessary so to do. The purpose, then, of this study is to provide a broad-ranging analysis of these and other issues arising in the context of the law relating to the interpretation and revision of decisions dealing with territorial and boundary disputes.

Finally, it will be appropriate to mention the type and range of decisions and tribunals examined in this work. The first and most obvious international tribunal is the International Court of Justice, but it is important to note that, in order to be as comprehensive as possible, this survey has sought to encompass both contentious decisions as well as advisory opinions of the Court. While it can be strenuously argued that advisory opinions are not binding on Member States of the United Nations – not least because they, as *individual* Member States, cannot seek them nor are they addressed by them – advisory opinions nevertheless have all the juridical and judicial weight of a judgment of the Court. Moreover, to exclude such opinions would be to lose the benefit of the Court's pronouncements in two valuable and relevant proceedings, namely, the *Jaworzina* and the *Monastery of Saint-Naoum* cases. The second set of tribunals to be included in this study is the category comprised of *ad hoc* arbitral tribunals. It is the case that tribunals instituted expressly for the purpose of resolving outstanding boundary and territorial disputes have made an impressive contribution to a doctrinal understanding of the notions of revision and interpretation, the three Argentina–Chile boundary cases collectively being only one prominent, and indeed complex, example thereof.

At the tertiary level come national tribunals, although it must be stressed that their contribution for present purposes is limited to a few national or domestic tribunals as examined or referred to below. Nonetheless, the motivation to include tribunals such as the United States Supreme Court is predicated on providing maximum coverage with a view to facilitating detailed discussion. In this, the guiding criterion has been the fact that, when the United States Supreme Court is seised of an original bill of complaint issued by one of the states of the American Union and issues of territory are involved, the Court expressly applies international law, the constitutional theory being that the territorial units of the Union are, in an important legal and political sense, sovereign entities co-operating in a federal structure. As the Court said in *Wisconsin* v. *Michigan*, the principles of international law apply also to boundaries between states constituting the United States;[9] and, in *Kansas* v. *Colorado*, the Court observed that, sitting as an international as well as a domestic tribunal, 'we apply Federal law, state law, and international law, as the exigencies of the particular case may demand'.[10]

At the fourth level, it is noteworthy that decisions of a national governmental body or an appointee thereof must be given all due weight especially where the decision in question is concerned with territorial rights and the limits of colonial entities and their sub-divisions. Accordingly, the Tripp decisions of 1 and 2 April 1956[11] and the Walker Report,[12] which subsequently led to the *Dubai–Sharjah Land and Maritime Boundary* case,[13] could not be excluded from this survey, and accordingly the latter arbitration has been analysed at the appropriate places below. In the following chapters, a more detailed presentation of these cases is provided with a

[9] 295 US 455 (1934), at p. 461. Indeed, the original jurisdiction of the Supreme Court to determine disputes over boundaries between States is grounded in the view that, in their sovereign capacity, the states made over to the United States a grant of judicial power over intra-state controversies; and hence 'the states waived their exemption from judicial power as sovereigns by their own grant of its exercise over themselves in such cases'. See Zipp, 'Original Jurisdiction of the United States Supreme Court in Suits Between States', 68 L Ed 2d 969, at p. 978.

[10] 185 US 125 (1901), at pp. 146–7. This case concerned the right of the state of Colorado to divert the waters of the Colorado River to the detriment of Kansas. For an incisive survey of the powers of the Supreme Court in this context, see *Mississippi* v. *Illinois*, 200 US 496 (1906), at p. 511; and *Rhode Island* v. *New Hampshire*, 12 Peters 657 (1838). In the *Trail Smelter* case, the authority of the decisions of the Supreme Court for the purposes of international arbitration was recognised by the Tribunal: 3 UNRIAA 1911, at pp. 1963–4. For a nuanced view of the application of international law in these circumstances, see Warbrick, 'The Boundary Between England and Scotland in the Solway Firth', 51 (1980) BYIL 163, at pp. 174–5.

[11] In the form of letters from J. P. Tripp, Political Agent to the Rulers of Sharjah and Dubai respectively, these decisions are reproduced in Schofield and Blake, *Arabian Boundaries: Primary Documents 1853–1957*, vol. XIV, *Trucial Coast: Internal Boundaries*, Archive Editions, Farnham Common, 1988, p. 691 and p. 697, respectively.

[12] The report of March 1955 is reproduced in *ibid*., p. 566.

[13] 91 ILR 543.

view to taking account of their doctrinal significance in the matter of the interpretation and revision of decisions dealing with territorial and boundary disputes. At this stage, it suffices merely to indicate in very general terms that various kinds of decision are relevant to this study, or, to put the matter in a different way, a decision of an international tribunal in contentious proceedings is but one kind of tribunal in one kind of dispute and that there are indeed several variations along the basic theme involving adjudication and arbitration.

Finally, it must be added that it is both impossible and fruitless to examine interpretation and revision as remedies before international tribunals in a complete juridical vacuum, that is, without taking into account decisions which deal with issues other than territory. Thus, from time to time, references to, and comparisons with, general judicial practice and the law on the matter have been made in order to provide perspective and depth. At the same time, an attempt is made to maintain a sharp focus on these remedies as they have been applied in boundary and territorial disputes. This approach is predicated on the view that important, but limited, points of reference and comparison ought to suffice, and that to delve more deeply and broadly into the law of revision and interpretation, as developed by international tribunals, would change the essential themes of this investigation. The whole purpose here is to scrutinise these remedies in the context of territorial and boundary disputes insofar as they generate problems peculiar to this area of the law.

PART II · THE SETTLEMENT OF TERRITORIAL AND BOUNDARY DISPUTES

2 Problems in settlement

I. Preliminary observations

The significance of territory in international law and relations is best described as being multi-dimensional, as opposed to multi-layered, in character. The distinction between the two ideas is predicated on the view that the latter conveys a notion of discrete strata lying one on top of the other, whereas the imagery of a multi-dimensional notion is more consistent with one in which a number of aspects, interests and considerations are interconnected in a composite whole. Clearly, the political significance of territory to a State lies at the very heart of the whole idea of statehood. Not only is territory the spatial extent of the existence of the State, the extent of territory is directly linked to the vital national interests thereof, that is, the interests of defence, security and, indeed, the survival of the State itself. It is, perhaps, crude to equate the extent of territory to the power and strength of the State, where the logic of the analysis dictates that the greater the extent of territory the greater the State's power.

Yet, this crude analysis of power is neither totally exaggerated nor totally untrue. For the bigger States do seem to enjoy a degree of security to which smaller States can only aspire. The sheer territorial magnitude of China and India is itself a bulwark against any adventurous use of armed force against them, their nuclear weapons notwithstanding. For this very reason, any diminution of territory is seen as a threat to security. Clearly, Turkey's earlier uncompromising policies towards the Kurdish nation were fuelled by such considerations. For, if Turkey were to allow the entire Kurdish nation to secede, Ankara would have to contemplate losing approximately one-third of its territory, a prospect far too catastrophic for Turkey realistically to accept. Similarly, Pakistan would be a seriously truncated State if Afghanistan's claims to the 'lost' territory of the Afghan nation were accepted and a new frontier put into effect between them.

The fact, of course, is that this equation between the territorial extent and the security of a State is not universally true, not least because military power and the security enjoyed by some smaller States (for example, that of Israel compared with its neighbours, and that of the United Kingdom compared with many other, larger States in the world) is also a multi-dimensional phenomenon. Even so, the situations described above tend to highlight another dimensional factor of territory, namely, self-determination. Nations living in the territory of a State for which they espouse no loyalty do sometimes find themselves struggling to secede with a determination matched only by that of the State seeking to preserve its territorial integrity. National liberation movements, it is well known, are not characterised by efforts to minimise the loss of life or damage to property; nor are they short-lived. Struggles for independence in the Basque region of Spain, Corsica, Chechnya, Sri Lanka and Western Sahara are not only decades old but provide no sign of hope for an early end to the misery endured by the inhabitants of these States.

Nor ought economic considerations in the notion of territory be underestimated. Indeed, in matters of maritime delimitation, they are fairly central. The unyielding determination of coastal States in the developing world to exercise maximal control over the rich living resources of the sea in areas adjacent to their coasts, particularly the western coasts of South America and Africa, was the defining reason behind the steady surge in the 1970s to secure a 200-nautical-mile exclusive economic zone. While this zone was finally confirmed in 1982 by the United Nations Convention on the Law of the Sea,[14] territory in the shape of the continental shelf had arguably become part of customary international law by the time the 1958 Geneva Convention on the Continental Shelf[15] was concluded. Importantly, the sovereign rights coastal States enjoy in the exclusive economic zone and the continental shelf are provided for the purposes of the exploration and exploitation of the living and non-living resources of the zone and the shelf. Hydrocarbon resources are, of course, of paramount consideration, and it is this set of factors which is avowedly at the centre of the present difficulties between East Timor and Australia with respect to delimitation of the continental shelf.

[14] 1833 UNTS 3; 21 (1982) ILM 1261.

[15] UN Doc. A/Conf.13/L. 52-L. 55; Misc. No. 15 (1958), Cmnd 584.

In this welter of considerations, historical, ethnic and religious factors can always be relied on to fuel the controversy. The existence of mutual distrust of, and on occasion hatred between, peoples living in close proximity to each other for centuries comes for most as a surprising fact of life; but, more importantly, it can also lead to the disintegration of States and a clamour for self-determination. Yet, it is one thing to demand and struggle for an independent State, it is quite another to commit genocide, ethnic cleansing and crimes against humanity in the name of the historic motherland for which on occasion all manner of sacrifice may be urged upon the patriots. It is true that the disintegration of Yugoslavia was preceded by Belgrade's wars with the breakaway republics of Slovenia and Croatia, but it was the ideal of self-determination which was seriously marred when Serbia's kinsmen in the self-proclaimed statelet of Srpska in Bosnia and Herzegovina effected the worst sort of ethnic atrocities in Europe since the end of the Second World War. Furthermore, while Yugoslavia's legal right to exercise territorial sovereignty over the historic Serbian heartland of Kosovo is nowhere in legal doubt, it is this very right which the Security Council will have to consider when it begins seriously to examine ways and means for securing a just and lasting solution to the problem of Kosovo's future.[16]

Significantly, religious fervour and denominational conflict were not unknown forces in Europe at an earlier period of time, and in fact were responsible for influencing the course of events which ultimately led to the emergence of the modern State system. As de Visscher describes it, in the period prior to the Treaty of Westphalia of 1648,[17] the Reformation had nationalised religion making the Lutheran princes the heads of territorial churches whose religion determined that of their subjects.[18] It is true, of course, that the Treaty, and the peace following it, reflected a growing awareness of the existence of political, and indeed sovereign, rights of the 300 or so princes attending the conferences, rights which were legally and politically different from the collapsing ideas of *imperium* and *dominium*; but equally significant is the fact that the Treaty ended three decades of sectarian bloodshed.

[16] See the text to notes 39–45 below.

[17] Parry, *Consolidated Treaty Series*, vol. I, Dobbs Ferry, 1969, p. 319 (Munster; English translation) and p. 198 (Osnabruck; English translation); Anon, *A General Collection of Treatys, Declarations of War, Manifestos and Other Publick Papers*, vol. I, London, 1710, p. 1 (Munster) and p. 374 (Osnabruck).

[18] Supra (note 1), pp. 3–21, at p. 6. Further, see Cassese, *International Law in a Divided World*, Oxford, 1986, pp. 34–8; and Gross, 'The Peace of Westphalia', 42 (1948) AJIL 20, especially pp. 21–3 and 27–34.

In other words, the Thirty Years War between the Protestants and the Catholic countries thus finally allowed for the emergence of a new kind of political reality in Europe, a reality characterised, *inter alia*, by burgeoning notions of independence of these princes from the Pope, determined as they were to assert even more strongly an evolving, and essentially non-feudal, kind of existence for their territorial entities of varying sizes. It was this which over time resulted in notions of territorial sovereignty and statehood. In relatively more modern times, religion has been employed to further claims to statehood or territory or both. The foundations of Irish independence were not only nationalistic in dimension but also denominational in character. Pakistan's claims to Kashmir, such as they are, are founded in the right of the former Muslim majority provinces of British India and the princely states of India to have acceded to Pakistan on or after the transfer of power in August 1947. Similarly, Israel's claims to parts of the West Bank and, prior to 2005, to the Gaza Strip and its occupation thereof in the form of settlements are steeped in ancient history and religion.

Nor would it be appropriate to underestimate the micro-level aspects of territory; this, indeed, is the most basic characteristic feature of all. Territory, it must be said, is nothing if it is not rooted in the idea of land.[19] The local user of land in all its various forms and manifestations is what gives territory its special status in the minds of its inhabitants. The right to till the land, the right to graze livestock, the right to mine and the right to build a house on one's property are no doubt everyday, mundane matters at one level, but they are of immense importance to local inhabitants. It is this set of proprietary interests which informs the policies of States, compelling them to provide their nationals with the security, stability and continuity they need with respect to these rights. In some cases, these interests will be heavily overlaid with economic considerations of the State.

Even so, the fact is that governments can hardly remain oblivious to the demands of the people who live and work on the land and who have come to depend upon its resources. Such considerations have a momentum and dynamism of their own, even if those considerations in and of themselves have little or no nationalistic dimension. The protection given to the inhabitants of the Falkland Islands is not predicated on a need to keep the British economy buoyant; on the contrary, the expenditure on defence and security is a disproportionate charge on the national exchequer, animated, no doubt, by a policy which, among other things, seeks to support the estab-

[19] Maritime territory is excluded from consideration in this specific context.

lished livelihood, lifestyles and national affiliations of a very small number of people. A similar kind of interest was obvious in the otherwise insignificant island of Sedudu or Kasikili in *Botswana* v. *Namibia*.[20] Turkey's occupation of the northern part of Cyprus and its support for the breakaway Turkish Republic of Northern Cyprus has led not only to the universal non-recognition of that entity as a State. Turkey's policies have also effectively led to the long-term impoverishment of that region of the island.

Finally in this context, the essential role of law needs strenuously to be emphasised. The substance of the point here is that legal aspects of geographical facts dominate the notion of territory. Of course, territory, both land and maritime, is a corporeal, measurable fact, but essentially it is, as noted above, a legal construct. In fact, it is difficult to appreciate the idea of territory without reference to law which is based essentially in the question of a right and of title to the land and the bodies of water which constitute the physical aspects of the State. As Kelsen observed, the territory of a State is legally nothing but the territorial sphere of validity of the natural legal order called a State.[21] In other words, territory is essentially the space in which the State exercises its sovereignty and control; and these aspects, importantly, are also facets of law.

The hybrid nature of the exclusive economic zone best conveys the role of law in territory. Not only does it have aspects of the high seas overlain in its notional existence, the zone is legally intertwined with concept of the continental shelf. Yet each is legally a distinct zone or part of the maritime space. Similarly, from a point of geographical fact, there is nothing distinctive in the column of water or the body of sea beginning at the thirteenth nautical mile from the waters at the twelfth. Even on land, the degree of powers of control exercisable by a State with respect to a portion of territory may be indistinguishable from the idea of sovereignty yet lack in law that quality. Both Hong Kong, and at least the New Territories, and Guantanamo Bay are examples of full but less than absolute plenary control. With respect to Guantanamo Bay, the United States Court of Appeal, in *Gherebi* v. *Bush and Rumsfeld*, distinguished between ultimate and residual sovereignty, where the former constituted temporal and not qualitative sovereignty.[22] The short fact is that it is law which gives these

[20] ICJ Reports 1999, p. 1045. [21] Supra (note 1), p. 307.

[22] 352 F 3d 1278 (2003), United States Court of Appeal for the Ninth Circuit. See also *Khalid A. F. Al Odah* v. *US*, 321 F 3d 1134, at pp. 1142–5 (2003); and *Johnson* v. *Eisentrager*, 339 US 763 (1950), with respect to Landsberg Prison in Germany following the end of the Second World War where the Supreme Court of the United States distinguished between territorial jurisdiction and sovereignty: *ibid*., pp. 768 and 777–9.

physical facts an existence which is known as territory; without law sovereign territory is only land or water or a river, as the case may be.

II. Territorial settlements: international law, armed conflict and self-determination

a. General

In view of the multi-dimensional nature of territory and title as described above, it is no surprise that territorial rights and sovereignty always succeed in attracting controversy. Quite clearly, territory at every stage is burdened by so many conflicting considerations that States find themselves more often than not in dispute with each other regarding their mutual territorial rights. Some of these considerations and interests are so tenacious that they refuse to die down even after States have made territorial adjustments or have begun to maintain the *status quo*. Where such adjustments and settlements are made upon the termination of international armed conflict, or in the context thereof, and where they are linked to issues of self-determination, these problems can become even more acute, ensuring thereby a continuance of dissatisfaction, to one degree or another, with the settlement or the *status quo*. Some of these controversial territorial settlements and developments have been singled out for examination below with a view to providing a few legal answers to such perennial issues, with the caveat that the answers are more akin to propositions than recognised principles of law. A disclaimer such as this is inevitable not only because of the limited number of problems examined but also because the main focus of the study lies elsewhere. The reason nevertheless for examining these issues is to show that, while international law tends towards a definitive end to disputes by requiring States to seek peaceful solutions to their disputes and to abide by the terms of such solutions, issues such as self-determination will at times frustrate the realisation of such ends.

However, before doing so, it is important to reiterate that the domain of law dealing with self-determination is both vast and complex and accordingly only a few representative problems, legal issues and arguments can be examined here. While territorial disputes are the focus of this study, the scrutiny begins with reference to locational disputes, that is, questions more concerned with the issue of where the alignment delimited should be drawn. Of course, all locational disputes are also territorial disputes to one extent or another.

b. *Post-conflict settlements: territorial and boundary issues*

By way of prefatory remarks, it is true of course to say that, historically speaking, States have employed both pacific and non-pacific techniques to resolve disputes of one kind or another, including territorial and boundary issues. Clearly, non-peaceful methods of settlement are no longer, in principle at least, an option: Article 2(4) of the United Nations Charter has made sure of that. Even so, territorial settlements arrived at by the use of such methods are not altogether beyond the legal horizon, as it were. A key to appreciating this point lies in maintaining a distinction between non-peaceful and non-legal means. Hence, territorial settlements may come about as a result of the lawful use of armed force, and such settlements are not *ipso facto* illegal. Thus, while the Declaration on Principles of International Law Concerning Friendly Relations and Co-operation stipulates that no territorial acquisition resulting from the threat or use of force shall be recognised as legal, it also provides a rider which states that this rule shall not be construed as affecting the powers of the Security Council under the Charter.[23]

Thus, when the Security Council decided, in Resolution 678 of 1991, that the Iraq–Kuwait boundary be demarcated pursuant to the delimitation provided in the 1963 Agreed Minutes between these two States, it was a measure which followed the Gulf War of 1991. Although it is the case that the United Nations Iraq–Kuwait Boundary Demarcation Commission was not mandated to *decide* the course of the alignment but only to *mark out* an *agreed* frontier, it is equally true that deciding where the agreed frontier actually lay was a difficult task and it effectively constituted determining the location of parts of the boundary anew.[24] More controversially, the Commission took it upon itself to demarcate the boundary in one sector for which there was no agreed line: the fact is that offshore areas were in fact not covered by the Iraq–Kuwait Agreed Minutes of 1963. In adopting this approach, the Commission was supported, perhaps even encouraged, by the Security Council insofar as it did not wish to keep any sector of the Iraq–Kuwait frontier undecided.[25] When the Security Council demanded in Resolution 833

[23] Sub-paragraph (b), tenth paragraph, Principle Forbidding the Threat or Use of Force, Resolution 2625 (XXV) of the United Nations General Assembly, 24 October 1970.

[24] For the Final Report of the Commission issued in 1993, see 94 ILR 1.

[25] Refer to Kaikobad, 'Problems of Adjudication and Arbitration in Maritime Boundary Disputes', 1 (2002) *Law and Practice of International Courts and Tribunals* 257, at pp. 269–72. Cf. Mendelson and Hulton, 'The Iraq–Kuwait Boundary', 64 (1993) BYIL 135, at pp. 178–86; Post, 'Adjudication as a Mode of Acquisition of Territory: Some Observations on the Iraq–Kuwait Boundary Demarcation in Light of the Jurisprudence of the International Court of Justice', in Lowe and Fitzmaurice (eds.), *Fifty Years of the*

of 27 May 1993 that both Kuwait and Iraq accept the boundary demarcated,[26] Kuwait accepted it with alacrity. Iraq also accepted the resolution, but its acceptance was delayed and its acceptance less than wholehearted.

Given this controversy, it is possible that over the years the problem of an 'unfair demarcation' exercise will continue to fester. As one commentator has asserted: 'For many Iraqis across the political and sectarian spectrum the UN demarcation of 1994 was forced on Iraq in defeat and failed adequately to deal with Iraq's practical need for unfettered access to the sea.'[27] Notwithstanding that, in terms of the law the problem is not difficult to resolve. For one thing, it can be argued that, even if it were granted that the Commission was acting beyond its powers, the resulting demarcation was probably not invalid, owing to the overriding powers of the Council in this respect. The law on the matter is clear, governed as it is by the rights and obligations of the United Nations Charter, particularly Articles 25 and 48(1) thereof. For another, the controversial demarcation is *in esse* a locational dispute, and, importantly, it does not raise issues of self-determination. Thus, although political sentiments of national honour and the like may become a cause for some concern, the dispute is not, by and large, intractable, and, given a modicum of good will on both sides, it will not engender acute tension.

It is less easy to resolve questions which are inherently territorial, as opposed to locational, in character and fuelled by sentiments of self-determination. It is of interest that a good number of territorial realignments and settlements, total and partial, including the creation and amalgamation of States, were put into effect after an end to protracted armed conflict of continental proportions. Indeed, this has been the experience of Europe for over 300 years. The Treaty of Westphalia of 1648,[28] the Treaty of Paris of 1763,[29] the 1815 Congress of Vienna[30] following the Napoleonic wars, the Congress of Berlin of 1878[31] and the territorial set-

International Court of Justice: Essays in Honour of Sir Robert Jennings, Cambridge, 1996, p. 237, at pp. 258–60; and Muir, 'The Iraq–Kuwait Border Dispute: Still a Factor for Instability?', 35 (2004) *Asian Affairs* 147.

[26] See paragraph E of this resolution which was adopted under Chapter VII.

[27] Muir (note 25), at pp. 147–8. He adds: '[The demarcation exercise of 1994 was] the exercise that the British never managed to pull off while they had responsibility for Kuwait's foreign policy and that the Iraqis and Kuwaitis had later failed to do for themselves. It perhaps required Iraq's ringing defeat in 1991 to achieve a demarcation putting Warba and Bubiyan and the coast south of Umm Qasr squarely inside Kuwait and dividing the Khor Abdalla waterway between the two countries, with both states having navigational access through it.' See p. 158.

[28] Supra, note 17.

[29] 1 BFSP 645.

[30] 2 BFSP 3.

[31] 69 BFSP 749.

tlements following the wars of 1914–18 and 1939–45 are all evidence of this phenomenon. The Treaties of Trianon, Saint-Germain-en-Laye and Lausanne,[32] the 1945 Yalta Declaration and the Potsdam Agreement[33] are just a few examples from the two latter wars. Certainly, it cannot be pretended that settlements engineered in such circumstances by the victorious States are underpinned by the consent of the vanquished freely given, reflecting as they do the long-term interests and objectives of the former. Yet these settlements are generally regarded as being lawful.

The theory underlying these territorial dispositions is, generally speaking, that the termination of a major protracted war causing monumental upheaval in the region justifies laying the foundations for fundamental territorial and boundary adjustments in the interests of reaching a fair, just and lasting peace, provided, of course, that the adjustments are validated at least by formal approval of all the parties in the region, especially the major powers thereof, where they are done collectively and are inherently equitable in nature.[34] Even so, the point of central concern here is that, despite elaborate adjustments and formal peace treaties, the dynamics of international society and the inherent nature of territorial matters are such that settled issues may become unsettled, fail to crystallise in the ways they were intended, or collapse when they are overtaken by events or predicated on policies and assumptions which were out of touch with the realities on the ground. Five of these settlements are of some interest here.

In the period following the end of the First World War, the question of the allocation of the Kurdish province of Mosul began to create severe difficulties for Turkey and Great Britain, the Mandatory of Iraq. The Treaty of Lausanne, concluded in 1923, left the matter to be settled by these two powers and, failing that, to the Council of the League of Nations. The Commissions of Enquiry set up by the latter revealed that the Kurdish nation did not want to join either Turkey or Iraq, and preferred independence. Despite this, after protracted proceedings, the Council finally settled the matter by adopting the so-called 'Brussels Line' in 1925 which

[32] Allied Powers Peace Treaty with Hungary, 4 June 1920; with Austria, 10 October 1919; and with Turkey, 4 July 1923: 15 (1921) AJIL (Supp.) 1; 14 (1920) AJIL (Supp.) 1; and 18 (1924) AJIL (Supp.) 1, respectively.

[33] Grenville and Wasserstein, *The Major International Treaties of the Twentieth Century*, vol. I, London, 2001, pp. 207 and 271, respectively.

[34] See Hill (note 1), pp. 195–6, citing the President of the Supreme Council (comprised of the five Allied and Associated Powers) in the context of a letter to the Polish Government in 1919, that there is a long-established procedure in European international law that the acquiescence of the great powers is necessary when a new state is created or when an existing state receives considerable territorial additions.

left most of the province to Iraq.[35] The Kurdish agitation for independence has not, of course, since died down and the territorial adjustment of 1925 has continued to bedevil both States since that time.

In the second place, reference may be made to the Middle East crisis. Great Britain, as the Mandatory of Palestine, was obliged by Article 2 of the Mandate[36] to implement the policy of a national home for the Jewish nation, but throughout its mission from 1922–3 to 1948 there was no reconciliation between the latter and the Palestinian people who were opposed to immigration in the territory, and this led eventually to the war of 1948–9 between Israel and its Arab neighbours. Importantly, the Palestinians failed also to be persuaded of the argument that partitioning Palestine east of the Jordan River and creating thereby a new entity, namely, the mandated territory of Transjordan, had in fact fulfilled their political aspirations to statehood.[37] This territory subsequently became the Hashemite Kingdom of Jordan. While the Israeli and Palestinian authorities recognised each other in October 1993,[38] albeit in guarded and carefully formulated terms, certain core issues, including those of the boundaries of the future State of Palestine and the status of Jerusalem still have to be settled.

The third settlement concerns territory which has caused difficulties for the Balkans for over a century. As a *villayet*, Kosovo had been part of Albania for centuries, and was hence under Ottoman rule until Serbia gained control over it by way of conquest in 1912.[39] It was decided in the London Protocol of 1913 to leave Kosovo within Serbia. It was then occupied by the Austro-Hungarians in 1914 following their war with Serbia, but, by 1918, the territory had reverted to Serb rule. Any resumption of Albanian control was not a realistic prospect in the geopolitics of the time, one aspect of

[35] Wainhouse *et al.*, *International Peace Observation: A History and Forecast*, Baltimore, 1966, pp. 43–7. [36] 17 (1923) AJIL (Supp.) 164.

[37] Stone, 'Peace and the Palestinians', 3 (1970) *New York University Journal of International Law and Politics* 247; reprinted in Moore (ed.), *The Arab–Israeli Conflict*, vol. I, Princeton, 1974, p. 581, at pp. 592–6.

[38] See the preambular paragraph to the Declaration of Principles on Interim Self-Government Arrangements, 32 (1993) ILM 1525.

[39] See, generally, Malcolm, *Kosovo: A Short History*, London, 1998; Glenny, *The Balkans 1804–1999: Nationalism, War and the Great Powers*, London, 2000, Chapters 3, 4 and 8; Hoffman, *The Balkans in Transition*, Princeton, 1963; The Independent Commission on Kosovo, *The Kosovo Conflict: International Response: Lessons to Be Learnt*, Oxford, 2000, pp. 33 *et seq.*; Calic, 'Kosovo in the Twentieth Century: A Historical Account', in Schnabel and Thakur (eds.), *Kosovo and the Challenge of Humanitarian Intervention: Selective Indignation, Collective Action and International Citizenship*, Tokyo, 2000, pp. 19 *et seq.*; and Wainhouse (note 35), pp. 29–33.

which was the unwavering Serb conviction that Kosovo had always been their national and religious heartland. In 1921, the Conference of Ambassadors delimited the border between Yugoslavia and Albania according to the line of 1913, with minor rectifications all in favour of Yugoslavia.

After the death of President Tito of Yugoslavia in 1989 and the abolition of Kosovo's autonomous status by Serbia in 1990, the movement among Albanian Kosovars for independence began to proceed apace with increasing levels of hostilities with Belgrade, resulting in NATO action in 1999. On 10 June 1999, the Security Council adopted Resolution 1244 which mandated the United Nations to maintain an interim administration in the disputed region. It is of some interest that, while it felt able directly to express the territorial integrity of the Federal Republic of Yugoslavia (Serbia and Montenegro),[40] and indirectly to contradict the idea of Kosovar independence,[41] by 2005 the Council had initiated the 'Final Status Talks' with respect to Kosovo[42] which included the option of full independence and autonomy.[43] The dilemma is that, while neither Belgrade nor certain influential European States will countenance Kosovo's independence, Kosovars overwhelmingly want nothing but their freedom from Serb rule.

The case of Taiwan[44] is the fourth example of a territorial adjustment, albeit partial or incomplete, colliding with issues of self-determination

[40] See, for example, the tenth and eleventh preambular paragraphs to Resolution 1244; and paragraph 8 of Annex 2 to this resolution.

[41] See Presidential Statement of the Security Council, 24 May 2002, in which it declared *ultra vires* and null and void a resolution adopted by the Assembly of Kosovo on 23 May 2002 on the matter of protection of the 'territorial integrity of Kosovo': S/PRST/2002/16. In effect, the Council rejected the notion of Kosovar, as opposed to Serbian, territorial integrity. Cf. its position in 2005, next footnote below.

[42] See Presidential Statement of 24 October 2005: S/PRST/2005/51; and see also the report of the Secretary-General of 7 October 2005, S/2005/635. While it supports the talks and the status, the Council does not state *expressis verbis* that it supports either independence or full autonomy. The UN Secretary-General has accepted the report of Ambassador Eide on the Implementation of Standards which has urged the starting of such talks. The official UN position previously was that Kosovo should progress towards 'substantial autonomy and meaningful self-determination' but not independence: see paragraph 8 of Annex 2 to Resolution 1244 of 1999; and the briefing of the Special Representative to the Security Council of 24 April 2002, 56 (2002) *UN Yearbook* 369.

[43] Per the UN Secretary-General, Report of 1 November 2005, *UN Daily News*.

[44] The issue of status remains controversial, and literature on the subject is considerable. Generally, see O'Connell, 'The Status of Formosa and the Chinese Recognition Problem', 50 (1956) AJIL 405, especially pp. 406–8; Crawford (note 1), pp. 143–51; Jain, 'The Legal Status of Formosa', 57 (1963) AJIL 25; Chen, 'Some Legal Problems in Sino-US Relations', 22 (1983) *Columbia Journal of Transnational Law* 41; Chen and Reisman, 'Who Owns Taiwan: A Search for International Title', 81 (1971–2) *Yale Law Journal* 599; and Kirkham, 'The International Legal Status of Formosa', 6 (1968) CYIL 144.

and the changing equations of power within international society. The United States, China and Great Britain issued the Cairo Declaration in 1943 seeking to assure China that the island of Formosa, among other territories, which Japan had 'stolen' from the Chinese, would be restored to it at the end of the war.[45] The Potsdam Agreement of 1945 reconfirmed the Cairo Declaration and limited Japan's territories to its principal islands.[46] In its Instrument of Surrender of September 1945,[47] Japan agreed to accept the Potsdam Declaration, thus agreeing indirectly to renounce its sovereignty over Formosa in favour of China. The Supreme Commander of the Allied Powers then directed Japanese forces to surrender to Generalissimo Chiang Kai-Shek and his Nationalists, who took control of the island in September 1945 as military occupiers,[48] and in the following month it was declared a province of China.[49]

However, after the Nationalists lost control of the mainland to Communists, the situation changed enormously. Clearly, the prospect of transferring Formosa to the People's Republic of China was unacceptable to the United States. Thus, in Article 2 of the 1951 Treaty of Peace,[50] Japan finally renounced all right, title and claim to its various territories, including Formosa, but there was no reference to the restoration of Chinese sovereignty over the island. Since then, the question of the status of Formosa or Taiwan has continued to cause concern.[51] It is China's position that the island is under the control of renegades from the mainland, whereas the Republic of China in Taiwan claims, in principle, to be the true Chinese Government currently in exile.[52] Matters will almost certainly come to a head if Taiwan were to proclaim itself an independent State.

The conflict in Viet Nam is further illustrative of the problem. In January 1973, the United States, the Democratic Republic of Viet Nam and

[45] For the text, see Whiteman, *Digest of International Law*, vol. III, Washington, DC, 1964, pp. 478–9; and see Jain (note 44), pp. 26–7.

[46] Whiteman (note 45), pp. 484–5.

[47] *Ibid.*, pp. 486–7. Chen refers to it as the legal basis for the post-war settlement with Japan: Chen (note 31), pp. 41–2.

[48] *House of Commons Debates*, vol. 536, Written Answers, col. 159, 4 February 1955. See also Heuser, 'Taiwan', 12 (1972) *Encyclopaedia of Public International Law* 367, at p. 368.

[49] Heuser (note 48), p. 368; and Kirkham (note 44), pp. 145–6.

[50] 158 BFSP 536; 46 (1952) AJIL 71.

[51] Further, see Wright, 'The Chinese Recognition Problem', 49 (1955) AJIL 320; Hungdah Chiu, 'Normalisation and Some Practical and Legal Problems Concerning Taiwan', in Hungdah Chiu (ed.), *Normalising Relations with the People's Republic of China: Problems, Analysis and Documents*, Baltimore, 1978, p. 51; and Whiteman (note 45), pp. 477–563.

[52] For these and related views, including the full independence of Taiwan, see Jain (note 44), pp. 27–38; and Kirkham (note 44), pp. 148–55.

South Viet Nam concluded an agreement to end the war in Viet Nam.[53] Article 9 confirmed the principle of self-determination as a sacred and inalienable right of South Viet Nam. Article 15 stipulated that reunification of Viet Nam would be gradual and by way of peaceful means, without coercion or annexation by either party and without foreign interference. In March of that year, a number of States, including the United States, the United Kingdom, Canada, the Soviet Union, the People's Republic of China and Poland, issued a Declaration in Paris acknowledging the Agreement to End the Viet Nam War. Article 2 recognised the right of self-determination for South Viet Nam, and Article 7 confirmed that any violation of the tripartite agreement would constitute a threat to peace and would require the States to consult one another for the adoption of necessary remedial measures.[54] Despite these assurances, South Viet Nam fell to the Democratic Republic of Viet Nam in April 1975 and was formally reunited with the North in 1976. As Crawford put it:

> Vietnam was probably never a unified independent State: if it possessed any formal unity that was in the period 1954–6, as a result of the Geneva Agreements and the absence of any claim to separate statehood on the part of the Democratic Republic of Vietnam. Despite its equivocations the Paris Peace Agreements of 1973 recognised the effective separation of Vietnam into two States – though, to be sure, that separation proved to be temporary.[55]

c. Concluding analysis

A few generalisations by way of propositions of law may be of some interest. In the first place, where a homogenous entity is divided to accommodate the power policies or post-war programmes of the more influential States but where such division does not arguably represent the wishes of the majority of inhabitants, as in the case of the Kurdish nation and Viet Nam, or where strong nationalist considerations against such territorial divisions persist, then those divisions may turn out eventually to be legally and politically unviable. It is easy to see that divisions of this kind, where they are solutions to political problems besetting the nation in the context of internal or international armed conflict, may turn out eventually to be only temporary solutions or more frequently solutions which create more problems than they solve.

Secondly, where, for similar reasons, an entity is deprived of its right to self-determination not because of considerations inherent in the

[53] 12 (1973) ILM 48. [54] Grenville and Wasserstein (note 33), vol. II, p. 632.
[55] Supra (note 1), p. 287.

problem, including geographical and political circumstances relating directly to the region, but because of policies extrinsic to it, then the longer the deprivation or frustration of that right the greater the legal and political momentum for achieving such a goal. This is particularly true of the Palestinian and Kosovar movements for statehood. By contrast, the failure of the Kurdish nation to secure statehood is essentially a regional problem spread out over five States with layers of Western, as opposed to Turkish, power policies complicating matters.

Thirdly, where the territorial division is merely a confirmation of the post-colonial or post-conflict *status quo* born out of uncertainty and/or military impotence, as in the case of Taiwan and Viet Nam, then the uncertainty will continue and indeed succeed in resisting any legal consolidation of the *status quo* until the matter is formally settled between the parties or where the *status quo* is overturned by one of them, or indeed both. It is important to note that the formal conclusion of treaties, especially those following armed conflict, cannot be a substitute for *bona fide* acceptance of such territorial settlements. A treaty can only aspire to create and perpetuate a legal regime but, if sincere political acceptance is missing, it can become a dead letter.

Fourthly, where the territorial division between neighbouring States is not complicated by matters of self-determination, as in the case of the offshore maritime division of the Iraq–Kuwait frontier line, then, arguably, it will cease in the long run to cause major perennial problems between them, provided, of course, other issues such as hydrocarbon resources do not come into play.

Finally, and in more general terms, some long-lasting territorial problems underline the fact that, despite the termination of hostilities and despite the existence of high-minded values in terms of justice and equity in some post-conflict territorial settlements, the clamour for rejection of such settlements and stalemates can on occasion continue for indefinite periods of time not least because the strength of feelings for territory, for the homeland, is unquenchable. The underlying theme common to all these kinds of situation is that certain territorial settlements, no matter how formally and legally correct they may be, will be governed by events over which the relevant States will have no control and it is this fact which serves to belie the very regime the treaty will have tried to create. Thus the basic paradigm reflects this relation between the legal and the political, that is to say, the greater the hiatus between, on the one hand, the law and the legal *status quo* and, on the other, the political realities on the ground, the weaker and less enduring the *status quo* will be, and equally, in converse terms, the greater the coincidence and compatibility between the legal and political situations – aspects which are inherent in any territorial or boundary regime – the stronger and more enduring will be the *status quo*. These observations are predicated in the view that the international law of title to territory aspires to maximise the effectiveness of territorial allocation and boundary adjustments and therefore abhors situations which are legally or politically ineffective.

While Parts III and IV constitute an account of two judicial remedies employed by States to resolve problems of law emerging from judicial decisions and arbitral awards, the premise here is that States are driven by the same fundamental sentiment in both situations, and this fundamental sentiment is, broadly speaking, an exaggerated sense of attachment to all things territorial.

III. Territorial settlements: peaceful methods, dissatisfaction and legal effects

a. General

Certainly, it is the case that peaceful methods based on diplomacy, compromise, good faith and goodwill constitute the first and preferred way forward, and in this context it is important immediately to emphasise that, despite all the border and territorial disputes between States, the simple expedient of negotiations continues to be the foremost, and perhaps the most underrated, dispute settlement technique. Great numbers of frontier problems have been adjusted by quiet diplomacy, evidence of which is reflected in various instruments, including territory and boundary treaties, agreed minutes, declarations and exchanges of notes. At times, these settlements are demarcated on the ground with the result that the basic treaty is thereafter supplemented by a detailed boundary protocol which accurately records the alignments in text, the co-ordinates of latitude and longitudes, maps and charts.

This diplomatic activity is not confined to independent States. Indeed, metropolitan powers did carry out many territorial adjustments and settlements between their respective adjacent colonial territories before their transfer to independence; the same was also done in the context of internal administrative regions. Significantly, such adjustments and treaties may be preceded by other peaceful means, for example by the mediation of other States and organisations, and by fact-finding missions and conciliation commissions. The fact-finding mission put into motion by the Personal Representative of the Secretary-General of the United Nations with respect to Bahrain in 1970 was extremely successful insofar as it showed that the inhabitants of Bahrain desired independence rather than a 'reuniting' with Iran.[56]

For present purposes, it is interesting to note that, while some States are able successfully to end all problems concerning the location of the line and the like, others are unable to agree to any compromise whatsoever. In these circumstances, some territorial problems are destined to continue, and for some States a treaty or any other formal legal arrangement may itself become the dispute between the States. The difference between these treaties and the territorial adjustments examined above is not only that they have no background of armed conflict. It is also the case that dissension from the territorial *status quo* comes by and large from conscious decisions to dispute the treaty or the contents thereof, whereas the difficulties referred to above are predicated in events over which the relevant States may have little or no control, especially with respect to the clamour for self-determination. Thus, concluding a treaty is no assurance of gaining *real* success in territorial settlements, either as a successor or as an independent State, in terms of disposing of troublesome issues. In other words, while the treaty will create valid rights and obligations, adverse political factors may serve to undermine respect for those rights and obligations.

b. Specific issues and disputes

Sentiments of dissatisfaction and dissension with territorial settlements are almost always clothed in categories of, and assertions based on, law. The disputes examined below are typical in the sense that they constitute the main categories in which this dissension is expressed. Given the vastness of the topic and the relatively narrow focus of this work, the discussion below does not pretend to be a comprehensive survey of this field of study. The basic aim here is to highlight the fact that territorial adjustments and settlements are on many occasions of little or no help in putting disputes to rest. This not only reinforces the basic thesis of this work, which is that, whenever either legally or factually possible, a State

[56] The Report of the Secretary-General favouring the independence of Bahrain was endorsed by the Security Council in Resolution 278 of 11 May 1970; see Al-Baharna, 'The Fact-Finding Mission of the United Nations Secretary-General and the Settlement of the Bahrain–Iran Dispute, May 1970', 22 (1973) ICLQ 541; Gordon, 'Resolution of the Bahrain Dispute', 65 (1971) AJIL 561; and El-Hakim, *The Middle Eastern States and the Law of the Sea*, Manchester, 1979, pp. 245–6: see also the text to note 84, *ibid*.

will not hesitate to seek to readdress settled issues of boundary and territorial matters to its advantage. Each of the categories considered below also provide opportunities to examine the difficulties from a legal perspective and to offer legal analysis with a view to reconciling these problems with international law in general.

1. Problems based on State and government succession

While a great many successor States and governments have not been straddled, as it were, with boundary disputes at independence, quite a few of them have found that colonial boundary treaties and/or dispositions have not brought continuity, stability or finality to the frontier. On the contrary, these settlements have become sources of prolonged tension and dissatisfaction with neighbouring States. The experience of China is particularly noteworthy because it has elements of both continuity and discontinuity of frontiers following a succession of States and governments. It is, however, only when the legal and factual circumstances attending these problems are examined that the true characteristics of its policy become clear and begin to shed light on the matter as evidence of State practice.

Continuity, it must be emphasised, constitutes the core of China's policy regarding boundary regimes with its neighbouring States, namely, Tsarist and Soviet Russia, the British and French Empires in India and Indo-China and Afghanistan. Accordingly, wresting a change in the location of the boundary has not constituted the sole policy objective of the Chinese Government. This is certainly true of the boundary treaties China has concluded with Pakistan, Nepal, Afghanistan,[57] Viet Nam and Burma,[58] where the existing boundaries, *de facto* and *de jure*, have largely been continued. However, if this appears to suggest that China's policy of concluding boundary treaties with neighbouring States was in effect a rejection, in principle, of the *uti possidetis* rule, then this would not be an accurate assumption. The fact of the matter is that Beijing considers some

[57] See, generally, Lamb, 'The Sino-Pakistani Boundary Agreement of 2 March 1963' 18 (1964) *Australian Outlook* 299; Cukwurah (note 7), pp. 143–8 (with respect to Pakistan he writes that Pakistan gave away more territory than it had gained in exchange; this, however, is not entirely accurate); Van Eekelen, *India: Foreign Policy and the Border Dispute with China*, The Hague, 1967, pp. 129–32; and Murty, *India–China Boundary: India's Options*, New Delhi, 1987, pp. 75–8 and 108–14. For its boundary treaty with Afghanistan, see Vertzberger, *China's Southwestern Strategy: Encirclement and Counterencirclement*, New York, 1985, pp. 107–11.

[58] See, generally, Lamb, *Asian Frontiers: Studies in a Continuing Problem*, London, 1968.

treaties, boundary or otherwise, as not being transmittable or binding because they were invalid in law. These 'unequal treaties' were products not of negotiation, compromise and consent but of imperialism and *dictat*. It was this sense of national humiliation which led China to adopt a policy predicated on seeking, on the one hand, formal discontinuity in matters of boundary and other treaties, while continuing, on the other, the existing alignment in practice. China's policy towards its boundary problems with the Russian Federation epitomises this approach.

As far as the history of the Sino-Russian frontier problem is concerned, there can be little doubt that it is a long and complex one. This complexity originates not only from the fact that over eleven boundary and territorial treaties and agreements, starting with the Treaty of Nerchinsk of 1689,[59] were concluded between Imperial Russia and the Chinese Government.[60] It also stems from a combination of factors, including its vast geographical extent, multinational groupings and the dynamism inherent in the international political system itself. Indeed, the positions adopted by these neighbours have been affected by the ebb and flow of empire, nationalism and communism over the nineteenth and twentieth centuries.[61]

China has always denied, in principle, the validity of these unequal treaties, particularly the Treaties of Aigun and Peking of 1858[62] and 1860,[63] the Protocol of Tarabagatai of 1864[64] and the St Petersburg Treaty of 1881.[65] By means of these instruments, China ceded nearly 800 square miles of territory to Russia.[66] However, the latter never respected its treaty obligations,

[59] *Hertslet's China Treaties: Treaties &c, Between Great Britain and China; And Between China and Foreign Powers*, vol. I, London, 1908, p. 437.

[60] See Jackson, *Russo-Chinese Borderlands*, Princeton, 1962, p. 111.

[61] See, generally, Tai Sung An, *The Sino-Soviet Territorial Dispute*, Philadelphia, 1973; Jackson (note 60), Chapters 1 to 4; Cukwurah (note 7), pp. 99–100; Smith, 'China–Russia (Soviet Union)', in Calvert (ed.), *Border and Territorial Disputes of the World*, 4th edn, London, 2004, pp. 157; see also Glenn, 'Central Asian Republics', in *ibid.*, p. 143; Schweisfurth, 'Boundary Disputes Between China and the USSR', 1 (1972) *Encyclopaedia of Public International Law* 49; and Garver, 'The Sino-Soviet Territorial Dispute in the Pamir Mountains Region', 85 (1981) *China Quarterly* 107.

[62] 53 BFSP 964.

[63] *Ibid.*, p. 970. It is important to bear in mind that, in the nineteenth century, it was Russia attempting to take back in terms of territory what it had earlier allegedly lost to the Chinese Empire over 150 years ago. See Miasnikov, *The Ch'ing Empire and the Russian State in the 17th Century*, trans. from the Russian by Vic Schneirson, Moscow, 1980, pp. 298–9.

[64] *Hertslet's China Treaties* (note 59), p. 472.

[65] *Ibid.*, p. 483.

[66] Camilleri, *Chinese Foreign Policy: The Maoist Era and Its Aftermath*, Oxford, 1980, p. 75. See also Anderson, *Frontiers: Territory and State Formation in the Modern World*, Cambridge, 1996, pp. 88–9. By contrast, in the Treaty of Nerchinsk of 1689, the Ch'ing Empire was able to gain from Tsarist Russia territory to which it was not allegedly entitled by way of an unequal treaty, concluded, as it was, under duress: Miasnikov (note 63), pp. 282–9, especially pp. 292–3.

for it went on to occupy territory in excess of its allocation. In addition, there were uncertainties in some sectors of the boundary. One aspect of this was the uncertainty in the Treaty of Aigun of 1858, on the basis of which territory on the left bank of the Amur River was ceded to Russia, and territory lying on the right bank of the Amur River up to the Ussuri River and to the south and west of these rivers was left to China, thus making the rivers themselves the boundary between the two States.[67] The question, however, of the boundary in the river was left undetermined. This uncertainty was compounded when Russia began to exercise control up to the right bank of the Amur. The Treaty of Peking reiterated this division and failed to remove the uncertainty.

This then led to problems regarding hundreds of islands in the river to which both States began to enter claims. These inequities were acknowledged by Moscow once the Tsarist government had been overthrown. Hence, in 1924, the Soviet and Chinese Governments drew up a treaty and agreed, in Article 3 thereof, that all treaties between the parties would be annulled at a future conference and that new agreements would be concluded on a basis of equality, reciprocity and justice.[68] Article 7 made clear that, pending re-demarcation, the present boundaries would be maintained. Attempts were made in 1926 to define a new boundary but were to no avail, and dissatisfaction on the Chinese side continued to characterise frontier relations between the two States.

The Sino-Soviet split of the 1960s became an obstacle to further agreement on the demarcation of the boundary, but, when relations improved, the disputing States embarked on two decades of border demarcation negotiations, a characteristic feature of which was China's acceptance of the territorial *status quo* as a basis for discussion[69] without foreclosing its position with respect to areas of particular concern. Clearly, the precise boundary in the Amur River and the islands therein were of the greatest concern. China took the position that the *thalweg* constituted the boundary in both the Amur and Ussuri rivers. Thus when the Russo-Chinese

[67] This was what Russian diplomacy had sought to secure in the negotiations leading up to the 1689 Treaty. Miasnikov quotes diplomatic sources when he writes that quarrels could be stopped 'if a border were fixed between the states along the . . . glorious Amur River . . . The border can run along no other line but the Amur, because otherwise subjects on both sides would begin crossing the border and creating all sorts of trouble.' The Russian Ambassador therefore wanted a left bank boundary on grounds of long possession and the ease of fixing the border along a natural frontier: Miasnikov (note 63), p. 244.

[68] 122 BFSP 263.

[69] Camilleri (note 66), p. 153; and Anderson (note 66), pp. 92–3.

boundary was finally agreed in principle in 1991,[70] one of the points agreed was that the line of the main channel in navigable rivers would constitute the boundary.

Demarcation was completed by 1997, and, although 2,444 river islands were mutually transferred, the question of sovereignty over some of the more controversial ones, especially Bolshoi Island in the Amur River, remained unsettled until October 2004 when the two sides agreed a boundary protocol which definitively settled the entire eastern sector alignment. This delimitation was subsequently reaffirmed in a treaty signed by the presidents of the two States in June 2005. By and large, however, the boundary agreed is not a radically new line. It follows the general contours of the lines established in, and maintains the territorial allocations of, the nineteenth-century treaties with modifications in important contested sectors. This is especially true in the case of Bolshoi Island which was 'returned' to China, albeit only partially: a little more than half was retained by Russia. Nevertheless, as Carlson observed in his perceptive study on the matter: 'At this time [namely, 1991] a new treaty was signed that established the exact location of the eastern segment of the border. The treaty in no way touched upon the enormous tracts of land China had claimed in the past. Instead, it essentially formalized the existing *de facto* location of the boundary between the two states.'[71]

China's frontier problems with India[72] are equally complex, but with one vital difference: Beijing claims that 'the two countries have never formally delimited this boundary and that there is a divergence of views regarding this boundary'.[73] It has challenged the only boundary

[70] 16 July 1991, Ministry of Foreign Affairs, People's Republic of China, www.learnedworld.com.

[71] See Carlson, 'Constructing the Dragon's Scales: China's Approach to Territorial Sovereignty and Border Relations in the 1980s and 1990s', 12 (2003) *Journal of Contemporary China* 677, at p. 688. See also Iwashita, *A 4000 Kilometer Journey Along the Sino-Russian Border*, Slavic Eurasian Studies No. 3, Sapporo, 2004, pp. 10 *et seq.*

[72] On Sino-Indian boundary issues, including Tibet, see Lamb, *The McMahon Line*, London, 1966, vols. I and II; Sharma, 'The China–India Border Dispute: An Indian Perspective', 59 (1965) AJIL 16; Rubin, 'The Sino-Indian Border Dispute', 9 (1960) ICLQ 96; Krishna Rao, 'The Sino-Indian Boundary Question and International Law', 11 (1962) ICLQ 375; Li, 'The Legal Position of Tibet', 50 (1956) AJIL 394; Van Eekelen (note 57), pp. 13–20, 144–5 and 211–15; and Vertzberger, *Misperceptions in Foreign Policymaking in the Sino-Indian Conflict, 1959–1962*, Boulder, CO, 1984, Chapters 2, 3, 4 and 6.

[73] See Note of the Chinese Ministry of Foreign Affairs to the Indian Embassy in China, 26 December 1959; and Statement of the People's Republic of China, 24 October 1954, in *The Sino-Indian Boundary Question* (Government Printer), Peking, 1962, p. 51, at p. 53 and p. 1, respectively (hereinafter referred to as *Sino-Indian Boundary Question*). For a more detailed account, see 'Report of the Chinese Officials on Their Statements and

agreement[74] between them, namely, the Simla Accord or Convention of April 1914. A product of a conference attended by the Chinese, British Indian and Tibetan authorities between 1913 and 1914, the Convention purported to provide a line dividing Inner Tibet from Outer Tibet, and, although the Sino-Indian frontier was not a matter fixed for discussion, the map accompanying the Convention did show, *inter alia*, a red line (the so-called McMahon Line) running east of Bhutan leaving China's Tibet to the north and India to the south. China has always argued that it had never signed, as opposed to initialled,[75] or ratified the Convention and that the Chinese Government had made it very clear that no agreement between Tibet and Britain would be recognised.[76] Accordingly, China argued that it was not bound by the terms of the Convention.

The McMahon Line had its origins earlier in March 1914 when it was agreed and drawn in an Exchange of Letters and accompanying map between the British and Tibetan representatives and, although it was agreed at the time of the Conference, China contends that it was done in secret behind its back. It followed that it could not have agreed to it, but, most importantly, it was an invalid boundary treaty inasmuch as Tibet, which was under the sovereignty of China, had no legal capacity to enter into treaties with other States independently of China.[77] While China has declined to accept these and other 'dirty unequal treaties',[78] tainted by

Comments Made During the Meetings of the Officials of the Two Governments' in *Reports of the Officials of the Governments of India and the People's Republic of China on the Boundary Question*, Ministry of External Affairs, Government of India, New Delhi, 1961, CR-1 *et seq*. Page references with the prefix 'CR' are used to refer to the Chinese part of the report.

[74] The 1842 treaty between Kashmir and the Tibetan authorities of China dealt with the areas bordering Kashmir and Sinkiang. China, however, has maintained that the agreement of 1842 is not binding on it because it is not a party to it. Nor did it actually provide delimitation: it only dealt with maintaining the *status quo* and with a non-aggression pact. The Kashmir/Ladakh–Tibet border covers only 20 per cent of the western sector of the frontier: Prime Minister of China to Prime Minister of India (note 73), p. 55; and Report of the Chinese Officials (note 73), pp. CR-14–15.

[75] The Chinese representative did initial the Convention, but his Government promptly repudiated it: see Lamb, *The China–India Border: The Origins of the Disputed Boundaries*, London and Oxford, 1964, p. 144.

[76] Note of the Chinese Ministry of Foreign Affairs of 26 December 1959, in *Sino-Indian Boundary Question* (note 73), pp. 57–8.

[77] Report of the Chinese Officials (note 73), pp. CR-19 to CR-32, especially pp. CR-25 to CR-27.

[78] Note of the Chinese Ministry of Foreign Affairs, in *Sino-Indian Boundary Question* (note 73), p. 58. It asks, on p. 58: 'The Chinese Government feels perplexed why the Government of India, which has likewise won independence from under imperialist oppression, should insist that the Government of its friend China recognise an unequal treaty which the Chinese Government has not even signed?'

invalidity, it has asserted that a traditional customary frontier, including the main chain of the Karakoram mountains and the southern foot of the Himalayas, has always existed between them and that, pending settlement, both sides should agree to maintain 'the line of actual control' and that the traditional *status quo* ought not to be altered unilaterally.[79] Importantly, this line of control accords by and large with the McMahon Line in the east and the main Karakoram watershed in the west.

The Indian Government, however, has insisted on complete and unquestioned succession to all boundary regimes maintained before independence in 1947. It has argued that the Simla Convention was a valid treaty creating legal obligations for both coterminous States and that the March 1914 agreement was not concluded behind China's back, that the Sino-Indian frontier was very much an issue at the Simla Conference and that China had over the years accepted Tibet's treaty-making powers.[80] India's inflexible 'no dispute and no negotiation' approach was then compounded by maintaining its controversial 'forward policy',[81] a policy designed to extend Indian control beyond the *de facto* alignment. Inevitably, this approach contributed to a heightening of tension and led ultimately to a brief war with China in 1962.

Defeated, India had to confront its loss of territory, including the keenly disputed Aksai Chin area in the western sector.[82] By late 1993, however, the Indian Government had finally begun to appreciate the strength of China's original proposals. Hence, in September 1993, the two parties agreed a treaty, Article 1 of which recorded: 'Pending an ultimate solution to the boundary question between the two countries, the two sides shall strictly respect and observe the [line of actual control] between the two sides.' The obligation is repeated in Article X of the Agreement on the Political Parameters and Guiding Principles for the Settlement of the India–China Boundary Question signed in April 2005.

[79] Statement of the People's Republic of China, in *Sino-Indian Boundary Question* (note 73), p. 2; and Note of the Chinese Ministry of Foreign Affairs of 26 December 1959, *ibid.*, p. 77. It also proposed a twenty-kilometre buffer zone along both sides of the line.

[80] Refer generally to the 'Report of the Indian Officials on Their Statements and Comments Made During the Meetings of the Officials of the Two Governments' in *Reports of the Officials of the Governments of India and the People's Republic of China*, in *Sino-Indian Boundary Question* (note 73), pp. 110–15.

[81] Xuecheng Liu, *The Sino-Indian Border Dispute and Sino-Indian Relations*, Lanham, MD, 1994, p. 2. See also Statement of the People's Republic of China, 24 October 1954, in *Sino-Indian Boundary Question* (note 73), pp. 2–3.

[82] Cukwurah (note 7), pp. 89–90; and 153–5.

For other States, historic ties have proven equally strong. In 1893, Afghanistan and the British Indian Government concluded a treaty delimiting the north-western frontier of India with Afghanistan.[83] The Durand Line was then comprehensively demarcated by 1895, save for a short stretch in the Mohammand sector. Thereafter, the Afghan and British Indian authorities confirmed the boundary in 1919, 1921 and 1930.[84] However, just before and soon after the United Kingdom transferred power to Pakistan in August 1947, Afghanistan began to agitate for its 'lost' territories, namely, Pakistan's North West Frontier Province and the tribal agencies, claiming that the agreement of 1893 did not bind Afghanistan.

One of its arguments was that the succession of British India to the independent States of Pakistan and India had nullified the nineteenth-century transfer of various semi-autonomous tribal homelands of the Pakhtuns to British Indian control and that the *rebus sic stantibus* principle applied to the 1893 treaty and all subsequent agreements which sought to confirm the Durand Line, with the result that the boundary was no longer legally effective.[85] Similarly, Somalia in the 1970s continued to stress the need to reunite with the Ogaden, now in Ethiopia, which it claimed historically had been inhabited by and been under the control of Somalis,[86] and that the colonial settlement of 1899 between Great Britain and Ethiopia could not prejudice its ancient rights. Historic claims, however, to Djibouti have now been abandoned.

The lessons that can be drawn are as follows. First, at the structural level, it is important to adopt a more sophisticated approach to incidents of State practice. The fact is that a superficial view of diplomatic activity can on occasion provide a skewed version of the principle or proposition behind the activity. China's experience shows that, for a correct appreciation of State practice, it may sometimes be necessary to delve more deeply into the detail.

[83] Aitchison, *A Collection of Treaties, Engagements and Sanads*, vol. 13, Calcutta, 1933, p. 256.

[84] For the Treaty of 1919, see *ibid*., p. 286; the Treaty of 1921, *ibid*., p. 288; and 104 BFSP 174; and the Exchange of Notes, 1930, Aitchison, *ibid*., p. 305 and 132 (1) BFSP 218.

[85] Anglo-Afghan Relations: Reg. P. Ext. 7593/46 in L/P&S/12/812 Coll. 3/208(1) and Pol. Ext. 7666/49, Telegram, Foreign Office to Kabul, 18 July 1949, L/P&S/12/1822, Coll. 3/214: India Office Records, India Office. Generally, see Davies, *The Problem of the North-West Frontier 1890–1908: With a Survey of Policy Since 1849*, 2nd edn, London, 1975; Spain, *The Pathan Borderland*, The Hague, 1963; Razvi, *The Frontiers of Pakistan*, Karachi, 1971, pp. 147 *et seq*.; and Lamb, *Asian Frontiers*, London, 1968.

[86] Generally, see Brownlie (note 7), p. 827; Anyangwe (note 8), p. 39; Latham Brown, 'The Ethiopia–Somaliland Frontier Dispute', 5 (1956) ICLQ 245; McEwen, *The International Boundaries of East Africa*, Oxford, 1971, pp. 113–28; and Whiteman (note 45), pp. 668–76.

Secondly, at the normative level, three points are noteworthy, the first of which is related to the above, which is that a holistic approach to State practice is important. In such an approach, the full range of considerations dictating a policy are taken into account; where there are two conflicting predicates, the more dominant ought to be given greater weight.

To the extent that it is possible to encapsulate China's approach to its border problems, it is true that the overriding characteristic is the acceptance of *de facto* continuity while maintaining the claim of *de jure* discontinuity. The significant fact here, from the point of view of law and State practice, is that, when States are willing to agree a boundary regime, they are more likely to accept an alignment which is the least disruptive of existing territorial arrangements, *de facto* or otherwise. The underlying fact is that China's position does not *necessarily* reflect dissatisfaction with the *location* of the various *de facto* alignments, but is simply a need to remedy perceived past injustices by asserting equality of treatment and to remove uncertainties attending these alignments. As Vertzberger writes:

> The boundaries, then, must be given new legitimacy and authority through renegotiation between the People's Republic and its relevant neighbour, 'taking into consideration the historical background and present actualities . . .'. It could very well happen that the new agreements would settle on borders geographically identical to the previous ones or would require just as many concessions on the part of China as on that of India, but these borders would be new in terms of symbolic significance, achieved from a position of equality and dignity.[87]

This can be contrasted with the positions adopted by Afghanistan and Somalia, where the territorial aspects are predominant insofar as it is the desire to regain lost homelands which motivates these States.

The second normative fact is that China's policy as described above is not necessarily incompatible with the doctrine of *uti possidetis*. Of course, unilateral rejection sits uneasily in a legal order fully imbued with the above doctrine, but it must be noted that the doctrine of continuity also applies to matters not settled conclusively or those tainted with legal problems. Hence, in matters of State succession for boundary regimes, there is a requirement of continuity not only of all legal and factual *certainties* but also of all *uncertainties*. Hence, problems of consent, consultation and capacity regarding treaties passed over from the predecessor regime cannot simply be brushed off. Furthermore, China's position regarding the maintenance of the *de facto* traditional alignment as the

[87] Supra (note 72), p. 155.

first provisional step is fully compatible with the *uti possidetis* doctrine and indeed closely resembles the considerations which informed the Latin American approach to the vexed question of uncertain administrative boundaries of the Spanish Empire. The legal effect of China's treaties with these neighbours was two-fold. On the one hand, the principle of *uti possidetis* was guardedly confirmed, and, on the other, China appeared not to prejudice its fundamental legal position, namely, that it was not bound by treaties which were either not formally valid or not binding because they were based on assertions of imperial power which created inequality between the contracting States and were therefore null and void.

The third normative fact is that, when confronted with boundary problems in the event of State and governmental succession, any resistance to the conducting of *bona fide* negotiations in a spirit of compromise cannot legally be justified, especially when the likelihood of a breach of the peace is sufficiently high. Article 33 of the UN Charter and the judgment of the International Court of Justice in the *North Sea Continental Shelf* cases[88] confirm this proposition of law. Thus intransigence demonstrated by India was neither diplomatically justified nor legally acceptable, especially given the fact that this intransigence resulted in armed conflict with China. Similarly, the untenability of Afghan and Somali claims can hardly be doubted, given the fact that the *rebus* rule is not applicable to boundary treaties. The principle articulated in Article 61(2)(a) of the Vienna Convention on the Law of Treaties is widely regarded as declaratory of customary international law, while Articles 11 and 12 of the Vienna Convention on the Succession of States in Respect of Treaties[89] also reflect customary international law inasmuch as they provide, in terms, for a continuity of boundary treaties and territorial arrangements in the event of a succession of States. Despite the strength of law behind the positions adopted by Pakistan and Ethiopia, there is, nevertheless, an obligation on all neighbouring States to discuss matters with a view to persuading the other side to settle or compromise or both. The maturity with which Moscow and Beijing have approached their border problems is exemplary in both law and diplomacy.

2. Problems based on unilateral renunciation

It is not, however, only boundary treaties of successor and established States which have been the source of unrest. States on occasion have simply

[88] ICJ Reports 1969, p. 3, at p. 47, where the Court referred to 'meaningful' negotiations.
[89] 1155 UNTS 331; and 17 (1978) ILM 1488.

renounced formal agreements concluded by them or rejected frontier alignments arrived at by impartial judicial, arbitral or non-judicial bodies, and, in keeping with past practice, it is usually a self-serving application or interpretation of the law which is relied upon to dispute their legal effects. One of the more striking examples of recent times is the renunciation by two coterminous States of two boundary treaties one after the other.

In 1969, Iran purportedly abrogated the 1937 boundary treaty with Iraq on the ground that the treaty, as a relic of the colonial era, was *rebus sic stantibus* and that, as a boundary river, the Shatt al Arab must be under joint sovereignty.[90] In 1980, Iraq announced the renunciation of the 1975 Baghdad Treaty which had delimited the riverain boundary along the median line of the *thalweg* of the Shatt al Arab. The latter renunciation was justified on the ground that the ongoing war with Iran had released Baghdad of all the obligations of the Treaty. In fact, it was the loss of the historic left bank of the Shatt al Arab which Iraq was unable to accept insofar as it was seen as a humiliating retreat from its ancient rights and control.[91]

From the legal point of view, however, it is undoubtedly the case that unilateral abrogation is viewed by States with disapprobation, because legally there is nothing to renounce: the treaty, once executed, is evidence of the location of the line, and of the transfer and disposition of territory; it becomes a muniment of conveyance, as it were. As the International Court of Justice observed in *Libya* v. *Chad* with reference to the boundary agreed in the Treaty of 1955:

> The establishment of this boundary is a fact which, from the outset, has had a legal life of its own, independently of the fate of the 1955 Treaty. Once agreed, the boundary stands, for any other approach would vitiate the fundamental principle of the stability of boundaries, the importance of which has repeatedly been emphasised by the Court . . . A boundary established by treaty thus achieves a permanence which the treaty itself does not necessarily enjoy. The treaty can cease to be in force without in any way affecting the continuance of the boundary.[92]

[90] Doc. S/9323, 11 July 1969: Letter from Iraqi Representative to the President of the Security Council, SCOR, Twenty-Fourth Year, 1969, p. 108, at pp. 113–17.

[91] See, generally, Schofield, 'Position, Function and Symbol: The Shatt al-Arab Dispute in Perspective', in Potter and Sick (eds.), *Iran, Iraq and the Legacies of War*, New York, 2004, p. 29; Kaikobad, *The Shatt al Arab Question: A Legal Reappraisal*, Oxford, 1988; cf. Lauterpacht, 'River Boundaries: Legal Aspects of the Shatt al Arab Frontier', 9 (1960) ICLQ 208; Al-Izzi, *The Shatt al Arab River Dispute in Terms of International Law*, Baghdad, 1972; Amin, 'The Iran–Iraq Conflict', 31 (1982) ICLQ 167; Edmonds, 'The Iraqi–Persian Frontier: 1638–1938', 62 (1975) *Asian Affairs* 147; and Whiteman (note 44), pp. 904–5.

[92] ICJ Reports 1994, p. 6, at p. 37. This is what Shaw calls the 'objectivisation of boundary treaties': see Shaw, 'The Heritage of States: The Principle of Uti Possidetis Juris Today', 67

Abrogation or any kind of modification of a boundary treaty must therefore proceed bilaterally, thereby making the renunciation or modification of rights and privileges a mutual affair. Indeed, as Iraq argued, Iran had 'no legal right unilaterally and arbitrarily to abrogate a treaty that was concluded in accordance with rules of international law', and that the Treaty of 1937, being a boundary treaty, '[is] considered final upon [its] conclusion, and boundaries cannot change as a result of alleged change of circumstances'.[93] The episode involving the unilateral rejection of an 'invalid' boundary agreement, namely, the Rio Protocol of 1942, by Ecuador in 1960 is instructive. The robust response of Argentina, Chile, Brazil and the United States, the four guarantor States of the Protocol, was that it was a basic principle of international law that the unilateral will of one of the parties was not sufficient to invalidate a boundary treaty or to liberate it from the obligations imposed therein.[94]

3. Problems based on unilateral rejection of boundary awards and decisions

Unilateral rejections are not confined to boundary agreements; they are also a phenomenon occurring with respect to territorial or boundary awards, some aspects of which are discussed in sections IV.c and IV.d below. At this point, it is appropriate to underline the fact that, while legal considerations are usually uppermost in terms of providing a statement of justification, the underlying political difficulties are always at the heart of the matter. Never fully reconciled to the 1899 award of the Arbitration Tribunal in the *British Guiana* v. *Venezuela* case, the Venezuelan Government decided unilaterally in 1945, and thereafter, that the award was null and void. One of the arguments was that the award was a 'diplomatic compromise' between members

(1996) BYIL 81, especially pp. 87–92; also see further *ibid.*, pp. 112–19; and generally see O'Connell, *International Law*, vol. I, London, 1970, pp. 373–4 (on dispositive treaties generally); and O'Connell, *State Succession in Municipal and International Law*, vol. II, Cambridge, 1967, p. 273; McNair, *The Law of Treaties*, Oxford, 1961, pp. 655–64; Kaikobad (note 91), pp. 85–92; Harastzi, 'Treaties and the Fundamental Change of Circumstances', 146 (1975-III) *Hague Recueil* 65; Tyranowski, 'State Succession and Boundaries and Boundary Treaties', 10 (1979–80) *Polish Yearbook of International Law* 115; Lester, 'State Succession to Treaties in the Commonwealth', 12 (1963) ICLQ 475, at pp. 492–5; and Fischer Williams, 'The Permanence of Treaties', 22 (1928) AJIL 89. See also Whiteman on the dispositive character of the Kiel Canal regime established by the Treaty of Versailles: Whiteman (note 45), vol. III, pp. 1256–71, especially pp. 1258–9.

93 Supra (note 90), p. 109 and p. 116.

94 See Whiteman (note 45), pp. 676–80, at p. 679. The boundary delimitation provision was contained in Article VIII.

of the tribunal as a result of pressure from the President of the Tribunal who had, in turn, allegedly been put under pressure by Russia and Great Britain.[95] Although the disputing States have concluded two treaties to maintain the *status quo* without prejudice to their respective positions, there has been no definitive settlement of the problem.[96]

In more recent times, the rejection by Ethiopia of the *Eritrea* v. *Ethiopia* boundary award is a case in point.[97] The award, handed down by the Eritrea–Ethiopia Boundary Commission in April 2002 after the United Nations had arranged a peace pact, namely, the Algiers Agreement of 2000, between the two warring States, was, in strict principle, a boundary delimitation exercise based on the 'pertinent colonial treaties' of 1900, 1902 and 1908. The Commission allocated the town of Badme to Eritrea, the first village militarily occupied by Eritrea and seen by Ethiopia as the *casus belli*. The Government of Ethiopia rejected the award and argued that the award was illegal, unjust, irresponsible and a blatant miscarriage of justice with respect to Badme and parts of the central sector.[98] The thrust of its arguments was that the Commission's delimitation was inconsistent, ambiguous, erroneous and self-contradictory.[99] Not only did it contend that the basis of the decision was unclear, the Government of Ethiopia claimed that the Badme sector was decided 'exclusively on the basis of maps even though the Commission itself ha[d] stated in the . . . Decision that "[t]he Commission is aware of the caution with which international tribunals view maps" '.[100] It also chose allegedly to ignore issues of administration and the continuous exercise of State authority, issues which constituted a key plank of the Ethiopian claim to Badme.[101] As far as the central sector was concerned, the Ethiopian Government argued that the Commission had adjusted the 1900 treaty line because of its mistaken identification of

[95] See Venezuela Foreign Ministry, Report on the Boundary Question with British Guiana Submitted to the National Government by the Venezuelan Experts, 1967, partially reproduced in Wetter, *The International Arbitral Process: Public and Private*, vol. III, New York, 1979, Chapter VIII, pp. 140, at pp. 141 and 143; and see *ibid*., pp. 333–52; Menon, 'Guyana–Venezuela Boundary Dispute', 6 (1972) *Encyclopaedia of Public International Law* 212; and Schoenrich, 'The Venezuela–British Guiana Boundary Dispute', 43 (1949) AJIL 523; cf. Child, 'The Venezuela–British Guiana Boundary Arbitration of 1899', 44 (1950) AJIL 682.

[96] See the texts of the treaties of 1966 and 1970 in Wetter (note 95), pp. 134–6 and 137–9, respectively. Further, see Pettisford, 'Guyana–Venezuela', in Calvert (note 61), pp. 117–20.

[97] 41 (2002) ILM 1057.

[98] Prime Minister of Ethiopia to the Secretary-General of the United Nations, 19 September 2003: www.ethiopiafirst.com.

[99] *Ibid*.

[100] Ethiopian Minister of Foreign Affairs to the Secretary-General of the United Nations, 16 October 2003: www.mfa.gov.et/Press/.

[101] *Ibid*.

the location of Fort Cadorna, yet it had failed to correct it in the award after discovery of the mistake, and stated:

> This is why Ethiopia has been insisting that the Commission has been arbitrary in its decision as well as illegal, unjust and irresponsible. Having moved a whole mountain 20 km from its natural position and having adjusted the boundary as an outcome of that error, the Commission insists that its decision will continue to be sacrosanct, regardless of the implication of this for peace and stability and for the lives of the affected people.[102]

The fact, of course, was that Badme was at the very heart of the dispute and had become 'symbolically important . . . for the people of Ethiopia who had paid so much blood to reverse the Eritrean Aggression', and that the 'decision was a recipe for continued instability, and even recurring wars'.[103] However, in November 2004, the Prime Minister of Ethiopia submitted a report on a new Ethiopian–Eritrean peace initiative in which the Ethiopian Government, for the sake of securing the objective of peace, accepted the April 2002 decision and agreed to begin negotiations on implementation thereof.[104] Notwithstanding the above, the two-year hiatus between delivery and acceptance of the award shows that, while underlying political factors can inform governmental policy seeking to reject an award on a thin veneer of legal grounds, its acceptance can also be a reflection of a need to normalise relations between the two States. At any rate, the offer of acceptance and negotiations has not been viewed favourably by Eritrea which expects a simple uncomplicated implementation of the award. At the time of writing, tension between the two States was rising and the fear of renewed hostilities palpable.

Be that as it may, the general legal position is similar to the rule prohibiting a unilateral rejection of a valid boundary treaty. International law will reject any situation which can validly overturn a judicial or arbitral award without either testing the claim before another tribunal, not unlike the award in the case of *Colombia* v. *Costa Rica*,[105] a decision which was rejected by Costa Rica on the grounds of *excès de pouvoir*, and which was subsequently examined, by mutual consent, in *Costa Rica* v. *Panama*[106] or by coming to an arrangement, either *ad hoc* or permanent. The guiding fact is that mutuality of consent is an essential element in the corpus of the law dealing with the settlement of disputes.

102 *Ibid.* 103 Prime Minister of Ethiopia to UN Secretary-General, supra (note 98).

104 Ethiopian Foreign Minister, 'Report on the New Ethio-Eritrean Peace Initiative Submitted to House of Peoples' Representatives', 25 November 2004: www.waltainfo.com.

105 92 BFSP 1038. 106 108 BFSP 439; 11 UNRIAA 528.

4. Problems based on constitutive legal considerations

At times, dissension can be so complex and problematic that, despite one or even two judicial or quasi-judicial decisions regarding the location of the line, the matter cannot realistically be considered as having finally and definitively been settled, and, equally importantly, rejection may come not from the disputant parties but from a mediating body. Of course, as noted above, all territorial and boundary problems are couched in law and therefore involve legal considerations to one extent or another whether or not they are interpreted justifiably. In this category, legal considerations are those which deal with issues going to the powers of the tribunal or quasi-judicial bodies and their effects on the final award. To that extent, these legal considerations are different from those which attend the categories discussed above.

A good illustration of this is the *Jaworzina Boundary* case.[107] The case shows how the application of certain legal criteria can prove to be an obstacle to closure and provide justification for reconsideration of the location of the line. This case deals with some of the boundary problems between Poland and Czechoslovakia in the districts of Spisz, Orava and Teschen after the conclusion of the Treaties of Versailles, St Germain-en-Laye and Trianon.[108] The general task of determining the Polish–Czech frontier fell to the Principal Allied and Associated Powers, and, by agreement between the two parties in July 1920 with respect to the disputed sector, to the Supreme Council of the Powers, which body instructed the Conference of Ambassadors to divide the districts.[109]

On 28 July 1920, the Conference decided the issue. In Article I(3) of its decision, the Conference described a line which divided the disputed districts of Teschen, Orava and Spisz between Poland and Czechoslovakia. The line was to be demarcated within one month by a Delimitation Commission. In Article II(3), the Commission was empowered to make proposals to the Conference for modifications to the boundary delimited by the Conference, provided they were justified by reason of the interests of the individuals or communities in the neighbourhood of the frontier, taking into account special local circumstances. Apart from considering it contrary to justice and equity, Poland claimed that the line remained subject to further delimitation and modification and final settlement in

[107] PCIJ Reports, Series B, No. 8 (1923), p. 6.

[108] See Articles 81 and 87, 112 BFSP 1; Article 91, *ibid.*, p. 317; and Article 75, 113 BFSP 486, respectively.

[109] Supra (note 107), p. 16.

the Spisz region (Jaworzina).[110] Czechoslovakia, however, took the position that the Conference had carried out its task by tracing the frontier line described in Article I(3), and that it could only thereafter 'effect slight modifications of the frontier line in accordance with proposals to be submitted by the Delimitation Commission'. Moreover, it was claimed, once it had exhausted its right to modify the frontier by rejecting the Commission's proposals, the Conference had no power to revoke the decision of 28 July 1920.[111]

The matter was referred in 1923 to the Permanent Court of International Justice by the Council of the League of Nations for an advisory opinion on whether the question of the delimitation of the frontier was 'still open' or whether it was 'already settled by a definitive decision', subject to demarcation and to modifications of detail for the purposes of adjusting to local circumstances.[112] The Court held that, while the frontier had definitively been settled by the decision of 28 July 1920, the latter had to be applied in its entirety and consequently the line in the Spisz region remained subject to the modifications allowed under Article II(3).[113] By definition, however, these modifications excluded 'a complete or almost complete abandonment of the line fixed by the decision of July 28th, 1920'.[114] The Court emphasised the fact that the Commission could only submit proposals to the Conference, the sole decision-making body. Any modification consistent with Article II(3) needed the unanimous consent of the Conference. Nor could consent of the disputant States on the Commission have any legal effect on the delimitation.[115] The Court added that the frontier was also subject to modifications of local detail arising out of a demarcation process.[116]

It is interesting, then, to note that one of the main questions of law was not in fact referred to the Court, and thus, when the advisory opinion was placed before the Council of the League on 17 December 1923, both Poland and Czechoslovakia accepted it,[117] but there were still lingering questions in some quarters with respect to the decision adopted by the Delimitation Commission on 25 September 1922 regarding the disputed boundary in the Spisz area. This came about as a result of a prolonged failure by the

[110] See the Case of the Polish Government, *ibid.*, p. 8. See also Appendix No. I to Document No. 114, Skirmunt to the Secretary-General of the League of Nations, 12 September 1923, Documents Relating to Advisory Opinion No. 8 (Jaworzina), *Publications of the Permanent Court of International Justice, Series C, No. 4 Fourth Session (Extraordinary)*, Leyden, 1923, p. 275, at pp. 279–82.

[111] See the Case of the Czechoslovak Government (note 107), pp. 9–10.

[112] *Ibid.*, p. 10. [113] *Ibid.*, p. 57. [114] *Ibid.*, p. 40. [115] *Ibid.* [116] *Ibid.*, p. 57.

[117] Hudson, *World Court Reports*, vol. I, Washington, DC, 1934, p. 253.

parties to agree a demarcation line. In an attempt to break this deadlock, members of the Commission from the Allied Powers proposed a line which ran along the crest of the Tatra mountain range. This proposal was designed to satisfy the economic interests of Poland and the military considerations of Czechoslovakia.[118] The latter, however, was not satisfied with the delimitation.[119] Hence, when the Delimitation Commission decided on 25 September 1922 to adopt this compromise line, the Czech member was the only Commissioner who voted against it and accompanied it with a letter of protest. This compromise line was forwarded for approval to the Conference of Ambassadors.

On 13 November 1922, the Conference of Ambassadors wrote identical letters to the Polish and Czechoslovak ministers, but reserved the taking of a formal decision on the compromise line. Nonetheless, it indicated that failing agreement between the two States with regard to Jaworzina, awarded by the Frontiers Treaty of August 1920 to the latter State, 'the Delimitation Commission could not compensate Czechoslovakia by allotting to her territories situated in a sector defined by the Decision of July 28, 1920 and awarded by that Decision to Poland'.[120] The anxiety was that, if the Treaty of 1920 came into force, the two lines in the Jaworzina area would not have coincided with each other.[121] The Conference took the position that it had suspended its decision of 28 July 1920 only on the condition that the two parties agreed a *bilateral* line, and that this was not the case here. Accordingly, the Conference asserted the right strictly to apply the delimitation contained in that decision and to resume its authority with respect to the delimitation of the Spisz area.[122] It was in this context

[118] The line is described and justified in President, Polish–Czechoslovak Frontier Commission to the Conference of Ambassadors, 12 September 1922, Document No. 92 in Documents Relating to Advisory Opinion No. 8 (note 110), pp. 237–8; and see also *ibid.*, 26 September 1922, Document No. 96, *ibid.*, pp. 243–4. Cf. the Polish position that it was 'unfavourable to Polish interests'. See Polish Delegate to the Secretary-General of the League of Nations (note 110), p. 294. See also Kellor and Hatvany, *Security Against War*, vol. II, *Arbitration, Disarmament, Outlawry*, New York, 1924, p. 598.

[119] See Annex H to the Statement of the Law Submitted to the Court by the Czechoslovak Government, Appendix to Document No. 118, Documents Relating to Advisory Opinion No. 8 (note 110), p. 315, at pp. 351–5; and Annex D, *ibid.*, p. 320, at p. 335.

[120] Document No. 98, Documents Relating to Advisory Opinion No. 8 (note 110), p. 247, at p. 249.

[121] Note by the Drafting Committee of the Peace Conference, 21 October 1922 as signed by M. Henry Fromageot: Document No. 97, Documents Relating to Advisory Opinion No. 8 (note 110), p. 245, at p. 246.

[122] Document No. 98 (note 110), p. 249. Kellor and Hatvany write that the Conference asserted that the Commission had exceeded its powers in marking out a frontier on 25 September 1922, but such a statement is nowhere in evidence in the letter of 13

that the question regarding the 28 July 1920 decision was put ultimately to the Permanent Court of International Justice.

By the time the question of the legality and effect of the decision of 25 September 1922 came before the Council of the League, the question had become more acute. Poland maintained that the Commission's proposals were in keeping with its powers of modification inherent in the Commission and that they were consistent with the interests of the different communities, private persons and local circumstances, and that accordingly the Council ought to approve the proposals and transmit them for adoption by the Conference.[123] Mr Benes, the Czech representative on the Council, argued: 'The Czechoslovak Government's contention was that this was not a modification of the line laid down on July 28, 1920, but almost an entire abandonment of that line.' Moreover, the Commission had exceeded its competence inasmuch as the proposals affected the old international frontiers of Hungary and Galicia (Sectors I and III) and they, as the Court had formally recognised, were not subject to modifications.[124] Both, however, agreed that it was for the Council to decide whether or not the proposals of 25 September 1922 were consistent with the Conference decision of 28 July 1920 and that its decision be transmitted to the Conference for a fresh and final initiative on the matter.[125]

The matter was referred to the Spanish member of the Council, Mr Quinones de Leon, who prepared a report on the matter.[126] The Council discussed the report on 13 December 1923 on the basis of which a resolution was adopted with minor modifications on 17 December 1923.[127] The Council took the position that, although the proposed line was based on considerations relating to the interests of individuals or communities in the neighbourhood, in proposing the line of 25 September 1922 the Delimitation Commission had in fact exceeded its powers. For one thing, the line superseded the former frontier throughout Sector I by an alignment which was located several kilometres east of this frontier. For another, the line proposed was not a set of modifications in that it did not coincide with the line topographically defined in the decision of 28 July

November 1922. The Polish Minister, however, in reply to the 13 November 1922 letter, did contend that it was 'morally impossible to treat as null and void' the decision of 25 September 1922: see Polish Minister to the Conference of Ambassadors, 29 November 1922, Document No. 100, Documents Relating to Advisory Opinion No. 8 (note 110), p. 254, at p. 255.

123 Sixth Meeting, 13 December 1923, 5 (1924) *League of Nations Official Journal* 345, at pp. 345–6. 124 *Ibid*., p. 346. 125 *Ibid*., pp. 346–7.

126 Annex 593, 13 December 1923, *ibid*., p. 398.

127 Tenth Meeting, 17 December 1923, *ibid*., p. 364.

1920 for about five kilometres and that the general lie of the 25 September 1922 line was in a north–south direction whereas the frontier in the Spisz territory as defined on 28 July 1920 ran from west to east for two-thirds of its length and north to south for the last one-third. The Conference of Ambassadors was invited to request the Commission to furnish fresh proposals in conformity with the advisory opinion.[128]

As a result, the controversial sector was re-examined by the Commission and a new line, based on a mix of Czech and Polish proposals for different sub-sectors, was recommended to the Council and justified by reference to communal interests and minimalist modifications. In his second report of 12 March 1924, Mr Quinones de Leon urged the adoption of this line,[129] and the Council then confirmed this line in a resolution adopted on the same day.[130] While Poland reluctantly agreed, the Czech Government welcomed and accepted the line proposed by the Council.[131] On 24 March 1924, the latter adopted a resolution accepting the delimitation proposals and also recommended that the two States agree an elaborate frontier regime entailing, *inter alia*, passport control regulations.[132] On 26 March 1924, the Conference adopted a resolution in which it stated that, upon approval of the Protocols by the Conference, the frontier would finally be fixed according to the resolution of 12 March 1924 adopted by the Council.[133] This detailed frontier regime was agreed on 6 May 1924, and the matter was finally put to rest.[134]

The sequence of events described above reflects, on the one hand, the fact that, despite ostensible agreement, political realities will continue to dictate its failure or success. From the legal perspective, however, there are some interesting points which need to be addressed. First, it is curious that one of the main issues attending the delimitation dispute was not referred to the Court by way of a specific question, that is, whether the decision of 25 September 1922 was *ultra vires* the Delimitation Commission. One speculative answer is that there was never any real legal uncertainty regarding its status, for it had always been clear that the final authority on all delimitation issues lay with the Conference of Ambassadors. If the Conference and the Council did not wish to waste the time of the Court by asking a question to which they both had an answer, then that, in itself, is unremarkable. The fact, however, is that the

[128] Draft Resolution introduced by M. Quinones de Leon, Ninth Meeting, 17 December 1923, *ibid.*, pp. 356–7. [129] Annex 616, 12 March 1924, *ibid.*, pp. 627–8.
[130] Fourth Meeting, 12 March 1924, *ibid.*, pp. 520–1. [131] *Ibid.*
[132] Kellor and Hatvany (note 118), p. 605. [133] Supra (note 110), p. 828.
[134] Kellor and Hatvany (note 118), pp. 604–5.

Conference and the parties were indeed exercised by the validity of the Commission's decision of 25 September 1922.

Even so, secondly, it is difficult to understand how the Conference could ever have been convinced that the Commission had exceeded its powers, for only decisions validly adopted by the appropriate decision-making body can or cannot be *ultra vires*. The action taken by the Commission on 25 September 1922 was in the form of a 'decision' but it was in law only a proposal which needed to be ratified by the Conference at its discretion to become a binding line. Insofar as the decision could not and did not create any legally binding rights and obligations, the question of *ultra vires* could never seriously have arisen.

Thirdly, the legal yardstick, by which the decision of 25 September 1922 became to be judged, was somehow in a state of flux. While *ultra vires* action was first heralded as a ground for dissatisfaction, the decision was then impugned in part by reference to the standards set by the Permanent Court of International Justice in the *Jaworzina* advisory opinion. The question asked of the Court by the Council at the urging of the parties was whether the decision in question was consistent with Article II(3) of the decision of 28 July 1920, 'the latter being interpreted in light of the opinion given by the Court'. The difficulty is that the September 1922 decision could not be judged by reference to standards established *ex post facto* by the Court; it could, strictly speaking, only be examined by the legal criteria set out in the July 1920 decision for the simple reason that the Court's interpretation of the July 1920 decision came over a year subsequent to the September 1922 decision, that is, on 6 December 1923. Of course, the Court did not set new standards and only clarified existing ones, but the fact is that any reference to the interpretation placed on the July 1920 decision by the Court could have no real legal meaning where the proposals were adopted before the latter opinion was given. Even if it is the case that no onerous obligations were placed on the parties by virtue of this opinion, to have *ex post facto* legal considerations brought in to judge decisions later in time is a proposition difficult to accept in law.

Fourthly, this whole episode shows in how much of a legal quandary the Conference found itself. On the one hand, the Delimitation Commission had acted on the basis of a *bona fide* and indeed urgent need to settle a matter which had caused so much difficulty between the parties amid rising tension. Moreover, inasmuch as the Commission had acted on the basis of a near unanimous vote, to have accepted the Czechoslovak position would arguably have appeared to grant it a veto over the matter. On the other hand, since there were strong arguments regarding the decision's *ultra vires* dimension, the Conference would have found it legally troubling to have approved a line which exceeded its powers insofar as it interfered with established borders. It was also concerned by the fact that the line decided by the unratified 1920 boundary treaty was different from the September 1922 alignment, a fact which would have required deft legal documentation to give the latter primacy over the former if and when it came into force. Finally, the Conference would have been conscious of the fact that a major contributor to the unsettled state of seemingly settled affairs was a lack of clarity in its decision of 28 July 1920, a state of affairs which was then exacerbated when the Conference stated in its letter of 13 November 1922 that the 'Jaworzina sector of the Polish–Czechoslovak frontier was not defined in the Decision of July 28th, 1920'.

c. Concluding analysis

By way of recapitulation, it needs to be highlighted that, although dissatisfaction with a boundary treaty or award, or any territorial settlement or regime for that matter, is a regular phenomenon in the relations between neighbouring States, the law adopts an extremely cautious approach to such phenomena. On the one hand, it shuns any attempt unilaterally to change the territorial *status quo prima facie* existing in terms of the location of the line or title to territory. The law's response is a strict one, for it cannot allow one-sided attempts to overturn the frontier or status of territory. Insofar as they create mutual rights and interests which run and remain directly with the land, settlements and awards enjoy immunity from such actions. By providing stability in territorial relations, then, the law provides a valuable service to the international community of States.

On the other hand, the law also accepts that from time to time there will be legal difficulties of status and location, despite, or because of, formal agreements and judicial and arbitral awards. Where such difficulties exist, the rules of international law require that they be addressed by negotiations conducted in good faith, and, where they fail, by any one or more of the methods identified in Article 33 of the United Nations Charter, including judicial or arbitral settlement, and at times the latter dispute settlement technique could be the second of two attempts. The point of course is that, once judicial or arbitral techniques are employed – and this may be the preferred route especially where there are a host of legal questions to be answered[135] – then the law, as opposed

[135] See, generally, Vallat, 'The Peaceful Settlement of Disputes', in *Cambridge Essays in International Law: Essays in Honour of Lord McNair*, London, 1965, p. 115, at p. 160.

to the element of compromise which is the cachet of negotiations, assumes centre-stage. While political dissatisfaction assumes a legal cloak, as it were, for the purposes of urging favourable changes to location or status, the law is relied upon to evaluate and sanction, wherever necessary, change, major or minor, to the territorial *status quo*. Thus, although the purpose of the law is to ensure and maintain stability and finality in territorial settlements, it cannot ignore the fact that providing legal and quasi-legal solutions to difficulties bedevilling the parties is also a function thereof. Where dissatisfaction, full or partial, is capable of being justified by such principles, then change appropriate to the legal requirement must be admitted as a valid measure. Stability, thus, is not an objective to be sought for its own sake, for if the status or location in question cannot be defended in law then the objective of stability ceases also to be relevant.

IV. The arbitration and adjudication of territorial and boundary disputes: dissatisfaction and international law

a. Arbitration and territorial disputes: historical background

While adjudication has gained great prominence today on account of the International Court of Justice, it is arbitration, of course, which is the older of the two techniques of peaceful settlement.[136] Indeed, it is safe to state that the history of arbitration is also, in a very real sense, the history of territorial settlements by such means. So closely linked are these two features that, when the representatives of Brazil and Argentina assembled

[136] Generally, on arbitration, see Verzijl, *International Law in Historical Perspective*, Leyden, 1976, Part VIII, *Inter-State Disputes and Their Settlement*, Leyden, 1976, pp. 180 *et seq.*; Simpson and Fox, *International Arbitration*, London, 1959; Nussbaum, *A Concise History of the Law of Nations*, New York, 1947, pp. 14–15, 25, 33–4, 212–18 and pp. 240–1; Moore, *History and Digest of the International Arbitrations to Which the United States Has Been a Party*, vol. II, Washington, DC, 1898, pp. 2109–22; Hudson, *International Tribunals: Past and Future*, Washington, DC, 1944, pp. 1–31; Bustamante, 'Arbitration in the Western Hemisphere', 7 (1929) *Foreign Affairs* 282; Sohn, 'Settlement of Disputes Relating to the Interpretation and Application of Treaties', 150 (1976-II) *Hague Recueil* 195; Muller and Mijs (eds.), *The Flame Rekindled: New Hopes for International Arbitration*, Dordrecht, 1994; Merrills, *International Dispute Settlement*, 3rd edn, London, 1998, pp. 88–120; Schlochauer, 'Arbitration', 1 (1972) *Encyclopaedia of Public International Law* 13; Soons (ed.), *International Arbitration: Past and Prospects*, Dordrecht, 1990; Ralston, *The Law and Procedure of International Tribunals*, 2nd edn, Stanford, 1926, pp. xxv–xl; Stuyt, *Survey of International Arbitrations 1794–1989*, 3rd edn, The Hague and Dordrecht, 1990, pp. vii–ix; and Strupp, 'The Competence of the Mixed Arbitral Courts of the Treaty of Versailles', 17 (1923) AJIL 661.

in Washington in 1889–90 for the First Pan American Conference, they were able to declare:

[t]hat international arbitration is a principle of American public law to which nations in this conference bind themselves, for decision, not only in their questions of territorial limits but also on all those in which arbitration be compatible with sovereignty.[137]

Perhaps even more striking, for present purposes, is the fact that arbitration for the settlement of territorial disputes is itself no stranger to controversy. The *British Guiana* v. *Venezuela* arbitration discussed above is merely one example. The point here is that, from time to time, both ancient arbitral adjustments and modern forensic awards have either been called into question or been revisited for confirmation or clarification; and, on many an occasion, they have been marred by problems of various kinds.

Thus, one of the earliest recorded arbitrations took place *circa* 4000 BC, between two ancient Sumerian cities, Shirpurla and Gishkhu, situated near a canal, the Shatt el Hai, and the dispute between them involved the question of territorial limits. Tod writes that, so bitter was the dispute between them, that not even war was able to resolve matters, and, eventually, Mesilim, the King of Kish, was called upon to arbitrate. In due course, the King defined the boundary between the cities and set up a stele to mark their territorial limits. A treaty of delimitation recording this has been discovered.[138] Tod then goes on to provide an illuminating account of the sophisticated legal nature of the international arbitral process among the Greeks, and observes that: 'By far the largest class of disputes submitted to arbitration in the ancient Greek world appears to have consisted of those which arose out of conflicting territorial claims.'[139] By way of clarification, he explains that some of these arbitrations did not deal exclusively with the allocation or status of territory and that some of

[137] Gonzalo de Quesada, *Arbitration in Latin America*, Rotterdam, 1907, p. 17. Cf. Moore, who wrote: 'It is proper, however, to point out that, in the settlement of boundary disputes by arbitration, there is nothing distinctively American. The same method has repeatedly been employed by European powers, both in Europe and elsewhere, for the determination of similar controversies.' See 'Application of the Principle of International Arbitration on the American Continents', in *Collected Papers of John Bassett Moore in Seven Volumes*, vol. III, New Haven, 1944, p. 58, at p. 65.

[138] See *International Arbitration Among the Greeks*, Oxford, 1913, pp. 170–1. This aspect of the account is based on the discoveries of L. W. King and H. R. H. Hall, *Egypt and Western Asia in the Light of Recent Discoveries*, London, 1907, p. 171. For a more critical view, see Fraser, 'A Sketch of the History of International Arbitration', 11 (1926) *Cornell Law Quarterly* 179, p. 185, note 20.

[139] Supra (note 138), pp. 53–4.

them also involved problems of demarcation of the boundary.[140] In a similar vein, Westermann, in his study of interstate arbitration in antiquity, observes:

> From 300 BC to 100 BC there are forty-six recorded cases which I think are to be classified as interstate arbitrations. In thirty-six cases, inscriptions discovered within the last century, most of them in recent years, form our source of information. The evidence is, of course, indisputable. The troubles adjusted are almost always boundary disputes.[141]

Verzijl cites an early example of Greek arbitration, *circa* 600 BC, carried out by Periandros, the tyrant of Corinth, between Athens and Mytilene regarding the town of Sigeion (also known as Sigeum) on the Hellespont;[142] and Schlochauer writes that, between 338 and 168 BC, a number of territorial disputes were submitted for arbitration, including the question of the estuary of the Danube and the territorial problems between the cities of Crete and the Aegean Sea island states.[143] In his study of Greek and Roman arbitration, Coleman Phillipson recounts a number of arbitrations in the Roman era which deal with boundary and territorial disputes.[144] He also provides some insight into the complexities and sophistication of territorial disputes in ancient Greece.

In one case, a dispute erupted between Corinth and Corcyra over the city of Epidamnus when the latter, a colony founded by Corcyra, managed to secure the assistance of Corinth to quell civil strife and barbarian attacks, whereupon Corcyra, herself a former colony of Corinth, began to assert herself over her former colony and agreed to submit the dispute to arbitration.[145] In the territorial dispute over some islands between Melos and Cimolos in 338 BC, Argos acted as arbitrator. The Argive functionaries included a president, a secretary and an assessor.[146] The frequency of territorial disputes is evidence of the fact that independent, impartial, third party settlement of such problems between States or discrete territorial entities was indeed central to the *raison d'être* of the process.

Notwithstanding this, dissatisfaction of one kind or another with the results of the arbitration itself is also arguably as old as this settlement

[140] *Ibid.* Other aspects of territorial claims included rights to territory falling short of absolute ownership and also disputes the focal point of which was a relatively small area of national or religious significance such as fortresses, temples, sanctuaries, springs, streams and harbours: pp. 54–7. See also Fraser (note 138), p. 187.

[141] 'Interstate Arbitration in Antiquity', 2 (1906–7) *Classical Journal* 197, at p. 207, and also p. 199.

[142] Supra (note 136), p. 72.

[143] Supra (note 136), p. 15.

[144] *The International Law and Custom of Ancient Greece and Rome*, vol. II, London, 1911, pp. 152–65.

[145] *Ibid.*, pp. 140–1.

[146] *Ibid.*, p. 141. See also the sophistication in procedure, pp. 148–50.

process itself. In this context, Westermann provides an interesting insight into 'a peculiar conclusion as to the results and value of Greek arbitration'. Relying on Victor Berard's research, he discloses the fact that four disputes/cases came up for reconsideration time and again. At least two of them were boundary or territorial disputes. The problem between the two Thessalian towns, Melite and Narthacium, involved disputed claims to a temple and its precincts. Decided in 385 BC, the award, which was in favour of Melite, was reaffirmed in 350 BC by the common council of the Thessalians, and was subsequently affirmed again by another arbitrator, Pyllos or the Epirote king, Pyrrhus. However, in AD 196, a ten-member Roman commission reversed the earlier awards and allocated the territory to the Narthacians, a decision subsequently ratified by the Roman Senate.[147]

The second arbitration, namely, the Samos–Priene territorial dispute, is better known. Ralston writes that the Roman envoy, Gnaeus Manlius Volso, who acted as arbitrator *circa* 180 BC, awarded the territory to Samos, but there were strong reasons to believe that he had 'received presents from the Samatians', the result of which was that Priene reopened the matter. A five-judge panel was then appointed by the people of Rhodes and, after very 'minute examination of the disputed district', the latter was awarded to Priene.[148]

Tod records three more arbitral proceedings between Samos and Priene on apparently the same frontier between 136 and 133 BC. In Arbitration No. LXIV of 136 BC, the ancient records establish the fact that: 'In view of the conflicting claims to a piece of land brought forward by Samatians and Prienian envoys, the Senate resolved to confirm the award of the Rhodian arbitrators recorded in No. LXII.'[149] In Arbitration No. LXV, which took place after 133 BC, the Mylasian (?) arbitrators confirmed 'the award and the frontier-delimitation of the Rhodians and [gave] an account of their restoration of the boundary tokens with the assistance of representatives of both states, who are highly commended for their services'.[150]

Westermann, however, observes that the Samos–Priene dispute was visited apparently nine times.[151] At any rate, both Tod and Westermann caution against hasty conclusions that arbitration in the Greek world was unsuccessful in resolving disputes. 'The sole ground', Tod wrote, 'for such a view lies in the fact that, in certain well-known cases an arbitral award

[147] Westermann (note141), pp. 207–8.

[148] See *International Arbitration from Athens to Locarno*, Stanford, 1929, p. 164.

[149] Tod (note 138), p. 43. [150] *Ibid*.

[151] Supra (note 141), p. 208. See also Coleman Phillipson (note 144), p. 147.

was not accepted by both sides as final and irrevocable, and consequently the same disputes were afresh submitted to arbitration.' This, however, he said, was an exception rather than the rule.[152]

Another account of questionable arbitration in ancient times also comes from Ralston. According to Cicero, he writes, Labeo was appointed by the Roman Senate to act as arbitrator of a boundary dispute between two Roman entities, Nola and Neapolis, *circa* 195–183 BC. Instead of allocating the contested territory to one of the disputant entities, the arbitrator advised them not to be 'greedy or grasping' and managed to get both parties to withdraw. Thereafter, he awarded the neutral tract to Rome.[153] These incidents of arbitration have, of course, to be seen in light of the caveat that the modern notions of international law, statehood and sovereignty were non-existent at that time. As Ralston points out, Rome recognised no other national group as its equal,[154] and hence incidents of 'international arbitration' in Mesopotamian, Greek or Roman times have to be viewed with a degree of caution.

Even so, it is the contest between Sparta and Messene over a mountainous district, referred to by Tacitus as the 'ager Dentheliates', which epitomises the perennial dispute and the recurrent arbitration. Coleman Phillipson writes that, in 338 BC, a court of arbitrators, which included representatives of Greece, found in favour of Messene and, accordingly, Philip of Macedon gave judgment pursuant to that finding. A century later in 221 BC, Antigonus provided a similar judgment for Messene, but only after he had defeated Sparta. The third 'decree', also in favour of Messene, was pronounced by Mummius. However, Sparta, ever dissatisfied by these

[152] Supra (note 138), p. 186. Tod calculates that out of thirty-three instances of arbitration, only eight cases were subject to further procedures. He goes on to observe that the dispute arising subsequent to the Samos–Priene arbitration did not relate to the disputed territory but to 'quite another question'; and that, after Lysimachus had awarded it to Samos, the Prienians never claimed it again. This may be so, but it conflicts with his own reports on the relevant arbitrations: *ibid.*, p. 43. His account on the disputed possession of the ager Dentheliates and the Melitea–Narthacium dispute over Medeus tends to highlight the longevity not only of territorial problems but also the arbitrations themselves: see pp. 185–6, on which see the text to note 147 above. Westermann observes that, not reckoning the four repeated arbitrations, the ratio of successful against failed arbitrations was thirty-two to seven: supra (note 141), pp. 208–9.

[153] Ralston (note 148), p. 170. Generally, see *ibid.*, pp. 153–73. Another example of a flawed arbitration is the award returned in the matter of the disputed tract of land between the Meliteans and the Chaldeans on the one side and Peumata on the other. The court of five arbitrators from Cassandrea allocated it to both parties, and hence the tract remained undivided: Tod (note 138), pp. 25–6, and note 1 on p. 26.

[154] Supra (note 148), p. xxv.

verdicts, appealed to the Roman Senate. In keeping with tradition and custom, the Romans appointed the city of Miletus as arbitrator.

After hearing claims and arguments from both sides, a court of 600 judges decided, by a vote count of 584 in favour to 16 against, to leave the ager Dentheliates to Messene. The court's decision was based on the fact 'that the territory in question having been in the possession of Messene before the arrival of L. Mummius in that province ought therefore to be judged to the Messenians.'[155] Despite this defeat, Sparta continued to agitate for Messene. Towards the end of the Republican era, the conflict revived and Atidius Geminus, the proconsul of Rome, arbitrated pursuant to the instructions of the Senate. 'Finally', Coleman Phillipson writes, 'in AD 25 both cities made a direct appeal to Rome through their ambassadors, and the senate pronounced its award in favour of Messene.'[156]

By the Middle Ages, however, the concepts of arbitration had begun to develop more quickly, not least because distinct territorial kingdoms were everywhere in Europe. In view, however, of the spiritual supremacy of the Vicar of Christ, it comes as no surprise that the Pope was called upon to 'arbitrate international' disputes, bearing always in mind that Papal arbitrators were more *amiables compositeurs* than judges in contemporary times.[157] Even so, some commentators have regarded one of the best-known incidents of dispositions of territory as an example of the Pope acting as an arbiter, namely, the Papal Bull of 1493 issued by Pope Alexander VI.[158] Seeking to demarcate the territories newly discovered by Christopher Columbus on behalf of Spain in the New World, the Pope drew a line 100 leagues west of the Azores and Cape Verde Islands; territories west of the line were Spanish and those lying to the east were to appertain to Portugal.[159]

It is, of course, clear that the Bull *Inter caetera* was not arbitration in the modern sense of the word, but this does not dispose of the matter. For the fact is that the 100-league line was devised by the Pope at the suggestion

[155] Coleman Phillipson (note 144), pp. 162–4, at pp. 163–4. [156] *Ibid.*, p. 164.

[157] Schlochauer (note 136), p. 16, with respect to Pope Innocent III and Pope Boniface VIII.

[158] See Vander Linden, 'Alexander VI and the Demarcation of the Maritime and Colonial Domains of Spain and Portugal, 1493–1494', 22 (1916) *American Historical Review* 1, referring to Grotius in *De Mare Libero*, Cap. III, p. 2. Cf. de Bustamante, *The World Court*, trans. E. Read, New York, 1926, pp. 3–4; and Moore, 'Brazil and Peru Boundary Question: The Acre (Aquiry) Territory', in *The Collected Papers* (note 137), p. 120, namely, that 'there was no actual concrete intention of dividing between Spain and Portugal the continents of North and South America'. See pp. 121–2. It was also geographically impossible to apply the fifteenth-century line of demarcation: *ibid.*, and see the next footnote below. [159] Hill (note 1), p. 205.

of Columbus who was keen to maximise territory, either already discovered or to be discovered, for Spain. Portugal's King John II was also fairly exercised over the extent and possible encroachment of Spain's discoveries over his possessions.[160] Thus, although the Bull favoured Spain, it was not as if the Pope were not fully cognisant of Portugal's claims in the 'Ocean Sea' in the equatorial zone and the 'southern Antipodes'.

On the contrary, the Bull of 4 May 1493,[161] which superseded the Bull of 3 May 1493 and which provided the definitive demarcation line, was a reflection of competing interests of the two sovereigns.[162] To that extent, then, this, and other similar Bulls, were, as Brownlie calls them, 'partitioning arrangements',[163] and clearly constituted third-party independent settlement of territorial claims. It is interesting, then, that, even in those times, dissatisfaction with respect to the partitioning was not unknown. It was because of this dissatisfaction that the kings of Spain and Portugal decided just over one year later, in 1494, by way of the Treaty of Tordesillas, to readjust the 100-league line by shifting it 370 leagues west of the Cape Verde Islands, a modification confirmed subsequently by the 1506 Bull *Ea quae*.[164] Nonetheless, Nussbaum was able to write:

> It is remarkable that the clause against papal dispensation, already included in the Treaty of Tordesillas, was elaborated in [the Treaty of Saragossa of] 1529 by these faithful Catholic rulers so as to prevent the use of a dispensation which the pope would grant on his own initiative (*motu proprio*). Thereafter, the practice of papal grants vanished.[165]

160 Vander Linden (note 158), pp. 12–13 and 18–19.

161 For a translated version of the Bull, see Commager (ed.), *Documents of American History*, New York, 1949, p. 2, reproduced from Davenport (ed.), *European Treaties Bearing on the History of the United States and Its Dependencies to 1648*, Washington, DC, 1917, pp. 75 *et seq*.

162 In this context, see also the excellent account in Bourne, 'The Demarcation Line of Pope Alexander VI', in *Essays in Historical Criticism*, New York, 1901, p. 193, at pp. 196–201. Further, see Greig, 'Sovereignty, Territory and the International Lawyer's Dilemma', 26 (1988) *Osgoode Hall Law Journal* 127, at pp. 140–3.

163 *Principles of Public International Law*, 4th edn, Oxford, 1990, pp. 147–8, at p. 147. Papal Bulls were also referred to as donations, and according to one authority were simply *ex post facto* legal conversion from possession to *justum dominium*: see von der Heydte, 'Discovery, Symbolic Annexation and the Virtual Effectiveness of International Law', 29 (1935) AJIL 448, at pp. 451–2.

164 Green and Dickason, *The Law of Nations and the New World*, Edmonton, Alberta, 1989, pp. 4–7, at p. 6. In his segment of the book, Green provides an excellent insight into the history of Papal Bulls, conflicting Royal patents, commissions and treaties in the struggle to control the New World: pp. 3–39. See also Bourne (note 162), pp. 201–2.

165 Supra (note 136), p. 53. On this, see also Lindley, *The Acquisition and Government of Backward Territory in International Law*, New York, 1926, pp. 124–8, at p. 125.

That they did eventually is not in doubt, but the point of significance here is that, even after the Treaty of Tordesillas, issues regarding the exact location of that boundary continued to vex the monarchs of Spain and Portugal for nearly 200 years, thus providing them with an opportunity to settle the dispute, at least at one point, by way of arbitration.

In truth, their territorial problems reflected in part the scientific inability to measure longitude with any degree of accuracy, but, more importantly, it was also a product of the hold which the Moluccas, or Spice Islands, 'the pearl of the precious Indies', exercised over Spain and Portugal at that time.[166] Thus, by 1524, it was 'agreed that each side should appoint three astrologers and three pilots as scientific experts, and three lawyers as judges of documentary proofs to meet in convention in March on the boundary between Spain and Portugal between Badajos and Yelves'.[167]

The Badajos Junta did meet, but owing to political considerations it was unable to decide matters definitively. While it was in Portugal's interest to delay matters, the lawyers in the Junta found no common ground with respect to the question of priority of possession of territories discovered. The line eventually drawn by the Spanish judges stood 375 miles west of San Antonio, a delimitation which went to the heart of the matter by allocating the Moluccas to Spain. Although the controversy was eventually decided to some degree of satisfaction in 1529, conflicting views regarding the location of the boundary between their empires then began to reflect their disputed claims to territorial possessions in South America. The line described in the Papal Bull of 1493 was finally consigned to history in 1750.[168]

By way of conclusions, it is the case that the origins of arbitration are closely intertwined with territorial disputes of one kind or another and this is as old as arbitration itself. Moreover, dissatisfaction with arbitral decisions on territory and boundary issues are equally as old, as is this dispute settlement procedure itself.

b. Arbitration and territorial and boundary disputes: consolidation

Arbitration as a dispute settlement technique began to take root, especially in the Americas. If the two main contenders for the first modern international arbitrations, namely, *New Haven [England] and New*

[166] Generally, see Bourne (note 162), pp. 201–9.

[167] *Ibid.*, p. 209. For a brief account, see Moore, 'Memorandum on Uti Possidetis: Costa Rica–Panama Arbitration, 1911' in *The Collected Papers* (note 137), p. 328, at pp. 334–5; and Greig (note 162), pp. 142–3, note 31.

[168] Generally, see Bourne (note 162), pp. 210–14.

Netherlands [The States General of the United Provinces of The Netherlands][169] and *Pennsylvania* v. *Connecticut* in 1782[170] are to be excluded from the reckoning, then the major watershed in the history of this dispute settlement process must be defined by the conclusion of the Jay Treaty between Great Britain

[169] There were several controversies between the Dutch plantation of Manhattan and the English colony of New Haven, which subsequently comprehended Connecticut, one of them being Dutch territorial claims stretching from Delaware to Connecticut and to Cape Cod. There followed a period of correspondence between the Dutch Governor, at first W. Keift and subsequently P. Stuyvesant, and the English colonialists regarding mutual claims and objections thereto, for which see Hazard, *Historical Collections; Consisting of State Papers, and Other Authentic Documents; Intended as Materials for an History of the United States of America*, Philadelphia, 1792, vol. II, pp. 54 *et seq*., especially Commissioners for the United Colonies in New England at New Haven, 9 July (?) September (?) 1646 rejecting Kieft's claim, via letter of 3 August 1646, to lands between the Delaware and the Connecticut rivers; and T. Eaton's reply of 12 August 1646 (Old Style): see pp. 54–6; and see the correspondence on pp. 154–6. In November 1647, the Dutch Governor proposed and the Governor of New Haven accepted arbitration by the Governors of Massachusetts and Plymouth to settle all differences between them. Although the Governors agreed and there was indeed talk of commissioners being set up for the arbitration, the proceedings were delayed for one reason or another, including the death of the Governor of Massachusetts, age, infirmity and 'indisposition to trauvile' of one of the commissioners, and the precise venue of the meeting. See letters of Governor Stuyvesant to Deputy Governor Goodyeare, 13 November 1647; Governor Eaton to Governor Stuyvesant, 16 November 1647; *ibid*., 11 April 1649 and *ibid*., 7 June 1649: refer to Hoadly, *Records of the Colony and Plantation of New Haven from 1638–1649*, Hartford, 1857, pp. 507 *et seq*. Eventually, Governor Stuyvesant wrote to Hopkins on 28 September 1650 (New Style) agreeing to arbitration by four arbitrators to decide on 'the basis of just and right according to their wisdom and integrity'. See Hazard, supra (this note), p. 169. The arbitration was carried out by the Delegates of the Commissioners of the United English Colonies and the Delegates of the Dutch Governor at Hartford, and, although it was described as 'Articles of Agreement', the instrument issuing from their deliberations on 19 September 1650 was clearly an award not a treaty, the text of which is in Hazard, supra (this note), pp. 710–73, and also on pp. 218–20. Paragraphs 1 and 2 of the award set out the delimitation in some detail. See also Miner, *History of Wyoming in a Series of Letters*, Philadelphia, 1845, Letter No. VII, 3rd section: www.rootsweb.com. The two parties met again in Boston in 1663 with respect to issues concerning limits, but by 1664 the Dutch had surrendered New Netherlands, including Fort Amsterdam, to the British: see Paper No. 788, Copies of Letters from the Governors of New York and New Netherlands, August 1664, in *Calendar of State Papers Colonial Series*, vol. V, *America and the West Indies 1661–1668*, HMSO, London, 1880; Kraus Reprint, Vaduz, 1964, pp. 225–6, at p. 226; see also Ralston, who writes that the matter was referred to the colony of Massachusetts for settlement: supra (note 148), p. 190.

[170] Article 9 of the Articles of Confederation of 1777 provided that the United States in Congress Assembled would be the last resort on appeal in all disputes between two or more States concerning boundary, jurisdiction or any other cause whatever. Although six cases came before the Congress, only one was decided by way of adjudication, the others being settled by political means, including bilateral negotiations: for text, see Annex 1 in Kelly and Harbison, *The American Constitution: Its Origins and Development*, New York, 1963, p. 987, at p. 991. The case, *Pennsylvania* v. *Connecticut*, dealt with

and the United States in 1794.[171] For it was in that treaty that the two parties provided for the settlement of certain disputes by way of arbitration, the point of significance here being that the settlements were to be effected not by diplomats and envoys of the two parties, but by commissioners appointed by the two governments acting impartially. For present purposes, three features of this 'new' technique are noteworthy.

First, the Commissioners were all nationals of the two States and accordingly there was no third party, or independent, element in the fledgling arbitral processes.

The rules informing the decision-making process constitute the second noteworthy feature. Indeed, it was this feature which gave the Jay Treaty prime position over the Treaty of Utrecht of 1713, nearly 100 years earlier, Article X of which required the 'commissaries' of France and Great Britain to determine the frontier between British possessions in Hudson Bay and the territories appertaining to the French in Canada.[172] Equally, it was this feature which also gave the Jay Treaty precedence over the Anglo-French Commissions agreed and established in 1749 with a view to determining the boundary in the same region, especially the great controversy over the

disputed territory, namely, the Wyoming lands, and was decided by five Commissioners sitting as a court in Trenton in favour of Pennsylvania in December 1782. The procedure followed was certainly legal: evidence was submitted and arguments were heard. While the basic contentions of the two states has been carefully recorded, the arguments are only stated as having been made by both parties. The judgment itself is unmotivated, as could be expected from arbitrators in the eighteenth century. See *Journals of the Continental Congress, 1774–1789*, vol. XXIV, Washington, DC, 1904–37, pp. 6–32; the judgment appears on pp. 31–2; the motions of the parties on pp. 12–23. If these two former colonies could be regarded as independent States having freely entered into a confederal arrangement dominated by the Congress, then the case could be seen as a product of a quasi-international arbitral process. See, generally, Ralston (note 148), p. 190; Frankfurter and Landis, 'The Compact Clause of the Constitution – A Study in Interstate Adjustments', 34 (1925) *Yale Law Journal* 685; McLaughlin, *A Constitutional History of the United States*, New York, 1935, p. 130, and, on state sovereignty, pp. 118 and 127 *et seq*.; and Caldwell, 'The Settlement of Inter-State Disputes', 14 (1920) AJIL 38, at pp. 53–4; and with respect to the early experience of the US Supreme Court, see *ibid*., pp. 58–64, where the predominance of inter-state boundary disputes is evident. 'It was not', he wrote, 'until 94 years after the adoption of the Constitution that the court was called upon to consider any other than a boundary dispute.' See p. 58, and p. 64 where he refers to the 'quasi-international jurisdiction of the Supreme Court'.

171 1 BFSP 784. Although this treaty is regarded traditionally as initiating the modern epoch of arbitration, some writers have questioned its seminal status: see Roelofsen, 'Comments: The Jay Treaty and All That', in Soons (note 136), pp. 201 *et seq*. His justification for querying this is predicated, *inter alia*, in the *Ostend Company* affair. See also Lachs, 'Arbitration and International Adjudication', in Soons (note 136), p. 37, at p. 38.

172 35 BFSP 815.

limits of Acadia, Nova Scotia. The distinguishing feature is the duty (and power) to decide the dispute impartially and with reference to principles of law and evidence. Indeed, the Anglo-French Commission failed precisely because there was no consensus with respect to the scope of powers of its members.[173]

The Jay Treaty provided for arbitration of three kinds of dispute, the first of which was the boundary dispute between the United States and Great Britain (on behalf of Canada). The Commissioners under the Jay Treaty were obliged by virtue of Article V of the Jay Treaty, 'impartially to examine and decide the said question' according to the evidence before them. The second category of dispute was concerned with the recovery of debts and the Commissioners were directed in Article VI to decide the matter 'according to justice and equity'. In the third category were maritime seizures and the rights of neutrals, and Article VII obliged the Commissioners to decide 'according to justice, equity *and the law of nations*'.[174] It is clear that the United States and Great Britain were seeking to provide different normative decision-making criteria for different categories of disputes; and, importantly, it is notable that, for the purposes of the boundary controversy, there was no reference to the law of nations. While this does not detract from the *River St Croix* award[175] given in 1798, it does indicate that, in 1794, the two parties were fully confident about the scope and content of the law of nations *only* with respect to maritime seizures and not title to territory, or indeed, for that matter, the recovery of debts.

Even so, there was reference in all three articles to *evidence*, and this showed that the parties did *not* contemplate the taking of decisions *devoid* of legal considerations, even if they were rudimentary in nature and perhaps not even principles of the law of nations. The full significance of this is examined shortly. At this juncture, it is relevant only to note that in *fact* the principles of decision relied upon by the three Commissioners

[173] For a detailed and illuminating account, see Savelle, *The Diplomatic History of the Canadian Boundary 1749–1763*, New Haven, 1940, Chapters 1 and 2, especially pp. 22–41. Cf. the instructions given to the British Commissaries in 1752, and it is clear from a perusal thereof that they were political in nature; indeed the very fact that the commissaries were given instructions with regard to their official positions indicates that their task was neither judicial nor arbitral: see 'Instructions for William Shirley and William Mildmay Appointed Commissary or Commissaries to be Appointed by the Most Christian King', 1750, in Wickham Legg (ed.), *British Diplomatic Instructions 1689–1789*, vol. VII, *France, Part IV, 1745–1789*, Camden Third Series, vol. XLIX, London, 1934, pp. 309–13. Elaborate written memorials were exchanged by the parties between 1751 and 1753; see Savelle, supra (this note), pp. 37–42.

[174] Emphasis added.

[175] 1 BFSP 807.

for the *River St Croix* award were those of negotiation and accommodation owing in part to the existence of geographical uncertainties regarding the source of that river.[176] Thus, given the perceived lack of developed rules and an absence of undisputed geographical facts, the two parties were able to accept and subsequently implement the award and to draw the boundary along the Chaputneticook River.

The third feature is of central significance here, not only because it constitutes the first 'modern' institutional impartial settlement of a boundary dispute, but also because it sets the mould for many other similar cases. For it was in Article V that the Commissioners were required to settle what in theory was already settled by an earlier treaty: they were required to identify 'what river was truly intended under the name of the river St Croix, mentioned in the . . . Treaty of Peace' of 1783 to serve as part of the boundary between Canada and the United States. In other words, the Commissioners were requested to interpret a boundary clause in a treaty, further reinforcing the central theme here that territorial settlements have an inherent tendency to become unsettled and to run into difficulties. No doubt, the parties in this case had genuine difficulties of interpretation, but the fact remains that it is not easy at times to be confident that a boundary treaty will lay to rest frontier problems, for the question of the precise delimitation of the frontier can lead to even more locational disputes, arising from vexed interpretations and disputed geographical features. It is for this reason that many coterminous States turn to arbitration and adjudication to resolve problems involving the meaning and scope of boundary provisions and treaties.

These observations are lent support by examining the provisions of the Treaty of Ghent of 1814[177] between the same parties. Following on from the Jay Treaty, this treaty provided for the settlement by arbitral commissions of four more outstanding boundary and territorial issues arising from the intent and provisions of the 1783 Treaty of Peace. While it is not intended here to provide a detailed account of these arbitral processes, it is important to note, for the purposes of this study, the following points.

First, the reference in Article IV to the impartial examination of evidence upon which the decision of the Commissioners was to be based for

[176] Cukwurah (note 7), pp. 171–3, at p. 173. The admission of a compromise serving as a basis for the settlement applied to the second part of the Commission's task. See Corbett, *The Settlement of Canadian–American Disputes: A Critical Study of Methods and Results*, New Haven, 1937, p. 8. In passing, it may be noted that the arbitration concerning the collection of debts owed to British creditors was less successful: see Simpson and Fox (note 136), pp. 2–3.

[177] 2 BFSP 357.

three of the four boundary and territorial problems[178] indicates that the parties were again committing themselves to a decision based on legal considerations, no matter how basic they might have been. This is significant not only because it established the juridical nature of the arbitral process. It also highlights the fact that decisions based on legal considerations began to be seen, especially by the Government of the United States, as a legitimate expectation of the parties.

Secondly, when in 1821 the Commissioners were unable, despite their best efforts, to settle the boundary dispute regarding the northwest 'angle' of Nova Scotia, the two parties decided to refer the matter to the King of the Netherlands. Article I of the Arbitral Treaty of 1827[179] provided the basis for a referral of the dispute to a friendly sovereign who would be invited to investigate and 'make a decision' on the dispute, a decision which Article VI stated was to be a sound and just one, and, to this effect, it empowered the sovereign to call, *inter alia*, for further evidence with respect to specific points in the statements of the parties. Importantly, the resulting award in the *Northeastern Boundary* case[180] was another milestone in the history of arbitration. For, if the Jay Treaty marks the era of modern arbitration, the *Northeastern Boundary* case is the first award which was formally rejected by a party to the proceedings. The problem, according to the assertions of the Government of the United States, was that the King had returned an award which was in excess of his powers; he had provided a delimitation which was practicable[181] and was thus a line based on convenience.

It would exceed the scope of this work to examine the veracity or otherwise of the allegations of the award, and only two points need to be

[178] The three disputes were (a) certain islands in the Bay of Passamaquoddy; (b) the northwest angle of Nova Scotia; and (c) the water boundaries in the Iroquois and other rivers and lakes and islands lying therein. Under Article VII, the two Commissioners were authorised merely to fix impartially and determine the fourth boundary dispute which concerned disputed sovereignty over various islands in the lakes and rivers between Lakes Huron and Superior to the Lake of Woods. [179] 14 BFSP 1004.

[180] 18 BFSP 1249.

[181] See Preble, US Envoy to The Hague, to Baron Verstolk de Solen, 12 January 1821: 22 BFSP 772. The matter was ultimately settled by diplomacy in the Webster–Ashburton Treaty, 30 BFSP 360; see Simpson and Fox (note 136), pp. 2–3; and Cukwurah (note 7), pp. 175–8 and 201–3; cf. Carlston, who agrees that, although the award was technically in excess of jurisdiction, it was also essentially mediatory in character: see *The Process of International Arbitration*, New York, 1946, pp. 89–90. Further, see Pinto, 'The Prospects for International Arbitration: Inter-State Disputes', in Soons (note 136), p. 63, at p. 71; and Fox, 'Arbitration', in Waldock (ed.), *International Disputes: The Legal Aspects: Report of a Study Group of the David Davies Memorial Institute of International Studies*, London, 1972, p. 101, at p. 102.

emphasised here. The first is that, insofar as the previous arbitral decisions between the United States and Great Britain (acting on behalf of Canada) were based, at least in principle and theory, on notions of impartiality, evidence, justice and equity, it could cogently be argued that the general trend towards decisions based on legal considerations, as opposed to *ex aequo et bono*, had begun to take root in international arbitration.

Some arbitral treaties appear to belie this proposition. Certainly, it is the case that, in 1869, Great Britain and Portugal agreed to refer their dispute over Bulama Island to arbitration and that they agreed in Articles 2 and 9 of the Lisbon Protocol[182] to grant the arbitrator, the President of the United States, the power to 'furnish an equitable solution' to the dispute in the event that he should be unable wholly to decide in favour of either party. This power, however, was intended to enable the arbitrator to dispose of the matter conclusively rather than to enable him to decide questions of title on practical, pragmatic or other non-equitable considerations. It is relevant that the report of Mr J. C. Bancroft Davis, the Assistant Secretary of State,[183] which formed the basis of the President's award in the *Bulama Island* case,[184] relied on various principles of international law, including the doctrines of Vattel, to decide the dispute. In the event, therefore, it did not prove necessary for the arbitrator to decide on the basis of the discretionary powers granted him.

Secondly, by rejecting the award in the *Northeastern Boundary* case, the Government of the United States had effectively given a crucial fillip to a doctrine which developed over time into two broad branches of the law. On the one hand, it reinforced the rule that, while they were admittedly binding and final, arbitral awards were also governed by fundamental precepts of international law. These included the rule that the decision-maker or tribunal could not exceed the powers stipulated in the arbitral agreement, and, if they did, then the decision, in principle, would be null and void, and accordingly not binding on the parties. The law of nullity of awards then began to develop more fully in the latter half of the nineteenth century and, by the first quarter of the twentieth, the right to

182 61 BFSP 1163. On the question of legal difficulties associated with the notion of decisions *ex aequo et bono*, see Scheuner, 'Decisions Ex Aequo et Bono by International Courts and Arbitral Tribunals', in Sanders (ed.), *International Arbitration: Liber Amicorum for Martin Domke*, The Hague, 1967, p. 275, especially p. 276; and Sohn, 'Arbitration of International Disputes Ex Aequo et Bono', in Sanders, *ibid.*, p. 330, especially pp. 331–2.

183 See Moore (note 136), pp. 1916–19. Mr Bancroft Davis was, of course, a jurist of renown.

184 *Ibid.*, p. 1920.

challenge arbitral decisions on a number of grounds was an accepted legal principle. The grounds developed included the denial of a fair hearing, duress or fraud perpetrated on the tribunal and the absence of a statement of reasons in the judgment.[185] Indeed, in certain quarters, the very integrity of the arbitral process had begun to be questioned. In a highly critical review of international arbitration as a dispute settlement technique, Dennis, writing in 1911, observed: 'it remains true that arbitration even at the Hague Tribunal [that is, the Permanent Court of Arbitration] still frequently results in compromise.'[186]

On the other hand, in addition to the rejection of the award of the King of Netherlands in the *Northeastern Boundary* case by the United States on the basis of *excès de pouvoir*, a different but not unrelated ground for questioning an arbitral decision began also to be championed by the United States. This related to the discovery of a decisive fact after the delivery of the award which, in the right legal circumstances, made the entire decision unsafe. Furthermore, over time, other States also began to accept that litigating parties had the right in principle to return to the tribunal and ask for clarifications of the award, a technique which was directed at times to a reconsideration of issues examined earlier by the tribunal. These categories of revision and interpretation constitute the main body of this work and are examined in Parts III and IV below.

[185] See, generally, Carlston (note 181), Chapters 2, 3 and 4; Simpson and Fox (note 136), pp. 250–9; and Fox, 'Arbitration', in Luard (ed.), *The International Regulation of Frontier Disputes*, London, 1970, p. 168, at pp. 168–72.

[186] 'Compromise – The Great Defect of Arbitration', 11 (1911) *Columbia Law Review* 493, at p. 501. An equally scathing attack is to be found in Wehberg, who wrote: 'If out of 170 decisions in the nineteenth century only six can be singled out as based upon good grounds, the facts speak for themselves.' See Wehberg, *The Problem of an International Court of Justice*, trans. C. G. Fenwick, Oxford, 1918, Chapter III, p. 19, and Verzijl (note 136), pp. 86–90, who writes that arbitration 'often shaded off into mediatory settlement' (*ibid.*, p. 87). The history of this 'defect' cannot be examined here; suffice it to say that the problem of international arbitration reflected deep divisions within two schools of thought on both sides of the Atlantic, divisions which involved questioning the essential function of arbitration, that is, whether arbitration was simply a dispute settlement technique, or a technique mandated to settle disputes only by reference to principles of law, i.e. 'judicial arbitration'. Ultimately, the latter view prevailed. For an excellent survey, see Pinto, 'Structure, Process, Outcome: Thoughts on the Essence of International Arbitration', in Muller and Mijs (note 136), p. 43, at pp. 44–62. For a cautiously critical position, see Strupp, who, while championing the cause of international arbitration, saw arbitral judges as 'humans [with] human sympathies': supra (note 136), pp. 661–2, at p. 662; but, for a more sanguine view, see Jennings, 'The Progress of International Law', 54 (1950) BYIL 334: that 'of the several hundreds of Awards and Judgments made in the last century or so, the ones which have not been carried out can be numbered on the fingers of one hand'. See *ibid.*, p. 340.

c. Sources of dissatisfaction and dispute: treaties and arbitral and judicial decisions

In the context of the present work, it is important to note that, by the beginning of the twentieth century, the juridical stage was set for States to rely on arbitration not only to *settle* boundary and territorial disputes but also to *continue* them in a different form, albeit, at times, justifiably so. This is not, of course, to imply that the resort to arbitration was less than genuine or *mala fide*. The point simply is that the development of the law on arbitration was such that it allowed parties to pursue their claims by exploiting the rules on nullity, revision and interpretation of arbitral decisions. It is also relevant that, in this domain of the law, as in some others, the contribution of North, Central and South American States was significant, espousing, as they did, the notion that awards, especially where they dealt with questions concerning the status of territory or the location of an alignment, or both, were not beyond challenge, provided always that the challenge submitted or reconsideration claimed was based on clear legal criteria. This approach encompassed questions of both nullity and revision.

This permissive approach to the matter was evidenced in the State practice. In the first place, the delegate of the United States at the first Hague Peace Conference in 1899 advocated vigorously for the right of revision to be included in the Hague Convention for the Pacific Settlement of International Disputes. An account of this aspect of the matter is presented below in section II.b of Chapter 7. On that basis, then, it needs only to be stated here that the United States adopted a position which caused some controversy at the Conference but was nevertheless accepted by other delegates (but not without some qualification), thereby allowing the inclusion in the Convention of the right of revision of decisions, provided always that certain criteria were fulfilled. By including this right, the general notion was, for the first time, formalised in a multilateral treaty, reinforcing the basic theory that the finality of awards was as much a matter of, and subject to, law as was the fundamental rule of *res judicata*.

Other treaties followed in this vein, both multilateral and bilateral. The General Treaty of Arbitration of 1901 between Bolivia and Peru provided in Article 12 that an award was binding unless it was based on a false or falsified document, or if it were, either in whole or in part, the consequence of an error of fact. Article 13 gave the parties three months in which to file an application for the revision of the award from the time when the notice of the decision was given.[187] The *Bolivia–Peru* arbitration was conducted on the basis of this agreement, although these provisions were not utilised.[188] Subsequently, the 1923 Central America Treaty of Arbitration also contained a clause on nullity and revision on the basis of several criteria including *nemo judex in sua causa*.[189]

In the second place, arbitration, and subsequently adjudication following on from the adoption of the Statute of the Permanent Court of International Justice in 1922, was, as far as territorial and boundary disputes were concerned, utilised in different ways. For present purposes, four can be identified, all of them extant. The first of these categories is the settlement of disputes by reference simply to the merits of the claims to title, as for example the classic arbitration under the aegis of the Permanent Court of Arbitration, namely, the *Island of Palmas or Miangas* case[190] between the United States and the Netherlands, and, in relatively more recently times, the *Minquiers and Ecrehos* dispute between the United Kingdom and France.[191]

The second class of cases constitutes a category in which litigating States are in dispute over the interpretation and/or application of a treaty or some other authoritative, binding instrument accepted by both parties, as for example the *Beagle Channel* case where Argentina and Chile were in dispute over the meaning of certain provisions of the Treaty of 1881 which delimited the boundary between them.[192] The third set of cases is a composite of the two categories mentioned above. In this category, thus, two types of questions are placed in alternative sequences, as for example the *Grisbadarna* case[193] where the Permanent Court of Arbitration was required to determine how far the maritime boundary had been determined by the provisions of the Boundary Treaty of 1661, and, to the extent that it was not, to determine the line accordingly. A similar kind of request was put to the arbitral tribunal in *Guinea-Bissau* v. *Senegal* with respect to the maritime boundary established by the Franco-Portuguese exchange of notes of 1960.[194] The fourth category, given its significance for this work, is discussed separately below.

[187] 95 BFSP 1018; and see Editorial Comment, 'The Arbitral Award in the Peru–Bolivia Boundary Controversy', 3 (1909) AJIL 949. [188] 3 (1909) AJIL 1029.

[189] See Article 1(3) read with Article 20, and Article 1(4): 130 BFSP 504. See also Article 11 of the 1921 Swiss–German Treaty of Conciliation, Arbitration and Compulsory Adjudication, 114 BFSP 820. [190] 22 (1928) AJIL 867.

[191] ICJ Reports 1953, p. 47. [192] 52 ILR 227; 17 (1978) ILM 734.

[193] 4 (1910) AJIL 226. [194] 83 ILR 1.

d. Arbitral and judicial decisions: nullity, revision and interpretation

The fourth category is of greater consequence for this work for it gathers together clusters of cases in which territorial or boundary disputes continue in one form or another after the handing down of the award or judgment. In the first cluster are cases in which one of the parties alleges that the judgment or award ought to be revised or clarified but does not claim nullity thereof, and this, as noted above, constitutes the main body of this work, and need not, therefore, be discussed at this stage. For the time being, reference need only be made briefly to the second cluster of cases in which the decisions of international tribunals are allegedly void inasmuch as they are defective in law and hence not binding. Clearly, this is a vast area of the law and detailed discussion lies outside the scope of this book. For the purpose, however, of relative completeness, it will be appropriate to present some thoughts on the matter in very general terms.

Parties objecting to a decision on the ground of nullity will rely on a number of legal considerations to make their claims. These claims can be placed in four general categories, but, importantly, they ought not to be seen rigidly, inasmuch as individual heads of claims to nullity have overlapping features. At any rate, the largest category in this context is that of *excès de pouvoir*,[195] and there are two aspects to this. In the first place, there is, what may be described as the geographical aspects to the exercise of excess jurisdiction. Where, for example, the tribunal delimits an alignment which is in excess of the claim line of one of the parties, the rule of *nemo judex non ultra petita* applies, and the affected party may be heard to argue that the decision rendered by the tribunal is void. The logic is persuasive: the tribunal must remain within the disputed area, although it need not slavishly follow the claim line of the litigant States, unless it is expressly required to choose between one of the two lines submitted;[196] or where the tribunal is required to attribute territory in a specific, defined manner to the exclusion of all other delimitations. In the *Chamizal* arbitration,[197] the United States Commissioner, followed later by his government, refused to accept the award of the International Boundary

[195] Generally, see Munkman, 'Adjudication and Adjustment – International Judicial Decision and the Settlement of Territorial and Boundary Disputes', 46 (1972–3) BYIL 1, at pp. 1–26.

[196] This was the requirement imposed on the arbitral tribunal by the *compromis* in the *Taba Boundary* case: 80 ILR 354.

[197] 5 (1911) AJIL 785. See Editorial Comment, 'The Chamizal Arbitration Award', 5 (1911) AJIL 709.

Commission on the ground that it was mandated by Article III of the 1910 Convention[198] to allocate the Chamizal tract either to the United States or to Mexico, and that it had decided to attribute part of it to each of the litigating States.[199] Claims in *Costa Rica* v. *Panama* were of a similar sort and are discussed in a subsequent part of this work.[200]

Another aspect of the *non ultra petita* rule is where the tribunal exceeds the geographical limits of its jurisdiction without necessarily awarding territory in excess of a State's claims. An example of this is the UN Iraq–Kuwait Boundary Demarcation Commission which, as noted above,[201] drew a line in the maritime sector of the boundary between the two States. Arguably, the demarcation was not null and void insofar as the Security Council supported and accepted the line so demarcated. The argument which Argentina relied on to assert the nullity of the *Beagle Channel* award was that the Permanent Court of Arbitration had allegedly allocated to Chile territory which it had not claimed and which was, it contended, clearly out of the disputed area.[202]

The 'legal' aspect to the excess jurisdiction rule is where the tribunal decides a matter or applies considerations which are expressly or impliedly ruled out by the parties. It was this fact which informed the allegations of the United States in the *Northeastern Boundary* case adverted to above. In the *Aves Island* arbitration,[203] the arbitrator, the Queen of Spain, was empowered by the 1857 Convention to decide the question of *sovereignty* over Aves Island disputed by Venezuela and the Netherlands. The Queen, however, returned an award in which she attributed the *proprietary* interest in the island to Venezuela and adjudged that the latter pay an indemnity to the Netherlands for the loss of its fishery rights. Although the award was clearly an *excès de pouvoir*, the two parties accepted the award.[204]

198 103 BFSP 588.

199 See Carlston (note 181), pp. 151–5; and Cukwurah (note 7), pp. 203–8.

200 Section IV.d of Chapter 5; text to notes 437–65.

201 See the text to notes 24–6.

202 This matter is referred to in the text to notes 915–18. A problem more structural in nature, as identified by McWhinney, is that the tribunal took the old positivist approach in which justice was based on the strict, logical style of earlier times in a setting where the parties were not expecting a mechanical restatement of the law: see 'The International Court as Constitutional Court and the Blurring of the Arbitral/Judicial Processes', in Muller and Mijs (note 136), p. 81, at p. 85. However, neither the author nor Schwebel agree with this view; for the latter's views, see 'Concluding Observations', in Muller and Mijs (note 136), p. 177, at p. 181.

203 Moore (note 136), vol. V, p. 5037.

204 See the exchange of letters between the Consulat Général des Pays Bas à Caracas and the Minister of External Relations, Central Session, No. 105, 5 May 1866. Interestingly, while the Dutch Consulate chose not to highlight the discrepancy in the Queen's

Similarly, in *Brcko (Final Award)*,[205] the independent presiding arbitrator, decided, after issuing two earlier interim awards, to create in effect a condominium out of the disputed *Opstina* or municipality of Brcko, that is, a territory to be 'shared' by the Bosnian Serb entity, Republika Srpska, and the Federation of Bosnia and Herzegovina. The difficulty, however, is that the arbitral clause of Article V(1) of Annex II to the Dayton Accords of 1995[206] did not envisage anything other than the determination by arbitration of the inter-entity boundary line. There can be little doubt that the arrogation of such powers was manifestly beyond the scope of authority vested in the tribunal by the Dayton Accords.

More disconcertingly, however, the arbitrator did not stop there. He also decided that the award could be revised if there were a lack of co-operation from one of the entities and that, in principle, the tribunal would not be *functus officio* until it was satisfied that the award had been implemented as certified by the Supervisor.[207] There are two problems with this kind of finding. First, it is not for the arbitrator or arbitrators to decide not to become *functus officio*; that is a matter for the parties to decide and stipulate in an agreement or in an arrangement evidenced by necessary implication. Once the award has been rendered, then, in the absence of agreement to the contrary, the tribunal ceases to function. Secondly, the tribunal cannot impose a regime of revision when the whole object and purpose of arbitration is to seek a solution predicated on the finality of the award and its consequences. Questions of compliance and implementation are *primarily* a matter for the relevant authorities of the two (or more) parties, and not the tribunal. Arguably, then, the award returned by the arbitrator was *excès de pouvoir*. As Schreuer observed:

> Traditionally, arbitration is perceived as a mandate that is narrowly circumscribed by the parties' agreement. A tribunal is entrusted with the specific task of answering a legal question defined by the parties. Digression beyond these parameters is often threatened by nullity. Once the tribunal has fulfilled its mandate it ceases to exist. In the Brcko Arbitration the Tribunal took a much broader view of its function. Despite its seemingly narrow terms of reference to determine the Inter-Entity Boundary Line, it took the task upon itself to find the

award between what was claimed by the parties to the arbitration and what was actually decided by her, it was the Venezuelan Foreign Ministry which effectively noted that the question of dominion and sovereignty was settled by a declaration on property rights over the island: *ibid*., pp. 5040–1. As the losing party, it was the Dutch Government which had, in theory, reason to challenge the award.

[205] 38 (1999) ILM 536. [206] 35 (1996) ILM 75.

[207] 38 (1999) ILM 547; paragraphs 65 and 68.

optimum solution as determined by the object and purpose of the Dayton Accords.[208]

At least one thing is clear from an award such as the one being considered. It highlights the difficulties of settling territorial disputes by 'judicial' arbitration and the need, at times, to resort to non-legal considerations and settlement procedures to resolve intractable conflicts. It also demonstrates the fact that even arbitrators expect that their own arbitral awards may become unsettled or settled imperfectly.

Failure of jurisdiction, the next category, provides a basis for objections predicated on the contention that the tribunal has failed fully or partially to carry out the task vested in it. The failure in contemplation is primarily a legal one, insofar as an award which has not been *delivered in concreto* cannot actually be null and void. Failures, thus, of the kind experienced by the parties in *Ecuador v. Peru*, where the arbitrator, the King of Spain, was advised in 1890 to delay rendering the boundary award owing to the occurrence of massive riots in Ecuador, are thus not *stricto sensu* failures of jurisdiction.[209] For there was in that case no *de facto* award which represented a failure of jurisdiction. An example of alleged failure of jurisdiction is better seen in the *Guinea-Bissau* v. *Senegal case*. In 1989, Guinea-Bissau requested the International Court of Justice to declare null and void the award in that case insofar as the arbitration tribunal had failed not only to reply to the second of the two questions put to it, but also because it had not actually drawn a boundary on the map which it had also been requested to provide.

In *Arbitral Award of 31 July 1989*,[210] the International Court of Justice held that, because the tribunal had decided the first question in the affirmative, namely, that the Franco-Portuguese Exchange of Notes of 1960 delimiting the boundary was effective and valid as between the two States, the second question did not have to be answered. Nor did the failure to draw a boundary on the map constitute a failure of jurisdiction: 'Since it did not reply to the second question, it did not have to define any other line. It thus considered that there was no need to draw on a map a line which was common knowledge, and the definitive characteristics of which [the tribunal] had specified.'[211] It also decided that there was indeed

[208] See 'The Brcko Final Award of 5 March 1999', 12 (1999) *Leiden Journal of International Law* 575, at p. 580; see also his earlier study, 'The Brcko Award of 14 February 1997', 11 (1998) *Leiden Journal of International Law* 71.

[209] Woolsey, 'Boundary Disputes in Latin America', 25 (1931) AJIL 324, at pp. 330–1; and Carlston (note 181), pp. 207–11.

[210] ICJ Reports 1991, p. 53.

[211] *Ibid.*, p. 74.

a majority vote for the award.[212] Similarly, one of the arguments put forward by Venezuela in support of its contentions regarding the nullity of the award in *British Guiana* v. *Venezuela* was that the arbitral tribunal had failed to determine the extent of the territories under the control of the Netherlands or Spain at the time of Great Britain's acquisition of British Guiana in 1814 which Article III of the Arbitral Treaty of 1897 had required it to do.[213]

In the third category are cases characterised by the argument based on a lack of jurisdiction in the tribunal. Parties may be minded to issue claims of nullity or allegations predicated on denying the legal effect of a judgment or award on the ground that the decision is devoid of any legal effect in view of considerations which go to the constitutive structure and powers of the tribunal. In *Arbitral Award of the King of Spain*, it was Nicaragua's contention that the designation of the King of Spain as arbitrator was not in conformity with the provisions of the Gámez–Bonilla Treaty, the arbitral agreement of 1894, and that the Treaty, which was in force only for ten years, had lapsed before he had agreed to act as arbitrator. The International Court of Justice rejected both contentions on their merits. There was no evidence to suggest that the two governments had not in fact complied with the procedural contingencies of the Treaty. The evidence showed also that the ten-year period began from the date of exchange of ratifications between the States in accordance with the intentions of the parties.[214]

Similarly, the right of the Council of the League of Nations to determine the Iraq–Turkey frontier in accordance with Article 3(2) of the Treaty of Lausanne was the chief matter in issue before the Permanent Court of International Justice in the *Mosul Boundary* advisory opinion.[215] The Court took the view that, although the decision to be taken by the Council could not be regarded as an arbitral award, it would, nevertheless, have binding legal effect, for such was the intention of the parties to the Treaty.[216] By providing such an opinion, albeit at the request of the Council of

[212] *Ibid.*, pp. 72–3. On these and related issues, see Rosenne, 'The International Court of Justice and International Arbitration', in Muller and Mijs (note 136), p. 99, at pp. 110–14; and Schwebel, 'The Majority Vote of an International Arbitral Tribunal' in Schwebel, *Justice in International Law: Selected Writings of Stephen M. Schwebel, Judge of the International Court of Justice*, Cambridge, 1994, p. 213.

[213] Venezuela's Report on the Boundary Question (note 95), p. 140; and see Wetter's comments, 'Analysis and Conclusion: Arbitration Itself is Here on Trial' (note 95), vol. III, p. 333, at pp. 344–5. For the text of the arbitral agreement, see 89 BFSP 57.

[214] ICJ Reports 1960, pp. 205–9. [215] PCIJ Reports, Series B, No. 12 (1925), p. 6.

[216] *Ibid.*, pp. 26–8.

the League, the Court was able pre-emptively to frustrate any possible post-decisional claim by the Turkish Government that the Council's decision regarding the frontier was in the nature and character of a recommendation, and accordingly devoid of any binding legal effect. As Wainhouse put it: 'The Council, anxious to avoid any charge that it might be exceeding its powers, decided to refer the question to the Permanent Court [of International Justice].'[217]

In the last category of claims lie factors which challenge the judgment or award by calling into question the intrinsic juridical worth of the decision without reference to the nature and scope of the powers of the tribunal as agreed between the parties. The lack of a motivated judgment is regarded as a sound basis for nullity, and indeed this was the basis of Guinea-Bissau's allegation that the award in *Guinea-Bissau* v. *Senegal* was without legal effect, an allegation which the International Court of Justice rejected in *Arbitral Award of 31 July 1989*. The substance of the Court's ruling on this claim was that the brevity of reasoning ought not to be seen as an absence of reasons.[218] The rule on motivated judgments, however, has to be seen in the context of intertemporal law: the fact is that a great many of the awards in the nineteenth century were devoid of reasons, including the *British Guiana* v. *Venezuela* award;[219] and that this rule materialised for the first time in the 1899 Hague Convention for the Pacific Settlement of Disputes, a matter discussed in section II.b of Chapter 3 below. Similarly, an award or judgment can be called into question on the ground that the tribunal had compromised its integrity. As seen above in the matter of *British Guiana* v. *Venezuela*, it was Venezuela's assertion, based on the Mallet–Prevost Memorandum, that the arbitral tribunal had been corrupted by pressure from the governments in London and Moscow, and that, accordingly, the award was devoid of legal effect.

[217] Supra (note 33), p. 46.

[218] ICJ Reports 1991, pp. 67–8. Similarly, the International Court rejected Nicaragua's claim that the award of the Spanish King in the *Honduras* v. *Nicaragua* boundary arbitration of 1906 (11 UNRIAA 111) was void owing to a lack or inadequacy of reasoning: *Arbitral Award of the King of Spain*, ICJ Reports 1960, p. 192, at pp. 215–16.

[219] The award in this case was totally unmotivated, and subsequently afforded Venezuela another ground for nullity: see Venezuela's Report on the Boundary Question (note 95), p. 140; and Wetter (note 213), pp. 343–4. It could be argued, however, that the award came on the cusp of the change in the law and that the new rule on motivated judgments had not yet settled into customary international law at that time, notwithstanding the fact that it had been included as Article 52 in the Convention for the Pacific Settlement of International Disputes in July 1899. Note that the award was delivered in October of that year. The *compromis* is silent on the matter. See note 737 below.

The *Buraimi Oasis* case of 1955 was afflicted with a similar sort of problem. The British Government, acting on behalf of the Sultanate of Muscat and Oman and the Trucial Sheikhdoms on the one hand, and the Saudi Arabian Government on the other, agreed to take the boundary issue of Buraimi Oasis and related villages to arbitration. After the submission of memorials, the member nominated by the United Kingdom to the tribunal, Sir Reader Bullard, decided to withdraw from the proceedings on the ground that the Saudi member of the tribunal, Mr Shaikh Yusuf Yasin, was allegedly conducting himself as if he were a representative of the appointing government. Thereafter, Dr de Visscher, the president of the tribunal, and subsequently Dr Dihigo, the Cuban member, also withdrew, and the proceedings were eventually abandoned.[220] In 1974 and 1990, the Saudi Government concluded agreements with the United Arab Emirates and Oman relinquishing its claims to the oasis in return for the United Arab Emirates providing Saudi Arabia with a corridor to the Persian Gulf just east of Qatar.[221] Buraimi is now divided between Oman and the United Arab Emirates.

Before summing up this part of the chapter, several important points need to be highlighted. First, the issues and problems discussed above are *representative* of the subject-matter; it is not meant to be a *comprehensive* statement thereof. Indeed, a large number of points have not been exhaustively discussed, including the problems of nullity, waiver, acquiescence and effectiveness, inasmuch as they all lie outside the compass of this work. Secondly, claims of nullity of awards and judgments are not effective merely upon their being issued by the dissatisfied State. The rules require that claims of this kind are examined either (a) by the same tribunal provided it is not *functus officio* or (b) by another tribunal provided a new agreement or some other legally binding agreement or arrangement by way of treaty or otherwise allows for such re-examination. Thirdly, in order to determine the nullity or otherwise of an award or a judgment, the precise terms of reference by which the dispute was put before the tribunal will, in most cases, need to be examined. In other words, the range of powers and considerations which the tribunal may or may not exercise or take into consideration will constitute a crucial fact which cannot be ignored.

[220] See Al-Baharna, *The Arabian Gulf States: Their Legal and Political Status and Their International Problems*, 2nd edn, Beirut, 1975, pp. 196–208; Kelly, *Eastern Arabian Frontiers*, London, 1964, pp. 200–4; Wetter (note 95), vol. III, pp. 357–87 (for a variety of materials on the matter, especially the Foreign Office statement issued on 5 October 1955, *ibid.*, pp. 375–7); Schwebel, *International Arbitration: Three Salient Problems*, Cambridge, 1987, pp. 235–45; and Schwiesow, 'Mediation', in Luard (note 185), p. 141, at pp. 144–8.

[221] Nyrop *et al.*, *Area Handbook for the Persian Gulf States*, Washington, DC, 1977, p. 289.

Fourthly, parties are free, in general, to waive any defect allegedly existing in the award, and may agree to implement the decision, especially if the defects are *de minimis*. Questions of nullity and voidability are precluded from consideration here. At this point, reference need only be made to the judgment in the *Gulf of Maine* case, where the Chamber of the International Court of Justice was partially but certainly *ultra petita*. The maritime frontier delimited by the Chamber in the first sector of the boundary from points A to B was in excess of the line claimed by Canada. While the United States Government was entitled in principle to object, it effectively waived its right and proceeded to welcome and implement the judgment. Clearly, its overall satisfaction with the delimitation of the continental shelf precluded the filing of any objections thereto.[222] Similarly, in *Land, Island and Maritime Frontier Dispute*, the Chamber was also marginally *ultra petita* in some sectors of the long Salvadorian–Honduran border, but the two parties were apparently happy to overlook this because the area in the aggregate was not extensive.[223] Fifthly, there is a small but complex degree of overlap between, on the one hand, revision and interpretation, and, on the other, some of the claims examined above, especially those dealing with questions of excess jurisdiction. Accordingly, these questions are considered in section IV.d of Chapter 5 below.

V. Concluding analysis: dissatisfaction, finality and reconciliation

In summing up, it will be appropriate to recall briefly that, for States and their inhabitants, territory represents a myriad of ideas, bound up as they are with history, nationalism, religion, folklore and tradition. Equally, territory represents security and stability. It is this cluster of factors which makes territorial disputes generally the most difficult and tenacious of all the problems States encounter in their dealings with other members of the international community. It is also for these reasons that there is, in fact, little or no overall recession of territorial and boundary disputes.

From, however, the point of view of international law, while there is no obligation to *settle* disputes, there is certainly a duty to *seek* a settlement

[222] ICJ Reports 1984, p. 246. For this, see the claim lines and maps on pp. 104 and 47. Although the map lines were for illustrative purposes, it does provide a good idea of the maritime alignments decided by the Chamber in that case. Further, see Kaikobad (note 25), p. 264, note 7.

[223] ICJ Reports 1992, p. 351. On this, see Kaikobad, 'The Quality of Justice Excès de Pouvoir in the Adjudication and Arbitration of Territorial and Boundary Disputes', in Goodwin-Gill and Talmon (eds.), *Reality of International Law: Essays in Honour of Ian Brownlie*, Oxford, 1999, p. 293.

and to conduct negotiations towards such a settlement in a *bona fide* manner.[224] Even so, it is the case that Article 33 of the United Nations Charter places special emphasis on certain kinds of dispute, that is, those which are likely to endanger international peace and security. In this kind of dispute, Member States are obliged *in principle* to seek a solution by one or more of the means specified in that article. The implications for States subject to these kinds of problem are obvious and need not be elaborated here. The essence of the point is that, despite various troublesome factors, many States do manage to resolve their disputes regarding the status of territory and the location of lines.

While the majority of such agreements are achieved by way of mutual goodwill, quiet diplomacy and effective negotiations, there are some agreements and settlements which are patently lacking in consent given freely; they are not the product of negotiations in the usual sense of the term. This state of affairs can arise where territorial adjustments are made by the Security Council under Chapter VII of the Charter, as it did with respect to the Iraq–Kuwait offshore areas, or where a peace treaty extracts territorial concessions from the vanquished. Apart from legal considerations of validity, referred to below, the inescapable fact is that, because territorial issues go to the heart of statehood, it is probably safe to hazard the proposition that, in these circumstances, any core, underlying, serious problems between the parties will continue and may even continue to bedevil good relations between them despite, and indeed because of, the existence of the Council's adjustments or the formal peace treaty.

Although the legal aspects of peace treaties cannot be examined fully here, it is appropriate to observe that State practice acknowledges in general the validity of territorial adjustments following a major conflict between States, provided that the changes are brought about by a congress of States, preferably those located in the region or sub-region, and, more importantly, are equitable in character. Where territorial concessions extracted from the losing State or States are *prima facie* exploitative of the military superiority of the victorious State, then in those cases the treaty is *prima facie* inequitable in its essential character. The same is generally true of bilateral peace treaties. On this view, then, for bilateral treaties, it could be argued that the endorsement of the United Nations is essential, especially where territorial concessions and adjustments are involved.

As far as multilateral peace treaties are concerned, it may be contended that, if there were to occur another major intercontinental armed

[224] See the *North Sea Continental Shelf* cases, ICJ Reports 1969, p. 3, at p. 47.

conflict, and if the United Nations were to survive that conflict in its present structure and with its present powers, then certainly the *imprimatur* of that organisation would be needed to give territorial adjustments a degree of legitimacy, provided, of course, that a need for such adjustments were established by independent and impartial investigation. Given, however, extreme national sensitivity over territorial issues, some adjustments can never be successful in resolving problems and may in fact contain the seeds for future unrest: the Versailles syndrome. Thus, new territorial issues may appear, even as old ones will die out, with the result that tension, and indeed bloodshed, could also continue.

Importantly, however, multilateral territorial adjustments arranged in conformity with principles of international law, including the Charter, are not the only adjustments which continue to cause problems between States: bilateral agreements, treaties, boundary protocols and demarcation commissions have all been known frequently to run into difficulties; this sort of dispute can be both intensely legal and factual, especially where it involves the interpretation of the terms of a treaty. It follows that, while *in theory* a treaty irons out the difficulties confronting the contracting parties, the *fact* is that they could well continue in a different form, and may only terminate when another 'more acceptable' agreement is made, or where, as is often the case, the matter is decided by arbitration or adjudication. Thus, tribunals may be mandated not only to decide issues of the status and location of territory and lines, but also vexed clauses in boundary or territorial agreements. International experience has shown that, even then, matters will not necessarily have reached their quietus; the remedies of interpretation and revision have on occasion been used to secure a better or more acceptable allocation or delimitation. The short point is that territorial problems are prone to surfacing in different contexts, formats and forms of relief claimed. The result, of course, is that this precludes an early end to mutual difficulties, leading to more negotiations for another agreement; or another round of proceedings of arbitration or adjudication, a sequence of events which reconfirms the general longevity of territorial and boundary disputes.

This, of course, is not an ideal situation, for international law abhors a state of affairs where parties are continually in serious dispute over all manner of issues, particularly where those issues are of the territorial kind, that is, one inherently susceptible to crisis and at times to armed conflict. In seeking to eradicate or minimise all sources of tension and dispute, international law has devised a simple principle of the most fundamental kind. This rule provides that, once a dispute is settled either by way of treaty or arbitral or judicial decision, the matter must be seen as being at an end. For territorial and boundary disputes, the rule comes in the form of the doctrine of finality and continuity of territorial adjustments.[225] By placing a legal impediment to continual adjustments, the doctrine precludes and discourages States from seeking such territorial changes.

The fact is, however, that some territorial disputes, as seen above, have the propensity to continue despite the existence of treaties and impartial third party decisions. This would seem to suggest that the doctrine is weak in terms of the actual practice of and implementation by States. These conflicting positions are easy to reconcile. The key fact is that even the most disputatious of States will accept the inherent sagacity of the doctrine. For, once the dispute is settled in accordance with that State's contentions or to its *bona fide* satisfaction, then that State will clearly be minded to place maximum reliance on that very doctrine of finality and continuity with a view to maintaining its gains and perpetuating the territorial regime. If this were not so, then no territorial or boundary settlement would ever be safe or final. A strong example of this is the position adopted by the United Kingdom regarding the *France–United Kingdom Continental Shelf (First Decision)* case, an arbitration discussed in detail in the following chapters. Suffice it to mention here that, despite the fact that there were errors in the arbitral award, the United Kingdom accepted it, not of course without demur, and confined itself to choosing the remedy of interpretation for the purposes of modifying the award at the expense of declaring it null and void.

Even so, although it is correct that the doctrine of stability and continuity of boundaries is a cornerstone of the law of title to territory, it is also the case that parties are always free to request reconsideration, but without creating any obligations for the other State to carry out the readjustments claimed. The essential point is that the doctrine in question is merely a general impediment designed to prevent a reopening of settled questions *as of right*, as opposed to readjustments freely entered into for various political considerations. It follows that, in order to succeed in reopening issues, the claimant State has to establish the *existence* of that right. Where the problems lie in conflicting interpretations of provisions

[225] Kaikobad (note 7), pp. 119 *et seq.*; Shaw (note 92.), pp. 87–92 and 112–19; Cukwurah (note 7), pp. 119–34; Jennings (note 1), p. 70; and Marston, 'The Stability of Land and Sea Boundary Delimitations in International Law', in Blake, G. (ed.), *Maritime Boundaries*, vol. 5 of Blake, G. (general editor), *World Boundaries*, 5 vols., London, 1994, p. 144. See also note 7 above.

in boundary treaties, there is no right in international law to *demand* independent, third party, impartial settlement. That can come about only by way of an existing or some other new agreement.

The same is true for the remedies of interpretation and revision, discussed below, the difference being that, in some situations, there may be a standing right of revision and interpretation, but these issues need not be pre-empted at this point. It will suffice to end here with the observation that, while legal principles attempt to impart a sense of finality to territorial issues fully and finally settled, they can only hope to succeed in this where the foundations of such settlements are also on firm ground corresponding to a sense of justice, equity and international law, especially where the *imprimatur* of the United Nations is clearly evident. That *imprimatur* may come in the form of active mediation, conciliation commissions, fact-finding, plebiscites and the like. The short point is that the greater the harmony between political reality on the one hand, and territorial arrangements on the other, the greater the chance of such arrangements continuing without problems.

PART III · JUDICIAL REMEDIES: INTERPRETATION

3 The interpretation of judgments and awards

I. Preliminary observations

The simple judicial process of interpretation[226] arises when litigating States empower an international tribunal to provide a judgment or award clarifying, on request, jointly or severally, the meaning, scope and effect of a judgment or award previously given by the same tribunal or some other tribunal. Despite this simplicity, complex legal issues can arise when a tribunal begins to supply a clarification of what it had itself meant to hold in a previous judgment or award, or in some cases what another tribunal had said or meant to say in its decision. Before these legal issues are scrutinised,

[226] Generally, see Hill, 'The Interpretation of the Decisions of International Courts', 22 (1933–4) *Georgetown Law Journal* 535; Collier and Lowe, *The Settlement of Disputes in International Law*, Oxford, 1999, pp. 179–80; Rosenne, *The Law and Practice of the International Court 1920–1996*, vol. III, *Procedure*, The Hague, 1997, pp. 1669–81; Grzybowski, 'Interpretation of Decisions of International Tribunals', 35 (1941) AJIL 482; United Nation's Secretariat, 'Commentary on the Draft Convention on Arbitral Procedure Adopted by the International Law Commission at Its Fifth Session', UN Doc. A/CN.4/92, New York, 1955, pp. 95–8; Zimmermann, *Interpretation of the Judgments of the International Court of Justice under Article 60 of the Statute*, Tübingen, 1989; Ralston (note 136), pp. 241–3; and see Simpson and Fox (note 136), pp. 245–7; Bowett, 'Res Judicata and the Limits of Decisions by International Tribunals', 8 (1996) *African Journal of International and Comparative Law* 577, at pp. 581–8; Reisman, *Nullity and Revision*, New Haven, 1971, pp. 192–208; Thirlway, 'The Law and Procedure of the International Court of Justice 1960–1989 (Part Thirteen)', 74 (2003) BYIL 7, at pp. 79–89; Plender, 'Procedure in the European Courts: Comparisons and Proposals', 267 (1997) *Hague Recueil* 9, at pp. 308–11; Bos, *A Methodology of International Law*, Amsterdam, 1984, Chapter VII; Jenks, *The Prospects of International Adjudication*, London, 1964, pp. 133 and 151; Fitzmaurice, 'The Law and Practice of the International Court of Justice, 1951–4: Questions of Jurisdiction, Competence and Procedure', 34 (1958) BYIL 1; Merrills (note 136), p. 162; Verzijl (note 136), pp. 573–4; Stone, *Legal Controls of International Conflict: A Treatise on the Dynamics of Disputes – and War – Law*, Sydney, 1959, p. 95; and Schlochauer, 'The International Court of Justice', in 2 (1972) *Encyclopedia of Public International Law* 1097–8.

it will be appropriate to provide some perspective by looking at the evolution of this concept in international law and State practice.

II. Evolution of the notion of interpretation

a. General

In marked contrast to the remedy of revision, which is examined in Part IV below, the evolution of this principle has been uneventful. It has crept into international law on the nod, as it were, because of the inherently uncomplicated and uncontroversial nature of the basic rule. The basic rule is that, if the judgment or award is not clear on a precise issue, then the tribunal can be approached to provide an explanation or clarification on the disputed passage or passages of the decision. Of course, it is the application of the remedy in specific cases which leads to difficulties and complexities of various kinds. These issues are discussed below.

b. The Hague Peace Conferences

The evolutionary development of the remedy begins not, as in the case of revision, in 1899 at the First International Peace Conference at The Hague, but at the Second Conference in 1907. The reason for this is simple. At the 1899 Conference, the remedy of interpretation as a principle or rule of procedure for the new Permanent Court of Arbitration does not seem to have crossed the minds of the juriconsults assembled there. It would not diminish the significance of this remedy in international law were it to be pointed out that the delegations of the forty-four nations were preoccupied with more urgent matters, that is, the entire issue of the pacific settlement of international disputes which, at the first multilateral institutional level, was in itself a great novelty. Thus, the Hague Convention for the Pacific Settlement of International Disputes of 1899[227] is silent on the principle of interpretation.

This matter first came into the frame when the First Commission of the Conference, which was mandated to consider the revision of the 1899 Convention, created a Subcommission, known as the First Sub-commission, to consider the matter.[228] Delegates submitted a good number of

[227] 91 BFSP 970.

[228] First Meeting, 25 June 1907: see Scott (ed.), *The Proceedings of the Hague Peace Conferences: The Conference of 1907: Translation of the Official Texts*, vol. II, *The Meetings of the First Commission*, New York, 1921, p. 203 (hereinafter referred to as '*Proceedings 1907*, vol. II').

proposals on various issues,[229] but it was the Italian delegation which put forward the draft which is of concern here.[230] Draft Article 52a provided thus:

Any dispute arising between the parties as to the interpretation and execution of the arbitral award shall be submitted to the decision of the tribunal which pronounced it.

The First Subcommission referred the matter, along with other proposals, to the Committee of Examination on 13 August 1907.[231] It was considered and adopted by Committee A of the Committee of Examination on 1 October 1907 at its seventeenth meeting. As the records of that meeting show, this provision, among others, '[gave] rise to no remarks and [was] adopted'.[232] Subsequently, the draft articles were referred to Committee C, the body responsible for studying issues of a technical character.[233]

It was here that the Italian draft article received some discussion. Sir Edward Fry, representing Great Britain, rejected the draft provision on the ground that a dispute on a question concerning the interpretation of the judgment constituted a new dispute and hence required a new *compromis* followed by a new arbitration.[234] The gravamen of his argument was that the right of a tribunal to interpret its judgment or award was not inherent in it, and, accordingly, if the parties needed clarification, a new separate agreement needed to be concluded authorising the tribunal to provide a formal decision explaining the meaning of the vexed passage or passages.

Mr Heinrich Lammasch, the representative of Austria–Hungary, intervened to provide a compromise by suggesting that the clause 'insofar as the *compromis* does not exclude it' be added to the draft provision.[235] In other words, the Lammasch proposal had the effect of putting the burden of excluding the remedy of interpretation onto the contracting States, and, by doing so, the said remedy would then become a standard, inherent power of the Permanent Court of Arbitration. This modification was accepted by other members of Committee C, and was adopted with some discussion on the matter of cross-reference to another draft article, making it clear that it was the *compromis* which decided the powers of the tribunal in this respect, and that it was advantageous to have the same judges for the purposes of the interpretation and revision

229 Annexes 1 to 17, *ibid*., pp. 851–73.
230 Annex 14, *ibid*., pp. 871–2.
231 Eleventh Meeting, *ibid*., p. 355, at p. 368.
232 *Ibid*., p. 575, at p. 588.
233 First Meeting of Committee C, 16 August 1907, *ibid*., p. 709.
234 Fifth Meeting, 2 September 1907, *ibid*., p. 727, at p. 731.
235 *Ibid*.

of judgments as were on the bench for the original proceedings and decision.[236] The draft article was then adopted by the Committee at its second reading on 11 September 1907 at its ninth meeting.[237] After another textual change at the tenth meeting,[238] Committee C adopted the provisional text of the draft convention.[239] The relevant article was formulated thus:

> Any dispute arising between the parties as to interpretation and execution of the award shall, provided the *compromis* does not exclude it, be submitted to the decision of the tribunal which pronounced it.

The First Commission then adopted without discussion the revised draft provision, along with other articles, on 7 October 1907 at the seventh meeting thereof.[240] Baron Guillaume, the Rapporteur of the First Commission, presented his report on the revision of the Convention of 1899 to Plenary at its ninth meeting on 16 October 1907.[241] In his brief commentary, he recorded the fact that the provision on interpretation was not adopted unanimously, and explained the position adopted by the British delegation and the compromise which was struck.[242] The Conference adopted the draft as a whole unanimously at that meeting.[243] It finally emerged as Article 82, the only change being the substitution of the words 'in the absence of agreement to the contrary' in place of 'provided the *compromis* does not exclude it'.[244] It is noteworthy that the discussion which took place in Committee C was probably the most this provision has ever had in its history at the multilateral level.

[236] *Ibid*. These were the observations of Mr Lange, the delegate from Norway.

[237] *Ibid*., p. 753, at p. 757.

[238] The French delegate, M. Fromageot, suggested that the word 'same' be deleted because it was superfluous: *ibid*., p. 760, at p. 765.

[239] 19 September 1907, Annex: Provisional Text of Article 20 and Following of the Convention of 1899 and of the Draft of a Supplementary Plan of the French Delegation, Adopted by Committee C, *ibid*., p. 768, at p. 775.

[240] *Ibid*., p. 109, at p. 131. The whole revised convention was also adopted: *ibid*., p. 133.

[241] *Proceedings of the Hague Peace Conferences: Translation of the Official Texts: The Conference of 1907*, vol. I, *Plenary Meetings of the Conference*, New York, 1920, Annex D, p. 325, at p. 395 (hereinafter referred to as '*Proceedings 1907*, vol. I').

[242] *Ibid*., p. 436.

[243] *Ibid*., pp. 329–30.

[244] Text of the Convention, *ibid*., p. 612. Cf. Hill, and the uncertainty surrounding its precise meaning, (note 226), p. 539. On this view, there is no uncertainty: see the text to notes 235–44 above; and section II of Chapter 5 below.

c. Developments since 1907 and the Great War: the Statute of the Permanent Court of International Justice

The next stage in the development of this notion as a remedy in international law was the Statute of the Permanent Court of International Justice, but it must also be noted that, in December 1907, that is, two months after the 1907 Hague Convention was adopted, the Governments of Costa Rica, Honduras, El Salvador, Guatemala and Nicaragua assembled for a conference in Washington and concluded the Convention for the Establishment of a Central American Court of Justice.[245] Article XXIV of the Convention allowed parties to a judgment of the Central American Court of Justice to request the tribunal to declare the interpretation which must be given to its judgments. It follows that the notion of allowing parties to a litigation to approach the tribunal for clarification had begun to take root immediately after the Hague Conference.

In any event, matters in Europe were also moving ahead. As a preliminary to the proceedings at the Council and Assembly of the League of Nations, the Advisory Committee of Jurists was commissioned to discuss the Statute of the proposed court,[246] and, not unlike the 1907 Conference, this principle did not receive much consideration. Meeting at The Hague, the Committee had before it a number of draft proposals as well as the 1907 Convention to serve as a basis for discussion and formulation of provisions.[247] At the thirtieth meeting on 21 July 1920,[248] the Committee adopted draft Article 21 on interpretation.[249] There was no discussion on the matter. The following day, at the thirty-first meeting, the draft article on interpretation was adopted, as was the record of the work of the Committee.[250] In its definitive report, the Committee formulated Article 58 as follows:

[245] 2 (1908) AJIL 231.

[246] See *Procès-Verbaux of the Proceedings of the Advisory Committee of Jurists, June 16–July 24, 1920 with Annexes*, The Hague, 1920 (hereinafter referred to as '*The Hague Advisory Committee Proceedings*').

[247] See the draft proposals submitted by the Five Neutral Powers and the Danish, Swedish and Norwegian Governments, all providing for interpretation: as outlined in Synopsis, Annex No. 7, Second Meeting, 17 June 1920, *ibid.*, p. 33, at p. 51, and the draft proposals on p. 91. For the full texts, see Permanent Court of International Justice, Advisory Committee of Jurists, *Documents Presented to the Committee Relating to Existing Plans for the Establishment of a Permanent Court of International Justice*, London, 1920, pp. 169, 203, 229, 237, 253, 291 and 309.

[248] *The Hague Advisory Committee Proceedings* (note 246), p. 617.

[249] See Annex No. 3 to the Thirtieth Meeting, *ibid.*, p. 637, at p. 642.

[250] *Ibid.*, p. 645, at p. 650. For the text of Draft Article 58, see Annex No. 2, *ibid.*, p. 669.

The Judgment is final and without appeal. In the event of uncertainty as to the meaning and scope of the Judgment, the Court shall construe it upon the request of any party.[251]

No commentary was provided. It may nevertheless be noted that the 'contrary agreement' clause was deleted because a regime for a permanent court was now being provided and the power of interpretation was deemed to be inherent in that tribunal. The draft was forwarded to the League, where the Council began deliberating its contents. At this stage, the Council was concerned with only the broad contours of the proposed court and with issues which were particularly controversial in nature, especially compulsory jurisdiction, discussed very briefly below. The Council held its tenth session at Brussels in October 1920 and introduced amendments made to the Advisory Committee's draft (also known also as the Hague draft), but, insofar as none of them were concerned with the notion of interpretation, they need not be examined here.[252]

The Brussels Draft, as the Council's amendments came to be known, was passed on to the First Assembly of the League, where the matter was assigned to the Third Committee and in turn to the Subcommittee thereof. However, in contrast to the provisions on revision, discussed in section II.C of Chapter 7 below, there was no discussion on the matter except that the word 'dispute' was substituted for 'uncertainty' in the clause 'In the event of uncertainty . . .' at the start of the second sentence.[253] The draft, as amended first by the Council and then by the Third Committee, was finally adopted unanimously by the Assembly in plenum at its twenty-first Plenary Meeting on 13 December 1920.[254]

However, before moving to the next stage of development, it may be interesting to take note of a little-known aspect of interpretation. It is little known, perhaps, because it failed to materialise in the definitive Statute of the Permanent Court of International Justice. One of the

[251] Annex No. 1, Thirty-Fourth Meeting, 24 July 1920, *ibid.*, p. 689, at pp. 743–4.

[252] Proces Verbaux (Extracts) of the 10th Session of the Council, 20–28 October 1920: Doc. 30 in *League of Nations Permanent Court of International Justice Documents Concerning the Action Taken by the Council of the League of Nations under Article 14 of the Covenant of the League of Nations and the Adoption by the Assembly of the Statute of the Permanent Court of International Justice*, Geneva, 1921, p. 42 (hereinafter referred to as *Documents on Action Taken*).

[253] See the Draft Scheme appended to the Report Submitted to the Third Committee by M. Hagerup on Behalf of the Sub-Committee, Doc. 48: Report and Draft Scheme Presented to the Assembly by the Third Committee, *ibid.* (note 252), p. 206, at pp. 214 and 221.

[254] *League of Nations, The Records of the First Assembly, Plenary Meetings*, Geneva, 1920, p. 478.

provisions in the Root–Phillimore Plan[255] related to the various heads of jurisdiction or competency exercisable by the proposed Permanent Court of International Justice.[256] Article 34, the draft provision which the Advisory Committee debated and finally accepted, stipulates as follows:

Between States which are Members of the League of Nations, the Court shall have jurisdiction (and this without any special convention giving it jurisdiction) to hear and determine cases of a legal nature concerning (a) the interpretation of a treaty; (b) any question of international law; (c) the existence of any fact which if established would constitute a breach of international law; (d) the nature and extent of reparation to be made for the breach of an international obligation; [and] (e) *the interpretation of a sentence passed by the Court.*[257]

It is, of course, paragraph (e) which is material here. In its final report to the League, the Committee advocated the adoption of this provision, but, as could be expected, the topic of concern was that of compulsory jurisdiction, an issue close to the heart of the Committee and, indeed, controversial to boot.[258] In point of fact, the time for such compulsory jurisdiction had not yet arrived, and, admittedly, is still some distance away. Accordingly, when the Council considered the Hague draft in Brussels, it cautiously rejected the notion of compulsory jurisdiction. Acknowledging the fact that this was an extremely useful development in the authority of the proposed court, the Council noted that it could not propose adopting a rule which did not have unanimous support; it could not propose a rule which was a modification effectively of Articles 12, 13 and 14 of the Covenant because modifications could only be introduced without danger when they had received unanimous support.[259] There was obviously no unanimity between Member States on this issue. It then proposed a new draft article which vested jurisdiction in the Court strictly on the basis of treaties in force between the States but without the need for a special

[255] Lord Phillimore, from Great Britain, and Mr Elihu Root, from the United States, jointly produced a draft which became one of the principal bases of discussions by the Third Committee.

[256] See the Twenty-Fourth Meeting of 14 July 1920, *The Hague Advisory Committee Proceedings* (note 246), p. 515: Annex No. 3, at p. 547. For a convenient text, see Scott, *The Project of a Permanent Court of International Justice and Resolutions of the Advisory Committee of Jurists*, Washington, DC, 1920, pp. 218–23.

[257] Draft Article 34, Report of the Committee, *The Hague Advisory Committee Proceedings* (note 246), p. 729 (emphasis added).

[258] Generally, see *ibid.*, pp. 726–9.

[259] Report Presented by the French Representative, M. Leon Bourgeois, and Adopted by the Council of the League of Nations at Its Meeting at Brussels on 27th October 1920: Doc. 32, *Documents on Action Taken* (note 252), p. 45, at p. 47; generally, see pp. 46–8.

agreement thereafter on the matter.[260] The main point of concern here is that, in amending and reformulating the provisions on compulsory jurisdiction, the Council deleted the Hague draft's reference to interpretation by the Court of its 'sentences'.[261] It may be that it felt that the remedy of interpretation was already provided in draft Article 60 of the Statute. In any event, the Subcommittee of the Third Committee accepted the Council's Brussels draft provision on the matter of compulsory jurisdiction and on the need for unanimity before such changes could be admitted. However, it also recommended the adoption of the optional clause scheme[262] and the Assembly in plenum accepted this proposal.

d. The Statute of the International Court of Justice

At the end of the Second World War, the United Nations Committee of Jurists, a body established pursuant to Chapter VII of the Dumbarton Oaks Proposals,[263] was commissioned to consider modifications to the Statute of the Permanent Court of International Justice.[264] As far as the interpretation rule is concerned, Article 60, along with Articles 57–64 of the Statute, 'were approved without objection' by the Committee,[265] and

[260] For the text, see Doc. 32, *Documents on Action Taken* (note 252), p. 47; and Draft Scheme for the Permanent Court of International Justice, Mentioned in Article 14 of the Covenant of the League of Nations, Presented to the Council of the League of Nations by the Advisory Committee of Jurists as Amended by Virtue of the Decisions of the Council: Doc. 35, *ibid.*, p. 54, at pp. 57–8.

[261] Annex 118 to Minutes of Tenth Council Session: Amendments Proposed by the Council to Certain Articles of the Scheme for the Permanent Court of International Justice: Doc. 31, *Documents on Action Taken* (note 252), p. 44.

[262] Seventh Meeting of the Subcommittee, 1 December 1920, Minutes of the Sub-Committee of the Third Committee: Doc. 82, *Documents on Action Taken* (note 252), pp. 142–4; and see Annex 14: Draft Submitted by the Subcommittee: Draft Article 36 (Brussels Article 33), *ibid.*, p. 170; and Annex 16: Report of the Third Committee by Mr Hagerup, *ibid.*, p. 172, at pp. 172 and 174: Annexes to the Minutes of the Sub-Committee, *ibid.*, p. 159. Further, see Report and Draft Scheme Presented to the Assembly by the Third Committee, Doc. 48, *ibid.*, pp. 210–11.

[263] Jurist 2, G/2, *Documents of the United Nations Conference on International Organization*, vol. 14, *United Nations Committee of Jurists*, San Francisco and London, 1945, p. 453 (hereinafter UNCIO).

[264] See the Report of the UN Committee of Jurists to the UN Conference on International Organization at San Francisco, Jurist 61 (rev.), G/49, 20 April 1945, and Jurist 86, G/73, 25 April 1945, UNCIO, vol. 13: *Commission IV Judicial Organization*, p. 648 and p. 821, respectively.

[265] Summary of the Seventh Meeting, 13 April 1945, Jurist 40, G/30: 13 April 1945, *ibid.*, p. 162, at p. 173. The brief discussion related to clarification regarding the power to consider appeals from other tribunals upon agreement as contained in the Rules of the Court between the parties and the rule of finality of the Court's decisions: see *ibid.*, pp. 173–4.

hence no modifications were recommended. At the Conference in San Francisco in 1945, the Committee's report was given over to Commission IV on Judicial Organisation, and the relevant Committee 1 for detailed consideration. At its sixth meeting, held on 11 May 1945, Committee 1 approved Articles 39–64 of the Statute *en bloc*, unanimously and without discussion.[266] The matter was then forwarded to the Co-ordination Committee and the Advisory Committee of Jurists. Both bodies accepted the modified Statute, and the unmodified Article 60.[267] The text of the Statute of the International Court of Justice was proposed by Plenary[268] and signed by the delegations on 26 June 1945.[269] Thus the rule on interpretation was transferred to the Statute without causing any difficulties or a need for further discussion.

e. Judicial contribution in the development of the notion

As far as the application of this remedy is concerned, it is clear that this constitutes the main scope of enquiry, and as such it will not be appropriate to survey its features here. Nor would it be useful to discuss these aspects in a section of a study which is concerned with the *evolution* of the notion of interpretation. It will, therefore, suffice here to note that the first application for interpretation came very early for the Permanent Court of International Justice. In *Interpretation of Article 179 of the Treaty of Neuilly*,[270] the Court gave a judgment in 1924 in a dispute between the Greek and Bulgarian Governments arising out the precise scope of jurisdiction of the arbitrator appointed under the Treaty of Neuilly of 1919. The Greek Government thereafter applied under Article 60 for clarification with respect especially to the question whether the judgment sanctioned the liquidation by Greece of Bulgarian property in Greek territory for the purposes of realising sums of money to be awarded by the arbitrator.

266 Summary Report of the Sixth Meeting, Doc. 264, IV/1/18, 12 May 1945, UNCIO, vol. 13, *ibid.*, p. 170.

267 Draft Statute Reviewed by the Advisory Committee, Doc. 1141, CO/180, 21 June 1945; and Draft Statute as Finally Approved by the Co-ordination Committee and the Advisory Committee, 22 June 1945, Doc. 1158, CO/180(1), 22 June 1945, UNCIO, vol. 15: *Co-ordination Committee; The Charter; Lists*, p. 126 and p. 148, respectively.

268 Doc. 1191, G/128, 25 June 1945, *ibid.*, p. 273.

269 *Ibid.*, p. 335. The corresponding provisions in the Rules of the International Court of Justice of 1978 are contained in Article 98 thereof, and, for commentary, see Rosenne, *Procedure in the International Court: A Commentary on the 1978 Rules of the International Court of Justice*, The Hague, 1983, pp. 203–4. Previous versions of this provision were contained in Articles 77 and 84 of the Rules of 1946 and 1972.

270 PCIJ Reports, Series A, No. 3 (1924), p. 4.

In its judgment in *Interpretation of Judgment No. 3*,[271] the Court, however, refused to grant the request for interpretation because the request dealt with questions not dealt with by the Court in response to the special agreement and the judgment. The rule was stated thus: '[A]n interpretation – given in accordance with Article 60 of the Statute – of the judgment of September 12th, 1924, cannot go beyond the limits of that judgment itself, which are fixed by the special agreement . . .'[272] In the *Jaworzina Boundary* and *Monastery of Saint-Naoum* advisory opinions, discussed in detail below, the Permanent Court of International Justice was faced with unorthodox requests for interpretation. However, in *Chorzów Factory (Interpretation of Judgments Nos. 7 and 8)*, the Court established the rule, among others, that clarification or interpretation must relate to points which had been settled with binding force in a judgment and that there must therefore exist a difference of opinion between the parties as to those points in the judgment in question which have been decided with binding force.[273]

Thereafter, the next request came in 1950, when Colombia asked for an interpretation of the Court's judgment in the *Asylum Case*[274] between Colombia and Peru. A clarification was provided in *Request for Interpretation of the Judgment of 20 November 1950*.[275] The next case in interpretation came via an unexpected route. In 1955, the General Assembly requested the Court to provide an advisory *opinion* on a previous advisory *opinion* of the Court. In the *Status of South-West Africa* case, decided in 1950, the Court had held in terms that 'the degree of supervision' exercised by the General Assembly should not exceed that which applied under the Mandates system of the League of Nations with respect to South-West Africa.[276]

Thus, when, in 1955, the Assembly adopted Rule F regarding the voting procedure on questions dealing with the Mandate, and requiring a two-thirds majority as an important question,[277] the Court was asked to advise whether Rule F was consistent with that opinion. In *South-West Africa Voting Procedure*, the Court held, *inter alia*, that the expression 'degree of supervision' should not be interpreted as relating to procedural matters, and that they related to measures and means of supervision.[278] There was a long period of time in which no requests for interpretation were submitted, until the request for such a remedy was put before the Court in respect of the *Tunisia–Libya Continental Shelf* case.[279] This and other litigation is scrutinised below.

[271] PCIJ Reports, Series A, No. 4 (1925), p. 4. [272] *Ibid.*, p. 7.
[273] PCIJ Reports, Series A, No. 13 (1927), p. 4, at p. 11. [274] ICJ Reports 1950, p. 266.
[275] *Ibid.*, p. 395. [276] ICJ Reports 1950, p. 128, at p. 138. [277] Resolution 844 (IX).
[278] ICJ Reports 1955, p. 67, at pp. 72–3. [279] ICJ Reports 1982, p. 18.

4 The classification of the notion of interpretation

I. Preliminary observations

The clarification sought by litigating States may range from a narrow point in a passage in the text of the award to wide-ranging issues arising from the original decision; this may and oftentimes does involve dealing with questions relating to the identification of geographical features described in the decision. Requests for interpretation may also raise issues regarding the effect of the decision on large tracts of territory, and the status thereof. The brief description provided above will have indicated that this study contemplates two kinds of interpretation, namely, incidental interpretation and main case interpretation. Both are examined individually below.

II. Interpretation as incidental to the main case

The first kind of interpretation is typical of the basic notion, namely, interpretation as a species of incidental jurisdiction. As such, it is a legal device which enables a State to request the tribunal which gave the decision to interpret its judgment or award in order to clarify aspects of the meaning and scope thereof. It is incidental in the sense that the interpretative process and subsequent decision is supplementary to the main proceedings and the judgment or arbitral award of the tribunal. It is also incidental in that the process springs either (a) from the basic arbitral agreement between the parties or (b) from a standing right vested in a permanent tribunal such as the International Court of Justice, the Court of Justice of the European Communities or the Court of Justice of the European Free Trade Area. Of course, given that the fundamental scope of this enquiry is confined to decisions dealing with boundary and territorial issues, it will be appropriate to refer to the powers exercised by the International Court of Justice and *ad hoc* international tribunals; the study will hence eschew the law and jurisprudence of the other two international tribunals mentioned above, except insofar as it may be useful to refer to the decisions of these and other tribunals for the purposes of analogous consideration.

By way of illustration, reference may be made to the *Tunisia–Libya Continental Shelf* case which was decided by the International Court of Justice in 1982 and which was then followed in 1985 by *Application for Revision and Interpretation of the 1982 Judgment*,[280] a case initiated by Tunisia on the basis of Articles 60 and 61 of the Statute of the International Court of Justice. In the latter case, Tunisia requested the Court to revise and interpret the judgment of 1982, details of which need not be discussed at this stage. The point to note here is that the Court provided a judgment which dealt with questions raised by both Tunisia and Libya, but this judgment was essentially ancillary to the main judgment: it did not go into the merits of the dispute again, and, to that extent, then, the use of the term 'incidental' describes the proceedings adequately.

Another example of interpretation essentially incidental in nature to the main proceedings is the *United Kingdom–France Continental Shelf Interpretive Decision* case where the Government of the United Kingdom filed an application to the Court of Arbitration for interpretation of its arbitral award in the *United Kingdom–France Continental Shelf Delimitation (First Decision)* case of 1977.[281] The United Kingdom requested the Court to provide clarification on certain aspects of the award which were causing difficulties of interpretation and application, and the Court provided another award clarifying these problems, without, however, going into the merits of the award which were, in any event, *res judicata*. It is in this context that the significance of interpretation, albeit as incidental to the main case, in matters of title to territory is captured well by Colson when he wrote:

> But the Decision of 14 March 1978 has more than interpretative value, because it enters new areas of maritime boundary doctrine which have heretofore been unexplored by international courts and tribunals. For the first time the general principles of international law relevant to maritime boundary delimitation are discussed together with the tools – charts, projections, and methods of calculation – that must be employed before any boundary becomes a reality. These matters, often considered 'technicalities', *are shown to raise legal issues of the first order and to have substantive consequences which may amount to many square miles of maritime area*. The decision demonstrates that traditional legal questions cannot be forgotten in the context of maritime boundaries.[282]

[280] ICJ Reports 1985, p. 192. [281] 54 ILR 142, and 54 ILR 6 respectively.

[282] See 'The United Kingdom–France Continental Shelf Arbitration: Interpretive Decision of March 1978', 73 (1979) AJIL 112, at p. 119 (emphasis added).

III. Main case interpretation

The second kind of interpretative process has tended to be ignored in the literature, not only because, perhaps, most writers have focused on interpretation simply as an aspect of incidental jurisdiction, but also because the category devised below is merely one way of grouping together a number of similar cases. On this view, nevertheless, all cases of interpretation are *not* aspects of jurisdiction incidental to the main case, and it is important that such a category be regarded as distinct from incidental interpretation inasmuch as the characteristic features of the two are distinct, although it is the case that the essential significant elements of the law are applicable to both categories of interpretation. This second kind of judicial process arises where a tribunal is called upon to provide clarification of a decision given by another tribunal and where such a process arises out of an agreement separate from the original *compromis*. From this perspective, then, this interpretative process is hardly incidental to the main proceedings, which may in fact be different from or remote from them in terms of time, the gravity of the issues and the nature of the claims. As the main cause of action itself, the judgment in proceedings of this kind cannot realistically be regarded as supplementary to the original decision, lying in the slipstream, as it were, of the main judgment. Depending, of course, on the circumstances of a particular case, it may be that issues discussed in the interpretative process will go to the merits of a dispute with consequential effects on title to territory.

Thus, when Argentina and Chile constituted by mutual agreement in 1991 an arbitral tribunal and vested it with the task of interpreting and applying the *Argentina–Chile Boundary Award* of 1902,[283] they were constituting a new international tribunal nearly a century later to resolve the disputed issues and flawed delimitation emerging from the award in 1902, and in that sense the case, decided eventually in 1994, was simply a contentious case, hardly incidental to the earlier dispute. Hence, the Arbitral Tribunal in the *Laguna del Desierto* case was able to state:

> This Tribunal is an autonomous judicial body, set up by the Special Agreement of 31 October 1991 within the framework of the *Tratado de Paz y Amistad* of 1984. It is neither the successor of King Edward VII, nor is it dependent upon any other arbitral agency, but is entirely autonomous. Its function is clearly set out in the Special Agreement and consists in deciding the course of the frontier between [Boundary Post] 62 and Mount Fitzroy as it was determined in the Award of 1902, which has

[283] 95 BFSP 162.

been recognised by the parties as *res judicata* and is not subject to any form of proceeding by way of revision, appeal or nullity.[284]

Interestingly, while *Laguna del Desierto* is what may be called main case interpretation, the subsequent *Request for Revision and Interpretation of the 1994 Judgment*[285] is an example of the incidental jurisdiction of the Arbitral Tribunal exercised in 1995 following an application filed by the Government of Chile asking for clarification and revision of the judgment in *Laguna del Desierto*. Earlier, in 1965, the same two States had constituted a tribunal, the Court of Arbitration, and vested it with the power to interpret, among other things, the unresolved parts of the 1902 award, a step which resulted in the *Palena* arbitration concluded in 1966.[286] Similarly, another instance of this kind of interpretation is the *Costa Rica* v. *Panama* boundary arbitration[287] of 1914 carried out ostensibly as an interpretative process with respect to an earlier arbitral award, namely, the *Colombia* v. *Costa Rica* case[288] decided by the President of France in 1900, Colombia being the predecessor State of Panama.

A further example is provided in the *Radcliffe India–Pakistan Boundary Award* delivered on 12 August 1947, that is, on the eve of the emergence of Pakistan and India as independent States with respect to their frontiers.[289] However, there arose disputes with respect to four sectors in the Bengal/East Pakistan frontier, and hence the two States constituted another tribunal, this time, however, as independent States, to proceed to the adjudication and final settlement of specific boundary disputes 'arising out of the interpretation of the Radcliffe Award and for demarcation of the boundary accordingly'.[290] In effect, the Tribunal was asked to clarify the lines drawn by a thick pen on a small-scale map by the Boundary Commission in 1947. The *Bagge India–Pakistan Boundary Award* was handed down by the tribunal in February 1950.[291] The point here is that, in all these cases, save *Request for Revision and Interpretation of the 1994 Judgment*, consent to interpretation came independently of the main *compromis* and as a result of prolonged mutual frustration.

284 113 ILR 1, at p. 42. 285 *Ibid.*, p. 194. 286 16 UNRIAA 111; 38 ILR 16.
287 8 (1914) AJIL 237. 288 92 BFSP 1038.
289 *Gazette of Pakistan Extraordinary*, 17 August 1947, reproduced in Razvi (note 85), p. 226. Further, see Spate, 'The Partition of India and the Prospects of Pakistan', 38 (1948) *Geographical Review* 5.
290 *Gazette of Pakistan Extraordinary*, 5 February 1950, reproduced in Razvi (note 85), p. 226, at p. 242. See further, Ahmad, 'The Indo-Pakistan Boundary Disputes Tribunal, 1949–1950', 43 (1953) *Geographical Review* 329.
291 *Gazette of Pakistan Extraordinary*, 5 February 1950: see above.

To be sure, there are other distinguishing characteristics between these two categories of interpretation, including the fact that, while incidental interpretative processes are usually limited by time to *ad hoc* arbitral tribunals, main case interpretation is unaffected by temporal limits, not least because the new tribunal is a creature of the sovereign will of two States and the contracting States have the right to disregard such limits by way of mutual consent. The fact that a large time gap exists between the first and the subsequent proceedings is also a distinguishing factor, especially where the law in the intervening years has changed enormously.

It is important, however, to note that there is also a *third* category of interpretative cases, although it is one which, given its characteristics, appears to fall as a subset of main case interpretation. In this third category, the task of the tribunal is more to do with determining the effects of the decisions at both the macro- and micro-levels. At the former level, the tribunal may be given the task of interpreting the decision to determine the overall status of the decision being interpreted and the boundary resulting therefrom; at the latter level, questions of location and allocation are resolved by reference to the terms of the previous decisions. It is not an independent category, however, because some of its characteristic features are only marginally different from main case interpretation. Yet, it is different in that the emphasis here is placed on finding a solution to an outstanding frontier problem despite the existence of a boundary decision which one of the parties may wish to ignore or underplay consistent with their political claims and demands.

Thus, in the *Dubai–Sharjah Land and Maritime Boundary* case, the interpretative process was a subtle one indeed, in that the *compromis* of 1976 authorising the Court of Arbitration to examine the boundary matter contained no reference to the interpretation of the decisions of the British Political Agent, Mr J. P. Tripp, with respect to the Dubai–Sharjah frontier, although this controversy stood at the centre of the dispute. This was because the Governments of Dubai and Sharjah were unable to agree with respect to the essential legal nature and effects of those decisions. While Dubai considered the Tripp decisions of 1956 and 1957 as part merely of the historic evidence of the frontier without admitting that they were either binding on the parties or *res judicata* of the issue,[292] Sharjah relied heavily on these decisions, arguing that they were arbitral awards and not merely administrative decisions. Inevitably, the issue of the Tripp decisions was one which the Court of Arbitration was obliged to address,

[292] 91 ILR 553.

inevitable because, although the *compromis* was silent, the two governments argued both for and against the legal effects of the decisions in their written and oral proceedings before the Court.[293] After deciding that they were administrative, binding decisions as opposed to arbitral awards, the Court went on to interpret the terms of the Tripp decisions and the Walker map and to identify and locate the disputed points along the boundary.[294]

A similar sort of situation prevailed in the *Qatar–Bahrain Hawar Islands and Continental Shelf* case,[295] but in this instance the question was less an interpretation of the terms of the administrative decision adopted by the British Political Resident in 1939, which allocated the Hawar Islands to Bahrain, and more a straightforward dispute regarding the legal status and effects thereof. Issues of a similar sort were before the Permanent Court of International Justice in two cases, namely, the *Jaworzina Boundary* and the *Monastery of Saint-Naoum*[296] advisory opinions. In both, the Court decided in favour of giving full legal effect to the decisions of the Conference of Ambassadors of 1920 and 1922 which delimited the boundaries of Poland and Czechoslovakia, and Albania and the Serb-Croat-Slovene State, respectively, and decided that the decisions were not administrative but binding arbitral awards. This required very careful examination of the terms of those two decisions as well as other relevant documentation.

In light of the classification adopted above, the following points are noteworthy. First, although it is essentially one kind of contentious case, a category in which certain cases with a common theme are grouped together, main case interpretation cannot be ignored in a study relating to institutionalised interpretation, that is, where interpretation is essentially a remedial measure exercised by a tribunal on the request of one of the litigating parties after the delivery of its judgment. To exclude this category would be to ignore an important and burgeoning area of the law. In any event, inasmuch as there is a close interplay of rules, there is little sense in losing the opportunity of discussing common principles and themes together. It is for this reason that the discussion below is not predicated in presenting the relevant legal problems by reference to

[293] *Ibid.*, pp. 556–7.

[294] *Ibid.*, p. 577; and pp. 595 *et seq.* On the tribunal's interesting approach to the matter, see Bowett, 'The Dubai/Sharjah Boundary Arbitration of 1981', 65 (1994) BYIL 103, at pp. 114–18, at p. 118; and his view that such a decision was one of novelty: p. 133.

[295] *Case Concerning Maritime Delimitation and Territorial Questions Between Qatar and Bahrain*, ICJ Reports 2001, p. 40.

[296] PCIJ Reports, Series B, No. 9 (1924), p. 6.

the two-fold classification offered above. Rather, the discussion below is arranged by reference to key doctrinal issues.

Secondly, and this stems from the point made above, it stands to reason that the law for both categories cannot be identical; clearly, certain procedural elements of incidental jurisdiction will be different. Even so, the substantive aspects of the law are the same, including the principle of *res judicata*, the rules on interpreting judgments and awards and certain propositions regarding the purpose and scope of interpretation. Thirdly, to classify a series of proceedings as incidental in character is not to trivialise it in any way. The broad general fact is that, in matters of territory, no issue is trivial. Nor, indeed, are the legal issues surrounding a controversy over interpretation, not least because differing interpretations will more often than not have territorial implications, in terms of loss or gain as the case may be. Indeed, the complexity or otherwise of the issues in interpretative proceedings is not dictated by the fact that they are scrutinised by a judicial or arbitral tribunal in a mode supplementary or incidental to the main case.

Finally, in order to provide maximum coverage within the overall theme, the study seeks to encompass all kinds of decisions. Thus, in addition to the judgment of a court, particularly the International Court of Justice, and the arbitral award of an *ad hoc* tribunal, it has seemed appropriate to include quasi-arbitral awards, administrative decisions and, importantly, the advisory opinions of the Permanent Court of International Justice. While a restricted approach would have yielded no benefits, a number of significant cases would have been excluded from consideration, thereby failing to enrich the discussion. In any event, there appears no compelling reason to exclude these kinds of decision. Given the current trends in the law, even if it is not an award, an administrative decision is nevertheless binding and not without concrete legal results. Moreover, they are useful insofar as they show to what extent the normal rules of interpretation are or are not applicable to them.

5 Legal issues regarding interpretation

I. Preliminary observations

Despite the inherent simplicity of this remedy, a number of complex problems can arise with respect to the scope and effect of interpretation. The problems and issues considered below are those which have arisen for tribunals dealing with boundary and territorial delimitation problems. They are discussed in the following five contexts: (1) interpretation and the role of consent; (2) the admissibility of requests for interpretation; (3) the scope and purpose of interpretation; (4) the relation between the interpretative process and *res judicata*; and (5) the basic principles of interpretation. Although discussed individually below, the problems, it is important to note, have been itemised chiefly for the purposes of presentation. Essentially, they are all doctrinally linked. Item (5) is examined later in Chapter 6.

II. Interpretation and the role of consent

By way of general observations, it must first be noted that the consent given by States for the adjudication or arbitration of an international boundary problem (or, for that matter, any international dispute) is distinct from the consent given by them allowing for the interpretation of the judgment or award rendered by that tribunal. This is of course particularly relevant in matters of interpretation as incidental jurisdiction. In other words, where States agree to resolve their dispute by way of an international tribunal, that agreement will not in principle extend to allowing that tribunal to give judicial clarification of a vexed portion of the award or judgment. In a nutshell, then, consent for jurisdiction is distinct from consent for the purposes of interpretation. Some writers assert that the power to interpret its decisions is inherent in the tribunal; one argument, among others, is that an unclear decision reflects a failure of the tribunal to fulfil its task. However, the better view is that, because the process of interpretation is a judicial one, it can only be carried out on the basis of consent freely given by the parties.[297]

Leading on from this, in the second place, are two related implications. The first is that, unlike the inherent power of a tribunal to rectify its material errors, a tribunal will not normally proceed *suo motu* to construe its judgment. It is clear that the tribunal will need to know the disputed section or sections which need construing. The second implication is that, for a successful request, consent must be evidenced: it may be demonstrated by reference to provisions granting consent on an *ad hoc* basis in arbitral agreements, or in multilateral treaties, especially, but not exclusively, in the statutes of international tribunals. Article 60 of the Statute of the International Court of Justice is instructive, for it provides: 'The judgment is final and without appeal. In the event of dispute as to the meaning or scope of the judgment, the Court shall construe it upon the request of any party.' The text of the article clearly shows that the International Court of Justice has standing powers to interpret its judgments. In other words, parties need not include a separate clause in their special agreements empowering the Court to clarify the meaning and scope of its judgments. Nor do they need to conclude a new *compromis* referring the matter once again to the Court.

In this context, it may be of some interest to comment upon the observations made by Thirlway on the matter. Writing on the law and procedure of the International Court of Justice, he observed:

> As regards interpretation, the only condition laid down by Article 60 of the Statute for the admission of a request for interpretation is that there is a 'dispute as to the meaning or scope of the judgment'. It is difficult to imagine circumstances in which one party would consent to an application for interpretation by the other party while at the same time maintaining that there was no such dispute. The question of the possible role of consent in this field is probably academic, not to say unrealistic.[298]

[297] See Hill (note 226), pp. 535–6; and Ralston (note 148), p. 103; cf. Bowett (note 226), p. 581; and Reisman (note 226), pp. 193–4.

[298] Supra (note 226), p. 13. Cf. his views on p. 80, and, generally, pp. 80–2. For brief commentary on the matter in general, see Stanczyk, 'Application for Interpretation of a Judgment Delivered by the International Court of Justice', 17 (1988) *Polish Yearbook of International Law* 193, at pp. 195–6, note 13. Further, see Zimmermann (note 226), pp. 75–9; and Hill (note 226), pp. 535 *et seq.*

It is difficult to agree fully with these observations. The fact of the matter is that, once the Court is vested with jurisdiction to hear a dispute between the parties, a litigant State need not seek *ad hoc* consent from the other litigant party to refer the dispute to the Court for the purposes of clarifying the meaning of the judgment. The reason is that consent to such a referral will be deemed to have already been given by virtue of the consent to refer the main dispute to the Court. As noted above, to vest the Court with jurisdiction to hear the case is to accept the fact that, by virtue of the Statute, the Court is empowered to provide clarifications of the judgment following a unilateral request by one of the parties. In other words, the problem raised by the commentator cannot arise under Article 60 of the Statute for the simple reason that there is no need for a disputing litigant party to seek *ad hoc* consent for the interpretation of the Court's judgment in view of the fact that consent to such proceedings must be understood to have been obtained when the parties initially agreed to vest jurisdiction in the Court. Further, the logic of the statement, although generally correct, is deceptive, for it does not convey a sense of the entire legal situation. It is, of course, only rational and obvious to assume that, once there is an agreement to refer the matter to the Court, there will also automatically be an agreement that a dispute in fact exists. However, this premise does not apply where consent is given *ante hoc* in multilateral treaties. In situations such as these, contracting parties are in effect agreeing in advance to take their disputes to the Court without having any way of knowing what those disputes may turn out precisely to be apart from knowing that the dispute must relate to the interpretation or application of that multilateral treaty. Nor can they be sure that contracting parties will even agree at the relevant time that a dispute does in fact exist between them. Indeed, this was one of the arguments adopted by the United Kingdom in the *Lockerbie* case when it contended that there was indeed no dispute between Libya and itself with respect to the Montreal Protocol of 1971. The Court did not accept this and ruled that, in fact, there was a dispute between the two States.[299] It follows, finally, that the consent rule is neither academic nor unrealistic. If Article 60 did not allow for interpretation and referred only to the finality of the judgment, then litigant parties would not be able to seek clarification of the Court's judgments because, once it delivers its judgment, the tribunal is in principle *functus officio*. Under Article 60, new agreements or evidence

[299] See ICJ Reports 1998, p. 9, at pp. 17–24, with reference to the position adopted by the United Kingdom.

of consent to refer the matter to the Court for clarification are not needed. Clearly, an important right vested in both litigant parties can hardly be described either as academic or unrealistic.

Similarly, Article 33(3) of the Statute of the International Tribunal for the Law of the Sea provides that, in the event of a dispute as to the meaning or scope of the decision, the Tribunal shall construe the decision upon the request of any party. Furthermore, Article 43 of the Statute of the Court of Justice of the European Communities[300] and Article 67 of the Statute of the Inter-American Court of Human Rights[301] empower the respective tribunals to interpret the decisions given by them. It is clear that consent *ante hoc* to the jurisdiction of these tribunals entails empowering them to clarify the meaning and scope of their respective decisions, where necessary, without the need for a new agreement for such purposes.

A number of multilateral dispute settlement treaties have also deemed it appropriate to include permissive provisions along these lines. The evolution of Article 82 of the 1907 Hague Convention on Pacific Settlement of Disputes has been described above. At this juncture, all that needs to be observed here is that Article 82 provided the template for Article 60 of the Statute of the Permanent Court of International Justice, and that, by creating a presumption in favour of the tribunal's power to interpret decisions, the Hague Conference was in fact adopting the position that such a power is indeed inherent in it. However, delegates to the Conference wanted to create, as shown above, as much uniformity on this and other aspects of international arbitration as was possible, so, although the Convention did not serve as a statute (as opposed to a background instrument)[302] of a

[300] See collectively Annex VI, and Article 12 of Annex VII (Arbitration), of the 1982 UN Convention on the Law of the Sea, UKTS (1999) 81, Cmnd 4524; and the Protocol to the Treaty of Nice, OJ C325, 24 December 2002. See also Chapter 8, Article 102, of the Rules of Procedure of the European Court of Justice, as amended April 2004, OJ L127, 29 April 2004. Generally, see Merrills, 'Reflections on the Incidental Jurisdiction of the International Court of Justice', in Evans (ed.), *Remedies in International Law: The Institutional Dilemma*, Oxford, 1998, p. 51, at pp. 66–70; and Plender (note 226), pp. 308–11.

[301] See 9 (1970) ILM 673. See also Article 38 of the Statute of the Central American Court of Justice of December 1992, 34 (1995) ILM 923; and Article 24 of the 1907 Convention for the Establishment of a Central American Court of Justice, 2 (1908) AJIL 231. Further, see Article 40 of the Draft Statute of the Pan American Court of Justice as formulated by the Fifth Pan American Conference held in Chile in 1923 and forwarded to the Commission of Jurists for the purposes of consideration thereof: text in 20 (1926) AJIL 374.

[302] Article 41 of the 1907 Hague Convention obliged contracting States to maintain the existing Permanent Court of Arbitration which was organised pursuant to Article 20 of the 1899 Convention; see Hudson, *The Permanent Court of International Justice 1920–1942: A Treatise*, New York, 1943, p. 6.

permanent tribunal, delegates were conscious of the need to create a regime where the standing rule was permissive of interpretation until overruled by way of contrary provisions in the *compromis*. Arbitrations relevant to this study have maintained this uniformity.[303]

Other provisions include Article 47 of the 1948 American Convention on the Pacific Settlement of Disputes (the Pact of Bogotá), which provides that parties may submit to the decision of the arbitral tribunal any differences they may have regarding the interpretation or execution of the award;[304] and Article 33 of the International Law Commission's 1958 Draft Rules on Arbitral Procedure, which states, in paragraph 1: 'Any dispute between the parties as to the meaning and scope of the award shall, at the request of either party and within three months of the rendering of the award, be referred to the tribunal which rendered the award.'[305] Further, Article 56 of the International Convention on the Settlement of Investment Disputes enables the same or a different tribunal to clarify the meaning and scope of an award.[306] To be sure, several inter-war bilateral treaties for the pacific settlement of international disputes also provided for the interpretation of decisions of international tribunals, including the treaties of arbitration concluded between Denmark and Norway, Finland and Sweden, Denmark and Finland, Romania and Switzerland, Denmark and Germany, Poland and the Kingdom of Serbs, Croats and Slovenes, and Italy and Lithuania between 1926 and 1927.[307]

As for *ad hoc* bilateral agreements pertinent to this study, it will be appropriate to note that a good number of them have enabled the tribunal to interpret the meaning and scope of the award, namely, Article 10 of the Guinea–Guinea-Bissau maritime delimitation arbitral treaty of

303 See the text to notes 308–19 below.

304 152 BFSP 73. See further Article 7 of the 1929 General Treaty of Inter-American Arbitration and Article XIX of the Costa Rica–Guatemala–Honduras–Nicaragua–El Salvador Treaty of Arbitration of 1923 and Article 44 of the Rules of Procedure, Annex B, in Habicht, *Post-War Treaties for the Pacific Settlement of International Disputes*, Cambridge, 1931, pp. 958, 46 and 52 respectively.

305 ILC Final Draft Articles, 1958 *Yearbook ILC*, vol. II, p. 83. See also Article 35 of the UN Commission on International Trade Law's (UNCITRAL's) Arbitral Rules, in General Assembly Resolution 15/12/1976; and Article 33(1)(b) of the UNCITRAL Model Law, in General Assembly Resolution 21/6/1985. Generally, see Carlston, 'Codification of International Arbitral Procedure', 47 (1953) AJIL 203, at pp. 221–2 and 248; and Bos, 'The International Law Commission's Draft Convention on Arbitral Procedure in the General Assembly of the United Nations', 3 (1956) *Nederlands Tijdschrift voor Internationaal Recht* 234.

306 4 (1965) ILM 532.

307 For the text of these treaties and Articles 10, 10, 10, 17, 11, 21 and 19 respectively, see Habicht (note 304), pp. 357, 362, 368, 373, 456, 495 and 621 respectively. Equally, a large number of such treaties do not have provisions allowing for interpretation.

1983;[308] Article 10 of the Anglo-French continental shelf boundary arbitral agreement of 1975; Article 13 of the Eritrea–Yemen arbitral treaty of 1996 regarding certain disputed islands in the Red Sea and the continental shelf between them;[309] Article 3(iv) of the Pakistan–India agreement of 1965 for arbitration over the Rann of Kutch;[310] Article XIII of the 1986 Egypt–Israel treaty for arbitration on the boundary dispute in the Taba sector;[311] Article 10 of the 1989 Franco-Canadian arbitral agreement regarding the continental shelf around St Pierre and Miquelon;[312] and Article XVIII of the 1991 Special Arbitral Agreement between Argentina and Chile in the matter of the Laguna del Desierto region of the boundary, read with Article 39 of Chapter II of Annex I to the *Tratado de Paz y Amistad* of November 1984.[313]

Of the six[314] arbitrations conducted under the aegis of the Permanent Court of Arbitration wherein boundary and territorial rights were in issue, two of them, namely, the *North Atlantic Coast Fisheries* (1910)[315] and *Grisbadarna* (1909)[316] arbitrations, incorporated certain provisions of the 1907 Hague Convention, including Article 82, in their arbitral agreements, while the *compromis* for the *Island of Palmas* (1928)[317] case specifically empowered the arbitrator to interpret and execute the award, not unlike the Eritrea–Yemen *Red Sea Islands and the Continental Shelf* (1996) and the Eritrea–Ethiopia (2002) awards.[318] Given the rebuttable presumption of Article 82, it was hardly necessary for the US and the Netherlands, or Eritrea and Yemen, respectively, to have done so, and that is perhaps why the Dutch and Portuguese Governments failed to mention this power in

[308] See 77 ILR 640, at p. 642. Cf. the 1985 Guinea-Bissau and Senegal arbitral treaty which does not have such a provision: see *Arbitral Award of 31 July 1989*, ICJ Reports 1991, p. 53, at p. 58.

[309] See 119 ILR 422, at p. 467.

[310] See 50 ILR 1, at p. 14. The right of interpretation is not explicitly stated: the clause refers to difficulties in the implementation of the award and the continuation of the tribunal, as opposed to being *functus officio* thereof.

[311] See 80 ILR 234, at p. 354.

[312] 95 ILR 650, at p. 650.

[313] See 113 ILR 16, at p. 20. Article XVIII stipulated that matters not dealt with in the 1991 arbitral agreement would be governed by the *Tratado* of 1984, and Article 39 of Chapter II to Annex I thereof provided for interpretation. See also Article 6 of the *Tratado*: 24 (1985) ILM 11.

[314] The *Lighthouses Administration Cases* are excluded from this count: 23 ILR 659.

[315] Scott, *Hague Court Reports*, p. 141. See Article 5 of the *compromis*, *ibid.*, p. 151.

[316] 4 (1910) AJIL 226. See Article 8 of the *compromis*: 102 BFSP 731.

[317] 22 (1928) AJIL 867. See Article 8 of the *compromis*, *ibid.*, p. 870.

[318] 119 ILR 417. See Article 13(3) of the *compromis*, *ibid.*, p. 467. Note, however, that there is no express reference to the 1907 Convention. Note also that the Eritrea–Ethiopia Boundary Delimitation Commission operated under the 1999 PCA Optional Rules for Arbitration Disputes: see Article 35 for interpretation.

their arbitral agreement for the *Island of Timor* (1914) case.[319] On this view, then, the large number of multilateral and bilateral treaties expressly providing for interpretation is evidence of the fact that such a power does not exist in the absence of permissive provisions. For, if there were an inherent power vested *ipso facto* in the tribunal, it would not have been necessary to include such provisions in either multilateral or bilateral agreements.

The third point involves examining the effect of consent on the legal powers and continued existence of the tribunal. On the one hand, given the open-ended right of interpretation provided in Article 60 of its Statute, the International Court of Justice does not become *functus officio* after rendering its judgment to the litigating States; it can be approached by either party to provide clarification of the meaning and scope of its judgment at any time provided there exists a dispute on such an issue.[320] The logic is that consent to jurisdiction of the Court constitutes consent to all the relevant powers of the Court. On the other hand, once a decision has been rendered by an *ad hoc* tribunal, it has in principle exhausted its jurisdiction, provided that, if there is a provision in the special agreement empowering the tribunal to interpret the meaning or scope of its judgment, then the tribunal continues to exist in law and does not become *functus officio* until the time period allowed for the submission of a request for interpretation has passed without the submission of such a request, or where any contingency provided for in the *compromis* does or does not take place.[321]

319 Scott, *Hague Court Reports*, p. 354. For the text of the *compromis*, see *ibid*., p. 387.

320 It has been suggested by Bishop that all the judges must be the same as those who decided the original case, but that may not be possible; nor is it necessary in law: see Bishop, *International Arbitral Procedure*, Washington, DC, 1931, at p. 87. See also Hill (note 226), pp. 545–6; and Zimmermann (note 226), pp. 99–101. On admissibility criteria, see section III of this chapter.

321 Generally, see Grzybowski (note 226), pp. 484–5; Carlston (note 181), pp. 240–1; Carlston (note 305), pp. 221–2 and 248–9; Hill (note 226), pp. 535 *et seq*.; Simpson and Fox (note 226), p. 245; Zimmermann (note 226), pp. 4–5; and Stone (note 226), p. 95, note 127. Cf. Bowett (note 226), p. 581; and also Rosenne, who writes that the 'power [of a tribunal] to interpret or revise a judgment derogates from the principle that the jurisdiction of an international tribunal to decide a dispute rests upon the consent of the parties'; in other words, tribunals have an inherent power to interpret a judgment, and hence consent is not needed. However, he suggests that, if consent is indeed needed for the purpose of interpretation, as the Permanent Court asserted in the *Jaworzina Boundary* advisory opinion, then that rule is applicable only in 'a particular type of arbitration . . . an *ad hoc* arbitration for the settlement of land frontier disputes'. See supra (note 226), p. 1670 (in reference to permanent judicial bodies); and Rosenne, *The International Court of Justice: An Essay in Political and Legal Theory*, Leyden, 1961, p. 332. Cf. also Reisman (note 226), pp. 192–4. Rosenne's position represents a minority view. See the observations in the text to notes 337 *et seq*. below. For questions of time limits, see section III.d of this chapter.

It is for this reason that some arbitral treaties expressly provide that the tribunal will not be *functus officio* until the award has been executed or implemented in full. By doing so, it reaffirms that the tribunal continues in law to be seised of the dispute.

Thus, Article XV of the 1971 *Compromiso* between Argentina and Chile regarding the Beagle Channel controversy stipulated that the Court of Arbitration would not be *functus officio* until it had notified the Government of the United Kingdom that, in its opinion, the award had been materially and fully executed.[322] Article XIV stipulated that there would be no appeal from the award, but this provision was subject to Article XIII of the 1902 General Treaty of Arbitration between the parties, and, although the latter provision was a saving for revision,[323] it establishes the general point that, in the absence of an express or implied clause allowing for interpretative or other proceedings, the delivery of the judgment terminates the jurisdictional tasks of the tribunal. Similarly, Article IX of the 1965 *Palena* arbitration treaty between the same two States prevented the Court of Arbitration from becoming *functus officio* until it had approved the demarcation and had notified the Government of the United Kingdom that the award had been executed.[324]

Of course, the tribunal may issue notices of clarification and the like, but the latter, in the absence of proven consent to interpretation, will have no determinant, dispositive or binding effect. Thus, in the *Jaworzina Boundary* advisory opinion,[325] the Permanent Court of International Justice was asked to state whether the delimitation of the Polish–Czech frontier was 'still open', or whether it could 'be considered as already settled by a definitive decision' on the matter decided by the Conference of Ambassadors on 28 July 1920.[326] The Polish Government took the position that the Conference, despite the above-mentioned Decision, had not

[322] 52 ILR 97.

[323] The Court of Arbitration rejected Argentina's 'Declaration of Nullity', reminding the State that it could have resorted to Article XIII of the 1902 Treaty, but that such a facility was now unavailable because it was out of time: see the communications from the Court to the parties and to the UK Secretary of State for Foreign and Commonwealth Affairs, 10 July 1978 and 8 March 1978: 52 ILR 283 and 281 respectively. For the text of the 1902 Treaty, see 95 BFSP 759.

[324] 38 ILR 24.

[325] PCIJ Reports, Series B, No. 8 (1923), p. 6. Although the Permanent Court cannot be described as an *ad hoc* tribunal, by providing a 'one-off' advisory opinion, its functions were similar to those of such a tribunal. Note also that the advisory opinion was given not to the States arguing their cases before them, i.e. Poland and Czechoslovakia, but to the Council of the League of Nations, and that it was not binding on the latter.

[326] *Ibid*., p. 10.

in fact carried out its task in its entirety.[327] The Court took note of evidence to this effect, including a note by the Drafting Committee of the Conference of Ambassadors bearing the date 21 October 1922 and two letters written to the representatives of Poland and Czechoslovakia by the President of the Conference on 13 November 1922; both sets of documents suggested that the frontier in the Jaworzina sector was undefined. Poland argued that the letter of 13 November 1922 was 'the most authoritative and reliable interpretation of the intention [of the Conference] expressed at that time, and that such an interpretation, being drawn from the most reliable source, must be respected by all'.[328]

The Court held that it is an established principle that the right of giving an authoritative interpretation of a legal rule belongs solely to the person or body who has the power to modify or suppress it. The Court went on to observe:

> Now the Conference of Ambassadors did not retain this power after the decision of July 28th, 1920, by which it fulfilled the task entrusted to it . . . The duties of the Conference . . . had some points in common with those of an Arbitrator entrusted by two States with the settlement of a frontier dispute between them. But in the absence of an express agreement between the parties, the Arbitrator is not competent to interpret, still less modify his award by revising it. The decision of July 28th, which was accepted by the Polish and Czechoslovak Governments, contains no mention of an agreement of this kind.[329]

Fourthly, consent, as noted above, may be given to a tribunal other than the one which returned the first judgment. Of course, if the tribunal is not a permanent body like the International Court of Justice, and/or if it is not *functus officio*, then any tribunal *stricto sensu* will effectively be a new tribunal, even though members of the new tribunal are those of the old. In any event, the point here is that consent for interpretation may be either direct or indirect, or express or implied, as the case may be, and again the *Jaworzina Boundary* advisory opinion is instructive. By way of the Spa Declaration of 10 July 1920, the Polish and Czechoslovak Governments vested the Conference of Ambassadors with the task of 'fixing the frontier' between the two States. In turn, the Conference, by way of a resolution of 27 July 1923, decided to put the delimitation dispute before the Council of the League of Nations for the purpose of finding a solution, and stated that: 'The . . . Governments [of France, Great Britain, Italy and Japan] would have no objection should the Council see fit to ask the opinion of the [Permanent] Court of International Justice on the legal question . . .

[327] *Ibid.*, pp. 7–8 and 34. [328] *Ibid.*, p. 37. [329] *Ibid.*, pp. 37–8.

raised by these difficulties.' Thus, when the Council requested the Permanent Court of International Justice to give an opinion on the precise status of the frontier in the Jaworzina district, it was also asking the Court to interpret the Decision of 28 July 1920. Accordingly, the Court observed:

[S]ince the instructions in question have been communicated to the Court, there is nothing to prevent the latter from using them as it may see fit for the purpose of *interpreting the principal document* in the question, namely the Decision of the Conference of Ambassadors of July 28th, 1920, adopted in consequence of the decision of the Supreme Council [of the Allied and Associated Powers].[330]

It went on to pose the question whether the modifications of the frontier permitted under Article II(3) of the Decision applied to the whole frontier between the two States in the Spisz district, including the two sectors formed by the former frontier between Hungary and Galicia, or only to the new dividing line described in the Decision itself. It held that Article II only referred to this latter portion, and observed:

It seems natural to *construe Article II* in light of the idea governing its first paragraph, which contains the essential and necessary provisions. It follows that the whole Article only relates to this new line.[331]

Notwithstanding this, it could be argued that the consent given by the disputant States was for the purposes of *fixing* the frontier and not for the purposes of *interpreting the decision fixing the frontier*. Such a distinction is consistent with the position adopted above, namely, that consent for jurisdiction is distinct from consent to the interpretative process. Even if it were arguable, and it is agreed that it is, that the Conference could not arrogate, strictly speaking, the power to ask the Court to interpret the Decision of 28 July 1920, it cannot be ignored that virtual consent by the two parties ultimately came in the form of full co-operation and assistance by way of written memoranda and oral statements.[332] It is also important to remember that the Court's jurisdiction was not based on the consent of the parties, for, in advisory, as opposed to contentious, proceedings, consent is not needed. However, it is almost certain that, if either one or both States had refused to come before the Court or to send their memoranda and documentation, the Court, in the exercise of its discretion, would have refused to provide an opinion,

330 *Ibid.*, p. 26 (emphasis added).
331 *Ibid.*, p. 42 (emphasis added).
332 See *ibid.*, pp. 7–10 for the cases submitted by the two States, and also see pp. 13–15. The Council requested Poland and Czechoslovakia to be prepared to assist the Court by furnishing it with all relevant documents or explanations: p. 10.

following the principle it had confirmed in the *Status of Eastern Carelia* case.[333]

Another good example of consent by conduct and implication is to be found in a study of the *Monastery of Saint-Naoum* case. While it had initially disputed the right of the Principal Allied Powers to settle its frontiers with Greece and the Serb-Croat-Slovene State, Albania voted in favour of the resolution adopted by the Assembly of the League of Nations on 2 October 1921 recognising the Powers, and not the Assembly of the League, as the appropriate body to carry out such a task. Acting as an agency of the Powers, the Conference eventually carried out the task of allocation and delimitation, the record of which was contained in a resolution adopted by it on 6 December 1922. The disputed monastery was allocated to Albania.[334]

In protest, the Serb-Croat-Slovene State argued that the Conference was obliged to settle the frontier in accordance with the Protocol of London of 1913 which had left the monastery to Serbia, and, because there were no special provisions regarding the monastery, the terms of the Protocol remained in force.[335] Albania resisted any claimed changes to the frontier, which it contended had been definitively fixed by the Conference. The League, acting on the request of the Conference, eventually asked the Court to investigate the question whether or not the Conference, by its decision of 6 December 1922, had exhausted its mission to delimit the frontier in the sector of the monastery. Both the Albanian and the Serb-Croat-Slovene Governments co-operated fully with the Court, furnishing it with memoranda and making oral statements.[336] It was by interpreting the resolution of 6 December 1922, and related instruments, including the Protocol of 1913 and the decision of the Conference of Ambassadors of 11 August 1913, that the Court was able to announce that the boundary had in fact been determined conclusively by the Conference, and that it had certainly intended to leave the monastery to Albania.

Be that as it may, it is important to note that, at times, States may be in dispute as to the precise scope of the consent given to the tribunal, that

333 PCIJ Reports, Series B, No. 5 (1923), p. 7. The Court refused to give an opinion inasmuch as Russia, as a non-member of the League, had not given its consent to the dispute settlement procedures open to such non-members at the invitation of the League. It said: 'Such consent was never given by Russia . . . The Court, being a Court of Justice, cannot, even in giving advisory opinions, depart from the essential rules guiding their activity as a Court.' See *ibid.*, pp. 27 and 29.

334 PCIJ Reports, Series B, No. 9 (1924), p. 6, at pp. 10–15.

335 *Ibid.*, pp. 16–18.

336 *Ibid.*, pp. 6–12. With respect to agreement by conduct in matters of admissibility, see *Interpretation of Judgment No. 3 (Interpretation of the Treaty of Neuilly)*: PCIJ Reports, Series A, No. 4 (1925), p. 4. See the text to notes 349 and 350 below.

is, whether the tribunal has been asked to interpret or to revise the boundary. These difficulties may arise as a result of an ambiguity in the *compromis* and conflicting interpretations of the latter before the tribunal. Difficulties of this sort were predominant in the matter of the *Costa Rica* v. *Panama* boundary arbitration where the precise scope and effect of the *compromis* were in dispute between the two States. This matter is discussed in some detail in section IV.d below. Suffice it say here that, as a general rule, the precise scope of the tribunal in terms of the task of interpretation must clearly be evidenced in the arbitral agreement; and that, where there is no *real* agreement as to what the tribunal is required to do despite the existence of a valid *compromis*, then that disagreement may well prove to have an effect on the entire dispute settlement process, leaving the boundary dispute to simmer on. The short point is that it is not enough to have a written agreement reflecting consent to an interpretative process and that such consent must be in evidence not only at the negotiating table but also before the bench.

Finally, it may be useful to consider the question of a possible hierarchy in the legal bases for consent for the interpretation of a judgment. It is not impossible, and indeed it has been the case, that a tribunal may find itself vested with the power to construe a judgment by reference to two enabling provisions in separate agreements. There may, on the one hand, be a valid special agreement between the parties which permits them to request the International Court of Justice to construe its judgment in case of a dispute regarding the scope and meaning thereof. On the other hand, the Court also has a standing right on the basis of Article 60 of the Statute to interpret its judgments provided, of course, that one of the parties makes a request for such an interpretation. The right to interpret a disputed judgment can hardly be in issue in such a state of affairs, but the question of precedence may arise where one of the parties argues that there can be no referral to the Court where one or more of the conditions of the special agreement allowing for interpretation are not allegedly met.

These issues arose in *Application for Revision and Interpretation of the 1982 Judgment*. Tunisia approached the Court for interpretation of the 1982 judgment under Article 60. It eschewed the option of applying to the Court on the basis of Article 3 of the Special Agreement, which provision allowed the parties to request the Court to provide 'explanations and clarifications' provided that no agreement on the rules and principles identified by the judgment of the Court had been agreed within three months. Tunisia's position was that obligations arising on the basis of Article 3 were subservient to those arising from the Charter and the

Statute which was integral to it, and that Article 103 of the former enabled Article 60 to override any conditions placed on the parties by Article 3 of the Special Agreement.[337]

Libya argued that the argument based on Article 103 of the Charter was irrelevant. 'The point', it said, 'is that Article 3 requires the parties to follow a certain procedure: that is, the evident obligation for them first to exhaust the remedy of seeking explanations and clarifications under Article 3 . . . For this reason, Libya considers that the Court does not possess the requisite jurisdiction to admit the Tunisian request for interpretation.'[338] The argument was that the request for interpretation had to be a mutual one, and it could be made to the Court only after efforts had failed to implement the judgment in good faith.[339]

Reaffirming the rule that the consent of States was the basis of its jurisdiction in contentious cases, the Court accepted that States could agree to any conditions for consent to jurisdiction provided that they were consistent with the Statute. A State may waive an objection to jurisdiction which it may otherwise have validly been allowed to raise. While it acknowledged that any conditions in special agreements and unambiguous waivers of jurisdictional objection needed to be examined for the purposes of Article 36 of its Statute, the Court held that the interpretative jurisdiction of the Court was a special jurisdiction deriving directly from Article 60, and it was bound to examine whether or not the conditions of such jurisdiction were fulfilled.

It took the position that, by becoming parties to the Statute, Libya and Tunisia had consented to the interpretative jurisdiction of the Court without any conditions. If Libya's arguments were accepted, then the effect of Article 3 of the Special Agreement would be to make the right to request interpretation subject to the prior employment of a procedure requiring the participation of both States.[340] The Court went on to rule that:

> [T]he exercise of the right of one party to seek an interpretation under Article 60 of the Statute would be effectively blocked by the other party, if that party chose not to co-operate. Whether or not such an agreement could validly derogate – as

[337] Tunisian Application Instituting Proceedings, *Pleadings, Application for Revision and Interpretation of the Judgment of 24 February 1982 in the Case Concerning the Continental Self*, 1984, vol. I, pp. 15–17. For the Libyan version of the translation, see *ibid.*, pp. 26–7. Generally, see Zimmermann (note 226), pp. 23–4 and 79–83.

[338] Libyan Observations to the Tunisian Application, *ibid.*, p. 73. See also the Argument of Mr El Maghur, the Libyan Agent, *ibid.*, p. 195.

[339] *Application for Revision*, ICJ Reports 1985, pp. 215.

[340] *Ibid.*, p. 216.

between the parties thereto – from the Statute, it is not lightly to be presumed that a State would renounce or fetter its right under Article 60 of the Statute to request an interpretation unilaterally.[341]

In effect, then, the conditions on which consent by States to a special agreement was meant to become operational could not, in the absence of countervailing circumstances, purport to oust the unconditional consent given by States when they became parties to the Statute. Although the Court hesitated to spell out the hierarchical aspect of the rule, it is fairly obvious that consent to the provisions of the Charter and the Statute will override contradictory obligations, regardless of whether they are based on the consent of the parties. As Stanczyk observed: 'For, the Court, passing over the issue of whether or not States could validly derogate from provisions of the Statute – and in this way the Court did not give an answer *in principio* – acknowledged that it cannot be lightly implied that a State waives its right ensuing from Article 60 of the Statute.'[342]

III. Admissibility of requests for interpretation

With respect to the admissibility of requests for interpretation, it appears that, at least four conditions must exist if the International Court of Justice, or a tribunal for that matter, is to carry out the task of interpretation of its judgment or award. First, there must be a dispute between the parties. Secondly, this dispute must relate to a passage or passages settled conclusively by the tribunal within the operative part of the decision. Thirdly, the dispute must relate to the meaning and scope of the judgment or award. And, fourthly, where the *compromis* provides for temporal limits, the request must be issued within the prescribed period of time.

These essential elements of a request for interpretation are examined individually below. At this juncture, the significant fact is that, before it begins its examination on the merits of the request, the tribunal will normally first consider the question of admissibility, although, unlike the process of revision, the procedural steps to be followed in case of a request for interpretation are not provided in most arbitral agreements. Hence,

[341] *Ibid.*, p. 216. Cf. the Separate Opinion of Judge Ruda, pp. 234–5. Further on this, see Thirlway, who describes the Court's position as reflecting 'a moderate interpretation of the special agreement'. Thirlway (note 226), p. 81.

[342] Supra (note 298), p. 199. For an earlier appreciation of this predicament, see Grzybowski (note 226), p. 493. Note also the dissent of Judge Gros on this matter in the main judgment, namely, *Libya–Tunisia Continental Shelf*, ICJ Reports 1982, p. 18, at pp. 143–7, especially p. 146.

the provisions of Article 61(2) of the Statute of the International Court of Justice are quite different from those of Article 60 which do not require a judicially determined statement on admissibility. However, where the facts and law of admissibility are closely linked to the merits, the tribunal may, at its discretion, examine them together. Accordingly, the Court of Arbitration in *United Kingdom–France Continental Shelf Interpretive Decision* held that questions of admissibility would be examined within the framework of the merits insofar as the former matters did not possess an exclusively preliminary character.[343]

a. The existence of a dispute

With respect to the first requirement, namely, the *existence of a dispute*, it is useful to note the observation made by the International Court of Justice in *Request for Interpretation of the Judgment in the Asylum Case*, namely:

> Article 60 provides, moreover, that interpretation may be asked only if there is a 'dispute as to the meaning of the judgment'. Obviously, one cannot treat as a dispute, in the sense of that provision, the mere fact that one party finds the judgment obscure when the other considers it to be perfectly clear. A dispute requires a divergence of views between the parties on definite points.[344]

The rule requires that an *actual* dispute ought to subsist between the parties as opposed to a *potential* one. In *Revision and Interpretation of the 1994 Judgment*, Chile recognised, when it had lodged its request, the fact that there was no dispute between Argentina and itself regarding the meaning of the 1994 award in *Laguna del Desierto*, but maintained that there was *potential* for a dispute because Argentina would be disposed to oppose Chile's interpretation of the boundary decided by the tribunal in the previous case; indeed, it requested the tribunal to transmit the request to that State so that Argentina may take a position on the matter either by accepting or by opposing it; the latter contingency would then create the dispute.[345]

It was Argentina's claim that it was contrary to Article 39 of Annex 1 to the 1984 *Tratado de Paz y Amistad* to initiate interpretation proceedings with a view to provoking a dispute subsequent to the submission of the request for interpretation.[346] The tribunal acknowledged the fact that there was no

[343] 54 ILR 165–6.

[344] ICJ Reports 1950, p. 395, at p. 403. Bowett suggests that the term dispute is somewhat stricter than the test proposed by the Permanent Court: Bowett (note 226), p. 582; and see Stanczyk (note 298), p. 202.

[345] 113 ILR 231.

[346] *Ibid.*

subsisting dispute when the interpretative request was received, and, accordingly, in law, there was currently no dispute between the two States regarding the interpretation of the 1994 award.[347] Nonetheless, it felt constrained to examine Chile's three heads of claim and then went on to dismiss the request for interpretation submitted on the basis of its merits.[348]

It is the case, however, that a State must be vigilant with respect to the question of the very existence of a dispute. If it fails to assert its right to insist that there is no real dispute, then it foregoes the opportunity of challenging the jurisdiction of the Court to proceed with the request on the merits. In *Interpretation of Judgment No. 3 (Interpretation of the Treaty of Neuilly)*,[349] the Permanent Court of International Justice took note of the fact that the Bulgarian Government had failed to exercise its option of disputing the jurisdiction of the Court to hear the Greek request for an interpretation of its judgment in *Interpretation of the Treaty of Neuilly*. It appears that Bulgaria, had it been so minded, could have argued that there was no definite dispute between Greece and itself on any aspect of the judgment.

The Court went on to observe that 'therefore the Court has jurisdiction to [give the requested interpretation] as a result of this agreement between the parties, so that there is no need for the Court to consider in the present case whether, in the absence of a definite dispute . . . the requisite jurisdiction could be based exclusively on the unilateral request made by the Greek Government'.[350] In other words, failing to challenge jurisdiction may, in the right circumstances, constitute either an implied agreement that a dispute does in fact exist, and/or that there is an implied submission to jurisdiction, or agreement thereto, allowing the tribunal to proceed to an examination of the request on its merits. It is also clear that, as noted above, failure to protest raises the implication of implied consent.

b. Operative part of the decision

With respect to the second requirement, the rule is that the request for interpretation must involve clarification of a passage within the operative part of the decision. It follows that it is not sufficient to show that the request concerns matters determined generally by the previous judgment; nor does it suffice that the request remains rooted to, but does not involve issues going beyond the limits of, the judgment itself.[351]

[347] *Ibid.*, p. 232. See also the Individual Opinion of Judge Galindo Pohl, *ibid.*, pp. 248–9.
[348] *Ibid.*, pp. 232–3. [349] PCIJ Reports, Series A, No. 4 (1925), p. 4.
[350] *Ibid.*, pp. 5–6. [351] *Ibid.*, pp. 6–7.

The rationale is that, since the *dispositif* constitutes the essence of the judgment and provides the precise findings of the tribunal, it is profitless to seek clarification of those parts of the decision which constitute part of the motivation of the judgment and are to that extent not integral to it. Hence, in general terms, the main body of the decision, including the reasoning thereof, is, *subject to the following*, excluded from the interpretation rule. In this context, *United Kingdom–France Continental Shelf Interpretive Decision*, discussed below, is significant on account of two facts.

First, it shows that a plea for interpretation may take several forms: thus, a request for interpretation may in fact be a way of asking the tribunal to rectify a material error. Hence, in all the appropriate circumstances, a party may ask the tribunal to interpret its judgment in such a way as to make clear that the alleged error in the judgment or on the accompanying map is erased, and to ensure, by way of such clarification, that the judgment represents in every way what the *tribunal* had in law and in fact actually decided and had indeed intended to state. Thus, by simply clarifying its findings in the operative part of its judgment, the tribunal will in effect excise any material mistake present therein. In his commentary on *United Kingdom–France Continental Shelf Interpretive Decision*, Bos was cautious in approving the approach adopted by the Court of Arbitration, where, after accepting the existence of a discrepancy between the reasoning and the *dispositif*, it proceeded to rectify it by adapting the reasoning instead of the *dispositif*. 'Or should', he questioned, 'the practical concern for consistency in judicial decisions find a natural stop where no material error in the operative part of a judicial decision is to be seen? Probably yes, since in that case rectification would serve an academic interest only.'[352] He went on to remark upon the chivalrous admission of the mistake by the Court of Arbitration:

> [I]n the course of interpretative proceedings [the Court of Arbitration] saw fit to rectify its *dispositif* and, thus, to arrive at a result not inconsiderably differing from that reached before. It came to its new result via an interpretation of its prior decision which here, for all practical purposes, should be considered *res judicata*. From the standpoint of the interpretation of judicial decisions it was interesting to note that the Court of Arbitration first of all sought to explain its original intention, and furthermore that consistency of its decision was a matter of course to its mind. Finally, the Court in setting forth its leading thought with regard to delimitation of the continental shelf took care to demonstrate its fitting

[352] Supra (note 226), pp. 211–12. For an incisive commentary on the whole case, see *ibid.*, pp. 205–11.

in with international law, thus practising the systematic method of interpretation *lato sensu*.[353]

He agreed with France that a dispute on the consistency of a judicial decision was not a dispute on the meaning and scope of the decision but on the binding force of the *dispositif*. 'Apparently', he wrote, 'in the Court's view, a request for interpretation could be made also in a case like this in which the interpretation of the decision involved was purely incidental to the remedy sought.'[354]

Secondly, a degree of flexibility is needed in the matter of the idea of the 'operative parts' of the decision. The reality is that, on most occasions, uncertainties in the relatively brief operative part of the decision will only be susceptible to clarification by referring to the reasons, the general *ratio decidendi* of the case.[355] This was the position taken by the Court of Arbitration in *United Kingdom–France Continental Shelf Interpretive Decision*, where a request for interpretation submitted by the United Kingdom made reference to three elements of the award, namely, the *dispositif*, the line drawn on the accompanying chart and paragraphs 202, 251 and 254 of the award pertaining to the Channel Islands sector of the boundary, and, where there were inconsistencies between the former two elements and the paragraphs located in the main body of the award (see Map 1). The position of the United Kingdom was that all three elements had to be consistent with each other. In other words, it wanted the Court to clarify and confirm the fact that the findings made in those paragraphs were reflected in the *dispositif* as well as on the map-line drawn by the Court's Technical Expert.

Accordingly, the Court of Arbitration was requested to interpret the above-mentioned paragraphs in such a way that any inconsistencies stood terminated. The difficulty was that paragraphs 202, 251 and 254 were not in the *dispositif* of the award. The Government of the United Kingdom claimed that these paragraphs were nonetheless operative in character in terms of having binding force.[356] The Court, it was claimed, had an inherent power under Article 10(2) of the Arbitration Agreement, which allowed the parties to request the Court to provide an interpretation of its decision, 'to rectify the chart and the *dispositif* to the extent necessary to

[353] *Ibid.*, p. 212. [354] *Ibid.*, p. 210.

[355] Generally, see Bos (note 226), pp. 193–213; Zimmermann (note 226), pp. 93–8; and Thirlway (note 226), pp. 82–5. Cf. Strupp, who, writing in the context of *res judicata*, noted that the concrete dispute is settled without its being necessary for the legal considerations given in the decision to share the quality of legal force: Strupp (note 136), p. 683. [356] 54 ILR 165.

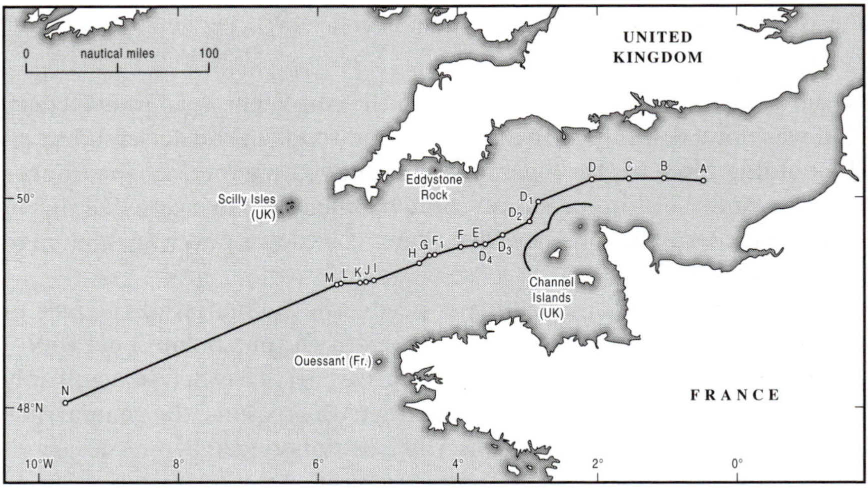

Map 1 *Anglo-French Continental Shelf* arbitration

give effect to the correct interpretation of its own Decision'.[357] The rectification entailed continuing the line westwards from Point M on the chart at an angle of 247° 09' 37'' as prescribed by the Court, by way of a 'geodetic' line instead of the loxodrome indicated in the *dispositif* and drawn on the chart.[358]

The French argument was a narrow one: it was claimed that the authority of *res judicata* indisputably attached only to the (precise) reply given by the Court to the question formulated in Article 2 of the Arbitration Agreement, that is, to the boundary delimited by the Court in the *dispositif* and drawn on the chart by the Technical Expert. The reasoning itself was excluded from the scope of any interpretation; the latter could only relate to the *dispositif* and the map-line drawn by the Court's Technical Expert. 'Article 10', the French Government claimed, 'does not contemplate that the right of [interpretation] should extend to the *reasoning* of the reply to the question, because the reasoning is not, in its view, the reply, which alone is envisaged by Article 10 as the subject of the right of recourse provided for in paragraph 2 [of Article 10].'[359] The United

[357] *Ibid.* [358] *Ibid.*

[359] *Ibid.*, p. 167 (emphasis added). Arguments of a similar kind were raised by the French Government in the context of the admissibility of the case when it asserted that the dispute did not really concern the contents of the decision at all but the alignment drawn by the Technical Expert. It asserted that the controversy related effectively to the paternity of specified parts of the decision, and hence, as France argued, that the pith

Kingdom replied that the key paragraphs were not part of the *reasoning* of the decision: they were themselves part of the *conclusions* reached by the Court on the question put to it. The list of co-ordinates provided in the *dispositif* represented no more than the Court's application of the principles set out in the body of the decision.[360]

In response to these claims, the Court of Arbitration held: 'That the words "the decision of the Court" should have been intended to refer only to the *dispositif* and the map-line was really inconceivable. To interpret the paragraph in such a way would run directly counter not only to the consistent and long established practice of the International Court of Justice but also to the object and purpose of the provision itself.'[361] Having regard to the close links which exist between the reasoning of the decision and the provisions of the *dispositif*, recourse may be had to the reasoning in order to elucidate the meaning and scope of the *dispositif*; but the subject of a request for interpretation must genuinely be directed to the question of what it is that has been settled with binding force in the decision, that is, in the *dispositif*.[362] The Court decided that its express findings in the reasoning constituted a condition essential to its decision and therefore the United Kingdom was justified in its contention that they should be included among the points settled with binding force. Consequently, recourse to the paragraphs in the decision containing the findings of the Court could properly be invoked as a basis for determining the meaning and scope of the *dispositif*.[363]

Furthermore, it was noted, the reasoning followed by the Court in the relevant paragraphs of the judgment was important because it indicated the process by way of which it had arrived at the findings essential to its decision and to the *dispositif*.[364] The Channel Islands sector boundary had been delimited so as not to allow the French continental shelf to encroach

and substance of the controversy raised by the United Kingdom was that certain parts of the decision were attributable to the Technical Expert rather than to the Court and that certain parts of the reasoning should prevail over the *dispositif* and the boundary line chart. The position taken by the Court is similar to that taken by it for the main substance of the case: *ibid.*, pp. 161–2. Given the close links between the admissibility question and the merits, the Court decided to examine them within the framework of the merits: *ibid.*, p. 166. [360] *Ibid.*, p. 168. [361] *Ibid.*, p. 169. [362] *Ibid.*, p. 170.

[363] *Ibid.*, p. 171; and see Bowett (note 226), pp. 584–5. Indeed, this is an accepted rule of international law, going as far back as the *Pious Fund of California* case, the first case to be examined by the Permanent Court of Arbitration. The Court held that all parts of the judgment concerning points debated in litigation enlighten and supplement each other, that they serve to render the meaning and bearing of the *dispositif* and to determine the points upon which there is *res judicata*, and which therefore cannot be put in question: 2 (1908) AJIL 898, at p. 900. [364] 54 ILR 171.

upon the established twelve-mile fishing zone of those islands, and it was to respect that principle that the Court had delimited the boundary from the *established* baselines of the Channel Islands territorial sea.[365] The task of the Court in *United Kingdom–France Continental Shelf Interpretive Decision* was merely to consider the consequences flowing from the finding that there was a contradiction between the expression of the Court's intention as stated in paragraph 202 of the decision and the *dispositif* and the accompanying chart.[366] If the intention of the 1977 decision was not to be defeated, the contradiction had to be resolved in favour of the findings in the reasoning.[367] The Court resolved to treat the matter as a material error in the decision. While it rectified the *dispositif*, the Court left it to the parties themselves to effect a corresponding correction of the boundary traced on the map.[368] The Court took support from the fact that France had not objected to the *substance* of the United Kingdom's plea with respect to this sector. This meant that France could be understood as having accepted as correct the basepoint positions made out by the United Kingdom.[369]

This was further borne out by the judgment of the International Court of Justice in *Interpretation of the Preliminary Judgment in the Cameroon–Nigeria Land and Maritime Boundary*.[370] It was Nigeria's allegation in that case that the preliminary judgment in *Land and Maritime Boundary between Cameroon and Nigeria (Preliminary Objections)*[371] was unclear as to whether Cameroon was entitled at various times after the submission of its Amended Application to bring before the Court new incidents involving alleged Nigerian responsibility; and that the Court ought to confirm by way of clarification that the dispute did not include incidents other than, at most, those specified in Cameroon's Application and Additional Application.[372] Cameroon not only questioned whether it was appropriate for Nigeria to request an interpretation of a decision in incidental proceedings concerned with the preliminary objections advanced by it in the first case. It also claimed that it was entitled to rely on all facts, irrespective of their date, which established the continuing violation by Nigeria of its international obligations, facts it could rely on for the purposes of the assessment of damage and adequate reparation.[373]

[365] *Ibid.*, pp. 173–4. The Technical Expert had failed to take into account certain low tide elevations and dry land features, all of which were part of the established baseline system: Bowett (note 226), p. 585. [366] 54 ILR 173. [367] *Ibid.*, p. 174.

[368] *Ibid.*, pp. 174–5; and see Bowett (note 226), p. 585. [369] 54 ILR 172–3.

[370] ICJ Reports 1999, p. 31. The preliminary judgment dealt with issues of jurisdiction of the Court and admissibility of the case. [371] ICJ Reports 1998, p. 275.

[372] ICJ Reports 1999, pp. 34–5. [373] *Ibid.*, p. 34.

In its judgment, the Court turned first to the question of jurisdiction, and, relying on the observations of the Permanent Court of International Justice in the *Chorzów Factory (Interpretation of Judgments Nos. 7 and 8)*[374] case, noted in its analysis of Article 60 that 'any request for interpretation must relate to the operative part of the judgment and cannot concern the reasons for the judgment except *insofar as these are inseparable from the operative part*'.[375] It was pointed out by the Court that Nigeria's sixth preliminary objection in the first case had dealt with the allegation that Cameroon's submissions and materials were so sparse and inadequate that it precluded the Court from carrying out a fair and effective judicial determination.

The Court went on to observe that it had rejected Nigeria's sixth preliminary objection, the reasons for which were set out in paragraphs 98–101 of the judgment. 'These deal', it noted, 'in detail with Cameroon's rights as regards the presentation of "facts and legal considerations" that it might wish to put forward in support of its submissions seeking a ruling against Nigeria . . . These reasons are inseparable from the operative part of the Judgment and in this regard the request therefore meets the conditions laid down by Article 60 of the Statute in order for the Court to have jurisdiction to entertain a request for interpretation of a judgment.'[376] It also held that Article 60 made no distinction as to the type of judgment concerned, and it followed that a judgment on preliminary objections, just as well as a judgment on the merits, could be the object of a request for interpretation.[377]

In any event, the Court ruled that Nigeria's request for interpretation was inadmissible.[378] It can be argued, then, that a flexible rather than a rigid approach to the problem is the more appropriate one for tribunals to adopt in these circumstances. Accordingly, the correct position in law is that, where the reasoning and the *dispositif* are so closely intertwined that a meaningful act of an interpretation of the relevant passage or passages cannot be carried out without having reference to the reasoning in the judgment, then the tribunal is permitted to resort to the latter to discharge its task of interpretation.

374 PCIJ Reports, Series A, No. 13 (1927), p. 4. See Judge Anzilotti's dissent: *ibid.*, p. 24; and Hill (note 226), p. 549 and Plender (note 226), p. 308.

375 ICJ Reports 1999, p. 35.

376 *Ibid.*, p. 36. See also Judge Weeramantry's dissent, *ibid.*, p. 42.

377 *Ibid.*, p. 35.

378 *Ibid.*, p. 39. For more on inadmissibility due to an absence of a connection with the *dispositif*, see the *Eritrea* v. *Ethiopia (Decision on Interpretation)* case, http://pca-cpa.org/PDF/EEBC/Decision24June2002.pdf, para. 16.

c. Meaning and scope of the decision

With respect to the third requirement for admissibility, namely, that the dispute must relate to the meaning and scope of the judgment or award, it is noteworthy that, as the Permanent Court of International Justice said in *Chorzów Factory (Interpretation of Judgments Nos. 7 and 8)*: 'A difference of opinion as to whether a particular point has or has not been decided with binding force also constitutes a case which comes within the terms of the provision in question, and the Court cannot avoid the duty incumbent upon it of interpreting the judgment in so far as necessary in order to adjudicate upon such a difference of opinion.'[379] Thus, litigant States may be in dispute whether or not a particular matter has indeed been conclusively settled by the tribunal.

In this context, reference may be made to *Application for Revision and Interpretation of the 1982 Judgment* between Tunisia and Libya (see Map 2). The International Court of Justice had to determine in the context of the Tunisian request for interpretation whether certain aspects of its 1982 judgment had actually been decided conclusively and with binding force. In that judgment, the Court had held that co-ordinates for the most westerly point on the shoreline of the Gulf of Gabes, reflecting as it did the change in the direction of the coast, would have to be settled by experts; but that it appeared that that point, would, approximately, be 34° 10' 30" north. While they were mentioned in the judgment, no co-ordinates, not even approximate, were indicated in the *dispositif*, although the Court did refer to the most westerly point of the Tunisian coastline.[380] Tunisia contended that, because they had not been mentioned in the *dispositif*, these co-ordinates did not have any binding character and accordingly Libya was wrong in insisting that they had to be applied; in fact the most westerly point on the Gulf shoreline was 34° 05' 20" north on the Carthage geodetic system.[381] Libya claimed that the point of change in the direction of the Tunisian shoreline had already been definitively located and defined by the Court with some precision, namely, 34° 10' 30" north.[382] More important, however, for Libya was the claim that Tunisia's request had an ulterior motive, namely, revision of the judgment.[383]

The Court noted that there was indeed 'a dispute between the parties as

[379] Supra (note 273), pp. 11–12. On this, see Hill (note 226), pp. 547–9.

[380] ICJ Reports 1982, p. 87.

[381] ICJ Reports 1985, pp. 221–2. See also the Tunisian Request in *ICJ Pleadings, Application for Revision and Interpretation* (note 337), pp. 27–9.

[382] ICJ Reports 1985, p. 222.

[383] *Ibid.*, p. 223.

to what, on a particular question, the Court [had] decided with binding force in the 1982 Judgment; and that it [was] also clear that Tunisia [was] asking the Court for "clarification of the meaning and scope of what the Court has decided" in that respect'. While it made clear that it would not give effect to an application which sought to obtain answers to questions not decided by it, or to achieve a revision of the 1982 judgment, the Court noted that 'within the limits of Article 60 of the Statute, the request was admissible'.[384] It is interesting to note that, while Tunisia had successfully identified for interpretation the operative section of the judgment of 1982, it had not fully accepted the implications of that operative part and was inviting the Court effectively to construe its judgment in such a way that it reflected its own desired set of co-ordinates. However, while it accepted that the co-ordinates were approximate, and thus rejected the Libyan position, the Court was also not persuaded by the Tunisian contention because the meaning it had wished to ascribe to that operative part was not fully consistent with what the Court had actually held in the *dispositif* and the judgment. Thus, the Court clarified the fact that reference to the change of direction of the coastline was not the governing criterion; it was in effect only descriptive, and the only key feature was the most westerly point on the shoreline of the Gulf.[385]

d. Restrictions *ratione temporis*

Here reference may be made to restrictions *ratione temporis*. A State must file for interpretation within the time limit allocated to it. In this regard, it is interesting to note that the law has not been static. Although neither the 1907 Hague Convention, the Statute of the International Court of Justice nor the Statute of the Court of Justice of the European Communities provide time limits for the submission of applications for interpretation,[386] it is the case that some modern treaties, particularly arbitral agreements

[384] *Ibid.*

[385] *Ibid.*, pp. 223–7. Generally, see Stanczyk (note 298), pp. 204–5; and Thirlway (note 226), pp. 88–9.

[386] Relatively modern treaties which do not provide time limits include Article 33(3) of the Statute of the International Tribunal for the Law of the Sea (see Annex VI to the 1982 UN Convention on the Law of the Sea, 1833 UNTS 3; 21 (1982) ILM 1261); and Article 12 of Annex VII (Arbitration) to the 1982 UN Convention on the Law of the Sea; and see Article 50 of the Washington Convention on the Settlement of International Investment Disputes, 575 UNTS 159; 4 (1965) ILM 532. Cf. Simpson and Fox, who write that the right of interpretation has usually been exercisable within a short time limit: Simpson and Fox (note 136), p. 246.

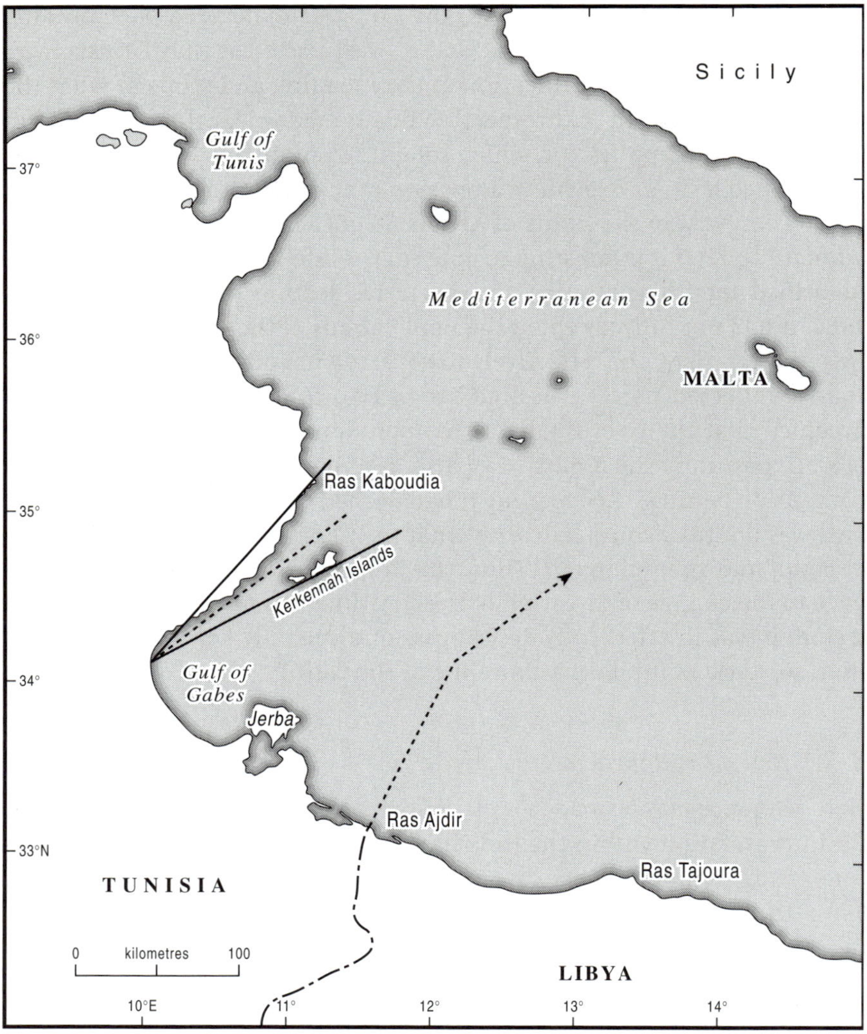

Map 2 *Tunisia* v. *Libya Continental Shelf* arbitration

for boundary disputes, have acknowledged the need to place relatively short restrictions *ratione temporis* where the parties have agreed in advance to allow interpretation.[387] Thus, it is relevant that Article XII of the 1986

[387] Treaties which provide time limits on requests for interpretation include the 1995 Statute of the Central American Court of Justice, Article 38 (30 days); UNCITRAL Arbitration Rules, Article 35 (30 days); and UNCITRAL Model Law, Article 33 (30 days). Article 33(1) of the Draft Rules on Arbitral Procedure provides a three-month period for interpretation.

Taba arbitral agreement allowed Egypt and Israel to submit requests for interpretation within a period of thirty days from the date of the award. A similar time period is to be found in Article 13(3) of the 1996 *compromis* leading to the Eritrea–Yemen *Red Sea Islands and Continental Shelf* cases. A relatively longer period of time, namely, three months from the date of the rendering of the award or notification thereof, is to be found in the agreements on continental shelf delimitation between Guinea and Guinea-Bissau, France and Canada, and the United Kingdom and France.[388]

There are various reasons for this modern[389] shift in favour of time limits for some *compromis*, one of which is the difficulty of reconvening the original arbitrators as the 'same' tribunal. This in fact was one of the reasons why Article 33(1) of the International Law Commission's 1958 Model Rules on Arbitral Procedure provided first for a one-month and then a three-month time limit, as opposed to none.[390] Even so, in matters of boundary delimitation, there is always an anxiety that an open-ended right to apply for interpretation would be conducive to uncertainty and inimical to the long-term stability of alignments, especially in view of the fact that requests for interpretation may lead to unwelcome modifications to a judgment boundary. This is discussed in section IV.d of this chapter. In any event, as the Court of Arbitration noted in *United Kingdom–France Continental Shelf Interpretive Decision*, where the time limits are 'comparatively short', in this case, three months, there is, in principle, no need to require undue formality, such as the exhaustion of

[388] Articles 10, 10(2) and 10(2) respectively. Cf. the earlier (1925) US–Netherlands *Palmas Island compromis* which failed in Article VIII to provide a time limit for interpretative requests. See 122 BFSP 979.

[389] Note, however, that the Statute of the Central American Court of Justice, which provided a thirty-day limit from the date of notification of the award, was concluded in 1907.

[390] No time limits were included in the reports and drafts for the proceedings of 1951 and 1952 (1951 *Yearbook ILC*, vol. II, p. 110, at p. 117; and *ibid.*, vol. II, p. 58), but, by 1953, the Commission had agreed to a one-month period following a suggestion made by Chile (*ibid.*, 1953, vol. II, p. 201; A/CN.4/68 and A/2456). However, there was also the matter of a three-month waiting period before the parties could approach the International Court, an issue which occupied members of the Commission. In 1955, the Dutch Government suggested that, in order to avoid ambiguity, both periods of time should be three months; Canada, however, stood against revision and interpretation altogether (General Assembly, Tenth Session, Annexes, *GAOR*, 1955, Agenda Item 52, p. 1, at pp. 15 and 3). At the tenth session of the ILC in 1958, Scelle provided for a one-month time limit (1958 *Yearbook ILC*, vol. II, p. 1, at p. 11, Draft Article 35), but, by the end of that session, the Commission had agreed to a three-month time limit, following suggestions by Zourek that one month was too short a period of time (*ibid.*, vol. I, p. 77; and see the debate at pp. 230–1).

diplomatic negotiations in establishing the existence of a dispute for the purposes of the interpretation of a judgment.[391]

The precise date on which time begins to run may cause difficulties. In *United Kingdom–France Continental Shelf Interpretive Decision*, France argued that the request for interpretation was inadmissible because it was submitted after the lapse of the three-month period allowed by Article 10(2) of the Arbitration Agreement, calculated from the date the Court *made* the decision, that is, 30 June 1977; and the United Kingdom asserted that time began to run from the date on which the award was actually handed down to the parties, that is, on 8 July 1977.[392] The matter turned on the meaning of the term 'rendering' of the award. If the latter date were taken, then the application was clearly in time.[393] The Court held, *inter alia*, that the term 'rendered' meant in the circumstances a handing down or delivering of the decision to the parties. It relied for this interpretation on the intention of the parties inasmuch as the text in the English version of the arbitral agreement used the word 'rendering', and the natural meaning of the word 'rendering' in the context of Article 10 implies handing down or delivering the decision, and, given that this accorded with common sense and fairness, it ruled that the request was not inadmissible on that basis.[394]

Nor was the Court prepared to accept the argument that, because the United Kingdom had agreed with France on a hiatus between the making

[391] 54 ILR 164. [392] *Ibid.*, pp. 156–60. Reasons for the delay are provided in note 394 below.

[393] An interesting exchange on the notion of rendering decisions took place between Messrs Fitzmaurice and El Khoury at the Tenth Session of the International Law Commission in 1958. Presciently, El Khoury suggested that time ought to begin to run from the day the award was *communicated* as opposed to the day it was *rendered* to the parties, on the ground that it could be weeks or months before the award was actually communicated to the parties. Fitzmaurice argued, wrongly as it appears in hindsight, that there was no difference between the day of communication and the day of the rendering of the decision; and, insofar as a fixed date was needed for the purposes of determining time limits, the fact that the award could be communicated to different parties on different days might lead to uncertainty as to when the time period could be understood to have begun. Other members of the Commission did not object to the reservations expressed by Fitzmaurice, and accordingly the distinction failed to be adopted. See 1958 *Yearbook ILC*, vol. I, pp. 230–1.

[394] 54 ILR 161. The Court observed that it had sought and obtained the agreement of the parties that the rendering of the decision be dispensed with at a formal session, and that, when ready, the decision would simply be transmitted to them. This was done to avoid the additional expense involved in maintaining the Court in session during the interval while the decision was being printed and the charts were being prepared: *ibid.*, p. 162. On this, see Rosenne, 'Some Procedural Aspects of the English Channel Continental Shelf Arbitration', in *Essays in Honour of Erik Castren* (Finnish Branch of the International Law Association), Helsinki, 1979, p. 96, at pp. 100–1.

and rendering of the decision, the former had effectively agreed to a diminution of the three-month period.[395] In the context of the International Court of Justice, the matter is simpler, for Article 94(2) of the Rules of the Court provides that the judgment shall be read at a public sitting of the Court and shall become binding on the parties on the date of the reading. Presumably, then, time limits also begin to run from that date.

Finally, where there is disagreement between litigant States, restrictions *ratione temporis* cannot apply if they appear in a special agreement referring matters to the International Court of Justice. This is because rights and obligations based in the Charter, or in the Statute, which is an instrument integral to the Charter, supersede obligations based on other treaties (see Article 103 of the Charter). As noted above, Article 60 of the Statute does not provide a span of time in which litigant States are allowed to file for interpretation, and, accordingly, the right to apply for clarification is open-ended. Any attempt to hold a party to obligations inconsistent with the Statute would arguably be to no avail even if it were legally distasteful to allow a State to escape from such obligations freely entered into in bilateral treaties. Article 103 of the Charter may be relied upon to negate such obligations, *provided, of course, that one of the litigant parties does not want to be held to the time-based obligations contained in the bilateral compromissory clauses.*

It may be useful to refer to *Application for Revision and Interpretation of the 1982 Judgment* and draw an analogy with the Court's approach to the matter in that case.[396] Although the precise issue there was rather different, insofar as it related to the question of following the stated procedure provided in Article 2 of the 1977 Libya–Tunisia Special Agreement before allowing them the right to approach the Court for interpretation, it is also the case that Article 3 permitted the parties to approach the Court for explanations or clarifications only after three months had elapsed following the delivery of the judgment of the Court. In other words, under Article 3, neither party could approach the International Court of Justice for an explanation before three months had elapsed. Nor, indeed, could either one of them have proceeded *unilaterally* to the Court, for that article provides that the two parties 'shall together go back to the Court and request any explanations and clarifications' with respect to its judgment.[397]

[395] 54 ILR 162. [396] Supra, text to notes 337–42.
[397] *Pleadings*, *Tunisia* v. *Libya Continental Shelf* case, vol. I (note 337), p. 26.

The Court, it will be recalled, was clearly uncomfortable with the idea that litigant States were able to renounce or fetter their rights under Article 60, and held that Libya could not insist that the stated procedure be followed *before* the Court could hear the request for interpretation.[398] The logic of the Court's position is sufficiently compelling to allow an analogy to be drawn with respect to limitations of time; and to come to the conclusion that the three-month time limit of the Special Agreement was of no legal consequence insofar as Tunisia was not bound under the Statute to wait for any length of time before it requested the Court to provide an explanation under Article 60, provided the other essential conditions discussed above and in the following pages were fulfilled, particularly with regard to the fact that a dispute did in fact exist between the parties. Nor, may it be noted in passing, was Tunisia obliged not to make a unilateral request, for Article 60 does not oblige Member States jointly to submit a request for interpretation.

e. Restrictions based in treaty interpretation

These are restrictions based on the fact that certain treaty provisions can prevent tribunals from providing an interpretative judgment. Clearly, an *ad hoc* arbitral treaty may preclude *expressis verbis* the tribunal from providing such awards. While this kind of restriction ought to be noted, problems of greater significance can arise by way of the operation of more general treaty provisions. While this has particular relevance for main case interpretation, it is not without effect for incidental interpretation. A good example of this is Article 6 of the Pact of Bogotá of 1948.[399] This provision, which is one of several provisions in Chapter One of the Pact qualifying or restricting the operation of the various dispute settlement procedures provided therein, stipulates that these procedures 'may not be applied to matters already settled by arrangement between the parties, or by arbitral award or by decision of an international court, or which are governed by agreements or treaties in force on the date of the conclusion of the present Treaty'. Thus, Article 6 attempts to restrict the operation of Articles 31 and 32 of the Pact, which vest the International Court of Justice with jurisdiction over disputes which the disputing parties have failed to resolve by conciliation or where the disputing parties have not agreed an

[398] ICJ Reports 1985, p. 216.

[399] 1948 American Convention on the Pacific Settlement of Disputes, 152 BFSP 73; and 30 UNTS 55.

arbitral procedure. It would also restrict the operation of Chapter Five, which outlines the procedure of arbitration.

It is in this context that reference needs to be made to *Costa Rica* v. *Nicaragua*[400] and *Nicaragua* v. *Honduras (Maritime Boundary)*.[401] Both cases, at the time of writing, are still ongoing. In the former application, Costa Rica requested the International Court of Justice to declare that it has perpetual rights of free navigation for commercial purposes in the San Juan River as stipulated in Article VI of the 1858 Treaty of Limits and as subsequently confirmed in the arbitral award issued by the President of the United States in 1888, namely, the *Cleveland Award*;[402] and that, accordingly, Nicaragua is precluded from interfering with such rights in the river by imposing restrictions and charges on Costa Rican boats and passengers, among other things.[403] Costa Rica claims jurisdiction on the basis, *inter alia*, of Article 31 of the Pact of Bogotá of 1948 read with Article 36(1) of the Statute of the Court.

In *Nicaragua* v. *Honduras*, the applicant State requested the Court to determine the single maritime boundary between the two States, which begins effectively at the point where the land boundary ends at the mouth of the Coco River. The latter point was settled by the King of Spain as arbitrator in *Honduras* v. *Nicaragua*[404] in 1906. Honduras' assertion is that delimitation already exists and that this line runs straight easterly on the parallel of latitude from the point fixed in the 1906 award at the mouth of the Coco River. Nicaragua claims that the Court has jurisdiction on the basis of Article 31 of the Pact of Bogotá read with Article 36(2) of the Statute. The question which thus arises with respect to both cases is whether Article 6 prevents the Court from exercising its jurisdiction.

It would, on the one hand, appear that one effect of Article 6 is that no State Party to the Pact can henceforth be allowed to rely on either adjudication or arbitration, both of which are procedures provided in Chapters Four and Five of the Pact, to resolve a dispute concerning the interpretation of an earlier judgment or award. This would appear to be fairly

[400] Application submitted by Costa Rica on 29 September 2005.

[401] Application submitted by Nicaragua on 8 December 1999. It has also submitted an application to the Court with respect to its dispute with Colombia regarding title to certain islands and keys in the Caribbean and with respect to a single maritime boundary between itself and Colombia. It contends that the Treaty of 1928, which Colombia contends settled the issue of the islands in the Caribbean, lacks legal validity and hence cannot provide a basis for Colombian title: see paragraph 2 of the Application submitted on 6 December 2001.

[402] 79 BFSP 555; and 1889 *Foreign Relations of the United States*, vol. I, p. 456.

[403] Nicaraguan Application (note 401), paragraphs 6–11.

[404] 11 UNRIAA 111.

straightforward; Article 6 prevents a litigant State Party from reopening a matter settled either by way of arbitration or adjudication, and this would be consistent with the rule of *res judicata*, a matter examined in detail in sections IV.d and V below. Suffice it to observe here that, where a matter has been settled between litigant parties, then both of them are precluded from bringing the same issue before the same or a different tribunal for the purpose of retrying issues on which a final decision has been given. To the extent that this prevents litigant States from reopening such issues, Article 6 is only reaffirming a rule axiomatic in character and, indeed, this was what was intended by the parties to the Pact. In the second place, it has been shown above that interpretation is based on consent, and, where it is plainly evident that consent for an interpretative judgment was either being withheld or was non-existent, then the right to make use of the procedures provided in Chapters Four and Five of the Pact would also have to be curtailed.

On the other hand, the better view is that Article 6 does not have such a preclusive effect, and there are several reasons why this is so. In the first place, as far as interpretation which is incidental to the main case is concerned, it has to be borne in mind that the right of the International Court of Justice to provide an interpretative judgment is part of the adjudicatory process, provided, of course, that there is a dispute regarding the scope and effect of the *dispositif* of the judgment and there is a request to that effect see Article 60 of the Statute of the International Court of Justice: *vide*. This means that agreeing to submit a dispute to the Court means agreeing, albeit indirectly, to the right of one of the parties to submit an application for the interpretation of the judgment in accordance with that provision. Thus, if a restrictive view of Article 6 is adopted, it would purport to take away a right clearly provided in the Statute. However, Article 92 of the United Nations Charter makes clear that the Statute is integral to the Charter, and accordingly any conflict between the two provisions must be redressed by reference to the governing principle contained in Article 103 which provides for superiority of Charter-based rights and obligations. This aspect of the matter was explained in section II above. Suffice it say here that it follows that, if the Pact of Bogotá attempts to restrict or withdraw or truncate the right to request an interpretation of the judgment as provided in Article 60 of the Statute, then the latter will prevail, and the Court may well be seised with the application for an interpretative judgment. Of course, the Court may decide not to admit the application if, for example, it could be shown that there was in fact no dispute between the parties regarding any of the operative parts of the judgment, but that will not be because of Article 6 of the Pact of Bogotá.

The second reason why Article 6 ought not to be seen as an obstacle for interpretation involves reference to the object and purpose of that provision. There can be no gainsaying that Article 6 was formulated in order to preclude litigant parties from seeking to revisit by way of adjudication and arbitration cases which had been settled by international tribunals insofar as the dispute concerned a reconsideration of the merits of the judgment or award. It has been seen above that the history of territorial and boundary judgments and awards is replete with litigant parties in South and Central America seeking reconsideration of the merits of the dispute on the basis of nullity of the original decision. However, the interpretative process does not address issues going to the merits of the original dispute; the sole purpose of this process, as shown above, is to seek and gain clarification with respect to disputed operative parts of the decision. It is not a remedy provided to States dissatisfied with the line delimited or territory allocated by the original tribunal. Clearly, the object and purpose of Article 6 was to reinforce the general rule of *res judicata*; it was not to foreclose procedures in relation to genuine, *bona fide* disputes the resolution of which is a simple clarificatory judgment or award which ignores the merits of the original case. A fact which supports this approach is that it maintains the subtle yet clear distinction between a dispute based on the merits of the case and a dispute regarding the scope and effect of the decision without doing violence to Article 6.

The third argument in favour of a non-restrictive approach to Article 6, that is, an interpretation which seeks not to preclude applications seeking interpretative decisions, is essentially a riposte to the consent argument. Of course, it is true that interpretation is based on consent of the parties and that Article 6 appears to convey the point that States Parties have reserved consent with respect to any dispute which has already been settled by a decision of an international court or arbitral body. The argument contradicting this would draw attention to the fact that Article 6 is fairly broad in scope: it is not limited to the *res judicata* rule. The fact is that it also seeks to preclude the application of all the other procedures provided in the Pact. It follows that the rule against the reopening of a dispute 'already settled' by way of mutual arrangement, judicial or arbitral decision or treaty applies not only to new judicial or arbitral proceedings, but also to the procedures of mediation and good offices outlined in Chapter Two of the Pact, and to the procedure of investigation and conciliation outlined in Chapter Three of the Pact.

If a restrictive view of Article 6 is adopted and interpretation is denied because of a lack of consent, then, by the same token, disputing States would not be able to rely on some of the very basic dispute settlement procedures, and the only pacific procedure left would be that of direct negotiation stipulated in Article 2 of the Pact. It is hardly conceivable that parties to the Pact would wish to prevent the use of good offices, mediation, investigation and conciliation if all that one of the parties wanted was a *bona fide* clarification of an operative part of the judgment or award. However, if a broad perspective of Article 6 were adopted, it would allow disputing parties to avail themselves of all the pacific dispute settlement procedures provided in the Pact but would not be able to seek adjudication and arbitration to reopen on the merits a dispute already settled by such a process. In short, Article 6 does not appear to exclude consent with respect to an application for an interpretative judgment; it cannot be seen to be a 'blanket exclusion' of consent regarding issues which do not go to the merits of a particular dispute but only to matters of clarification of that decision.

As far as the *Costa Rica* v. *Nicaragua* application of 2005 is concerned, it is clear that Costa Rica has not requested a reopening of the merits of the case; and that the gravamen of its claim is that the *Cleveland Award* elaborates and clarifies the rights of navigation already provided in the 1858 Treaty. Thus, reliance on the award of 1888 by Costa Rica is essentially by way of support for its fundamental position regarding its rights in the San Juan River. Costa Rica seeks clarification by way of declaration to the effect that the rights claimed by it in the river are consistent with those stated in the award; it is hardly a dispute which is attempting to reopen the basic controversy settled by the President of the United States and duly accepted by the parties over 100 years ago.

Similarly, in *Nicaragua* v. *Honduras*, the applicant State does not seek to reopen the merits of the arbitration concluded in 1906; the award is relevant insofar as it informs the parties as well as the Court of the starting point of the maritime boundary. It is of course the case that the parties will need to rely on the award of 1906 to determine how much or how little was actually decided by the arbitrator, but these issues ought not to take the Court beyond the text of the award, and, where either of the parties invite the Court to re-examine issues beyond those of providing clarification, then it would appear that the latter body would seek to reject such a request, and limit itself to questions of clarification and reaffirmation of the end-point of the land boundary to the extent that it may be necessary so to do. In short, it would appear that the Court will not find in Article 6 of the Pact an obstacle which would prevent it from exercising jurisdiction in both cases. By contrast, in *Nicaragua* v. *Colombia*, the Court will necessarily have to deal with questions regarding the validity of the Treaty of March 1928 and accordingly it will almost certainly be requested to consider issues going to the substance of matters settled by way of treaty, and by so doing the restriction imposed by Article 6 of the Pact will come in to play. It is safe perhaps to hazard that the latter provision will prove to be an obstacle to the Court's jurisdiction in this case.

IV. Purpose and scope of interpretation

As regards the purpose and scope of interpretation, the following rules and propositions are noteworthy.

a. Bona fide need for clarification

Perhaps the most fundamental of rules is that the purpose of interpretation must always be a *bona fide* need for clarification of an operative part of the decision; the process of interpretation cannot be seen as another, or a second, attempt to convince the tribunal to change its mind. The underlying objective of a request for the interpretation of a decision must be limited to obtaining clarification of the meaning and scope of a particular passage or passages in the operative part of the decision, or the reasons thereof, provided, as noted above, that the latter are integral to and/or inseparable from the former. Accordingly, the tribunal cannot, strictly speaking, accommodate any request for interpretation which either goes beyond the purposes of clarification or which is inconsistent with such an objective. As the International Court of Justice noted in *Request for Interpretation of the Judgment in the Asylum Case*, the process of interpretation cannot in any way go beyond the limits of the judgment itself as fixed in advance by the parties themselves in their submissions.[405] It follows that a request for interpretation of a decision cannot be a *pretext for the revision* of the decision and/or, for present purposes, a process for the modification of the boundary delimited by that tribunal in its decision. As Judge Weeramantry, Vice-President of the International Court of Justice, observed in *Interpretation of the Preliminary Judgment in the Cameroon–Nigeria Land and Maritime Boundary*:

[405] ICJ Reports 1950, p. 403.

They [i.e. States Parties] may not, for example, under the guise of an application under Article 60, attempt to seek revision of a judgment or reopen a matter which is already *res judicata*. Nor are parties entitled, in any circumstances, to use a request for clarification as a device for gaining time. All of these are to be discountenanced, and the Court will in no way lend its assistance to such procedures.[406]

An opportunity to reflect on the general principle came before the International Court of Justice in *Application for Revision and Interpretation of the 1982 Judgment* with reference to Tunisia's claims to the second sector of the maritime boundary and the most westerly point on the Tunisian shoreline. As noted above,[407] Tunisia argued that the Court's co-ordinates did not have any binding effect because they did not appear in the *dispositif*, and that in actual fact the most westerly point was 34° 05' 20" North, on the Carthage system.[408] In effect, then, Tunisia's version of that point would have had the Court abandon in total the geographical co-ordinates suggested by it in its reasoning.

The Libyan objection was essentially similar to the reservations it had made regarding the first sector, namely, that the real object was to effect a substantial revision and modification of the judgment of 1982. The Court observed: 'It is however a condition of admissibility of a request for interpretation . . . not only that there be a dispute between the parties as to the meaning and scope of the judgment, but also that the real purpose of the request be to obtain an interpretation – a clarification of that meaning and scope.'[409] It accepted that there existed a dispute between the parties as to what had been decided with binding force in 1982, and that Tunisia needed clarification on the meaning and scope of what the Court had decided then. However, it added: 'So far as the Tunisian request for interpretation may go further, and seek "to obtain an answer to questions not so decided", or to achieve a revision of the Judgment, no effect can be given to it; but within the limits defined by Article 60 of the Statute, it is admissible.'[410]

In a more forthright statement, Judge Oda observed, in his Separate Opinion, that, while the judgment could be criticised in places for having caused confusion, there was no ambiguity in the drawing of a straight line connecting two unequivocal points, that is, the land frontier at Ras Ajdir and the mid-ocean point 33° 55' North, 12° East. Tunisia's reliance on co-ordinates, different from the Court's but consistent with its own petroleum concessions boundary, had led to new methods which were

406 ICJ Reports 1999, p. 43. See also Stanczyk (note 298), p. 200; and Bos (note 226), p. 212.
407 See the text to notes 380–3. 408 ICJ Reports 1985, p. 224. 409 *Ibid*., p. 223.
410 *Ibid*.

'entirely different from what the Court had in mind, and has thus made its request for interpretation of the 1982 Judgment *in fact* a plea for revision of the Judgment'.[411] He was equally forthright about the second sector in the Gulf of Gabes. He wrote that Tunisia was *not* seeking an interpretation of the judgment; it was attempting to '*replace* the concrete indication given by the Judgment by its own interpretation as to the location of the most westerly point of the Gulf of Gabes', and that 'Tunisia's requests for interpretation of the Judgment are simply disguised requests for revision'.[412]

Earlier, in 1978, the Court of Arbitration, in *United Kingdom–France Continental Shelf Interpretive Decision*, had had a similar opportunity to reflect upon the limited scope and purpose of the process of interpretation. One of France's objections to the request submitted by the United Kingdom for interpretation of the Court's decision with respect to both sectors was that the powers of interpretation possessed by the Court by virtue of Article 10(2) of the Arbitration Agreement permitted the Court to elucidate the meaning of an obscurity in the decision without allowing it to modify its contents in any way; and that the measures requested by the United Kingdom were predicated on reconciling certain elements obtaining in the decision and in the *dispositif*, including the boundary drawn on the map by the Court with the help of the Technical Expert. France also claimed that, if the Court accepted these claims and adopted these measures, then it would constitute exceeding its powers given under the agreement.[413] The Court took the position that interpretation was:

> a process that is merely auxiliary, and may serve to explain but may not change what the Court decided with binding force as *res judicata*. It poses the question, what was it that the Court decided with binding force in its decision, not the question, what ought the Court now to decide in light of fresh facts or fresh arguments. A request for interpretation must, therefore, genuinely relate to the determination of the meaning and scope of the decision, and cannot be used as a means for

[411] *Ibid.*, p. 241 (emphasis in original).

[412] *Ibid.*, p. 245 (emphasis in original). See also the Separate Opinion of Judge Ad Hoc Suzanne Bastid, who held that Tunisia's interpretation 'winds up with an interpretation which in fact constitutes a new text, conveyed in its submissions of 14 June 1985, the only logical place for which would be in submissions on the merits of a claim for revision'. See *ibid.*, p. 251. Cf. Bowett, who writes that, although it did not expressly accept that Tunisia had raised a genuine point of interpretation, or deny that it had, the Court also did not accept the Libyan argument that the Tunisian Government was in reality seeking revision: Bowett (note 226), p. 586.

[413] 54 ILR 165.

its revision or amendment, processes of a different kind to which different considerations apply.[414]

b. Restrictive aspects of interpretation

The second important rule follows naturally from the first, that is, the process of interpretation must be seen restrictively. This has several aspects to it. First, interpretation, even where it is for *bona fide* clarification purposes, is not a licence to seek and secure the revision of the judgment and judgment boundary. Any plea for interpretation of a decision where it is based on a genuine need for clarification must be kept within the strict limits of this notion. As Stanczyk noted: 'It does not seem, however, that a request for interpretation is to become a routine motion of States bringing their disputes before the Court.'[415]

Here, reference may again be made to *United Kingdom–France Continental Shelf Interpretive Decision*. In section III.b above, it was pointed out that the United Kingdom had objected to the way the boundary in the *dispositif* and map had been drawn in the Atlantic sector. The main offending fact was that, in the sector west of Point M, the Technical Expert, who was responsible for drawing the line described by the Court, had erred in not making the required corrections in the Mercator projection. In reply to a question posed by the Court, the Government of the United Kingdom further refined its claim and asked the Court to substitute the loxodrome for the 'geodetic' line drawn on the chart by the Technical Expert.[416]

The French position was, *inter alia*, that the Mercator projection accorded with the practice of the users of the sea; that the geodetic line westwards of Point M, as proposed by the United Kingdom, was itself not a strict mathematical rendering of the equidistance line; that a strict equidistance geodetic line would have involved the use of all relevant basepoints and that these lines would not be simple middle lines, but complex lines involving several arcs of circles with turning points reflecting some changes in the basepoints.[417] The Government of the United Kingdom, in turn, contested the French Government's version of a strict equidistance line: it did not accept the selection by France of

[414] *Ibid.*, pp. 170–1. For commentary on this, see Bowett (note 226), pp. 586–7. This rule has been adopted by other tribunals, including the Iran–United States Claims Tribunal, for which see Brower and Brueschke, *The Iran–United States Claims Tribunal*, The Hague, 1998, pp. 243–4, especially note 1163. [415] Supra (note 298), at p. 210. [416] 54 ILR 165.

[417] *Ibid.*, pp. 177–9.

certain basepoints, particularly Longships, lying northwards off Land's End.[418] With respect to the argument advanced by the United Kingdom, that the Court ought to have used the most modern and sophisticated scientific techniques for the purposes of delimitation, 'the French Government state[d] that this might have been a proper subject of discussion before the Court's Decision but not now when it has given its judgment'.[419] It went on to assert that the Arbitration Agreement did not oblige the Court to follow the method now advocated by the Government of the United Kingdom.[420]

The reasons why the Court rejected the United Kingdom position have been stated above. It will be appropriate, nevertheless, to add here that the Court held that the issue before it was not 'what in light of fresh facts and fresh arguments ought to have been the Court's decision regarding the boundary in that region. It is, and is exclusively, the course of the boundary that was laid down by the Court in the Decision of 30 June 1977.'[421] It went on to add:

> But even if the techniques used in the calculation of a half-effect boundary were to be considered as being incompatible with the method described by the Court and it were open to the Court to review the problem of appropriate techniques for applying the half-effect solution, this could only be done after a fresh examination of all pertinent factors and considerations as well as of the several possible techniques and the courses of the boundaries resulting from their use. The Decision of 30 June 1977 regarding the Atlantic region was a particular one, on the basis of the applicable rules of international law providing a particular equitable solution and after studying the boundaries resulting from the application of other techniques. To reopen the question of the method applied by the Expert and the Court in the proceedings in 1977 appears, in consequence, to go beyond the function of interpretation entrusted to the Court under Article 10 of the Arbitration Agreement as well as beyond its inherent power to rectify a material error.[422]

By way of analogy, then, it is interesting to take note of the *Laguna del Desierto* arbitration between Argentina and Chile in 1994. After having failed to convince the tribunal of its claims, Chile filed a petition for the revision and interpretation of the decision. In its subsidiary request for interpretation, Chile asked the tribunal:

> to interpret its judgment [so] that the geography as it is in reality on the ground shall prevail over the line identified by the Expert [appointed by the tribunal]; that is to say, that the true location of the local water-parting shall be determined by the Demarcator on the ground and, that, in any case where this shall not be

[418] *Ibid.*, p. 196. [419] *Ibid.*, pp. 187–8. [420] *Ibid.*, p. 188. [421] *Ibid.*, p. 192.
[422] *Ibid.*, p. 202.

possible, he shall trace a straight line joining the last point of the water-parting coming from the north to the next point to the south where it shall again be possible in practice to determine the course of the said water-parting.[423]

In its award in *Request for Revision and Interpretation of the 1994 Judgment*, the tribunal held that the case law on the matter made it clear that interpretation could not go beyond the scope of the judgment itself.[424] Citing the views expressed by the Court of Arbitration in *United Kingdom–France Continental Shelf Interpretive Decision*, and by the International Court of Justice in *Application for Revision and Interpretation of the 1982 Judgment*,[425] the Tribunal highlighted the fact that the Expert was given all necessary instructions to ensure that the course of the line of the frontier should accord with the 'precise intent' of the tribunal.[426] It observed that the 'Expert's Report shows that at no point was it impossible to identify the local water-parting. On the other hand, to accept that a straight line should be drawn in place of the water-parting would constitute a real modification of the Judgment, going well beyond mere interpretation.'[427]

The other restrictive aspects are discussed in Chapter 6 below in the context of the various basic principles relating to interpretation. At this juncture, it will be appropriate to discuss the rationale for adopting a restrictive approach to interpretation. It is not difficult to appreciate why it is that the process of interpretation ought normally to be seen narrowly and put into effect restrictively, that is, kept confined strictly within the scope of clarification, as opposed to a reconsideration of the merits of the case or part thereof. There are at least three reasons for this proposition of law.

First, any kind of judicial or arbitral dispute settlement process is based on the consent of States, whether it is given *ad hoc* or *ante hoc*. It is usually the case that a court or tribunal vested with jurisdiction over a dispute between States will also have before it the precise question or questions on which it will be expected to provide a set of answers. This is particularly true of *ad hoc* arbitral tribunals. In these circumstances, the tribunal cannot, in its interpretative phase, provide answers to questions not contemplated by the parties in the original proceedings; it is well received that consent for all issues must either categorically, or by necessary implication, be given by the parties to the tribunal in the *compromis*.

Secondly, a matter decided with final effect by the tribunal is *res judicata* and cannot be revised or modified on the pretext of interpretation of the

[423] *Request for Revision and Interpretation of the 1994 Judgment*, 113 ILR 194, at p. 196.
[424] *Ibid.*, p. 230. [425] *Ibid.*, pp. 230–1. [426] *Ibid.*, p. 232. [427] *Ibid.*, p. 232.

scope and meaning of that decision. This aspect of the matter is discussed in subsection c below.

Thirdly, a re-examination of issues may entail the production of evidence and the hearing of fresh arguments on new matters not predicated on clarification but revision of the boundaries. Clearly, a situation such as this is incompatible with the notion of interpretation and can hardly be encouraged.

c. Tests for interpretation

In the preceding subsection, it was maintained that the tribunal has to view its task of interpretation rather restrictively. This means that the process of interpretation of judgments and awards in territorial and boundary cases should be undertaken narrowly and confined within the terms of the judgment lest the exercise become that of modification and adjustment of the frontier delimited by the tribunal. Be that as it may, the question remains whether the standard required to admit the request and produce an interpretative judgment ought to be set high in order to reduce the number of clarifications sought and obtained, or set low in order to encourage parties to seek clarification. It appears that, in terms of admitting the request and providing an interpretative judgment, there are two propositions and considerations of law which pull in opposite directions.

On the one hand, it is readily arguable that, in principle, there is a lawful expectation that a decision will be implemented by the parties without inordinate delay and indeed as soon as possible. This is in fact a three-way expectation, namely, an expectation held by the two States Parties to the litigation and the tribunal as well. In some cases, delays in implementation will have a direct effect on the level of international tension and friction, especially where relations between the parties are generally fragile. Equally important, delays can also call into question the general efficacy of a judgment, and continued postponement can even have adverse repercussions on the authority of the tribunal itself. Hence, any proposition of law, which allows a lawful moratorium on the full and effective performance of obligations arising from a judgment, must, in normal circumstances, be viewed with a large degree of circumspection. 'The question', the International Court of Justice observed in the *Interpretation of the Preliminary Judgment in the Cameroon–Nigeria Land and Maritime Boundary* case, 'of the admissibility of requests for interpretation of the Court's judgments needs particular attention because of the need to avoid impairing the finality, and delaying the implementation, of these judgments.'[428]

At the same time, it is also the case, as seen above, that the implementation of a decision can in some cases be difficult if not impossible in the absence of some clarification by the tribunal. In those cases, a denial of clarification could perpetuate difficulties and eventually lead nowhere. It is obvious therefore that it would not be in the best interests of either party to require the tribunal to set too high a standard for admitting the request, and hence if there is a genuine need for clarification, a need based on *bona fide* confusion rather than a desire either to delay implementation or to seek modifications to the boundary line, then an interpretation by the tribunal ought to be viewed more as a necessity and less as a source of annoyance. It was this predicament which Judge Koroma seemed to address in his Dissenting Opinion in *Interpretation of the Preliminary Judgment in the Cameroon–Nigeria Land and Maritime Boundary*, when he asserted: 'The lack of clarification regarding the meaning and scope of the Judgment could lead to an unnecessary and conceivable prolongation and confusion of pleadings that could have been obviated by the Court's interpretation of its Judgment.'[429] Vice-President Judge Weeramantry went further, and asserted that, where there was a dispute as to the meaning or scope of the judgment, the Court was under an obligation to construe it under Article 60 at the request of the party seeking clarification. He went on to observe:

> A judgment, however well crafted, could well embody phraseology which, in the context of a given set of circumstances, may require some clarification. It is one of those incidents of litigation which the judicial experience of ages has shown may arise from time to time, and it is precisely for this reason that Article 60 . . . made such clear provision for the right of interpretation. Indeed, the Article was drafted so strongly as to cast the Court's duty in imperative terms [i.e. 'shall'] . . . I refer in this context to the *Factory at Chorzów* case where the Permanent Court [of International Justice] observed that, where there is a difference of opinion as to whether a particular point has or has not been decided, this comes within the terms of the provision in question . . . '[A]nd the Court cannot avoid the *duty incumbent upon it* of interpreting the judgment in so far as necessary, in order to adjudicate upon such a difference of opinion . . .' This is part of a passage in the *Factory at Chorzów* Judgment which, in the words of Rosenne, has become the classic statement of the law on this point.[430]

[428] ICJ Reports 1999, p. 36. See further Judge Ajibola in his Dissenting Opinion, p. 56. See Rosenne (note 226), p. 1679. [429] ICJ Reports 1999, p. 52.

[430] *Ibid.*, pp. 47–8 (emphasis in original in the Judge's quotation). See also the declaration of Judge Ad Hoc Caicedo Castilla in the *Request for Interpretation of the Judgment in the*

This approach is also evident in Judge Ajibola's Dissenting Opinion, where he accepted that the Court should not agree to any delay being caused in the matter and that the case should be disposed off expeditiously because of the prevailing situation of the parties at the frontier. 'But', he wrote, 'at the same time there is need for caution; this should not be done at the expense of justice and proper procedure.' He agreed that a judgment was necessary to enrich the jurisprudence of the Court and to serve as a guideline to litigants with regard to the limitations imposed on the content of the applications.[431]

d. Modification, revision and res judicata

The process of interpretation raises interesting questions of law with respect to the revision and modification of judgments. It was noted above in sections IV.a and IV.b that tribunals generally adopt a restrictive approach to interpretation and that they look for a *bona fide* need for such a remedy before considering the request on its merits. It was also noted that the International Court of Justice was cautious with respect to Tunisia's request for interpretation in *Application for Revision and Interpretation of the 1982 Judgment*, and, although it admitted the request, it was not willing to accede to the terms thereof, and rejected the Tunisian version of the geographical co-ordinates for the most westerly point of the Gulf of Gabes on the ground that the request sought a revision of the 1982 judgment. Attention was also paid to the *dicta* of the Court of Arbitration in *United Kingdom–France Continental Shelf Interpretive Decision*, in which it highlighted the general rule that a request for interpretation could not be used as a means for the revision of a judgment, and that the request must genuinely relate to the determination of the meaning and scope of the decision. At the heart of the matter, of course, is that the fundamental rule of *res judicata* precludes the reopening of issues conclusively settled between the litigating parties.

The fact, however, is that, at times, a request for the interpretation of a decision *will* involve the modification of a boundary delimited by a tribunal. Indeed, the very purpose of submitting such a request will be to

Asylum Case, ICJ Reports 1950, p. 395, at p. 404, where it is noted (in the third person) that he was 'unable to concur in the Judgment of the Court because, in his opinion, Article 60 of the Statute can be interpreted more liberally, as shown by the Permanent Court of International Justice in the Chorzów Factory case. He recognises, however, that it is open to the Parties to come before the Court if a divergence of views satisfying the precise conditions required by this Judgment were to be submitted to it.'

[431] See ICJ Reports 1999, p. 60.

secure a revision of the location of the judgment boundary. It is also the case that, unlike the situations described above, some tribunals have admitted and interpreted decisions which have led to the revision and modification of the judgment boundary. In a nutshell, then, there may arguably be a blurring in some cases between interpretation and modification/revision, not in terms of the general notions, but in terms of actual legal effects. Revision, of course, is a distinct judicial remedy provided on request by one of the parties upon discovery of a hitherto unknown fact. (Revision is discussed in Part IV below.) The point here is that, since the two remedies are distinct in law, and despite the fact that the two may overlap, there can be no revision in the guise of interpretation. It is intended here to look at the various ways in which requests for interpretation have sometimes led to a revision and modification of the judgment boundary and thereafter to attempt to reconcile in legal terms this state of affairs.

As observed above, it is the case that, at times, to provide an interpretation of a decision is to modify the judgment boundary to an extent. This is particularly true where there are material errors in the decision. Thus, States may request the tribunal to interpret its judgment and by so doing clarify and confirm the allegation that a minor clerical error was made in the decision. If the error is established, the tribunal can then rectify its mistake simply by clarifying its position. This exercise may entail modification or revision of the judgment and/or the judgment boundary. The request of the United Kingdom in the Channel Islands sector in *United Kingdom–France Continental Shelf Interpretive Decision* comes easily to mind as an example of this point. It was an acknowledgment of this fact which prompted the Court of Arbitration to observe:

> Where, as in the present case, the request for interpretation must, if upheld, entail some adjustment – to use a neutral term – of the *dispositif*, the task of determining whether the remedy sought in the request falls within the ambit of the process of 'interpretation' or amounts to a demand for 'revision' may be a difficult one. The determination of this question necessarily depends on the particular facts of each case.[432]

The Court, of course, rejected the claims of the United Kingdom for adjustment in the Atlantic sector, and so the problems of rectification in that sector did not, in fact, materialise. It did, however, accept that an adjustment had to be made for the Channel Islands sector and that these adjustments reflected rectification of a material error, an oversight. While it

[432] 54 ILR 171.

rectified the boundary in its judgment, and followed the line composed of segments of arcs of circles of a twelve-mile radius drawn from basepoints A to M on the baselines of the Bailiwick of Guernsey, the Court left the drawing of the line as an act of correction to the parties. The change, therefore, posed no problems. The central point here is that the Court was clearly concerned that a request for interpretation of an operative part of the judgment entailed the prospect of its revision and that there was a blurring of the categories in terms of effects. It was for this reason that Gray and Kingsbury went so far as to say that the Court 'took an extensive view of what is covered by interpretation, and commentators have suggested that both [the *Palena* and the *United Kingdom–France Continental Shelf*] cases really allowed revision in the guise of interpretation'.[433]

The revision and modification of judgment boundaries may also arise in the context of allegations of essential or serious errors. On the one hand, in such situations, disaffected States may choose to pursue judicial remedies based on allegations of nullity, not unlike Nicaragua's application before the International Court of Justice in the *Arbitral Award of the King of Spain*.[434] On the other hand, litigating States may decide to eschew allegations of nullity, and pursue the alternate remedy of interpretation of the award or judgment before the same or another tribunal. The advantage in choosing interpretation lies not only in the fact that the latter remedy, predicated as it is in the continuation in law of the boundary despite the error, is less disruptive than allegations of nullity. It is also true that, because no special consent is required where interpretation is a right rooted in the *compromis*, it may be easier to seek this remedy rather than secure consent for a new case altogether.

Be that as it may, it must be noted that subsequent clarification of the ambiguities and rectification of the errors may have implications in terms of relocation of the boundary and changes in the text of the decision or parts thereof. One of the better examples of this is the *Palena* case which Argentina and Chile brought before the Court of Arbitration with a view

433 See 'Developments in Dispute Settlement: Inter-State Arbitration Since 1945', 63 (1992) BYIL 97, at p. 130, note 224. For the *Palena* case, see section V.b of this chapter.

434 (*Nicaragua* v. *Honduras*), ICJ Reports 1960, p. 192. In that case, Nicaragua contended that the land boundary award was null and void owing, *inter alia*, to essential error: the Spanish King, acting in the capacity of arbitrator, had allegedly erred in the evaluation of the documents and other evidence submitted to him. Rejecting this plea, the Court held that a distinction had to be maintained between an essential error and the arbitrator's *evaluation* of documents and other kinds of evidence submitted to him. *Appraisal* of the probative value of documents and evidence appertained to the discretionary power of the arbitrator, the exercise of which was not open to question: *ibid*., pp. 215–16. Allegations of nullity were also raised by Guinea-Bissau in *Arbitral Award of 31 July 1989*, ICJ Reports 1991, p. 53, *passim*.

to resolving the problems of 'fulfilment' of the 1902 award grounded in the seriously flawed geographical knowledge of the area. The law and facts of this case are discussed below in section V.b of this chapter, and, in order to avoid repetition, it will suffice here to note that the Court's interpretation of the award of King Edward VII led to changes in the alignment in the disputed area. This, of course, has to be seen in light of the fact that the task of the Court was not limited to interpretation of the 1902 award; it was also required to effect the fulfilment thereof, which meant, in terms, the application or implementation of the award on the ground, and, given the nature of the geographical errors, a certain amount of modification was inevitable. As the Court noted in this respect, the expression 'interpretation and fulfilment' was 'a comprehensive [one] which authorises the Court to examine the demarcation of 1903 as well as the 1902 Award itself and authorises, nay requires, the Court, while avoiding any revision or modification of the 1902 Award, nevertheless to supply any deficiencies therein in a manner consistent as far as possible with the Arbitrator's intention'.[435] Bos' remarks are thoroughly relevant, for he wrote:

> In other words, depending upon the magnitude of the task of completing an arbitral award, completion may sometimes be practicable in the guise of interpretation, and sometimes may be not. But in all circumstances it should be considered as something different from interpreting a *res judicata*.[436]

A greater controversy surrounded the *Costa Rica* v. *Panama* boundary arbitration[437] (see Map 3). For a proper appreciation of this complex case, some detail is essential. In 1880 and 1886, two arbitral treaties between Costa Rica and Colombia, Panama's predecessor State, were concluded but not given effect.[438] In 1896, these two parties agreed to submit their boundary

[435] 38 ILR 91.

[436] Supra (note 226), p. 205. Cf. Strupp, who viewed the *dispositif* alone as having the quality of *res judicata*, with the result that the legal considerations given in a decision do not share the quality of legal force: Strupp (note 136), p. 683. He was writing in the context of revision of judgments and awards.

[437] See, generally, Carlston (note 181), pp. 101–11; Anderson, 'The Costa Rica–Panama Boundary Dispute', 15 (1921) AJIL 236; Ireland, *Boundaries, Possessions, and Conflicts in Central and North America and the Caribbean*, Cambridge, MA, 1941, pp. 24–43; Cukwurah (note 7), pp. 208–11; Woolsey (note 209), pp. 329–30; Nelson, 'The Arbitration of Boundary Disputes in Latin America', 20 (1973) *Netherlands International Law Review* 267, at pp. 287–8 and notes 126 and 127; and Moore, 'Memorandum on Uti Possidetis: Costa Rica–Panama Arbitration' (note 167), p. 328.

[438] 71 BFSP 215 and 1014 respectively. The Treaty of 1880 was ratified, but in 1881 the Government of the United States protested on the ground that it had acquired certain rights and privileges concerning transit across the Isthmus of Panama, and that

dispute to arbitration by the President of France.[439] In September 1900, President Loubet delivered his award in *Colombia* v. *Costa Rica*, in which he drew the boundary from Cape Mona on the Atlantic to Punta Burica on the Pacific Ocean. In between these two points, Loubet delimited a line which, in the northern, or Atlantic, sector, ran north of the mouth of the River Sixaola or Tarire, thereafter along the counterfort of the Cordillera and then along the main watershed up to a point about 9° North. By so doing, the valley of this river was allocated to Colombia.[440] While the latter accepted the award as fully valid and binding, Costa Rica found itself unable to accept the allocation in the Atlantic sector. These views are discussed below. It is important to note at this stage that the southern, or Pacific, sector of the Loubet frontier extending south of 9° North to Punta Burica was acceptable to both parties.

On 23 November 1900, Costa Rica, in a letter to the French Minister of Foreign Relations, M. Delcassé, urged the President to adopt a boundary shown therein as an interpretation of his award. The Loubet line, as Costa Rica interpreted it, started at Punta Mona, ran along a ridge leaving to its north the Sixaola/Tarire River valley; it then ran south-westwards on the left bank of the Sixaola to the point where it met the Yorquin River to the 82° West meridian. After crossing the Sixaola/Tarire River, it ran south along the Yorquin–Uren watershed and continuing south it lay on the main Atlantic–Pacific watershed up to 9° North latitude. It was also claimed that, 'unless the line followed the [Yorquin] and not the [Sixaola], it would include, within the area awarded to Colombia, territory not in dispute'.[441] The point was that the Sixaola–Tarire–Yorquin was the 'real' *status quo* boundary and hence an alignment north of it would have been in excess of territory actually claimed. Colombia's position was that, as long as the boundary was in the disputed territory as described in the failed arbitral treaty of 1886, which it was, it did not matter where the frontier was actually delimited by the arbitrator, President Loubet.

accordingly the Governments of Costa Rica and Colombia were required to declare that such rights would remain intact despite any arbitral decision. For this reason, the designated arbitrator, the King of the Belgians, declined the invitation. While the King of Spain agreed to carry out this task, he declared that the matter would be addressed only after the pending arbitration between Colombia and Venezuela was concluded, but thereafter the King of Spain died and the two disputing States were compelled to agree the Treaty of 1886, in which they agreed that the Government of Spain was competent to proceed with the arbitration. However, despite extending the time periods for the arbitration, the latter government failed to provide a decision. Thereafter, Colombia took the position that the two agreements had lapsed but remained in principle favourable to arbitration of the dispute. See Ireland (note 437), pp. 30–1.

439 92 BFSP 1036. 440 *Ibid.*, p. 1038. 441 Ireland (note 437), pp. 32–3.

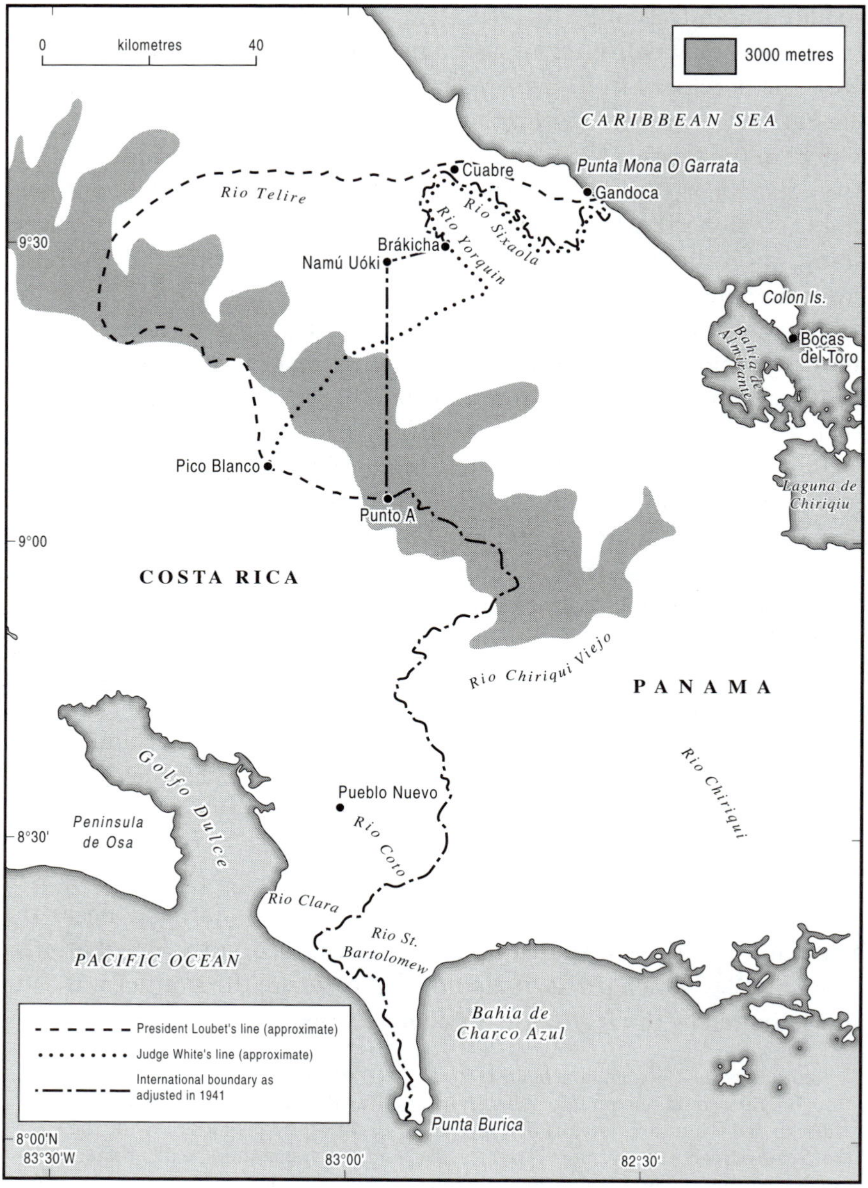

Map 3 *Costa Rica* v. *Panama Boundary* arbitration

Delcassé denied Costa Rica's request, and stated that, insofar as precise geographical criteria were unavailable, only a general line, drawn strictly within the disputed territory agreed in the 1886 Convention between the parties, could be fixed.[442] The dispute festered, but, in March 1910, Costa Rica and Panama agreed in the Porras–Anderson Treaty,[443] to refer the dispute to arbitration, and appointed the Chief Justice of the United States Supreme Court as arbitrator as arbitrator. The formulation, however, of the precise task to be carried out by Chief Justice White was fraught with difficulties and led to problems after the arbitration was over. This is discussed presently. Suffice it to note here that, despite the delicate balance struck by the United States, the litigating States continued to maintain mutually incompatible positions regarding the basic object and purpose of the arbitration.

Clearly, then, the terms of Article I of the *compromis* are important. They required the arbitrator to determine the boundary most in accordance with the 'correct interpretation' and 'true intention' of the award of 1900. Article I also authorised the arbitrator to take into account, apart from the facts and circumstances attending the controversy, 'the limitation of the Loubet award expressed in the letter of His Excellency Monsieur Delcassé, Minister of Foreign Relations of France to . . . [the] Minister of Costa Rica . . . of November 23, 1900, that this boundary line must be drawn within the confines of the territory in dispute as determined by the [Colombia–Panama] . . . Convention of Paris . . . of 20 January 1886'. As far as the Pacific sector was concerned, the two disputants agreed that the frontier south of the 9° North latitude was 'clear and indisputable'.

For Panama, the starting point was always going to be the Loubet award, and an interpretation of that award was all that was required of Chief Justice White; the binding and conclusive character of the Loubet decision was not in issue. 'No question', it said, 'is made as to its validity, none as to its correctness, but only as to its interpretation. To submit to arbitration the interpretation of the award necessarily involves the affirmance of its validity and correctness.'[444]

[442] Minister for Foreign Affairs of Costa Rica to Minister for Foreign Affairs of Panama, 1 March 1915, Subinclosure 2, Document B, Minister Hale to the US Secretary of State, 3 April 1915, 1915 *Foreign Relations of the United States* 1138 and 1142, at p. 1144. See also Carlston (note 181), p. 103; and Ireland (note 437), pp. 32–3. This is an abbreviated version of the Costa Rican interpretation.

[443] 6 (1912) AJIL 1; 103 BFSP 404.

[444] Minister of Panama to the US Secretary of State, 20 October 1914, 1914 *Foreign Relations of the United States* 994, at p. 995. See also Panama to Costa Rica, 17 October 1914: Inclosure 1 in Chargé, American Legation to US Secretary of State, 18 October 1914, *ibid.*, p. 1016, at pp. 1016–17; and Minister of Foreign Affairs of Panama to Minister for Foreign Affairs of Costa Rica, 30 January 1915, Subinclosure 1, Document A, Minister Hale to US Secretary of State, 3 April 1915, 1915 *Foreign Relations of the United States* 1138, p. 1138, at p. 1139.

For Costa Rica, the matter was more complex. On the one hand, the question involved not only deciding which one of the two interpretations of the Loubet boundary award was correct. It was Costa Rica's allegation that Panama was wrong in interpreting the award as having allocated the valley north of the Sixaola River to its predecessor State, Colombia, and that a correct interpretation of the decision showed that the valley had been left to Costa Rica.[445] On the other hand, Costa Rica also contended that, by drawing such a line, the arbitrator had encroached into undisputed Costa Rican territory and that the decision was flawed by uncertainty and geographical defects.[446] Not only did it call into question the obligatory nature of the award,[447] Costa Rica also attempted to show that the Loubet award was in need, hence, of modification, amendment and correction.[448] Accordingly, while Panama continued to press for a literal interpretation of the award, Costa Rica claimed, in the words of Anderson:

> that the scope of the arbitration was enlarged beyond the mere interpretation of the Loubet award, in a verbal sense, by permitting the intention attributable to the former arbitrator to enter into the interpretation of the award, and by requiring the arbitrator in deciding this question to take into account all the facts, circumstances and considerations having a bearing upon the case, thus insuring that the award should be reformed and the boundary fixed in accordance with the merits of the controversy.[449]

Anderson also points out that, in addition to the new republic being advised by the United States, there was no intention of limiting the arbitral task to mere interpretation; and that Panama had agreed that, if it were demonstrated that the Loubet alignment passed through undisputed Costa Rican territory as fixed by the 1886 Convention, that part of

[445] See Minister for Foreign Affairs of Costa Rica to the Minister for Foreign Affairs of Panama, 1 March 1915, Subinclosure 2, Document B: 1915 *Foreign Relations of the United States* (note 442), pp. 1144–5.

[446] Carlston (note 181), pp. 103–6; Anderson (note 437), pp. 236–7; and Ireland (note 437), pp. 32–6.

[447] Carlston (note 181), p. 104.

[448] Costa Rica to Panama, 30 October 1914: Inclosure 2 in Chargé, American Legation to US Secretary of State, 18 October 1914: 1914 *Foreign Relations of the United States* (note 444), p. 1017, at p. 1020. In a letter to the Panamanian Foreign Minister, his Costa Rican counterpart claimed that his State 'could have had a thousand reasons for [disregarding the Loubet Award], but it preferred to sacrifice the clearest rights rather than assume an attitude which might be interpreted as disrespectful of the sanctity of the covenant'. See letter of 1 March 1915, Subinclosure 2, Document B (note 445), p. 1144. Panama conceded that the arbitrator had the power to correct the award insofar as he may find it outside the jurisdiction vested in the French President: see Panama to Costa Rica, 18 October 1914: 1914 *Foreign Relations of the United States* (note 444), p. 1017.

[449] Supra (note 437), pp. 236–7.

the boundary would require modification consistent with what was most in accordance with the true intention of the award.[450]

In the event, the arbitrator held 'that the fundamental question to be decided [is] whether the boundary line fixed by the previous arbitration was within the previous treaty or treaties. And, if it was not, it must follow that its correction is within the scope of the authority conferred by this treaty; and if it was, no power here obtains to revise it.'[451] He decided that, in fact, the Punta Mona–Cordillera alignment was not within the disputed territory, and went on to observe: '[I]t is conceded by both parties that under this treaty there is the power and duty to substitute for the line set aside, a line within the scope of the authority granted under the previous treaty "most in accordance with the correct interpretation and true intention" of the former award.' That line, he decided, was based on the Sixaola–Yorquin River boundary, and he then went on to declare the counterfort alignment as 'non-existing'.[452] It was now Panama's turn to declare the award *excès de pouvoir* and hence null and void.[453] It was contended that the arbitrator had made a 'real revision of the Loubet award instead of the interpretation called for by the Arbitral Convention, and had fixed a frontier line totally strange to the former award'.[454]

This was a difficult question, with arguments on both sides being persuasive. On the one hand, it could be argued that Chief Justice White's award was null because his line was in fact hardly a true 'interpretation' of what President Loubet had decided or had intended to decide, it being understood that interpretation here means simply a clarification of the meaning and scope of the decision. It is interesting that Chief Justice White refused at one stage of the award to consider whether certain ridges, spurs and occasional peaks about sixteen miles from a small eminence which is Punta Mona on the Atlantic could mistakenly constitute Loubet's 'counterfort', on the ground that he was 'not called upon to consider' such a question;[455] but that, indeed, was exactly what he had been asked to do in the *compromis*, that is, to determine the true intention and correct interpretation of the Loubet award. Nor admittedly did Chief

[450] *Ibid.*, p. 238. See also US Secretary of State to Minister in Panama (Price), 15 March 1921, 1921 *Foreign Relations of the United States*, vol. I, p. 184, at pp. 187–8.

[451] 8 (1914) AJIL 932. [452] *Ibid.*, pp. 937 and 940–1.

[453] See Minister of Panama to US Secretary of State, 20 October 1914 (note 444), pp. 994–5; Panama to Costa Rica, 17 October 1914 (note 444), pp. 1016–17. Further, see Panamanian Minister of Foreign Affairs to the American Minister, 18 March 1921: Enclosure in a letter from the US Minister in Panama to US Secretary of State, 12 April 1921, 1921 *Foreign Relations of the United States* (note 450), p. 190. [454] Ireland (note 437), p. 38.

[455] 8 (1914) AJIL 930.

Justice White acquaint himself fully with the record kept rigorously by the previous arbitrator.[456] By looking *expressis verbis* at the 'merits of the controversy', the arbitrator was arguably exceeding his powers, a matter compounded by declaring the Atlantic sector of the Loubet line as legally non-existent. Moreover, Panama had never conceded that Chief Justice White had the power to 'substitute' the alignment made by Loubet; on the contrary, Panama had always claimed that the arbitrator had no powers of substitution of the line.

On the other hand, there is also some merit in the view that, once it had been agreed in Article I that the line had to be drawn within the confines of the territory in dispute as determined by the 1886 Convention, '[i]t would seem to be obvious', as Anderson writes, 'that in the discharge of his duty it was incumbent upon the arbitrator to decide what were the confines of the territory in dispute, as determined by the Convention . . . in order that he may comply with the terms of submission as to the drawing of the boundary line within these confines. Mindful of this obligation, the arbitrator did consider and determine . . . what were the confines of the territory in dispute . . . Having made the determination as to the extent of the territory in dispute, he was bound by explicit provisions of the submission to draw the boundary line within that territory.'[457]

Thus the logical outcome of the decision made by the arbitrator to the effect that the Atlantic sector line was *ultra petita* could only be an obligatory redrawing of the alignment to the extent of the excess with a view to keeping the boundary within the confines of the 1886 Convention. As Anderson stated: 'It was, therefore necessary for the Chief Justice to lay down a wholly different line', and to fix 'as the boundary the dividing line between the disputed territory and the undisputed territory, thus approaching, as nearly as possible, the line of the Loubet award which had to be discarded because it ran through undisputed territory'.[458] It could also be argued that Panama had effectively come to accept, albeit in guarded fashion, that some modification would have to take place, a modification which, only by stretching the notion, could be regarded as an interpretative process.[459] Also noteworthy in this context is Costa Rica's allegation that Panama's rejection of Chief Justice White's award

[456] Panamanian Minister of Foreign Affairs to the American Minister, 18 March 1921: 1921 *Foreign Relations of the United States* (note 450), at p. 199.

[457] US Secretary of State to the Minister in Panama, 27 April 1921: 1921 *Foreign Relations of the United States* 207, at p. 210.

[458] Supra (note 437), p. 238.

[459] See Costa Rica to Panama, 30 October 1914 (note 448), p. 1020; and Panama to Costa Rica, 17 October 1914 (note 444), p. 1017.

was based on domestic politics rather than on any substantial (legal) ground.[460]

Moreover, it cannot be ignored that, had the arbitrator carried out his task strictly according to the terms of the *compromis*, he would in effect have reinforced the Loubet alignment, which in fact was the very bone of contention between the two States, and such a course of action would not have led to a final resolution of the underlying problems between Costa Rica and Panama. This would hardly have been consistent with the rule of effectiveness. A treaty must be interpreted in a way in which the intentions of the parties are made effective: *ut res magis valeat quam pereat*. The trouble, however, here is that the real intentions of the parties were neither common nor agreed, but in fact obscure.

Nonetheless, it is also the case that, had Chief Justice White been unable eventually to provide an award on the ground of conflicting jurisdictional tasks, then that would have constituted a failure to exercise jurisdiction – yet another unenviable predicament for him. Costa Rica was correct then to claim that Panama's suggestion that the arbitrator ought to have abstained from rendering a decision was '*an alarming novelty in general jurisprudence*. The true doctrine is precisely the contrary.'[461] Nonetheless, on balance perhaps, it appears that, in principle, the arbitrator did exceed his powers[462] in redrawing, instead of clarifying, the meaning of the award. It is one thing to go into the merits of the controversy to interpret the meaning and intent of the text of the judgment; it is quite another to re-examine the controversy and substitute one boundary for another,

[460] Minister of Costa Rica to US Secretary of State, 9 March 1915, in 1915 *Foreign Relations of the United States* 1134, at p. 1137. The White award was finally executed in 1921 following pressure from the United States: the latter could not countenance any argument based on the claim that the Chief Justice of the Supreme Court had provided an imperfect award: see US Secretary of State to Minister Price, 28 April 1915, in 1915 *Foreign Relations of the United States* 1147; and, generally, see the correspondence with Panama, in 1921 *Foreign Relations of the United States*, vol. I, pp. 175 *et seq.*; Cukwurah (note 7), p. 211; and Ireland (note 437), pp. 39–41. An agreement adjusting the White delimitation was concluded in 1938: Ireland (note 437), pp. 41–2; and finalised in 1941. The 1941 line was drawn from the mouth of the Sixaola river, and, following the valley of the Yorquin upstream, the boundary then left the river at Brákicha and proceeded southwestwards to Namú Uóki at the meridian 82° 56' 10" West. From this point the line was delimited due south along this meridian up to Point A at which point it ascends the main watershed and continues onwards to Cerro Pando. Thereafter, the boundary is consistent with the Loubet/White line. See Article 1 of the May 1941 treaty: 144 BFSP 751; and see the official delimitation in (Government) *Comision Del Atlas de Panama* (Panama City?), 1975, opposite Lámina 2.

[461] Costa Rica to Panama, 30 October 1914 (note 448), p. 1021 (emphasis in original).

[462] Nelson (note 437), pp. 287–8.

especially when one of the States vigorously denies that the arbitrator is empowered to modify the line. Notwithstanding the above, the short point being canvassed here, of course, is that, in all the appropriate circumstances, including the precise text of the *compromis*, an interpretative decision can become a convenient peg on which to hang an exercise in modification. As Panama asserted in a letter to Costa Rica, 'the Arbitrator has, in short, made a revision of the Loubet Award instead of interpreting it, as he was by the arbitration convention called upon to do'.[463] Indeed, the controversial text of the *compromis* of 1910 proved to be the source of all the difficulties faced by the litigating States.

In order to reconcile these conflicting positions, the following points are important, and the first step in this direction is to take very brief account of these two judicial remedies. Thus, although they have overlapping features and effects, interpretation and revision are fundamentally distinct from each other. Each has its own defining legal characteristics. The simple fact is that, while interpretation is based on the idea of a dispute between the parties over some general or particular aspect of the meaning of a part of the decision, revision is grounded in the discovery of a crucial fact after the tribunal has adopted its decision. Similarly, while the primary, ostensible purpose of interpretation is clarification of a passage or passages in the decision, regardless of whether or not it entails modification, the objective of revision is, by definition, the modification of the judgment and judgment boundary, and, characteristically, of course, a modification which is in favour of the applicant State.

It follows that, while interpretation might appear to be an act of modification or revision, the latter can only take place if there is a discovery of a fact of a decisive nature; and, where these criteria are not fulfilled, there can be no revision. 'It does not follow', writes Bowett, 'that once a tribunal goes beyond its legitimate power of interpretation it is therefore engaged in revision. The process of revision is entirely dependent upon the discovery of new facts, so that if the applicant's arguments are not based upon new facts there is no question of any revision.'[464]

The second point is the more important one, and it is this. Any kind of modification, major or minor, of a judgment boundary by way of interpretation or revision or both is allowed where the litigating parties consent thereto. States have the right to agree to an arrangement, political or judicial, whereby outstanding or stubborn boundary problems are conclusively settled. As an aspect of their sovereignty, they may agree to

[463] Letter of 17 October 1914 (note 444), p. 1017. [464] Supra (note 226), p. 591.

reconsider any point or points along the boundary or permit an arbitral tribunal or court to do so. This is particularly true with respect to main case interpretation, that is, an interpretative process which is not incidental to the main case but is the main case itself.

Viewed in this light, then, there is no conflict of any sort and therefore no need to seek reconciliation between the rules of continuity of a judgment boundary on the one hand and, on the other, the fact of modification resulting from interpretation and/or revision. It is on this proposition of law that changes to the judgment boundaries in the *Palena* and *Costa Rica* v. *Panama* cases can easily be understood. As indicated above, the crux of the Costa Rican position was that Panama had agreed to empower the arbitrator to *redraw* and not only *interpret* the Loubet alignment. The difficulty was that that precise task was not clearly spelt out in Article I of the *compromis* of 1910. No such difficulty was experienced in the *Palena* case, where Argentina and Chile clearly agreed to vest the Court with the power to interpret and fulfil that part of the boundary which had not been settled since 1902, and, given that it was impossible in terms of geography to demarcate that boundary, a change in the location of the boundary was inevitable and understood. This approach to the problem has the advantage that the *res judicata* rule is neutralised: where States agree to accommodate the modification of a judgment boundary by further litigation, then any restrictions imposed by that maxim are of no consequence.[465]

Thirdly, it may be possible to reconcile the situation by drawing a distinction between, on the one hand, a revision of the judgment boundary as the underlying purpose for interpretation, whether *bona fide* or otherwise, and, on the other, the revision or modification of the decision as simply an inevitable *effect* of the interpretation of the relevant operative part or parts of the decision. Thus, on this view of the matter, limited adjustments to a boundary may be an acceptable *consequence* of a request for interpretation where it is motivated by a *bona fide* need for clarification of the meaning, purpose or scope of the decision, as opposed to a request which seeks to employ the interpretative process merely as a legal device for the purposes of reconsideration of the decision. Admittedly, it may not always be easy to distinguish between these two aspects of a request, not unlike the situation created by the arguments advanced by the United Kingdom in the *United Kingdom–France Continental Shelf Interpretive Decision* case. Yet, on other occasions, as *Laguna del Desierto* and *Request for Revision*

[465] See further with respect to the *res judicata* rule, section V below.

and Interpretation of the 1994 Judgment show, the distinctions are easy to discern, for, in the latter case, the request for interpretation and revision was hardly credible; while, in the former, remedying the defects of the 1902 award was the sole purpose of the interpretative proceedings. It may be noted that this part of the analysis does not seek to answer at this stage the questions raised by the *res judicata* rule, and that an attempt to do so is made in section V of this chapter.

e. The admission and rejection of requests: anomalous features

It will be useful to note three anomalous features in relation to the admission and rejection of requests for interpretation. First, the simple fact without more that the request for interpretation as formulated by the petitioning State would constitute a re-examination of the judgment boundary decided by the tribunal and/or that it tends to go beyond the narrow and restrictive scope of interpretation is not reason enough to reject the request *in limine*. In other words, a request for interpretation, which if accepted by the tribunal as urged by the petitioning State would lead to modifications in the boundary decided by the former, need not, for that reason alone, be declared inadmissible. For one thing, it has been seen above that, at times, simple clarifications of binding parts of decisions may entail *de facto* modifications in the boundary line. It is inescapable, then, that modifications may have to be seen as a matter of law and not only exclusively of fact. The point here is that a tribunal may in the circumstances have to take into consideration factors other than modification which militate against admission. For another, the tribunal may consider the request admissible and yet may go on to reject the interpretation placed on the operative parts of the decision by the requesting party. By thus doing, it will preclude modification.

Secondly, the tribunal may decide to rule the request inadmissible and yet proceed indirectly to provide an explanation, by way of the reasoning in its judgment or award, of what it had decided in the first or earlier judgment.[466] As Merrills noted, since the rejection of a request always requires a judgment, even a decision like that in the *Asylum* case may constitute an oblique interpretation of the original judgment if the former shows that something lies outside the latter judgment.[467] 'Thus', he writes, 'even a refusal to interpret a judgment can itself say something about the parties' legal rights.'[468]

[466] See Merrills (note 300), pp. 65–6. [467] *Ibid.*, p. 65.

[468] *Ibid.*, pp. 65–6. See also Thirlway (note 226), p. 88; and Zimmermann (note 226), p. 24.

An anomalous clarification was provided in the *Portendic Claims* case. In 1783, Great Britain ceded the River Senegal, its dependencies and five of its forts to France. It retained, however, the liberty of carrying on the gum trade from the mouth of the River St John to the bay and fort of Portendic, provided that 'the English' did not 'form any permanent settlement of what nature soever in the river St John, upon the coast, or in the bay of Portendic'.[469] In 1834, France ordered its warships to arrest and then expel British merchant vessels from trading in the bay, arguing that casting anchor and landing goods for the purposes of exchanging them for gum constituted a settlement; and that the treaty of 1783 required British ships to keep under weigh and precluded crew from going onshore. France also contended subsequently that the ships were supplying an insurgent tribe in Senegal against whom the French had imposed a blockade in the bay. The British Government took the position that the blockade had not been notified to it and hence was unopposable to it.

In 1842, the parties eventually decided to refer the matter to arbitration. The King of Prussia was requested to determine whether certain British subjects had suffered injury as a result of being excluded from trading in the bay and whether France was bound to indemnify Britain for such loss.[470] In his award of 1843,[471] the King decided that injury was established and that indemnity was indeed due to the British Government. The three States, that is, Great Britain, France and Prussia, set up a Commission for Liquidation, but only paltry sums of money were awarded with respect to two of the ships.[472] Dissatisfied, the owners approached the British Government and claimed further indemnity. It was asserted that the scope of the arbitration was limited to examining the issue of formal French notification of the blockade and hence the sums awarded were essentially nominal in character. However, the admissibility of a portion of the claims depended upon examining the legality or otherwise of the blockade itself,[473] and this had not been done.

Although it was confident that the King had considered the legality of the blockade, the British Government agreed to request the Prussian

[469] See British Statement Relative to the Claims Arising out of Measures Adopted by France in the Years 1834 and 1835, Inclosure in Earl of Aberdeen to Earl of Westmoreland, 4 April 1843, 34 BFSP 1071, at p. 1072; and, generally, Parry (ed.), *A British Digest of International Law Compiled Principally from the Archives of the Foreign Office*, Part III, *Territory International Waterways Rights in Foreign Territory*, vol. 2b, London, 1967, pp. 658–65.

[470] Declaration of 14 November 1842, 34 BFSP 1064.

[471] 42 BFSP 1377.

[472] Parry (note 469), p. 663; and, for the full award of liquidation, see Ward to Earl of Aberdeen, 9 October 1844, 34 BFSP 1088, at pp. 1091 and 1093. The two ships were *The Governor Temple* and *The Industry*.

[473] Parry (note 469), p. 663.

Government to provide an explanation. The position of the Prussian Government was that an interpretation of the award could scarcely take place but by means of a formal act which would finally require the express sanction of the King himself. Even so, the Prussian Minister of Foreign Affairs asserted that 'there is no question here of such interpretation; the elucidations which [the British Government wish] to obtain, relate only to the manner in which the King and his Government have understood the Declaration . . . by which England and France submitted their difference to the arbitration of His Majesty.'[474]

Eventually, therefore, it was the 'Cabinet of the King' which, 'being perfectly able to supply these elucidations in an authentic manner', clarified the point that the King had pronounced upon all aspects of the British claims; and that this demonstrated the fact that the scope of the arbitral process was not a restrictive one. The Cabinet also explained that the legality of the blockade of 1835 had been examined and, indeed, the award was founded upon the result of such an examination. In effect, therefore, while an 'authentic' explanation was no doubt provided, albeit indirectly, the Prussian Government maintained the position that the arbitrator was unable (directly) to provide an elucidation without following a formal sovereign procedure. The main legal feature of this is that, because the elucidation was provided by the *Cabinet* of the King, the interpretation was in fact an *executive*, as opposed to an *arbitral*, explanation of the award. Simpson and Fox have commented on this by writing[475]

> Arbitrators have, however, sometimes felt able, at the request of one party, to make statements, which, while not formally 'interpretations', served to clarify the award. [In] the *Portendic* case, where the King of Prussia, while professing to be unable to give an interpretation save at the request of both parties, in effect, satisfied the wish of the United Kingdom for an interpretation, by stating how he had understood his terms of reference.

In short, a tribunal may proceed to reject a request for interpretation and/or may even deny that an interpretation is being given, and may still provide a *de facto* clarification. This cannot, of course, be an ideal technique, and yet it may nonetheless be an unintended consequence of the tribunal's decision. It was this inadvertent and partial clarification which came under the scrutiny of Judge Koroma in the *Interpretation of the*

474 *Ibid.*, p. 664.

475 Supra (note 136), p. 245. Further, see Bos, who wrote that, 'for all practical purposes the *Portendick Case* may serve as a valid example of the interpretation of *res judicata* along procedural lines less strict than those maintained by the International Court': Bos (note 226), p. 202.

Preliminary Judgment in the Cameroon–Nigeria Land and Maritime Boundary case. Adverting to the fact that the Court had declared in its majority judgment that the Nigerian request was inadmissible, Judge Koroma noted in his Dissenting Opinion that the Court had nonetheless made clear in its (interpretative) judgment that it drew no distinction between the notions of 'incidents' and 'facts' referred to in its preliminary judgment. This, he stated, 'can be read as an oblique, though, in my view, unsatisfactory "interpretation", which does not clarify the meaning and scope of that judgment. Regrettably, by taking this position the Court would, on the one hand, seem to be trying to meet the object of the request while at the same time rejecting the request itself.'[476] He went on to criticise this by noting that, while this explanation 'would appear to provide a measure of interpretation, it still [left] open the possibility of misconstruction and confusion, which, if not clarified, could even be at variance with the relevant provisions of the Statute and Rules of Court'.[477]

Conversely, a tribunal may rule a request admissible and still manage to avoid providing formal clarification in its interpretative phase, relying instead on other aspects of its judgment as a basis for clarification and indirect fulfilment of its task. It was thus in *Application for Revision and Interpretation of the 1982 Judgment* as regards the first sector of the boundary. Tunisia claimed, *inter alia*, that it needed clarification 'as regards the hierarchy to be established between the criteria adopted by the Court, having regard to the impossibility of simultaneously applying these criteria to determine the starting-point of the delimitation line as well as the bearing of that line from due north'.[478] Offering its own interpretation of the judgment, Tunisia argued that the boundary which ought to be taken into consideration for the establishment of the delimitation line could only be the south-eastern boundary of the Tunisian petroleum concession permit.[479]

In its view, the co-ordinates through which the line was to run as indicated in the 1982 judgment had no 'intrinsic significance'. Hence, they did not have any binding force insofar as they were based on the mistaken belief that the Libyan petroleum concessions lines in the south-eastern corner of the first sector of the boundary were perfectly aligned with the Tunisian petroleum concession permit of 1961. It is clear that, had it confirmed Tunisia's interpretation of the relevant passage, the Court

[476] ICJ Reports 1999, p. 49.

[477] *Ibid.*, p. 51. On this, Thirlway wrote: 'On all three Nigerian submissions, the Court in fact is giving an interpretation of the kind given by Pontius Pilate: *quod scripsi, scripsi*': Thirlway (note 226), p. 88.

[478] ICJ Reports 1985, p. 219.

[479] *Ibid.*

would have had to replace the boundary 'indirectly'[480] provided by it in the 1982 judgment. It was for this reason that Libya contested Tunisia's claims by stating that 'the essence of the Tunisian request is not interpretation, but something quite different . . . Such a request is nothing more than a bald plea for a revision of the Court's Judgment and for the elimination of a key part of paragraph 133 C (2) of the Court's *dispositif* . . . In this manner, Tunisia attempts to alter what the Court has already decided with binding force.'[481]

While the Court examined the substance of Tunisia's claims regarding the first sector of the boundary, it did so without reference to any *ulterior purposes* behind its application for interpretation, an approach in contrast with that adopted by it in connection with the second sector of the boundary, reference to which has been made in section III.c above. In any event, rejecting Libya's arguments regarding the inadmissibility of the request, and deciding that there was indeed a dispute on a question of interpretation of the judgment between the parties,[482] the Court turned to the substance of Tunisia's contentions. It accepted that there was indeed some weight to Tunisia's claims regarding the need for clarification of the meaning and scope of part of the judgment's operative clause, namely, the matter of the precise co-ordinates through which the boundary ought to run.

The Court held that, while the line had to be determined with precision by the technical experts, the co-ordinates were not in themselves approximate,[483] and that reference to the petroleum concessions in the *dispositif* was chiefly by way of an explanation; these considerations were not part of the description of the delimitation line itself.[484] Thus, the 'request for interpretation', the Court ruled:

is therefore founded upon a misreading of the purport of the relevant passage of the operative clause of the 1982 Judgment. The Court therefore finds the Tunisian request for interpretation in the first sector to be admissible, but is unable to uphold Tunisia's submission as to the correct interpretation of the Judgment in this respect; and since it has been possible for the Court to clear up the misunderstanding in the course of its reasoning on the admissibility of the request for revi-

[480] Strictly speaking, the International Court of Justice was not requested by the parties to delimit the continental shelf boundary, but only to indicate the rules and principles applicable to such a delimitation. The 'delimitation' provided by the Court was in effect an application of the principles, and hence not a line of delimitation properly so called.

[481] *Pleadings, Application for Revision and Interpretation* (note 337), p. 74. See also the majority judgment, ICJ Reports 1985, p. 217.

[482] ICJ Reports 1985, pp. 217–18.

[483] *Ibid.*, p. 209.

[484] *Ibid*. Cf. the Separate Opinion of Judge Ad Hoc Bastid, *ibid.*, p. 252.

sion, the Court considers that there is nothing to be added to what it has already said as to the meaning and scope of the 1982 Judgment in that reasoning.[485]

It follows therefore that, in all the right circumstances, a State Party may be able to evoke, in howsoever an irregular manner, an explanation from the tribunal, which, even if it does not conform to the interpretation placed on an operative part of the judgment advocated by one of the parties, clarifies the confusion even in its rejection. This dialectic acquires significance when viewed in light of the advantages to be gained in imparting greater continuity to judicial boundary delimitations and minimising disruption caused by requests for interpretation.

f. Interpretation in the context of the general task of the tribunal

The final point here involves reference to the fact that the limits of the interpretative process are conditioned not only by the operative part or parts of the first decision, but also by the scope of the request for interpretation itself. This means that the tribunal will not accede to a request for interpretation of the relevant parts of the judgment where the request in essence has no direct bearing on the general or central task of the tribunal, even though it may have a direct connection with the *dispositif* and/or relevance to the general matter of delimitation. When in *Application for Revision and Interpretation of the 1982 Judgment* Tunisia requested the Court 'altogether subsidiarily' to order an expert survey for the purpose of ascertaining the exact co-ordinates of the most westerly point of the Gulf of Gabes, Libya failed specifically to protest against such a request.

Even so, the Court reviewed the request in order to dispose fully of the case. It noted that, although Article 50 of the Statute allowed the Court to order at any time the carrying out of an enquiry or of commissioning of an expert opinion, 'this provision must be read in relation to the terms in which jurisdiction is conferred upon the Court in a specific case; the purpose of the expert opinion must be to assist the Court in giving judgment upon the issues submitted to it for decision.'[486] The Court observed that the present case was concerned with interpretation of the 1982 judgment and that it could not add anything to the original decision which had acquired the force of *res judicata*. It held that it would have been appropriate to accede to Tunisia's request 'only if the determination of the exact co-ordinates of the most westerly point of the Gulf of Gabes

485 *Ibid.*, p. 220. 486 *Ibid.*, p. 228.

were required to enable the Court to give judgment on the matters submitted to it'.[487] Insofar as this was not the aim of the proceedings currently before it, the Court felt unable to agree to the ordering of an expert survey.

The brief discussion above demonstrates the fact that the notion of interpretation, especially its scope and purpose, is a complex one which resists simplification. While it is agreed that interpretation cannot be used as a guise for a re-examination of the decision and a relocation of the boundary, it is also the case that, in some instances, interpretation without re-examination of the judgment and/or the boundary may be neither desirable nor, indeed, possible. The tension between the two can be effected by looking, *inter alia*, at the *ex tunc* effects of the original decision. This is discussed presently. It needs to be repeated that the mere fact that a request for interpretation will lead to modification/revision of the boundary is not sufficient reason to dismiss the request *in limine*. A fuller discussion on the matter appears in the concluding part of this work.

It would appear, therefore, that, as in most cases, a correct balance must be struck, and thus, where a narrow approach predicated on a strict test can only prolong the dispute and complicate matters, then, in those circumstances, an approach based on the reality of the legal situation would recommend itself. Where the dispute arises clearly from a *bona fide* source of confusion over the meaning of an operative passage or passages, then an interpretative judgment ought not to be denied only on the basis that the implementation of a judgment cannot be postponed. In other words, the balance must be struck in favour of providing an interpretative judgment, and less weight would need to be placed on the need simply to avoid delay in the decision's implementation.

V. Interpretation and the principle of res judicata

The fourth important aspect of the notion of interpretation involves evaluating its relation to the *res judicata* rule. This will be done in two stages. The first stage is predicated on supplying an account of the various points of contact between these two categories of the law. Analysis at the second stage is concerned with an attempt to reconcile these apparently conflicting rules of law.

[487] *Ibid*. It made a reference to *Interpretation of Judgments Nos. 7 and 8 (Factory at Chorzów)* (note 273), p. 21.

a. General points of contact

As far as the interlocking points of contact are concerned, the first arises logically from the observations made above in sections II and III above. It was seen there that a tribunal can provide an interpretative decision only in respect of those parts of a judgment or an award which have been settled with binding force by the previous tribunal, and are therefore dispositive in character. It is crucial, therefore, that, in order to carry out its task, the tribunal must be able to identify those parts of the judgment which have indeed been conclusively settled by it. It follows that an interpretative decision is available exclusively in respect of passages which are in effect *res judicata*. Conversely, then, *res judicata* is a defining characteristic for the purposes of interpretation.

This approach was evident in *Request for Interpretation of the Judgment in the Asylum Case*, where the International Court of Justice observed: '[T]he object of interpretation must be solely to obtain clarification of the meaning and scope of what the Court has *decided with binding force*.'[488] Hence, although, as noted above, interpretation can only be provided for points decided primarily in the *dispositif*, as the Court of Arbitration observed in *United Kingdom–France Continental Shelf Interpretive Decision*, 'if findings in the reasoning constitute a condition essential to the decision given in the *dispositif*, these findings are to be considered as included among the points settled *with binding force* in the decision'.[489]

Similarly, in the *Laguna del Desierto* boundary case, the tribunal stressed the fundamental rule that '[a] judgment having the authority of *res judicata* is judicially binding on the parties to the dispute',[490] and went on to note: 'The force of an international judgment as *res judicata* relates primarily to its operative part (*dispositif*), that is to say that part in which the tribunal rules on the dispute and establishes the rights and obligations of the parties.'[491] It added that the 'jurisprudence has likewise accepted that propositions contained in the grounds of judgment ("considerations") which constitute the necessary logical antecedents to the operative part have the same binding force as the latter'.[492]

[488] ICJ Reports 1950, p. 402 (emphasis added).

[489] 54 ILR 170 (emphasis added). See also the Secretariat's Commentary on Arbitral Procedure (note 226), pp. 96–7; and Lowe, 'Res Judicata and the Rule of Law in International Arbitration', 8 (1996) *African Journal of International and Comparative Law* 38.

[490] 113 ILR 43.

[491] *Ibid.*, pp. 43–4. See also the dissent of Judge Galindo Pohl, *ibid.*, pp. 82–7.

[492] *Ibid.*, p. 44.

The corollary to this, as Rosenne observed, is the 'general principle – which applies with equal force to the preliminary question of the admissibility of the request for interpretation – . . . that interpretation cannot go beyond the limits of the judgment. That derives from the basic notion of *res judicata*.'[493] The converse of this is simply that points *not* conclusively settled by the tribunal are not binding on the parties and are accordingly not *res judicata*. It would follow that, in these circumstances, the tribunal can hardly be requested to supply a judicial explanation regarding matters on which it has not provided a binding and conclusive decision, or on matters to be conclusively decided upon in a different set of proceedings by the same tribunal or a different one. Clearly, such parts of a decision need not be the focus of judicial attention inasmuch as nothing turns on them.

The second point of contact for interpretation and *res judicata* is that the latter constitutes a rationale for the rule (discussed in section IV.b above) which states that the interpretative process is to be seen restrictively and that the latter process cannot be used to reopen matters conclusively settled by the tribunal in its original judgment. This is particularly true of judgments and awards dealing with territorial disputes and boundary delimitation. Thus *res judicata* provides, in general principle, immunity from further, subsequent judicial re-examination in the guise of interpretation. As an important principle informing and governing the interpretative process, the *res judicata* maxim provides a kind of impediment to an unencumbered interpretative process.

An important lesson in this respect comes from the *dicta* of the Court of Arbitration in *Dubai* v. *Sharjah*, where the Court drew a distinction between boundaries established by way of treaties and arbitral or judicial proceedings, and a frontier established, as in that case, by way of administrative decisions. It held: 'In the first hypothesis, except in a case of nullity, the principles of *pacta sunt servanda* or of *res judicata* could be invoked to prevent the boundary so settled being called again into question.' Interestingly, although the boundary established by the latter process reflected political and economic considerations, that is, non-legal criteria, the Court warned that this was 'not to say that such administrative decisions may be lightly set aside'.[494] The very fact, then, that a case before a tribunal is concerned with a frontier created by way of a valid administrative process will invite the tribunal to exercise a

493 See Rosenne (note 226), p. 1670.

494 91 ILR 579. See Dubai's submissions on the matter, *ibid.*, p. 553. Further, see *Eritrea* v. *Ethiopia (Decision on Interpretation)*, supra (note 378), para. 16.

measure of caution in favour of continuity. This measure of caution reflects a more general rule with respect to boundaries, a rule which appears along the gamut of the law of title to territory, one aspect of which is *quieta non mouvre*. As the Permanent Court of Arbitration observed in the *Grisbadarna* case, 'it is a settled principle of the law of nations that a state of things which actually exists and has existed for a long time should be changed as little as possible'.[495] *A fortiori*, a boundary established by an award will be *res judicata* for the purposes of modification by way of the interpretive process.

The question of *res judicata* was raised in *New Hampshire* v. *Maine*[496] in the context of a judgment given in 1977 in the form of a consent decree of the United States Supreme Court in which the middle of the main navigable channel of the Piscataqua, the boundary river, was the agreed frontier line between the two New England states. The case is discussed in detail in Chapter 6, section VI below in the context of acquiescence and estoppel. Suffice it to say here that one of the grounds of objection maintained by Maine and the United States Government (as *amicus*) was that the case rested *vel non* on the issue of *res judicata*, commonly called claim and issue preclusion.[497] The argument phrased by the latter was that:

> Because the Court's resolution of those issues was clear and essential to its decree, New Hampshire is precluded from relitigating them, and, in particular, from now claiming that its boundary with Maine along the Piscataqua River is at the low water mark on the Maine shore. A decree of this Court adjudicating the boundary between two States is intended to constitute a permanent determination on which the respective States and numerous private parties may rely. Where, as here, the Court's decree also expressly sets forth the Court's determination of underlying issues of law and fact on which the decree itself is predicated and which the Court and the parties therefore found necessary to address, the decree must be understood, absent a strong showing to the contrary, to constitute a definitive resolution – and to bar relitigation – of those issues as well. New Hampshire has made no contrary showing here.[498]

The Court, however, decided that the *res judicata* doctrines of both claim and issue preclusion were not the precise controlling criteria, and dismissed the petition of New Hampshire by reference to and in favour of the application of the doctrine of judicial estoppel.[499] This is discussed presently.

[495] 4 (1909) AJIL 226, at p. 233. [496] 532 US 742 (2001).
[497] *Ibid.*, pp. 4–5; and see Brief for the United States as Amicus Curiae, pp. 14–19.
[498] Brief for the United States as Amicus Curiae (note 497), p. 20. Footnote number deleted.
[499] 532 US 742, at p. 749 (2001).

By contrast, the doctrine of *res judicata* defined the Court's approach to the problem in the Atlantic sector in *United Kingdom–France Continental Shelf Interpretive Decision*. Although the facts have been stated above,[500] it will, for the purposes of convenience and presentation, be useful briefly to indicate some of the main contentions of the United Kingdom appropriate to this aspect of the study. The United Kingdom Government's position was that the Court had identified the principles and method of delimitation in paragraphs 251, 253 and 254 of the 1977 decision, but that the line delimited in the *dispositif* and traced on the Boundary-Line Chart were both at variance with these three paragraphs which, it was claimed, 'embodied' the decision of the Court on the matter.[501] Insofar as the latter two representations of the boundary could not be reconciled with the findings of the Court in the said paragraphs, the United Kingdom argued that the 1977 decision 'should be interpreted so as to resolve the contradiction in favour of the evident intention embodied in these paragraphs; and that "the Boundary Line Chart and, as necessary, the text of the Decision should be rectified accordingly".'[502]

France's contention was that there was no contradiction between the decision and the chart: the boundary delimited was in perfect accord with the Court's reasoning in paragraphs 249–51.[503] More important for present purposes is the fact that France objected to the request on the ground that the interpretative process would in fact constitute a revision or modification of the decision, as opposed to the mere correction of a material error.[504] France also claimed that, if a strict application of the half-effect method were to be employed, basepoints other than those used by the Court would have to be taken into account.

The Court accepted the French argument that the half-effect solution was not an application of, but an equitable variant of, the equidistance principle expressing a necessarily approximate appreciation of diverse considerations;[505] and that the method for implementing it was devised as a modified, rather than a strict, application of the equidistance method.[506] Accordingly, the Court held that there was no incompatibility between paragraphs 251, 253 and 254 on the one side and the method of calculating the course of the line between points M and N employed by the Expert and adopted by the Court in the *dispositif* on the other. 'It follows', it added, 'that the principle of *res judicata* applies, and that it is

[500] See section III.b of this chapter. [501] 54 ILR 175–6. [502] *Ibid*., p. 177.
[503] *Ibid.* [504] *Ibid*., p. 193. [505] *Ibid*., pp. 195, 197 and 201. [506] *Ibid*., pp. 201–2.

not open to the Court to entertain the request of the United Kingdom for the rectification of this segment of the boundary.'[507] In effect, the Court clarified the misunderstanding evident in the position adopted by the United Kingdom, and thus in one important sense fulfilled its task, but rejected the claim made by that State by relying on the *res judicata* rule as a justification for not modifying its finding.

The International Court of Justice in the *Interpretation of the Preliminary Judgment in the Cameroon–Nigeria Land and Maritime Boundary* case forcefully confirmed this approach. Discussing the admissibility of the Nigerian request, the Court noted in general terms that:

> The question of the admissibility of requests for interpretation of the Court's judgments needs particular attention because of the need to avoid impairing the finality, and delaying the implementation, of these judgments. It is not without reason that Article 60 of the Statute lays down, in the first place, that judgments are 'final and without appeal'. Thereafter, the Article provides that, in the case of a 'dispute as to the meaning or scope of the judgment', it shall be construed by the Court upon the request of any party. The language and structure of Article 60 reflect the primacy of the principle of *res judicata*. That principle must be maintained.

The Court went on to reiterate the principle it had:

> previously held [in the *Request for Interpretation of the Judgment in the Asylum Case*], namely that [t]he real purpose of the request must be to obtain an interpretation of the judgment. This signifies that its object must be solely to obtain clarification of the meaning and the scope of what the Court has decided with binding force, and not to obtain an answer to questions not so decided. Any other construction of the Statute would nullify the provision of the article that the judgment is final and without appeal.[508]

It rejected Nigeria's request for interpretation because the latter's version of what the Court had meant to state, namely, that the dispute before the Court did not include any alleged incidents other than, at most, those specified in Cameroon's Application of 29 March 1994 and Additional Application of 6 June 1994, was a submission which the Court had categorically rejected in its judgment of 11 June 1998.[509] 'The Court', it held, 'would

[507] *Ibid.*, pp. 202–3.

[508] ICJ Reports 1999, pp. 36–7. See also the Dissenting Opinion of Judges Koroma, *ibid.*, p. 52, and Weeramantry, *ibid.*, p. 43. Cf. Thirlway, who questions the logic of the Court's observations by stating that it is in no way a contradiction or qualification of the principle of *res judicata* to recognise a possibility of authoritative interpretation: Thirlway (note 226), p. 79.

[509] *Land and Maritime Boundary between Cameroon and Nigeria (Preliminary Objections)*, ICJ Reports 1998, p. 275.

therefore be unable to entertain this first submission without calling into question the effect of the Judgment concerned as *res judicata*.'[510]

The third point of contact between interpretation and *res judicata* involves the meaning and definition of words and phrases. The proposition here is that new or different meanings cannot be given to words and phrases used by the original tribunal, for to do so may result in the alteration of the judgment and judgment boundary. As the Tribunal in *Laguna del Desierto* observed succinctly, 'the meaning of the terms used in an arbitral award also forms part of the *res judicata* and neither of the parties can change it'.[511] Meanings, it observed, could not be modified by usage subsequent to the judgment nor by any linguistic developments or by the activities or the decisions of one of the parties to the dispute.[512] It was in light of these observations that the Tribunal undertook its consideration of the meaning of the term 'water-parting' as used in the award of 1902, and 'local water-parting' as used in the Report of the Technical Commission.[513]

Argentina attempted to persuade the Tribunal that the notion of a 'water-parting' ought to be interpreted in light of the 'common meaning' held at that time when the notion was used in the award, and that it simply meant a continuous orographic line separating fluvial basins.[514] The Chilean Government argued that the award had used the descriptive term 'local' to distinguish it from the 'continental' water-parting. Its view was that, while the former geographical feature separated rivers which ran into one ocean alone, the continental water-parting was an orographic line separating all the waters flowing into the Atlantic from those flowing into the Pacific.[515] Argentina countered by claiming that the terms 'local' and 'continental' were not significant: they were merely 'accessory notions' to the simple geographical concept of the watershed,[516] the main feature of which was that the line could not cut across rivers and lakes if it were to qualify as a water-parting. Chile, however, said that, given the history and circumstances of the dispute, the latter criterion was not as crucial or determinant as the requirement of the local–continental divide of a watershed. The Argentine line, it claimed, lay partly along the continental divide as opposed to the local water-parting stipulated in the Report; and, inasmuch as there was no continuous local water-parting between the two recognised points, Boundary Post 62 and Mount Fitzroy, the Report did not coincide with geographic reality.[517]

[510] ICJ Reports 1999, p. 38. [511] 113 ILR 44. [512] *Ibid*., p. 62.
[513] See, generally, *ibid*., pp. 60–8. [514] *Ibid*., p. 61. [515] *Ibid*. [516] *Ibid*.
[517] *Ibid*. See also the dissent of Judge Galindo Pohl, *ibid*., pp. 134–46.

In its examination of these issues, the Tribunal discovered that Chile, too, had asserted before the British arbitrator in 1902 that a water-parting must be understood in light of the customary meaning it had acquired in various treaties and that it could not cross any watercourses within the extent of the territory covered by it.[518] It was the Tribunal's view, therefore, that the two parties were actually in agreement at that time regarding the meaning of the expression 'water-parting', a notion which fulfilled an essential function in the award of 1902.[519] If its meaning were changed, the substance of the award would also change, and, accordingly, the Tribunal held 'that the expression "water-parting" in the Award of 1902 forms part of the *res judicata* and is not susceptible of any subsequent modification by usage, by linguistic developments, or by the activity or the decisions of one of the parties to the dispute'.[520]

The Tribunal also dismissed another Chilean argument, namely, that the tribunal ought not to apply the 1902 award in light of modern geographic knowledge of hitherto unexplored frontier areas, for to do so would constitute revising the award by way of a retrospective consideration of new facts. The Tribunal rejected this claim by taking the view that, in the disputed sector, with which it was only concerned, the frontier followed a natural feature which did not depend on accurate geographical knowledge of the area, but only on its true configuration. The ground remained as it had always been, and consequently the 'local water-parting' existent in 1902 was the same water-parting which could be determined at the time of the arbitral proceedings in 1994. It noted that the purpose of the proceedings was not for raising questions dealing with the retrospective application of geographical knowledge acquired subsequently.[521]

The last point of contact is the rule that, despite the *res judicata* immunity from re-examination of the judgment, States are free to agree to vary the terms of the decision. This matter was discussed in section IV.d of this chapter in the context of modification and revision, and the basic rule is applicable here as well. It will suffice to refer to *Application for Revision and Interpretation of the 1982 Judgment* where the Court examined Tunisia's request with regard to the ordering of an expert survey to determine the exact co-ordinates of the most westerly point on the Gulf of Gabes. Although it could have done so, the Court observed that it had elected not to determine this point in the 1982 judgment. Nor did it agree to order an expert survey for this purpose. It went on:

[518] *Ibid.*, p. 63. [519] *Ibid.*, p. 67. See also p. 72. [520] *Ibid.*, pp. 67–8.
[521] *Ibid.*, p. 75.

Nevertheless, it did not do so, preferring to leave this task to the experts of the parties. Its decision in this respect is covered by the force of *res judicata*. This does not, however, mean that the force of *res judicata* is such as to prevent the parties returning to the Court to present a joint request that it should order an expert survey to establish the precise co-ordinates of the most westerly point of the Gulf of Gabes. But they would have to do so by means of an agreement.[522]

It must be emphasised that this aspect of Tunisia's application was not one which fell into the category of either a request for interpretation or revision of the judgment. Nonetheless, the proposition in general terms is that the rule of *res judicata* is a general rule which precludes re-examination of an issue decided with binding force, but, should the States wish to override this rule and request the tribunal to reopen one or more issues decided, then the tribunal will not be likely to reject the request on the strength of the *res judicata* rule alone, provided that there are no other countervailing factors preventing the tribunal from acceding to this request, including – and this is particularly true of the International Court of Justice – abuse of process, or where reopening the issues would not further clarify or shed new light on the various points in issue.

b. Reconciliation and harmonisation

It was noted above in section IV.d above that, at times, the interpretation of a judgment may lead to the modification or revision of the judgment and judgment boundary, and that therefore this process may appear to conflict with the *res judicata* rule. Given this problem, it is important to reconcile these two categories of the law. An attempt at reconciliation entails reference to the following facts.

First, it is important to distinguish between effects *in law* and effects viewed in light of the *physical facts and acts* on the ground. Once this dichotomy between law and fact is understood, then reconciliation between the modification/revision of a judgment boundary by way of interpretation presents little difficulty. The proposition here is predicated on the fact that the remedying of defects and ambiguities in the original decision by way of interpretation may entail, on a factual and realistic basis, modifications in the judgment and the judgment boundary (where relevant); but these modifications cannot, in terms of law, constitute a revision of the decision or the boundary, not least because the interpretative decision merely clarifies the status and location of the boundary as

[522] ICJ Reports 1985, p. 228.

it always had been understood to have existed. As the Permanent Court of International Justice observed in *Chorzów Factory (Interpretation of Judgments Nos. 7 and 8)*: 'The interpretation adds nothing to the decision, which has acquired the force of *res judicata*, and can only have binding force within the limits of what was decided in the judgment construed.'[523] To that extent, then, the 'new' boundary emerging from the interpretative decision will have effects *ex tunc*. By way of abundant caution, effects *ex tunc* would normally only be applicable where the second tribunal is vested with the power to *interpret* the first decision, as opposed to the power to *delimit* the line *de novo*.[524] This is particularly true of material errors. While the Court in the *United Kingdom–France Continental Shelf Interpretive Decision* case ruled out making adjustments to the boundary in the Atlantic sector on the ground, among others, of *res judicata*, it did not hesitate to adjust the line in the Channel Islands sector once it was shown to the satisfaction of the Court that the adjustments were in the nature of rectification of a material error. It held:

> The function of the Court under Article 10, paragraph 2, is to declare definitively the meaning and scope of its Decision of 30 June 1977, rather than to decide anew the course of the boundary. This function of the Court of Arbitration considers it will duly discharge if it now prescribes with binding effect the nature of the rectification required to harmonize paragraph 2 of the *dispositif* with the Court's findings in paragraph 202 of the Decision.[525]

The logic is that, when States elect to empower a tribunal to *interpret* a decision and remedy the ambiguities and errors, or both, contained therein, they manifest an interest in preserving, as opposed to nullifying, the first decision. Changes to the boundary made in light of the interpretative decision do not constitute modification or acts of revision but adjustments which most closely accord with the intentions of the original decision, provided that (i) the interpretative process is not used as a *pretext* for securing modifications or adjustments; and (ii) the request for interpretation cannot realistically be fulfilled without reopening the proceedings on the basis of fresh arguments not addressed in the original decision.

The *Palena* arbitration is a case in point (see Map 4). In 1965, after having failed to resolve their differences arising out of the flawed 1902 award and the resulting demarcation impasse between Boundary Posts 16 and

[523] Supra (note 273), p. 21.
[524] States, to be sure, may decide to attribute such effects even in *de novo* delimitations where they are so minded.
[525] 54 ILR 174.

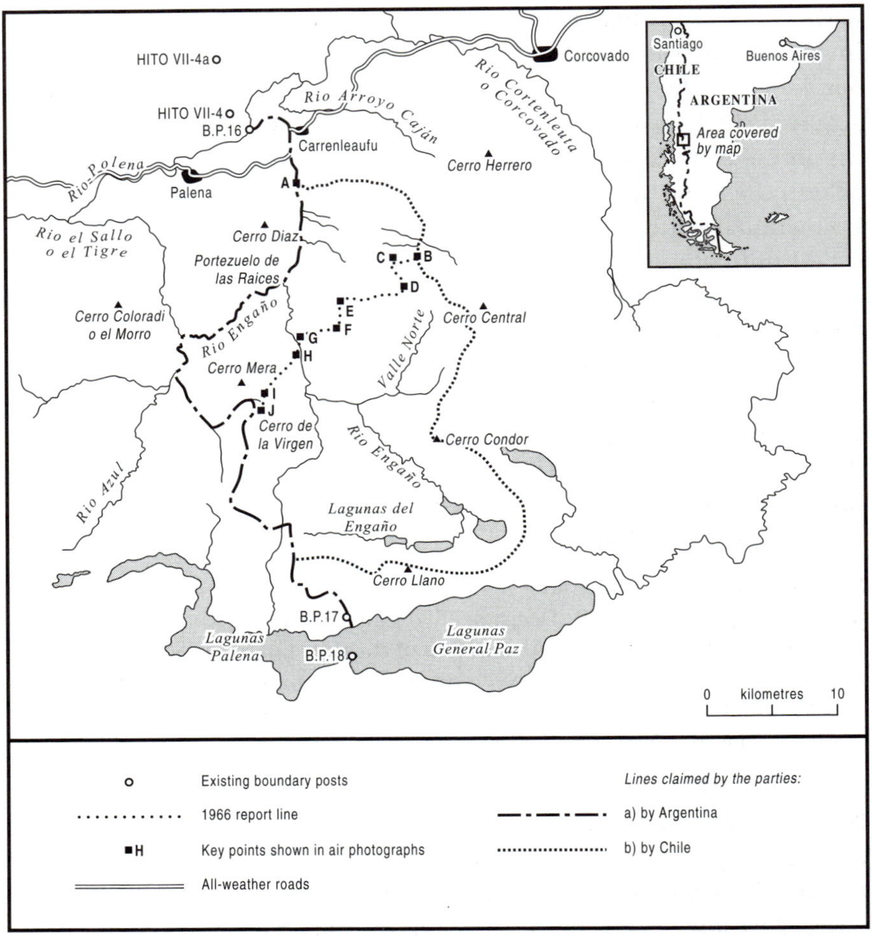

Map 4 *Argentina* v. *Chile (Palena)* arbitration

17, Argentina and Chile referred the matter to the Court of Arbitration to consider, *inter alia*, the question of the 'proper interpretation and fulfilment of that Award' with a view to delimiting a boundary in that sector.[526] The Court observed that the phrase 'interpretation and fulfilment' was a comprehensive expression which authorised it to examine the demarcation of 1903 and its antecedent, the award of 1902, and that it also authorised, nay required, the Court, while avoiding any revision or modification of the 1902 award, nevertheless to supply any deficiencies therein in a manner consistent as far as possible with the

[526] 38 ILR 23.

arbitrator's intentions.[527] When the Court thereafter drew the line between Boundary Posts 16 and 17, the delimitation was in law and fact the first time ever that the boundary had actually been delimited between the two States in a manner which accorded with the geographical realities on the ground; yet, it was neither a new nor a revised boundary in the legal sense; it was, to be sure, a modified or adjusted boundary as compared to what the arbitrator had delimited in 1902.

Similarly, in *Laguna del Desierto*, the same two parties requested the Arbitral Tribunal to decide the course of the frontier line between Boundary Post 62 and Mount Fitzroy by way of interpreting and applying the award of 1902, in accordance with international law.[528] The Tribunal, as noted earlier, made it clear that it was not a successor to King Edward VII who had handed down the 1902 award; and that the latter, it was agreed, was not subject to any form of proceeding by way of revision, appeal or nullity.[529] The role of the Tribunal was only one of interpretation; its decision was declaratory of the meaning and content of the award. It concluded: 'Consequently, the Judgment of this Tribunal, by its very nature, has effects *ex tunc*, and the line of the frontier decided upon is the same as that which had always existed between the two States Parties to the present Arbitration.'[530] The legal position then in these circumstances is that the adjusted boundary is the one which reflects more faithfully the original decision. As Judge Galindo Pohl asserted in *Request for Revision and Interpretation of the 1994 Judgment* in the matter of effects *ex tunc* of the 1902 award:

> This . . . reflects a principle of law whereby the interpretation of a judgment is deemed to be incorporated in the original decision. In this case, the interpretative decision contained in the Judgment is deemed incorporated in the Arbitral Award of 1902, and as a result it may be said that the precision now introduced into the Award has existed as between the two States ever since 1902. In this way the Tribunal has applied a general principle of law with regard to the effects of an interpretation over time.[531]

Another aspect of this reconciliation of these two notions is the fact that, in some interpretative proceedings, both States may be prepared to go into hitherto unexamined issues when driven by a genuine desire to find a lasting, final and definitive solution to a festering sore of a problem between them, and, in such a case, they may simply decide to come to terms with the facts and reality of adjustments; the *Palena* and *Laguna del*

[527] *Ibid.*, p. 91. [528] Articles I and II of the Special Arbitral Agreement: 113 ILR 20.
[529] *Ibid.*, p. 42. [530] *Ibid.*, p. 76. [531] *Ibid.*, p. 242.

Desierto cases are examples of this kind of policy and approach. In contrast to this, where, owing to disagreement or oversight, the tribunal is not empowered with a relatively extensive right of interpretation, as was the case, for example, in *United Kingdom–France Continental Shelf Interpretive Decision*, then the tribunal will have no option but to rule out those requests which tend to go beyond the scope of interpretation. In short, the element of consent plays an important part in laying down the limits of the interpretative request, and it is this element which, in all the appropriate circumstances, relegates *res judicata* to the background.

6 Principles of interpretation

I. Preliminary observations

It will be appropriate now to state some of the basic principles of interpretation. These are the rules tribunals have relied on to guide them in the interpretation of judgments and awards of international tribunals, including their own earlier pronouncements. A few preliminary points are noteworthy in this context. First, the rules relating to the interpretation of treaties constitute a close parallel to the interpretation of the decisions of international tribunals; there is a clear analogy, albeit limited, between these two categories, and it is the case that the analogy is not lost on tribunals, not least because the rules of treaty interpretation serve as a general source of guidance to tribunals when clarifying disputed passages in the text of decisions. There is of course some difference between these two kinds of interpretative processes.

For one thing, while the rules of interpretation are well developed in the corpus of international law, in terms of both customary as well as conventional law, the Vienna Convention on the Law of Treaties[532] being the best example of the latter source of law, the interpretation of decisions is relatively less well developed, at least in the field of law currently under examination. For another, there is the intrinsic nature of the subject matter of interpretation. A treaty, of course, is a product of negotiation and compromise, and it usually represents the lowest common denominator in terms of agreement between the parties. However, the judicial or arbitral decision is exactly the opposite, for it is based on law and a judicial appreciation of the legal rights and obligations of the two States. Indeed, if it were *ex aequo et bono*, it would clearly be null and void, provided, of course,

[532] Supra, note 89.

that a settlement based on compromise and other non-legal considerations was not expressly permitted.

The essential point is that seeking clarification of the true meaning of a clause in a treaty is quite different from discovering what a tribunal actually decided in its decision, the difference lying in the nature of the sources and materials relevant to treaty interpretation and decision-based interpretation. Whereas, in treaty interpretation, the tribunal seeks to understand what, as the Court of Arbitration said in the *Palena* case, was the common will of the parties concluding the treaty,[533] in the interpretation of decisions, the tribunal is asked to clarify what was actually decided by the first tribunal by reference to the discovery of the law and facts of the case. Where incidental jurisdiction is the relevant process, and where it is asked to indicate what it had meant to say in the previous decision, the tribunal may find its task relatively easy, as compared with attempts by it to pass on rights and obligations decided by way of bilateral or multilateral treaties between international entities, namely, States and international organisations.

A rider is necessary here in order to highlight the fact that what the tribunal may have *meant to decide* in terms of its findings in the *dispositif* ought, in most cases, to be a direct reflection of what it was *required to decide* as stated in the *compromis*. In other words, a dispute on the meaning of a passage in a decision of an international tribunal may wholly or partially depend upon the interpretation of a clause in a treaty, where the *compromis* contains the precise corresponding question asked of it in the arbitral agreement between the parties. It may well be that a tribunal, mandated to provide some clarification of such an issue, will find itself having to examine the *travaux préparatoires* of the arbitral agreement and indeed the entire diplomatic history of the boundary dispute. Certainly, this is at the heart of the controversy between Canada and the United States with respect to the Dixon Entrance (this issue is discussed below in section III). Suffice it to state here that the dispute regarding the status of the Entrance and adjacent waters cannot fully be resolved without reference to the arbitral agreement of 1903 between the United Kingdom and the United States which requested the arbitral tribunal to answer and decide various questions dealing with the boundary established by the Anglo-Russian Convention of 1825 off the coast of Canada, including the point of commencement of the boundary line therein. Nor would it be fruitful if the circumstances attending the Convention of 1825 were ignored.

[533] 38 ILR 89.

Secondly, the process and principles applicable to interpretation will be influenced by the legal nature of interpretation. Where interpretation is an aspect of the tribunal's incidental jurisdiction, then the task of interpretation might not be as complex and burdensome as where the interpretation is effectively a new case and the award or judgment is itself the cause of action, that is, what has earlier been referred to as main case interpretation. This observation is predicated on the view that a tribunal will more easily be able to clarify what it had meant to say in its original decision, and, if current State practice is an indication of trends in temporal limits, then that tribunal may be asked to perform its task in about one month's time. Depending, of course, upon the complexity of the claims and counterclaims, it may be that the full panoply of rules and propositions of law relating to interpretation will have a reduced role to play; it will also be relatively easier for the tribunal to be more forthright and categorical in its decision.

The International Court of Justice's approach in *Application for Revision and Interpretation of the 1982 Judgment* illustrates this point. It clarified the fact with a measure of confidence that what it meant by the most westerly point on the Gulf of Gabes was 'simply the point on the shoreline which is further to the west than any other point on the shoreline', that, by referring to this point, the Court had 'meant exactly what it said', and that, had it meant otherwise, 'it would have said so'.[534] By contrast, main case interpretation, which could well take place years after the original decision, and before a tribunal different from the one which passed the original decision, may, relatively speaking, be more taxing, in that the tribunal will, in all probability, have to pay greater attention to a good number of preliminary questions regarding the approach, the scope and the limits of the task of interpretation. It may also have to confront issues such as evolving rules of international law.

Thirdly, it is very much the case that the principles applicable will be a direct reflection of the claims and counterclaims, and law and facts of the case, and to that extent it is neither advisable nor appropriate to be very dogmatic about the application and relevance of these principles. It is nevertheless the case – and this may be stated with some certitude – that the

[534] ICJ Reports 1985, at p. 225. The task of the Court was no doubt simplified by the fact that seven of the judges in 1985 (Judges Nagendra Singh, Oda, Ago, Lachs, Sette-Camara, Schwebel and Elias) were on the bench in 1982 when the original judgment, *Tunisia–Libya*, was handed down to the parties. Some counsel were the same in both proceedings (Messrs Bowett, Vallat, Dupuy, Virally and Colliard). On the changed composition of the Court, see Zimmermann (note 226), pp. 99–110.

principles of law relative to the interpretation of arbitral and judicial decisions in the matter of land boundaries and maritime territory are all the same. On this view, then, Judge Galindo Pohl's views in his Dissenting Opinion in the *Laguna del Desierto* case cannot be supported. His view was that: 'Those interpretative processes which have been applied in areas of the law which are in the course of development and reorganisation – for example some areas of the Law of the Sea – have no application here.'[535] To the extent that his reference is to issues relative to the adjudication of title to maritime territory, there is nothing to suggest that there is any criterion of distinction which can be sustained. In truth, the basic rules and governing rules of land title are applicable in equal measure to maritime title. The rules governing the interpretation of maritime title cases are those governing land territories. In light of these observations, the following basic principles are noteworthy.

II. Words, meanings and the general practice of international tribunals

The rules of treaty interpretation clearly have relevance here. Thus, as far as basic textual interpretation is concerned, tribunals will be guided by relevant principles dealing with interpretation in accordance with the ordinary meaning of the terms used in the decision and in light of the true intention of the tribunal. One aspect of this was set out by the Permanent Court of International Justice in the *Jaworzina* case, where it held that full effect must be given to the perfectly clear language of the decision being interpreted, and that authoritative, albeit subsequent, statements which contradict the decision could not be allowed to outweigh the text of the decision.[536] Where, similarly, there is ambiguity in the text or usage, the tribunal may hold back in deciding either way. Thus, in *Monastery of Saint-Naoum*, the Court was invited by the Yugoslav argumentation to interpret the French language term '*jusqu'à*'. This term had been used in the London Protocol of 11 August 1913, an instrument the Yugoslav Government was relying on to aver that the Conference of Ambassadors had decided to leave the monastery to it. It argued that the region from, *inter alia*, the southern shores of Lake Ochrida from the village of Lin '*jusqu'à*', or 'as far as', the monastery, had been allocated to it by the Conference of Ambassadors. It noted that, in the same paragraph, side by side with the expression '*jusqu'à Saint-Naoum*' was to be found

[535] 113 ILR 84. [536] Supra (note 107), p. 36.

the expression *'jusqu'à Phtelia'* which was shown by the facts to mean 'Phethelia inclusive'.

The Court also noted that the term had been used in numerous instances in both exclusive and inclusive senses, and therefore held that it was not able to affirm that the meaning of the word in connection with a place like the Monastery of Saint-Naoum necessarily implied either its inclusion or exclusion. The Court thus avoided making a definitive decision on the strength of an interpretation which had not been unequivocally employed.[537] The key proposition appears clearly to be that vexed issues of territory ought not to be decided solely by reference to plain, ordinary meanings of ambiguous words in a decision.

Importantly, words and the text in decisions are to be seen in light not only of consistency but also of context. Accordingly, in *Application for Revision and Interpretation of the 1982 Judgment*, the International Court of Justice confirmed that all statements and references made in the original decision must be read in its (proper) context with a view to establishing whether the Court had intended it as (i) a precise statement, (ii) an approximation for working purposes or (iii) a simple indication subject to variation.[538] By doing so, the Court was able to clarify the fact that, although the 1982 judgment was in principle binding on Libya and Tunisia, the precise effect of different segments of the judgment boundary depended, *inter alia*, on whether the Court had provided the geographical co-ordinates of the alignment as either approximate or definitive.

It is also arguable that greater care ought to be taken in attempting to understand and clarify the meanings of words and phrases used in the text of a *decision*, as opposed to the interpretation of an *agreement* between States. In the *Palena* case, the Court of Arbitration observed that it is proper to apply stricter rules to the interpretation of an award determined by an arbitrator than to a treaty which results from negotiation between two or more parties, where the process of interpretation may involve endeavouring to ascertain the common will of those parties.[539] The nub of the logic is that a judgment is intrinsically a legal instrument, both in terms of creation and effect, whereas a treaty is essentially a political process which only upon its conclusion creates a set of legal rights and

[537] PCIJ Reports, Series B, No. 9 (1924), p. 6, at p. 20. It should be noted that the Court had not been requested to provide an advisory opinion on this Protocol but on the Decision of the Conference of Ambassadors of 6 December 1922, that is, whether the Conference of Ambassadors had finally settled the Albanian–Yugoslav boundary by this decision. In order to do this, however, the Court found it necessary to interpret the relevant paragraphs of the London Protocol of 1913.

[538] ICJ Reports 1985, p. 192, at p. 219.

[539] 38 ILR 89. Cf. Bos (note 226), pp. 204–5.

obligations for the contracting parties. This intrinsic difference is reflected in an approach predicated in exercising stricter vigilance in interpreting the words and phrases of a judge or arbitrator as opposed to the compromise language of a treaty.

In *Laguna del Desierto*, the Tribunal endorsed this proposition[540] and another *Palena* rule, namely, the rule on general practice. This rule requires an interpretative tribunal to be conscious of the value, for the purposes of interpretation of a judgment, of an examination of the technique adopted by the original tribunal. Thus, where a judgment systematically treats in a similar manner, or where terms or expressions appear to be used repeatedly with the same meaning, then this can provide a useful guide to interpretation.[541] It held that there was nothing in terms of general practice in the 1902 award to allow 'local water-partings' to cut across rivers, and consequently Chile's interpretation of such water-partings could not be sustained. Moreover, the meanings of things such as water-partings could not be modified by usage subsequent to the judgment; nor by linguistic developments or activities, nor by decisions of the parties.[542] If this restriction were not maintained, then meanings different to those which the tribunal had originally ascribed to them would become applicable. This would not only distort the original meaning of the disputed text or passage. By effectively sanctioning a new meaning to a term in the decision, the interpretative process would fly in the face of the *res judicata* rule. This matter was discussed in sections IV.d and V.a of Chapter 5 above.

III. Presumption against a breach of the law

One of the rules tribunals are guided by is the rule of presumption against an interpretation which would constitute a breach of international law. Thus the decision ought to be interpreted in such a way that any meaning ascribed to it is consistent with, and does not amount to a breach of, international law, especially where the clarification sought by one of the parties would effectively imply that the previous award was wholly or partially null and void. The *Laguna del Desierto* case is instructive (see Map 5). Argentina claimed that the Chilean interpretation of the award line would effectively give it territory greater than that it had actually claimed before the Tribunal in 1902. The maximum claim line then advanced by Chile was the continental watershed, whereby the Atlantic basins would be allocated to

[540] 113 ILR 72. [541] *Ibid.* [542] *Ibid.*, p. 62.

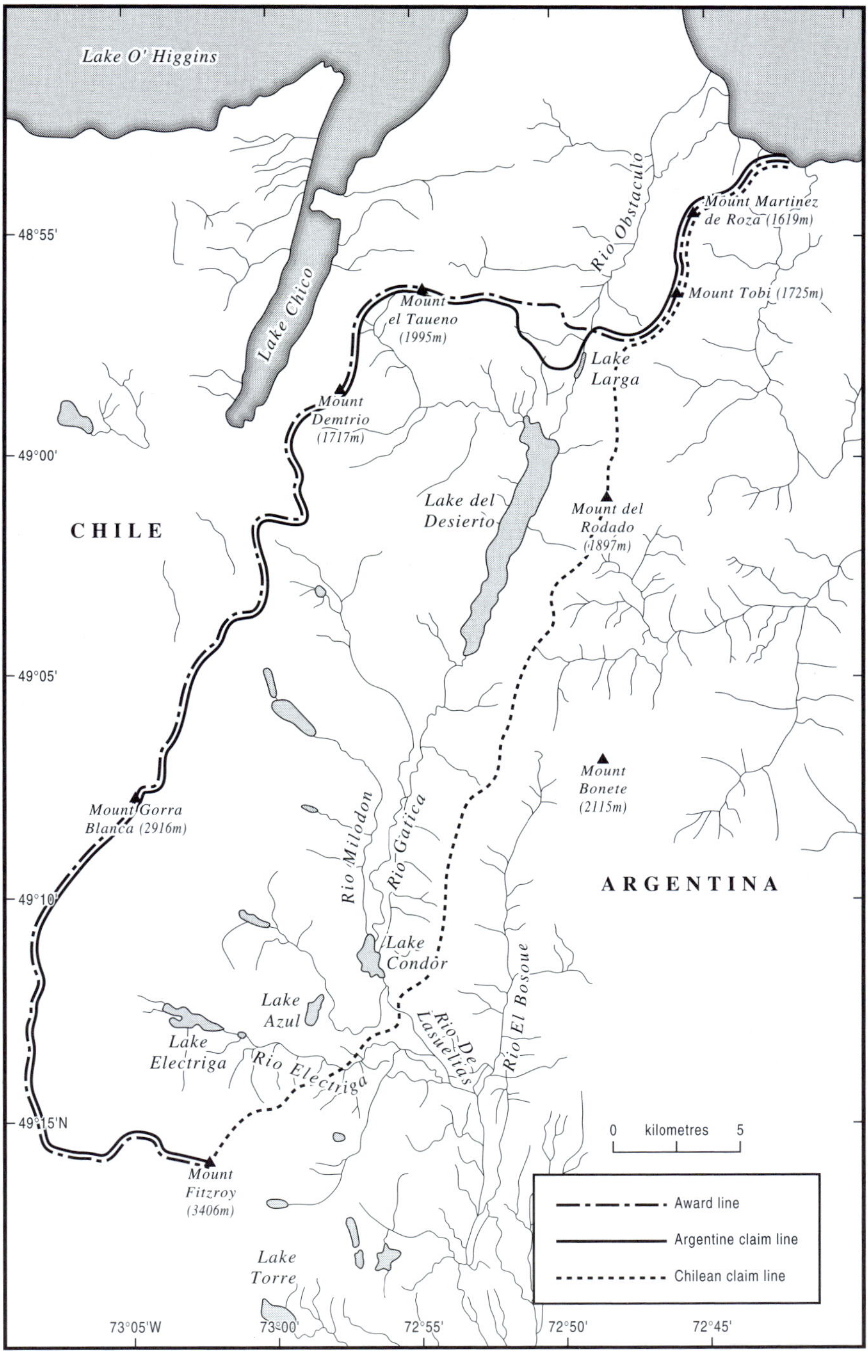

Map 5 *Argentina* v. *Chile (Laguna del Desierto)* arbitration

Argentina and the Pacific basins would go to Chile. However, before the 1991 Tribunal, Chile entered claims which gave it part of Rio Gatica, or de las Vueltas, an Atlantic basin. The point was that, if the Chilean interpretation were the correct one, then it would have meant that the arbitrator had granted Chile even more territory than it had actually claimed, and consequently the award would have been *ultra petita* and hence null and void. The Tribunal of 1991 could not countenance such an interpretation.[543]

Chile retorted that its territorial contentions in 1898–1902 were essentially based on claim lines drawn on maps in 1898 and not on the continental *divortium aquarum* principle. A comparison of the claim lines would show that its present claim did not exceed the maximum claim line of 1902. To counter the allegation that its present claim line exceeded the continental watershed, Chile argued that its claim line of 1902 could not be interpreted on the basis of current geographical knowledge.[544] The Tribunal held that Chile's claim line in 1902 was the line of the *continental divortium aquarum* as the frontier established by the Treaty of 1881 and the Protocol of 1893.[545] It went on to observe that Chile, in 1898–1902, had accepted that the principle of the continental watershed would prevail over its cartographic representations, particularly where the regions were either totally unexplored or insufficiently explored, and that a lack of knowledge of a region could not serve as a pretext for not applying this criterion.[546] The Tribunal discovered that Chile's maximum claim line included Lake San Martin (a tributary of the Pacific) and its entire basin, and that it left the basin of the Rio Gatica or de las Vueltas, which drains into Lake Viedma, a tributary of the Atlantic, to the Argentine side of the frontier;[547] and that, in 1902, Chile had in fact intended that the frontier effectively fulfil the function of separating the basin of Lake San Martin from that of the Rio Gatica.[548] The Tribunal held:

> Consequently international law will not permit us to attribute to the terms used by the British Arbitrator [King Edward VII] to define the frontier between the point on the southern shore of Lago San Martin where [Boundary Post] 62 stands today and Mount Fitzroy any meaning which grants Chile territory which, because it lies outside the said line, exceeds its maximum claim. To do so would amount to ruling that the 1902 Award infringed international law by violating the rule *non ultra petita partum*.[549]

It was explained that, in fulfilling its judicial role, a tribunal charged with interpreting a legal instrument must not only ensure that its decision has

[543] *Ibid.*, p. 46. [544] *Ibid.*, pp. 48–9. [545] *Ibid.*, p. 51. [546] *Ibid.*, pp. 55–6.
[547] *Ibid.*, p. 57. [548] *Ibid.*, p. 58. [549] *Ibid.*

the support of and conforms with international law, but it must also exclude any possibility of producing results contrary to international law.[550]

A similar situation arose in *Honduras* v. *Nicaragua* before the Honduras–Nicaragua Mixed Commission where the Chairman returned a quasi-judicial decision with respect to a twenty-kilometre segment of the boundary between these two States.[551] This was a case dealing with the interpretation of the Spanish monarch's arbitral award of 1906 after it was held valid and binding by the International Court of Justice in 1960. The Mixed Commission comprised one member each from the two States, while the Chairman, Mr Sanchez Gavito, was a Mexican national serving as Chairman of the Inter-American Peace Committee. The task of the Commission was to fix the boundary pursuant to the terms of the 1906 award. According to the latter, the boundary in the second sector started from the junction of the rivers Poteca and Guineo and then followed the boundary of an estate or land grant, the Sitio de Teotecacinte, demarcated in 1720, leaving it entirely to Nicaragua. The line terminated at a pass, Portillo de Teotecacinte.[552]

In the course of demarcation proceedings, a dispute arose with respect to part of the second sector, from a point called Murupuxi to the Portillo. Honduras contended that all the boundaries of the Sitio formed international boundaries, and that the 1906 boundary ran from Murupuxi due south in a straight line to Cruz San Bravo, the south-western corner of the Sitio, and then in a north-westerly direction to the Portillo. Nicaragua's claim was that the alignment ran in a south-westerly direction from Murupuxi straight to the pass.[553] It is crucial to note that neither interpretation of the boundary did violence to the relevant passage in the award of 1906.

One of the arguments which the Nicaraguan Government advanced against the Honduran claim line was that, in 1901, and then subsequently during the arbitral proceedings before the Spanish King, Honduras had requested recognition of the fact that from the Portillo de Teotecacinte the frontier continued downstream in the bed of the Limón River, the headwaters of which arose in the Portillo, until it joined the Guineo. The former river flowed in an arc just south of the Murupuxi–Portillo line claimed by Nicaragua as the boundary.

[550] *Ibid.*, p. 45. After delimiting the disputed region, the tribunal confirmed the fact that the line decided by it did not exceed Chile's maximum claim in 1898–1902, and, consequently, that, under international law, it did not imply that the 1902 award violated the *ultra petita* rule: *ibid.*, p. 77.

[551] 30 ILR 76.

[552] *Ibid.*, pp. 76–8.

[553] *Ibid.*, pp. 78–9.

Nicaragua asserted that the earlier Limón River line claimed by Honduras did not correspond at all with the line claimed by it before the Commission; the territory claimed earlier by Honduras was smaller in terms of extent when compared with its claim line before the Commission in 1961. The result of this discrepancy in the two claim lines was that, if the Honduran claim line of 1961 before the Commission were accepted as the correct interpretation of the 1906 award, it would have constituted giving Honduras more territory than it had claimed before the Spanish King, the arbitrator. As Nicaragua put it, the claim of the Government of Honduras regarding the line connecting Murupuxi and the Portillo was '"contrary to the very essence of the Award and to the judgment of the International Court of Justice" since it would make "the decision of King Alphonso XIII, as it pertains to the demarcation of the western region of the Sitio de Teotecacinte, a judgment that is defective by reason of what is known in law as *ultra petita*, inasmuch as it would appear to give more than it officially requested"'.[554]

The response of Honduras was that this contention was not within the competence of the Commission whose function was simply to demarcate the frontier established by the award of the King of Spain in 1906 in accordance with the demarcation of 1720. Fully aware of the difficulties regarding the legitimate sphere of action of demarcation agencies, the Chairman took the position that his Commission's task was essentially that of demarcation in accordance with the Honduras–Nicaragua Basis of Arrangement, a task complicated by the fact that, as Chairman, he had the final decision in the event of disagreement between the national representatives. He thus held that the Commission was incompetent to decide the issue, and '[c]onsequently, no attempt will be made to resolve any question of a techno-juridical nature. No pronouncement will be made on the Nicaraguan thesis of *ultra petita*.'[555] The Chairman then drew the frontier straight south for a short distance (600 metres) in the direction of Cruz San Bravo until it reached the Limón River, and then from there drew it upstream along the latter river and along one of its headwaters to the Portillo.[556]

Although it is not difficult to appreciate the cautious approach adopted by the Chairman, the fact is that the Honduran thesis was not in principle sustainable in law. The reason is that demarcation is impossible without some sort of consensus on what the terms of the award (or treaty, for that matter) actually mean. Where there is no consensus, a

[554] *Ibid.*, pp. 86. [555] *Ibid.*, p. 86–7. [556] *Ibid.*, pp. 87–9.

demarcation commission may be empowered to decide between the two disputed versions, and this was precisely the situation in this case where the Basis of Arrangement of 1961 vested the Commission with the power to decide on the location of the line in the event of disagreement between the representatives of Honduras and Nicaragua. Hence, although the ultimate task of the Commission was indeed demarcation, it is disingenuous to say that it was not competent to decide which of the two versions was the correct one or whether a third line best reflected the true meaning of the 1906 award. The point is that, where there is confusion stemming from the decision's findings, including relevant reasoning, then interpretation constitutes a crucial step in fulfilling the task of demarcation. If this is correct, then the Commission is also empowered to carry out all the tasks which further the ultimate aim of the Commission, and this includes the task of ruling out one or both interpretations of the judgment boundary on the basis of the law and facts involved. This includes deciding the *ultra petita* argument urged by Nicaragua.

In any event, it is also easy to understand Honduras' competence argument when viewed in light of the history of Central American boundary arbitrations, and clearly the problems arising from the *Costa Rica* v. *Panama* boundary arbitration and the resultant discord could not but have discouraged the Commission from embarking on this exercise. Although there are parallels of the latter case with the one under examination here, there is one crucial difference between them. In *Costa Rica* v. *Panama*, the dispute did not really turn on the question of which of the two versions of the Loubet award was the correct one; the real dispute was whether Loubet's line was void owing to *excès de pouvoir*.

The difficulty for Chief Justice White in *Costa Rica* v. *Panama* was that his task as arbitrator had not been framed in such terms; the Chief Justice was asked to interpret the Loubet line but not without an ambiguous statement hinting at broader powers, a fact relied on by Costa Rica and rejected by Panama. By contrast, the two versions before the Honduras–Nicaragua Mixed Commission were perfectly compatible with the 1906 award in terms of the delimitation provided; the problem was that the 1961 Honduran version would have been *ultra petita* by reference to the 1906 award. All that Nicaragua was asking the Commission to do was to take into account this fact in the course of the interpretative process. In this, the argument is identical with that advanced by Argentina before the Argentina–Chile arbitral tribunal with respect to the 1902 award in *Laguna del Desierto*. Had Nicaragua requested the Commission to decide whether the 1906 award was *excès de pouvoir*, then such a request would itself have been an invitation to provide a decision *excès de pouvoir*, in other words another nullity. It is clear of course that this was not the case. In other words, there is no reason why an arbitrator or judge is precluded from employing a canon of construction with a view to interpreting the earlier award or judgment, without actually deciding the issue of *ultra petita* or excess powers of that tribunal.

Similarly, the long-standing dispute between the United States and Canada in the Dixon Entrance and Hecate Strait off the coast of British Columbia is instructive.[557] In 1825, Great Britain and Russia concluded a treaty in which they delimited the boundary between Alaska and Canada's British Colombia. After Alaska was sold to the United States, the two neighbouring States sought to execute the treaty, but there was no agreement with respect to certain provisions therein, namely, Articles III, IV and V. Article III provided a line commencing from the Prince of Wales Island at the Dixon Entrance and terminating at a point where the 141 ° West longitude met the 'Frozen Ocean' in the north. Articles IV and V clarified issues of allocation, including, importantly, the allocation of Prince of Wales Island to Great Britain, and the location of the mountain line. In January 1903, the parties agreed to refer the matter to an arbitral tribunal and requested it to provide answers to five questions arising from their disagreements.

The *Alaska Boundary* Tribunal in the *Alaska Boundary Case*[558] delivered its award in October 1903, but that was not the end of the matter. In 1909, the United States challenged Canada's claim with respect to exclusive jurisdiction in the Hecate Strait. The argument of the United States was that the award was concerned with the *allocation* of land and island territory and that the tribunal did not contemplate providing a *frontier* for maritime territory. Hence, the line of contention is that the waters in the Strait and the Entrance beyond the three-mile limit are not Canadian/British waters.[559] Canada's claim is that the Strait and Entrance are the territorial waters of the province of British Colombia and that that the line delimited by the tribunal applied not only to *terra firma*, but also to the maritime possessions of the two States.

This contention is supported by the fact that, in 1909, the Committee of the Privy Council of Canada reported that the treaty of 1825 and the

557 For commentary on the dispute, see Bourne and McRae, 'Maritime Jurisdiction in the Dixon Entrance: The Alaska Boundary Re-examined', 14 (1976) CYIL 175; and Morin, 'Les eaux territoriales du Canada au regard du droit international', 1 (1963) CYIL 82, at pp. 130–4; Morin, 'La zone de pêche exclusive du Canada', 2 (1964) CYIL 77, at pp. 93–6; and Morin, 'Le progrès technique, la pollution et l'évolution récente du droit de la mer au Canada, particulièrement a l'égard de l'Arctique', 8 (1970) CYIL 158.

558 15 UNRIAA 485.

559 Bourne and McRae (note 557), pp. 176–7.

award of 1903 had drawn a line of demarcation between the possessions of the United Kingdom/Canada and Russia/the United States upon the coast of the continent and the islands of North America to the north-west, and because 'possessions include territorial waters as well as land, it is inferred that the waters on either side of the line (A–B) are territorial'.[560] In other words, all the islands and maritime spaces south of the line starting from point A at Cape Muzon, at the southern tip of the Prince of Wales Island, point B, and running straight east to the Portland Channel, were under the sovereignty of Canada.[561] The Committee reasoned that, if this were not a correct interpretation of the award line, it would mean that the United States would 'own 3 miles out to sea off Cape Muzon, or 3 miles on the Canadian side of the boundary-line'.[562]

The matter was referred by Canada for advice to the Law Officers of the Government of the United Kingdom, who adopted a relatively more cautious approach to the problem. They took the position that the interpretation of the Canadian Government could not be justified in international law, and wrote:

So far as the general principles of international law are concerned, we think that any international tribunal would certainly hold that the great spaces of water intervening on the north and east between Queen Charlotte Island and the nearest land [that is, the coast of Alaska/British Columbia] are open sea, over which neither the United States nor Great Britain or Canada can claim exclusive jurisdiction . . . [I]t is contended in the report [of the Canadian Privy Council] . . . that the effect of this demarcation was to assign the sea as well as the islands and mainland lying north and south of that line to the high contracting parties respectively. This is not the construction which would be given to the treaty if due regard be had to the well-known rule of international law as to the freedom of the open sea and to article I of the treaty . . . The line of demarcation as drawn by the arbitration tribunal under the convention of 1903 is referred to in the convention and in the Canadian report as a 'boundary line', and an inference is thereupon sought to be drawn that, whatever lies to the north or south of that line, whether land or water, would be within the territory of one or the other of the contracting parties. This, however, is to construe the expression 'boundary line' in rather too literal a sense. If it were treated literally as a 'boundary line', it would have the effect of allocating to Canada part of the territorial water at the extreme points of the line where it rests upon the coasts of Alaska and at all

560 Report of the Committee of the Privy Council of Canada, 6 July 1909: Further Correspondence etc., Part VII, July to December 1909: (Conf. 9698) Inclosure 2 in No. 92, in Parry (note 469), pp. 38, 39 and 40–4, at p. 42.

561 *Ibid.*, pp. 42–3; and see Bourne and McRae (note 557), pp. 176–7.

562 Parry (note 469), p. 42.

intermediate points where it is drawn within three miles of such coasts. This cannot have been intended.[563]

It is amply clear that the essence of the matter involves ascertaining whether in 1903 the parties were contemplating drawing either a frontier in terms simply of allocation of the land and islands in the disputed zone or a maritime frontier as well. It is equally clear that, to clarify this, reference has to be made to the award of 1903, the treaty of 1825, the negotiations which led up to them and the conduct of the parties before and after the award. Bourne and McRae have attempted to do this. After an exhaustive examination, they are unable to arrive at a definite conclusion and are perhaps equivocal on the matter. They appear to establish that, while there is a degree of uncertainty about these issues, the preponderance of evidence perhaps suggests that the 1825 line was primarily a line of allocation. Nor is the conduct of the parties on the issue entirely conclusive.

Be that as it may, it is important to point out that, regardless of the evidence of negotiations and conduct leading up to the 1825 Treaty and thereafter, the general presumption must be that the 1903 Alaska Boundary Tribunal did not deliver an award which was in whole or in part a breach of the law. If this is correct, then it follows that extensive claims to maritime territory could not have been sanctioned or contemplated by the Tribunal and hence the award would have to be interpreted accordingly. The question then turns on whether, at the time when the award was made, there were restrictions in terms of international law as regards the extent of maritime territory claimed by coastal States, and the answer to that clearly lies in positive terms.

While it is accepted that the precise extent of the territorial sea was still a matter of some controversy in the early part of the twentieth century, that is, when the award was delivered, it was generally agreed that extensive claims of the *mare clausum* era were over two centuries ago.[564] The real debate among States was one which focused on the spatial limits of territorial seas, a debate on limits ranging between three and twelve nautical miles.[565] Nonetheless, it is more pertinent for present purposes to note

[563] Sir W. Robson and Sir S. Evans to Colonial Office, 22 December 1909: Further Correspondence etc., Part VIII, January to June 1910: (Conf. 9737) Inclosure in No. 5; LOR 1909 (Conf. 9638), No. 10A: reprinted in Parry (note 469), pp. 44–6.

[564] See, generally, O'Connell (note 92), pp. 454–7; Colombos, *The International Law of the Sea*, 6th edn, London, 1967, pp. 47–65; Hershey, *Essentials of International Public Law and Organisation*, 2nd edn, New York, 1930, pp. 321–5; and Smith and Phillipson, *International Law*, 5th edn by Coleman Phillipson, London, 1918, pp. 109–15.

[565] Refer to Colombos (note 564), pp. 91 *et seq.*

that both protagonist States had always strictly urged the three-mile limit, and, in view of that, it is not conceivable that the tribunal would have considered, in principle, maritime areas beyond the three-mile limit as appertaining to either the United States or Canada. Equally, however, while the Entrance is about thirty-five nautical miles wide and thus hardly constitutes land-locked waters,[566] the Strait can be regarded as *inter fauces terrae*, and hence internal waters, a notion consistent with the principles of the law of nations prevailing at that time.

These are all clearly questions going to the merits of the dispute and cannot be exhaustively examined here. Even so, at this stage, two points are of central concern, and the first is this. If the treaty and award had indeed allocated land and also defined the maritime frontier in the circumstances described above, namely, an award the effect of which constituted a breach of international law, then any interpretation given by Canada which is consistent with that breach is unacceptable in law in terms of allowing that State to rely on it with a view to furthering its claims. More importantly, in the second place, if it were fully accepted that the effect of the award would constitute a breach of the law, then the question of nullity and effectiveness arises, but that is a matter lying outwith the scope of this study as outlined in Chapter 1 above.

It will, therefore, suffice to note here that, where full or partial nullity of a decision is established by a process of law, then that decision cannot create lawful rights and obligations to the extent of the nullity, and cannot accordingly prejudice the claims of either party, provided also that there is no evidence of acceptance of the award despite, and in full knowledge of, that breach of the law. Pakistan's acceptance of the award rendered in the *Radcliffe India–Pakistan Boundary* proceedings is an apposite

566 Although examining the merits of this dispute is beyond the scope of this study, two interesting facts, which detract from the Canadian claim, are noteworthy. First, internal waters need to be *geographically* landlocked in order to constitute *inter fauces terrae*, and, in the case of the Entrance, not only is it too wide at approximately thirty-five nautical miles, it is really a confinement which, on the south side, is one of geography and, on the north, one of law, that is, a line drawn in law. Secondly, both natural entrance points are not exclusively under the sovereignty of one State. The Canadian presence at the starting point, Cape Muzon, is one more of logic and cartography, and less of law, given that that point, and indeed the entire island, is attributed to the United States. Arguably, the degree of Canadian presence at Cape Muzon is not sufficient in law to be such that it could be said that both the northern and the southern entrance points are in Canada. The closing line along the mouth of the Rio de la Plata between Uruguay and Argentina is controversial precisely because the natural entrance points are in two different States and the mouth is greater than twenty-four nautical miles, that is, 118 nautical miles. See Francalanci and Scovazzi, *Lines in the Sea*, Dordrecht, 1994, pp. 68–9.

example. Despite irregularities in the drawing up of the award of 1947, which could, arguably, have rendered it void, the Government of Pakistan decided not to challenge its validity, and considered the decision binding.[567]

The last proviso is itself also subject to the rider that the award does not affect the rights and obligations of third States. By way of illustration, the award in *Brazil* v. *British Guiana* is noteworthy.[568] Acting as arbitrator, the King of Italy held that the Anglo-American Arbitral Tribunal, when deciding the boundary in *British Guiana* v. *Venezuela*, 'adjudged to the former the territory which constitutes the subject of the present dispute, [and hence the award of 1900] cannot be cited against Brazil, which was unaffected by that judgment'.[569]

For the purposes of completeness, it may be noted that, in 1973, the United States proposed referring the matter to the International Court of Justice with a view to requesting the latter to provide a judgment on, *inter alia*, whether Canada had any greater rights to Dixon Entrance and adjacent waters by virtue of the award of 1903 than it would have under the appropriate principles of international law, and whether the award line A–B, that is, the line joining Cape Muzon and Portland Channel, separated

[567] The Punjab–Bengal Boundary Commissions were constituted by the Viceroy of India, Lord Mountbatten, in June 1947 and were headed by Sir Cyril Radcliffe. The four Indian members, all of whom were senior justices, represented the two main political and religious movements for independence from British rule. Official records, independent sources and statements by retired officials of the (British) Indian Civil Service have now established without doubt that the Viceroy had in his possession a copy of the award on 8 August, that is, four days before it was published, and that, on 11 August, three days before the transfer of power, the British Governor of the Punjab requested Mountbatten to '[e]liminate salient', a reference to the loop in the boundary in the Ferozpur sector. A modification of the line was deemed necessary to give an independent India access to Kashmir; all other routes lay through Pakistan. The modification, however, would have adversely affected Pakistan's irrigation systems and defence considerations. Thereupon, the Viceroy prevailed upon Sir Cyril to alter the line accordingly. Key leaders in the Muslim League were aware of these developments. The award was published on 12 August 1947. The Governor-General of Pakistan, Mr M. A. Jinnah, characterised the Radcliffe Award as an 'unjust, incomprehensible and even perverse award', and that, had it been so minded, the Government of Pakistan could have argued that it was null and void. However, in October 1947, the Government of Pakistan accepted it on the ground that it had agreed in advance that it would be binding on the Government. In 1950, the *Bagge India–Pakistan Tribunal Boundary* award was delivered to the disputing States as clarification of the Radcliffe Award. For an account of this, see Razvi (note 85), pp. 35–9, especially note 3 on pp. 37–8; and Ahmad (note 290), pp. 329 *et seq.* The two awards are Appendices I and II in Razvi (note 85), pp. 226 and 241; see *Gazette of Pakistan Extraordinary*, 17 August 1947 and 5 February 1950, respectively; and Sadullah *et al.* (eds.), *The Partition of the Punjab 1947: A Compilation of Official Documents*, vol. III, Lahore (Government Printer), 1983, p. 281.

[568] 99 BFSP 930.

[569] *Ibid.*, p. 931.

only land under the sovereignty of the United States and Canada, or whether it constituted a maritime boundary between the two States.[570] Canada rejected the offer.[571] The current position of the United States is that the maritime boundary in the Entrance ought to be determined by reference to the equidistance principle between the coasts and islands of the United States and Canada,[572] while the latter has now developed claims of historic waters in the Strait and the Entrance.[573]

An important qualification to the commentary presented above is that these propositions will not apply where the law evolves *after* the decision of the tribunal has been delivered. Thus, the rule of presumption against a breach of international law applies with respect to the law existing when the decision was made. There is no gainsaying that, if the decision is not interpreted in light of the prevailing law, a number of complications can arise, the most important of which, for present purposes, is that the boundary decided by the tribunal can become undone, as it were, and that is not a satisfactory state of affairs in either law or international politics.

Accordingly, in situations where there has been an evolution in the rules of international law, the principle of interpretation is that the normative reference point is the earlier, as opposed to the later, rule of law. In other words, where the law has so evolved and is putatively at variance with international standards currently accepted by States in the international legal system, then that fact alone cannot be an adequate reason to abandon the judgment boundary in favour of an interpretation of the award which is more consistent with contemporary international law. The rule here is that an award or judgment must be seen, clarified and applied in light of the law existing at the time when that decision was made. Indeed, this is the simple rule of intertemporal law.

This was the point of law accepted in 1897 by the Swiss Federal Court in *Schaffhausen* v. *Zurich*.[574] In this case, the canton of Schaffhausen claimed that the left bank of the Rhine constituted the boundary, leaving the entire Rhine to it, whereas the canton of Zurich argued for a middle line. The Federal Court was obliged to refer to the Confederate Award of 1555, by which decision the left bank was held to be the boundary between the

[570] Letter from the US Department of State to Canada, 27 June 1973: 1973 *Digest of United States Practice in International Law* 465–7.

[571] See 1974 *Digest of United States Practice in International Law* 672–3.

[572] See D. D., 'US–Canada Flag State Enforcement Arrangements: Dixon Entrance', 1981–8 *Digest of United States Practice in International Law*, vol. II, pp. 1928–30. (Entry by Donna Darm?)

[573] Bourne and McRae (note 557), p. 178.

[574] Schindler, 'The Administration of Justice in the Swiss Federal Court in Intercantonal Disputes', 15 (1921) AJIL 149, at p. 167.

two cantons. It is appropriate to note that, in the sixteenth and seventeenth centuries, a boundary river in Europe was treated either as a condominium of the riparian entities or divided along the geographical middle.[575] However, the practice of such States helped to change that position, and, by the latter half of the eighteenth century, the line was usually stated as being in the middle of a *navigable* boundary river, with the understanding that the middle of the river was not the geographical middle, that is, the *medium filum acquae*, but the line of the main navigable channel, or the *thalweg* of the river. Thus, by 1897, boundaries along either the right or left bank were not the preferred methods of delimitation among European States.

One of the points in issue before the Federal Court was whether Zurich could argue that developments in international law could not be ignored, and, if so, whether the left bank boundary ought to be modified in favour of an alignment drawn along the centre of the Rhine. In other words, the crucial issue was whether changes in international law ought to be taken into account in applying an award in which the boundary line decided by the tribunal was at variance with current standards of international law. The Federal Court took the following position:

> The circumstance that now, in accordance with the development of objective law, more importance is attached to the doctrine of international law, according to which the boundary of two States divided by a river is usually found in the middle of the said river, and less importance is attached to the actual possession and events of feudal law, cannot now effect any change in the juridical condition determined in such an authentic way anymore than it could have done so previously. For the principal question to be decided today is whether the present dispute has not already been decided, at least to a certain extent, in a legally binding manner, and whether thereby a condition has been created which must be guarded according to the principles of acquired rights, regardless of how the dispute would be decided according to the now prevalent norms and conceptions.

Thus, the presumption against a breach will apply, but it will apply with reference to the law which existed at the time of the award, and not at the time when the award is being interpreted. The rationale is clear. If the rules require the decision to be interpreted in light of current norms of law, then a State may be tempted to request interpretation once it is convinced that the law has evolved in a way beneficial to its claims and aspirations to the territory and location of boundary. In view of the fact that the law is always dynamic, sometimes imperceptibly so, there would be

[575] See, generally, Verzijl (note 136), vol. III, pp. 538 *et seq.*; and *Iowa* v. *Illinois*, 147 US 1, at pp. 5–11 (1893).

great potential for uncertainty if in these kinds of circumstance a retrospective interpretation of the law were ruled out in favour of a prospective one.

IV. Materials, conduct and relevant circumstances: admissibility and probative weight

As a general principle, facts and materials which throw light on the meaning of the decision may be taken into consideration, and it would be unhelpful to suggest that evidence in the nature of treaties, instruments, official reports and the like ought to be admitted restrictively. Although a tribunal has the right to refuse to take into consideration certain kinds of materials, and may in fact decide so to do, the fact is that it is unrealistic to provide an overarching, strict test for the admissibility of such materials as evidence. A claim regarding the interpretation of a judgment boundary is, in the final analysis, simply another contentious case, or advisory opinion for that matter, and all materials may, within limits, be admitted. The interpretative decision will therefore necessarily reflect and be a product of the law, facts and circumstances of the main case. It is necessary to keep in mind the fact that, although the task of interpretation is a narrow one, it cannot be carried out in a vacuum. It is for this reason that a wide range of materials and circumstances have from time to time been used by tribunals to understand, clarify, interpret and apply the terms of the decision. As the Court of Arbitration observed in *Dubai* v. *Sharjah*:

> The parties have submitted to this Court a dispute relating to their boundaries and have asked this Court to determine those boundaries. The Court could not properly undertake this task or accomplish this function if it deprived itself for one reason or another of the opportunity of examining the totality of the evidence submitted to it.

One way of classifying the materials is by reference to the date of the decision, and hence a tribunal may have to examine materials and evidence arising or occurring both before and after the decision was handed down. It may, relatively speaking, be easier to take into account material which existed *prior to* the original decision for the simple reason that a tribunal would be expected to have taken cognisance of all the facts and circumstances which agitated the States and which subsequently led them to begin proceedings before the original tribunal. Clearly, the materials admitted as evidence will depend, among other things, on the provenance thereof; but, equally importantly, the materials admitted in evidence may in fact be an extension, as it were, of the decision being interpreted and may hence require interpretation as well.

Thus in the *Monastery of Saint-Naoum* advisory opinion, the Permanent Court of International Justice not only had to pass upon the definitive status of the Conference of Ambassador's decision of 6 December 1966. The Court discovered that in order to fulfil its task it had in fact also to give judgment on two earlier decisions of the Conference, namely, the decision of 11 August 1913, also referred to as the London Protocol, and the decision of 9 November 1921. The Serb-Croat-Slovene State maintained that 'the [latter] decision . . . conferred a vested right upon it, by establishing the principle that the frontier was to be that fixed in 1913, except as otherwise expressly provided; and that, since no special provision was made as regards the Monastery of Saint-Naoum, the terms of the Protocol of 1913, which attributed it to Serbia, remained in force. It is clear that this contention is indissolubly connected with the question whether the Albanian frontier at the Monastery of Saint-Naoum was actually fixed in 1913 or not.'[576]

Thus, the Court was obliged to examine the extent to which the decisions of 1913 and 1922 of the Conference of Ambassadors had actually sought to delimit the frontier. Indeed, it interpreted the terms of the 1913 decision with great precision, and discovered that the usage of terms, as discussed above, was equivocal and hence inconclusive: an analysis of the texts emanating from the London Conference led to no definite conclusion one way or the other. However, the decision of 6 December 1922 was not equivocal, leaving, as it did, the Monastery (clearly and categorically) to Albania. Once that task was performed, the Conference had exhausted its mission and the frontier between Albania and the Serb-Croat-Slovene State stood established.[577] 'The decision', the Permanent Court of International Justice held, 'of December 6th, 1922, which, in the view of the Conference, constituted an act necessary for the fulfilment of the mission entrusted to it, is based on the same powers as that of November 9th, 1921; it therefore has the same definitive character and the same legal effect as that decision.'[578] Clearly, then, all the relevant instruments anterior to the decision had to be examined carefully before the Court was able to provide an opinion with respect to the question asked of it by the Council of the League of Nations.

In a similar vein, it is a fact that tribunals will invariably need to carry out a careful appreciation of the general history or evolution of the

[576] Supra (note 296), p. 16. Paragraph omitted. [577] *Ibid.*, p. 21. [578] *Ibid.*, p. 15.

boundary issues. So it was then that, in *Costa Rica* v. *Panama*, the arbitrator, Chief Justice White, discussed extensively the positions adopted by the parties by way of negotiations and attempted negotiations, the previous cartographical records showing the alignments and the nature and extent of occupation and settlement of the territory during the period of dispute.[579] The arbitrator also relied on the positions taken by both parties just before and during the proceedings to establish that in fact there was no question of a counterfort boundary because both States had always maintained a river alignment, namely, the Chiriquí by Costa Rica and Yorquin/Sixaola by Colombia.[580]

Similarly, in the *Jaworzina* advisory opinion, the Permanent Court of International Justice noted that, in the resolution adopted by the Supreme Council of the Principal Allied Powers on 11 July 1920, the last paragraph contained mutual undertakings on the part of the Powers to send to each of their delegates at the Ambassador's Conference confidential instructions regarding boundary issues between Poland and Czechoslovakia. The Court added that, 'since the instructions in question have been communicated to the Court, there is nothing to prevent the latter from using them as it may seem fit for the purpose of interpreting the principal document in question, namely the Decision of the Conference of Ambassadors of July 28th, 1920, adopted in consequence of the decision of the Supreme Council and the instructions above-mentioned'.[581]

It went on to take into account also the circumstances attending this decision, chief of which was that the Principal Powers, who were confronted with a serious dispute, were of the opinion that it 'necessitated a speedy solution' and that only 'by a settlement emanating from a duly authorised body could the whole dispute be disposed of without leaving any important point for subsequent decision'.[582] It follows that the transmission and admission of evidence to the tribunal will in principle allow the latter to evaluate it for the purposes of interpretation. The weight it

579 8 (1914) AJIL 913, at pp. 917–22.

580 *Ibid.*, pp. 922–31. In *Dubai–Sharjah*, Dubai claimed that '[i]nternational law requires that the Court, in general, place greater weight on evidence of conduct by the Parties in recent times in preference to evidence of more distant dates', and that '[n]ormal tests of evidence should be applied by the Court when weighing the evidence before it. Direct evidence from a witness is to be preferred to indirect evidence, whenever the former is available. The witnesses' means of knowledge is critical.' The Court preferred to pay attention to written documents from the period in question which afforded a more reliable source of evidence: see 91 ILR 553 and 590.

581 Supra (note 107), p. 26.

582 *Ibid.*, p. 29.

ascribes to such materials is, of course, a matter for the tribunal. This is discussed presently.

However, materials and evidence arising *subsequent* to the judgment or award can present problems. It would appear that, normally, this category of materials could have no bearing on what the tribunal may have meant to hold in its original decision. This is, of course, the position adopted by the Permanent Court of International Justice. In *Chorzów Factory (Interpretation of Judgments Nos. 7 and 8)*, it held that 'the Court, when giving an interpretation, refrains from any examination of facts other than those which it has considered in the judgment under interpretation, and consequently all facts subsequent to the judgment. It confines itself to explaining, by an interpretation, that upon which it has already passed judgment.'[583] Importantly, the Court of Arbitration in the *Palena* case confirmed the general rule. It distinguished between treaty interpretation and the interpretation of judicial decisions, and held that it was not necessary to look outside the three documents comprising the award of 1902 for the purposes of interpretation. It then went on to state: 'As for subsequent conduct of the parties, including also the conduct of private individuals and local authorities, the Court fails to see how that can throw any light on the Arbitrator's intention.'[584]

In *Laguna del Desierto*, the Tribunal held to this position, and observed that subsequent conduct was not a factor bearing directly on the mandate of the Tribunal in that it related to facts which had occurred after the judgment was adopted by it. Referring to the post-decisional practice of the Argentina–Chile Mixed Boundary Commission, the Tribunal accepted that the latter's work could be relevant in relation to the interpretation of the award of 1902, and to an analysis of the legal position in the sectors where the work had been carried out. However, the Commission's operations could clearly have had no influence on the intention of the arbitrator in 1902, or on what was decided by him in

[583] Supra (note 273), p. 21.

[584] 38 ILR 90. The three sets of documents referred to by the Court of Arbitration constituted in the first place the award made by the British monarch, King Edward VII, as arbitrator, on 20 November 1902; this award was based on the report of 19 November 1902 of the arbitration tribunal and constituted the second instrument; and the third set were the maps on which the boundary was delineated by the arbitrator. See also Bos, who, while agreeing with the Court on this matter, observed that the principles applicable in matters of treaty interpretation, including the teleological, sociological, comparative, restrictive and extensive methods, will normally have no place and, consequently, that the grammatical, historical, systematic and logical methods are the only ones applicable: Bos (note 226), p. 213.

respect of the sector between Boundary Post 62 and Mount Fitzroy; nor could they have affected the conclusions reached by the Tribunal in that regard.[585]

Similarly, questions of reliance on subsequent conduct and the practice of the parties were raised in *Dubai* v. *Sharjah*. With respect to the coastal terminus in the Al Mamzer–Abu Hail region, the Court of Arbitration ruled that 'the very precise wording of the Tripp decision appears to support the view of the Government of Sharjah, and any maps or documents which may have been drafted subsequently are not relevant where they conflict with this wording: it may be added that, according to a Foreign Office memorandum dated 16 June 1969, "strictly speaking only the letters of award have real validity" '.[586] It is important to note that the Court did not rule out the significance of subsequent conduct of the parties as a factor in deciding whether or not the administrative, as opposed to judicial/arbitral, decisions could be set aside.[587]

It could, nonetheless, be argued that conduct, practice and experience of all kinds ought not to be excluded in certain circumstances. Thus, where not only *subsequent*, but also *current* and, indeed, *earlier*, experience and conduct cast significant light on relevant matters and clarify issues relative to the validity of the methods of delimitation employed, then it may be that the tribunal will be positively inclined to refer to such materials. A good example of the wide range of facts and materials relevant for interpretation comes from *United Kingdom–France Continental Shelf Interpretive Decision*. The Court of Arbitration took into account the past and present practice of geographers regarding the use of the Mercator projection in order to ascertain the proper scope and effect of the use of this projection by the Technical Expert in drawing the Boundary Line Chart. In fact, during the session in December 1977, the Court asked the parties to provide written replies to the following questions:

> What is the general practice in regard to the nature of the charts used for the delimitation of continental shelf and other maritime boundaries? Are charts based on Transverse Mercator Projection in general use in Hydrographic Departments?[588]

The Court took note of the fact that it was common practice to delimit equidistance boundaries dividing the territorial sea or internal waters on standard navigational charts on Mercator projections without correction

[585] 113 ILR 77–9. [586] 91 ILR 543, at p. 596.

[587] *Ibid*., p. 611, for which see *ibid*., pp. 611–22. State conduct was also crucial in the Nahada Amair/Hadib Azana sector, on which see Bowett (note 264), pp. 118–21 and 121–3; and the text to notes 591–6 and 658–60 below. [588] 54 ILR 155.

for scale error, and went on to hold that State practice does not permit the conclusion that the delimitation of maritime boundaries by loxodrome on the Mercator projection was obsolete.[589] The question, the Court said, was whether the Technical Expert's construction of the course of the boundary by reference to two loxodromes was compatible with the simplified frame for applying the half-effect solution or whether his omission to allow for the scale of error inherent in Mercator rendered it incompatible with this frame.

Having come to the conclusion that the use of the Mercator projection without scale error correction was admissible in law, and that its use was not so outmoded in practice that it was open to challenge, the Court held that the techniques used in the calculation of the half-effect boundary could not be considered incompatible with the method of delimitation laid down in paragraphs 251, 253 and 254 of the decision.[590] Thus evidence of State practice regarding the general use of the Mercator projection was a crucial element in clarifying the relevant paragraphs of the 1977 decision. The point to note is that 'general practice' referred to in this case includes both past as well as current practice.

In other circumstances, subsequent conduct may also be relevant to show the extent of the judgment's effects on the ground, which in turn will cast light on, and clarify matters regarding, the meaning of a judgment or award. In *Dubai* v. *Sharjah* (see Map 6), the Court of Arbitration ruled that the Tripp decisions were not judgments; nor were they arbitral awards, as Sharjah had claimed. Even so, the instruments were binding administrative decisions not devoid of legal effect,[591] and hence the boundary could not be established *de novo*. The Court acknowledged that there would have been no value in examining the evidence produced by Sharjah if the task of the Court were confined to interpreting or applying these decisions.[592]

Accordingly, the Court ruled that it would examine the effect these decisions had had on the legal situation on the ground in order to explain the subsequent attitude of the parties. The Court explained that, if the

[589] *Ibid.*, p. 200. On the Court's failure to give instructions to the Technical Expert on the projection to be used and other more suitable projections, see Bowett (note 226), p. 587, note 35.

[590] 54 ILR 202. Cf. the Separate Opinion of Judge Sir Humphrey Waldock. While he accepted the fact that the use of the Mercator projection without correction of scale error was not so outmoded as to make it obsolete, Sir Humphrey emphasised the point that such a state of affairs was inappropriate where extensive seaward projections of maritime territory were being contemplated: *ibid.*, pp. 207–8.

[591] 91 ILR 577.

[592] *Ibid.*, p. 583.

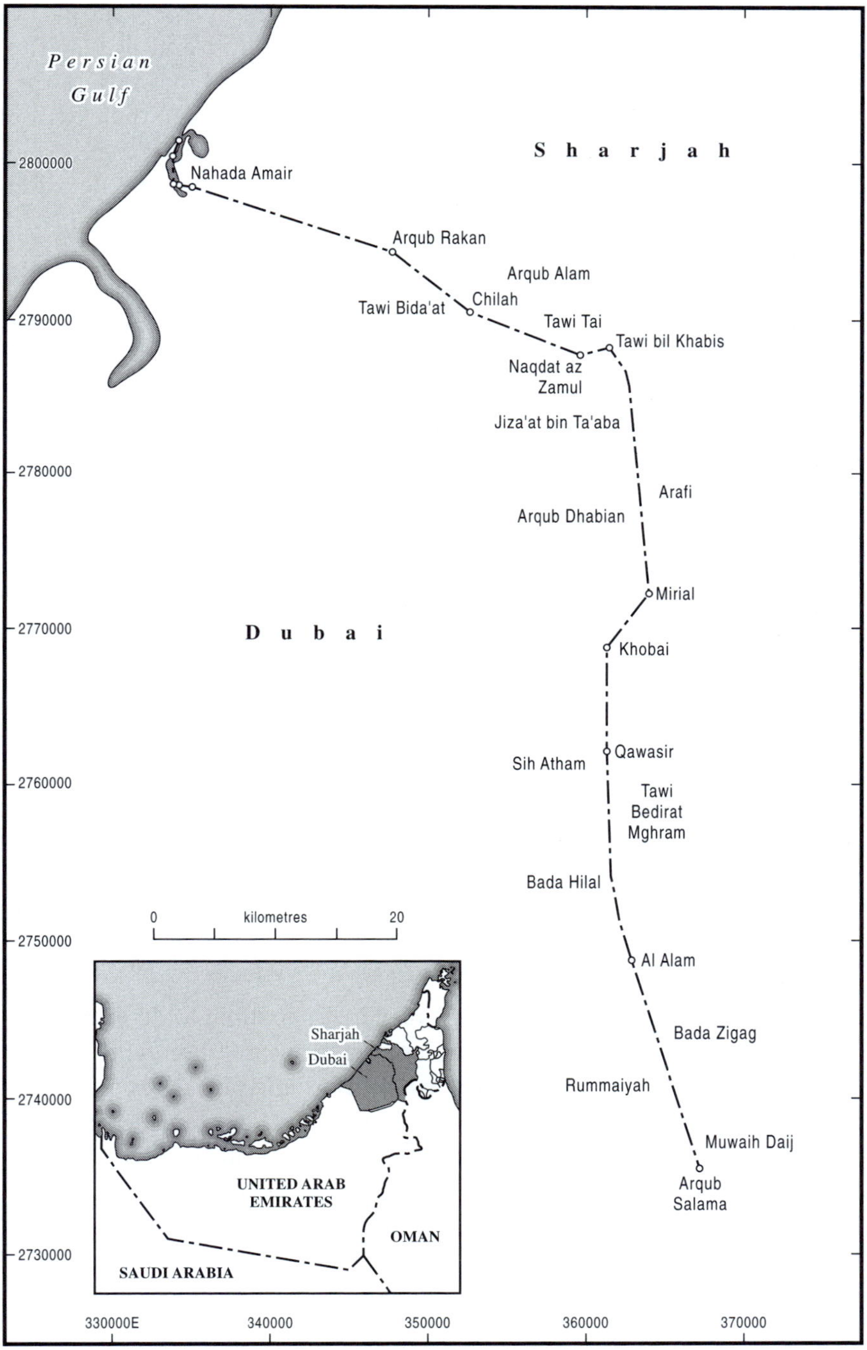

Map 6 *Dubai* v. *Sharjah* arbitration

boundary had either in whole or in part been rejected by one of the parties as contrary to legal title at the time of the decisions, and was neither recognised nor effectively applied in practice by Dubai or Sharjah, then the Court would have the right to set aside the decisions to the extent of its non-application. However, if the boundary had been recognised or applied in subsequent years, then the Court would give the decisions effect despite the fact that they may be at variance with the legal situation in the disputed areas at the relevant time.[593]

It went on in this vein to hold that, in the coastal sector, with regard to the Al Mamzer peninsula, the subsequent behaviour of the parties was as though 'there had never been the [Tripp] decision [of 1956]', which had given the disputed peninsula to Sharjah and of which Dubai had always remained in full possession and control.[594] Accordingly, the Court set aside the Tripp terminal point which ran approximately between Dubai Creek and Khan Creek and replaced it with a starting point which began at the tip and ran south along the eastern low water line of Al Mamzer peninsula.[595]

By contrast, in the next sector, namely, the Nahada Amair–Hahdib Azana sector, the Court accepted the arguments of Sharjah that it had full effective control in the area, that it had both recognised and applied the Tripp decision and that it had fully established that the boundary passed through Nahada Amair.[596] Of course, subsequent conduct was employed here to determine the status and effect of the Tripp decisions, but the fact remains that, by doing so, the latter also stood clarified in those very terms. The short point being conveyed here is that it is in general difficult to negate the legal significance of subsequent conduct in the interpretative process, with the caveat that *Dubai* v. *Sharjah* was not concerned with the interpretation of arbitral, but administrative, boundary decisions, namely, the Tripp decisions of 1956 and 1957.

Further, in some circumstances it may be impossible to determine the true meaning of a decision without looking into the subsequent conduct of the parties. Thus, while it is admitted that some post-decisional materials cannot have any direct bearing on proving the intention of the tribunal, where the boundary cannot be demarcated on the ground owing to the existence of geographical inaccuracies, subsequent conduct may have to be relied on with a view to resolving some of the complexities. Indeed, the award in the *Palena* case is not without its equivocal characteristics. While it expressed a degree of cautiousness in admitting

[593] *Ibid.*, p. 585. [594] *Ibid.*, pp. 595–621. [595] *Ibid.*, p. 625. [596] *Ibid.*, pp. 626–8.

post-decisional materials evidencing intention, and while it maintained that it was for the Court alone to perform the task of interpretation and fulfilment of the award of 1902, it also admitted that the Court could 'naturally . . . expect to derive some assistance in its task from the manner in which the parties have attempted to interpret and fulfil the Award'.[597] As Fox observed in this regard, 'before excluding from their deliberations all evidence other than the text of the Award', those individuals

> whose task it is to construe local boundaries should peruse the reasoning of the Court of Arbitration to its finish. For though in general terms, [Members of the Court] dismiss as irrelevant evidence of the subsequent conduct of the parties, in their detailed study of the meaning of the Award they admit evidence of a very similar nature.[598]

One aspect of this task was to determine whether the boundary ought to follow the Southern Channel, as urged by Argentina, or the Eastern Channel, as urged by Chile, after it had become clear that it was impossible in terms of geography to demarcate the frontier described in the 1902 award. In order to determine which of the two channels constituted the major channel, the Court had to turn to both historical and geographical criteria. The former included post-decisional reports of official boundary surveyors, maps and governmental correspondence showing the Eastern Channel as the major channel. By way of confirmation, the Court applied geographical and scientific criteria, including length of channel, size of drainage area, and annual rate of volume of discharge, and concluded that the major branch of the Encuentro in this sector was the Eastern Channel.[599] The Court, however, emphasised that it 'must never lose sight of the fact that it was the *intention* of the Arbitrator to make the boundary follow a river as far as Cerro de la Virgen'.[600]

Similarly, despite its restrictive views on the work of the Mixed Boundary Commission, the Tribunal in *Laguna del Desierto* was not without some ambivalence with respect to subsequent conduct. Referring to the latter, it held, 'both parties have submitted evidence of such conduct to the Tribunal, attaching to it differing degrees of importance. While seeking to avoid any discussion of the matters so raised which would divert it from strict compliance with its function, the Tribunal cannot omit all reference to this aspect of the case.'[601]

[597] 38 ILR 91. [598] Supra (note 185), pp. 179–80.

[599] 38 ILR 91, at pp. 93–8 (emphasis added). It must, however, be noted that the task of the Tribunal was not limited to interpretation and that part of its task constituted 'fulfilment' of the award to the extent that it had not been fulfilled by the parties.

[600] *Ibid.*, p. 93. [601] 113 ILR 78.

Accordingly, while it gave no weight to the work of the Commission, the Tribunal did take into account the official post-decisional cartography of Argentina and Chile. It noted that Chile's maps showed the frontier running along the northern edge of the basin of the Rio Gatica, or de las Vueltas, thus leaving it to Argentina, and came to the conclusion that Chilean official cartography did not in fact support its claim that it was entitled to a portion of the basin. Similarly, it admitted subsequent conduct in the form of effective control and administration of the disputed area. However, it declined to give any weight to it on the ground that the acts in question were neither consistent nor unequivocal in nature; they also lacked the effectiveness necessary to give them legal consequences of relevance to the Tribunal's proceedings.[602]

It was this equivocal approach which Chile tried to exploit in the interpretative proceedings following the *Laguna del Desierto* case. In *Request for Revision and Interpretation of the 1994 Judgment*, it argued that the Tribunal in 1994 had failed to take into account conduct subsequent to the 1902 award. By confining itself to events prior to the arbitrator's decision, the Tribunal, Chile argued, had committed an error of law.[603] The response of the Tribunal in 1995 was relatively more robust. It held that, despite the fact that subsequent conduct was not a factor of direct relevance to its mandate, it had nevertheless examined this head of evidence in some detail. It explained that post-decisional cartography, the effective exercise of jurisdiction in the disputed area and the work of the Commission had all been discussed in the award of 1994, but none of the items discussed were of sufficient force to affect the Tribunal's conclusions in relation to the interpretation of the 1902 award.[604]

Referring to the cartography submitted by Chile, the Tribunal clarified the position it had adopted, and observed that it had refrained from taking further points adverse to Chile's position insofar as it was unnecessary so to do: the simple reason was that, after examining every map submitted by Chile, the Tribunal became convinced that Chile's cartography did not support the claim that the Rio Gatica basin was left to Chile and not to Argentina. However, in view of the criticism Chile had made, the Tribunal undertook a still more detailed examination of the cartography, but this only confirmed the decision it had already reached, namely, that there was no omission of any kind in relation to its analysis of the cartography which might be regarded as an attack on the stability of frontiers or on Chile's rights.[605]

[602] *Ibid.*, pp. 78–9. [603] *Ibid.*, pp. 201–2. [604] *Ibid.*, pp. 202–3. [605] *Ibid.*, p. 203.

In sum, then, materials and evidence going to intention, meaning and implementation cannot in all the appropriate circumstances be ruled out simply because they relate to a period of time following the delivery of the decision. As Judge Galindo Pohl observed in his Dissenting Opinion in *Laguna del Desierto*: 'The parties' subsequent conduct is evidence of how they understood the Award, and can accordingly be useful for the purposes of confirming an interpretation based on the component elements of the Award.'[606] The fact is that reliance on such post-decisional materials can become a necessity where there are major geographical inaccuracies and other similar problems in the award or judgment, and also where careful examination of the 'real' intention of the previous Tribunal constitutes an essential step in the resolution of the dispute.

Even if there is in general principle no reason to preclude States from relying and submitting materials which seek to prove their respective contentions in the interpretative process, the precise probative weight to be attributed to such materials is quite a different matter. The first of three tests affecting the probative weight of the materials is concerned with the contemporaneity of knowledge. In *Laguna del Desierto*, the Government of Chile argued, *inter alia*, that the Tribunal should determine the frontier claimed by it during the proceedings of 1898–1902 only by reference to the geographic knowledge prevalent at that time.

The Tribunal responded by observing that Argentina and Chile had set out their maximum claims in accordance with criteria which had defined and justified their aspirations and had clarified the documents submitted to the arbitrator. What was decided in 1902 could not be interpreted on the basis of criteria relied on at the bar of the Tribunal established in 1991 but which were not invoked in the original proceedings. Since these materials were, it said, not available to the 1902 proceedings, they could not now be used as a basis of interpretation.[607] In its view, the natural and effective water-parting was the true line decided by the arbitrator in the disputed sector, and the task of Tribunal was simply to determine that local water-parting.

Judge Galindo Pohl observed in his Dissenting Opinion, 'as a *sine qua non* for an understanding of the meaning of the Arbitrator's decision, that we place ourselves in the era of the judgment and seek to comprehend, and of course to respect, the circumstances in which he was operating. Particularly in disputes relating to frontiers, judgments must be

[606] 113 ILR 123. See also the dissent of Judge Benadava, *ibid*., pp. 190–1.

[607] 113 ILR 49–50. See also the Dissenting Opinion of Judge Benadava, *ibid*., pp. 185–6.

understood by reference to the geographical knowledge, the information and the arguments presented to the court at the time in question. Any other approach would risk the *res judicata* and the stability of frontiers.' Placing emphasis on the basic objective and purpose of interpretation, he wrote: 'The end in view determines the means employed; and since the end is to ascertain the meaning of the Award of 1902, we must examine the case and its consequences in light of the elements of opinion, fact and law available to the Arbitrator for the purposes of his opinion.'[608]

In the subsequent *Request for Revision and Interpretation of the 1994 Judgment*, the Tribunal clarified the fact that it had indeed complied with the principle of contemporaneity by referring to the natural and effective water-parting, but that the course of the alignment was to be determined not in accordance with geographical knowledge prevalent at that time, but with the simple, true, geographical configuration prevailing then and now in the disputed region.[609]

Another factor affecting probative weight concerns the circumstances in which the conduct occurs and in which the parties carry out the practice. Reference is being made here to the *Alaska Boundary Case* and the dispute between the United States and Canada regarding the true scope and effect of the award of 1903. During the proceedings in the *Atlantic Coast Fisheries* arbitration,[610] the President of the Tribunal enquired of Mr Charles Warren, counsel for the United States, whether the *Alaska Boundary Case* had 'a direct bearing on the extent of maritime limits, or of the limits of territorial waters'. Mr Warren replied: 'None whatever.' 'Was it a question', the president pressed, 'concerning the boundary on the sea or the boundary on land?' The reply in effect was that the dispute was concerned with the boundary on land.[611]

The *North Atlantic Coast Fisheries* arbitration is, of course, not an interpretative decision of the *Alaska Boundary Case*, but it is worth noting here because it clarifies the point that evidence relied upon depends upon the circumstances in which statements are made and conduct is carried out. Although it is not by any means conclusive, this exchange is relevant because it reinforces the fact that the United States was conscious of its claims regarding the nature of the award of 1903, and that, at the appropriate opportunity, counsel for the United States did not prejudice his government's position on the matter; but what is equally important is the fact that, had he stated otherwise, it would in all probability still not be seen

[608] *Ibid.*, pp. 49–50. [609] *Ibid.*, p. 212. [610] 4 (1910) AJIL 948.

[611] *Proceedings of the North Atlantic Coast Fisheries Arbitration*, vol. X, Washington, DC, 1912, p. 1094 and pp. 1094–5, as quoted and cited by Bourne and McRae (note 557), p. 211.

as a crucial admission by Washington, chiefly because a single statement, made in legal proceedings for the purposes of clarification of a point which, although important, was not crucial to the Government's position in an unrelated case, cannot prejudice the definitive position adopted by that State in terms of the territorial claims it purports to assert.

These issues are best discussed in section VI below. Nonetheless, the two general points worth noting here are that, on the one hand, statements such as these are essentially indicative of the general understanding of the parties prevalent at the time the decision was made and soon thereafter. On the other hand, while such statements would, in most cases, be taken into account by a tribunal seeking to determine the question of the nature, scope and effect of the decision in question, the precise probative weight of such evidence will vary from case to case and depend upon all the circumstances thereof.

The second test involves determining the intentions motivating the previous tribunal: materials adduced for the purpose of proving what the previous tribunal had intended to say in the disputed texts of the decision may carry great weight for the interpreting tribunal. Clearly, relevant materials will include the subsequent conduct of the parties insofar as they shed light on the interpretation placed by them on the decision or award. The significance of the subsequent conduct of the parties has been alluded to above, particularly the *Dubai* v. *Sharjah*, *Palena* and *Laguna del Desierto* cases, and it will suffice merely to take note of those observations at this stage.

The third test is associated with provenance and contemporaneity of the *practice of tribunals* and authoritative *bodies* as opposed to the subsequent conduct of the *parties*. This practice may be both anterior and posterior to the decision being interpreted. As far as subsequent situations are concerned, one school of thought would suggest that, once the decision has been definitively made and communicated to the parties, then any subsequent act or statement purporting to interpret the decision adopted by it will have no weight and will probably not even be admitted. In this context, it will suffice to reiterate the *functus officio* rule described earlier, and the strict position adopted by the Permanent Court of International Justice in the *Jaworzina* case.

It will be recalled that, in that case, Poland relied, *inter alia*, on the letter of 13 November 1922, addressed by the President of the Conference of Ambassadors to the Polish and Czechoslovak ministers, in which the President stated that the frontier in the Jaworzina sector 'was not defined in the decision of July 28th, 1920'. Poland asserted that the Conference, which had already taken the decision of 28 July 1920, was 'the most authoritative and reliable interpretation of the intention expressed at that time, and that such an interpretation, being drawn from the most reliable source, must be respected by all, in accordance with the principle: *ejus est interpretare legum cujus condere*'.[612] The Court held that it was an established principle that the right of giving an authoritative interpretation of a legal rule remained solely with the person or body vested with the power to modify or suppress it.[613] Inasmuch as it had not been authorised to interpret the decision, the Conference of Ambassadors was *functus officio* after the decision had been made, and accordingly the purported interpretation had no probative weight for the Court.

However, the Permanent Court of International Justice gave full weight to other materials which tended to throw light on the question of the status of the decision of 28 July 1920. The Court held that maps could not be regarded as conclusive proof independently of the text of the decisions, 'but in the present case they confirm in a singularly convincing manner the conclusions drawn from the documents and from a legal analysis of them'.[614] It held that the Treaty of Sèvres was of 'interest' inasmuch as it was a document contemporary with the July 1920 decision and because it *emanated from the source, namely, the Conference of Ambassadors*. According to Article I of that Treaty, the frontier in the districts of Orava and Spisz was to be formed by the old frontier of Galicia and Hungary, except at those points where the decision of 28 July 1920 had departed from that frontier and had set up new alignments.

It held that the new alignment was in conformity with that found on the large-scale map annexed to the decision of 28 July 1920 showing the three disputed districts.[615] Similarly, the decree subsequent to the July 1920 decision, namely, that of 7 August 1920, issued by the International Sub-Commission of Spisz and Orava which governed the handing over to Poland and Czechoslovakia of the districts allocated to them, mentioned by name the communes separated by the new frontier, including Jaworzina. The Court held that it was evident that the Commissioners who were directly responsible for the carrying out of the decision of 28 July 1920 did not doubt that the whole territory of Spisz had been divided by that decision.[616]

612 Supra (note 107), p. 37. 613 *Ibid.*, pp. 37–8. 614 *Ibid.*, p. 33. 615 *Ibid.*, pp. 33–4.

616 *Ibid.*, p. 34. Cf. the map produced by the Yugoslav Government in *Monastery of Saint-Naoum* advisory opinion and which was excluded from consideration. It was alleged that the map represented the delimitation of the London Protocol of 11 August 1913. Even admitting, the Permanent Court said, that the map line represented the

Materials and documentation may also not be taken into consideration or be given great probative weight where the said materials are unreliable for one reason or another; it stands to reason that the interpreting tribunal will look upon them with circumspection, even if the documents being relied upon are authoritative in provenance and contemporaneous with the decision. In *Dubai* v. *Sharjah*, Dubai relied on the Walker map of either 1956 or 1957 which, it argued, was the basis of the Tripp decision of 1956[617] and which established the location of Hadhib Azana well to the north of Nahada Amair and close to Sharjah's industrial zone. Sharjah's position was that no map was attached to the Tripp decision of 1956, 'and therefore, the maps produced in evidence and referred to above cannot be considered as an integral part of that decision'. It also adduced in evidence another Walker map which may also have served as the basis of the Tripp decision, and which showed Hadhib Azana located a good way to the east of Nahada Amair.[618] The Court of Arbitration held that 'it is necessary to set aside both of the maps prepared by Mr Walker, in so far as the location of Hadhib Azana is concerned, since, although prepared by the same person, they are mutually contradictory on the general line of the boundary in this area'.[619]

The dispute over the interpretation of the award of 1903 in the *Alaska Boundary Case* provides an opportunity for viewing materials anterior to the award. It will be useful to refer once again to the Canadian argument, that the decision of 1903 was a decision which provided a proper maritime frontier in addition to allocating land and islands to the two disputing parties. Reflecting on this view, Bourne and McRae note that, in its 1909 report to the Canadian Government, the Committee of the Privy Council observed that, in the Treaty of 1846, the United States and Great Britain had drawn the frontier along the middle of the Strait of Juan de Fuca, treating waters on either side as territorial.[620] The Strait is between ten and twenty miles in width. Subsequently, a dispute arose regarding the 'correct' canal along which the boundary ought to run in the Strait, and the matter was referred to the German Emperor for arbitration.[621]

delimitation provided in the first paragraph of this decision, it did not necessarily represent the Albanian frontier. Moreover, it held, the map was unsigned and its authentic character was not established. See supra (note 296), p. 21.

617 Walker, the Assistant Political Agent, carried out the necessary enquiries for the purposes of determining the Dubai–Sharjah frontier. He produced a number of sketches in 1955 which Dubai alleged formed the basis of the map in question. His report and map informed the Tripp decision of 3 July 1956: 91 ILR 628–9. He submitted a further report in 1964. See note 11 above.

618 91 ILR 629.

619 *Ibid.*, p. 630.

620 Supra (note 557), pp. 218–19; and see Report of the Committee of the Canadian Privy Council (note 560), pp. 41 and 43.

621 Supra (note 557), pp. 218–19.

In the *San Juan de Fuca* arbitration conducted in 1872,[622] the arbitrator decided that it was the Haro Canal, as urged by the United States, as opposed to the Rosario Canal (or Strait), as advocated by Great Britain, which constituted the true boundary.[623] Thus the division by the parties (as well as the arbitrator) of the Strait was a division of both maritime and land areas and this constituted evidence that extensive maritime territory could be understood as appertaining to coastal States. When the Law Officers in London pointed out that the waters of the San Juan de Fuca Strait were *inter fauces terrae*,[624] the Committee responded that, in both cases, namely, the Dixon Entrance and the Hecate Strait on the one side, and the San Juan de Fuca Strait on the other, the waters could not be regarded as territorial (in the strict sense of the three-mile limit claimed by Great Britain), but that, in the phraseology of Bourne and McRae, 'in both cases international law of the time would not have appeared to prohibit a claim by the coastal States to jurisdiction'.[625] They went on to contend:

> To argue that the parties could not have intended to divide the waters of Dixon Entrance in the manner contended for by Canada because to do so would be contrary to international law would [be to] weaken the position of both states in their assertion of jurisdiction in the Strait of Juan de Fuca.[626]

Although that may not be an absolutely accurate analysis of the law given that the assertion of jurisdiction by both States has been in effect for over 100 years without challenge by other maritime States, the general position is that at times earlier decisions of other tribunals on by and large the same subject-matter may throw light on the true intentions of the parties, and more importantly, the meaning of an arbitral award or judgment. They will not, however, be conclusive of the matter.

As far as subsequent authoritative third party materials are concerned, Bourne and McRae also refer to the *North Atlantic Coast Fisheries* arbitration,[627] decided seven years later in 1910. One of the arguments urged by the United States was that, while a maritime State could renounce its treaty rights to fish in foreign territorial waters, it could not renounce its natural right to fish on the high seas.[628] The Tribunal, however, rejected this argument, and observed that, while it could not grant a right to fish on the high seas, a State could, within certain definite limits, abandon such a right. France and Spain had abandoned their fishing rights in the

[622] 62 BFSP 188. [623] *Ibid.* [624] Supra (note 469), p. 45; and see *ibid.*, pp. 38–9.
[625] Supra (note 557), p. 218. See the Treaty of 8 May 1871: 61 BFSP 40.
[626] Supra (note 557), pp. 218–19. [627] 4 (1910) AJIL 948. [628] *Ibid.*, p. 978.

waters in question in 1763. 'By a Convention', it held, 'between the United Kingdom and the United States in 1846 the two countries assumed ownership over waters in Fuca Straits at distances from the shore as great as [seventeen] miles.'[629]

The implication Canada would seek to exploit is that, by referring to the 'ownership' of waters, the tribunal in effect confirmed the understanding of both parties at that time that the 1846 line, as clarified by the 1903 award, purported to divide maritime areas and attribute sovereignty accordingly. Thus an *obiter* statement made by a subsequent tribunal may be relied on by a State to establish a meaning or to clarify the scope and effect of a tribunal's decision.

Finally, in this context, it would appear that the propositions put forward above are in direct conflict with the rule enunciated by the Permanent Court of International Justice in *Chorzów Factory (Interpretation of Judgments Nos. 7 and 8)*, cited above. However, the position adopted by the Court can be reconciled by distinguishing the circumstances and putting them in context. The Court in that case was conscious that, despite the fact that it was asked to provide an interpretation of a disputed judgment, the proceedings on the merits in the case concerning the compensation claimed by the German Government on the basis of Judgment No. 7, that is, *Certain German Interests in Polish Upper Silesia*,[630] were still pending before the Court. It was also aware that the Polish Government would have tried to rely in that case on the result of the municipal litigation brought by it before the Tribunal of Katowice against the Oberschlesische.

'At all events', the Court noted, 'the obligation incumbent upon the Court under Article 60 of the Statute to construe its judgments at the request of any party, cannot be set aside merely because the interpretation to be given by the Court might possibly be of importance in another case which is pending. The interpretation adds nothing to the decision, which has acquired the force of *res judicata*, and can only have binding force within the limits of what was decided in the judgment construed.'[631] In effect, the Court was stating that, whatever the outcome of the case before the Polish tribunal, it could not have any effect on the what it had already observed in the previous judgment in terms of clarifying its meaning and scope. Seen in this light then the propositions put forward above do not conflict with the *dicta* of the Permanent Court of International Justice.

[629] *Ibid*. See also the reference to this in Parry (note 469), generally pp. 38–9.

[630] PCIJ Reports, Series A, No. 7 (1926), p. 4.

[631] Supra (note 273), p. 21.

V. The principle of effectiveness

Overarching and wide-ranging in application, this rule guides tribunals in a variety of situations, including treaty and decision-based interpretative processes. In simple terms, a tribunal will tend to interpret a decision of an arbitral or judicial tribunal in a way which gives maximum effect to the judgment or award. The rationale of the principle of effectiveness is rooted in the basic logic of the matter, a guide to which is evident from the converse of the rule. Hence, when interpreting a passage in a decision, the tribunal will be motivated by the fact that any interpretation, which is neither substantially meaningful nor possessed of utility, is to be avoided for obvious reasons. 'The so-called rule of the *effet utile*', the Tribunal held in *Laguna del Desierto*, 'which is founded on the unvarying and uninterrupted practice of the courts, provides that an instrument must always be interpreted so as to give it some effect. Applying this rule to the matter at issue, it follows that the term "local water-parting", as used by the 1902 Arbitrator, ought to be interpreted here so as to give it some effective meaning. Accordingly, the definition of local water-parting as a line which separates waters which flow into the same ocean, presented as self-evident in the Chilean Memorial, cannot be accepted by the Tribunal.'[632] If this definition were applied to the award line of 1902 which fixed the line along the local water-parting between Boundary Post 62 and Mount Fitzroy, the result would be that there would not be any local water-parting between these two points and that consequently the award could not be applied on the ground. 'The fact', it held, 'is that [Boundary Post] 62 is situated in a Pacific basin while Mount Fitzroy is on the Atlantic side. Hence, for at least part of its course the water-parting joining them separates waters draining into different oceans.'[633]

The Argentine thesis, however, gave full effect to the award boundary, a thesis based on simply giving the expression its normal or usual meaning and following the water-parting regardless of the ocean in which the waters eventually flowed – a view which was accepted by the Tribunal as being the correct interpretation. It instructed the Expert Geographer to identify the local water-parting.[634]

[632] 113 ILR 70; and p. 72; and see general comments, pp. 44–5.
[633] *Ibid.*, p. 70.
[634] See, generally, *ibid.*, pp. 60–77.

VI. The doctrine of acquiescence, recognition and estoppel

The principle of acquiescence and the related procedural rule of estoppel are closely related to the observations made in section IV above, but are treated separately insofar as the crucial issue of a foreclosure of positions, as entailed in a discussion of acquiescence and estoppel, is not of crucial relevance to that aspect of the law. Even so, these rules, under the general banner of a doctrine, are, it may be emphasised, central to the law of title to territory, manifesting themselves in a variety of ways in the corpus of the law on the matter. It is no wonder, then, that these rules have found relevance and application in matters dealing with the interpretation of judgments and awards in territorial and boundary disputes.

Where a tribunal is requested to interpret a decision of an arbitral or judicial body, then, in the course of its examination, it may consider it appropriate to apply rules of law related to, or which are founded on, the general principle that a State Party to the litigation cannot be allowed to blow hot and cold on the same matter at the same time or on different occasions. It is the case that a situation prevailing on the ground for a reasonably long period of time cannot lightly be called into question, for it benefits from an approach which tends to favour the *status quo*, especially where both parties have by their acts and/or omission conveyed the notion of acceptance and agreement. It also benefits from the proposition that, even if a territorial situation is not entirely consistent with the law, or where a territorial allocation is inconsistent with the terms and obligations of a boundary treaty or other binding rule of law, then that situation acquires in effect a degree of validity, despite its legally controversial origins, provided that it is subsequently accepted by the parties in express terms or by necessary implication.

The important point here is that the principle of acquiescence and estoppel has a threefold effect. In the first place, the application of the principle creates substantive rights for one party against the other in all the appropriate legal circumstances. In the second place, acquiescence and recognition can shed light on the true meaning and implementation of the earlier decision. Thirdly, acquiescence and estoppel can effectively vary the alignment to the extent of the acquiescence manifest by the State in question. *New Hampshire* v. *Maine*[635] (2001), in which the Supreme Court of the United States was requested to decide a boundary dispute in the

[635] 532 US 742 (2001). For a general review, see Reed, *Shore and Sea Boundaries*, Washington, DC, 2000, vol. III, pp. 168–71.

Piscataqua River, is instructive in terms of providing perspectives on the matter. Of fundamental importance to the dispute was the decree issued by King George II in 1740. In order, however, fully to appreciate the legal character of this instrument, it is appropriate to take brief note of the historical provenance of this dispute.[636]

In the early part of the eighteenth century, the Province of New Hampshire was in a major dispute regarding its boundaries with Massachusetts. Although the dispute focused on the Merrimac River which lay to the south and south-west of New Hampshire, there were also boundary issues to the north and north-east with Maine which was then an integral part of Massachusetts.[637] Unable to settle the dispute, the representatives of the colonies of New Hampshire and Massachusetts Bay approached the King of England in 1731 for a settlement of the problem. The matter was referred to the Board of Trade, which body recommended the formation of a panel of commissioners from the other New England colonies to decide the issue.

This panel, appointed in 1737, heard argument, examined evidence and decided that the 'Dividing Line' passed up through the mouth of Piscataqua (later, Portsmouth) Harbor and up the middle of the river to the furthest head thereof. The line seaward of the harbour was also drawn through the middle of the harbour and by doing so the offshore islands to the south and southeast of the Dividing Line were allocated to New Hampshire and those to the north and north-east to Massachusetts Bay.[638] Neither province, however, was satisfied and appealed to the Lords of the Committee of the Privy Council for Hearing Appeals from the Plantations. The following year, the Committee of the Privy Council summarily affirmed the panel's decision, whereupon the King issued the decree of 1740 in which he drew the boundary through the mouth of the Piscataqua, then along the middle of the river and the harbour between the islands, to the sea on the southerly side.[639]

[636] This part of the history is based on *New Hampshire* v. *Maine*, 426 US 363 (1976) and the Brief for the United States as Amicus Curiae submitted in that case: supra (note 497), pp. 1–6.

[637] Brief for the United States as Amicus Curiae (note 497), p. 3. It is useful to note that, by 1691, Massachusetts had fully acquired Maine after nearly half a century of proprietary and governmental expansion. It was finally admitted to the American Union as a state in 1820.

[638] The relevant part of the report of the Commissioners is reproduced in Brief for the United States as Amicus Curiae (note 497), p. 4.

[639] 426 US 363 (1976), at pp. 366–7; and Brief for the United States as Amicus Curiae (note 497), pp. 5–6.

In effect, therefore, the dispute, which developed subsequently in the 1970s between the two states regarding the location of the mouth and the middle of the Piscataqua river and the middle of the harbour,[640] was a controversy regarding the terms of a royal decree based on a decision reached first by an arbitral process and confirmed subsequently by an appellate body, albeit summarily.[641] Thus, in 1973, New Hampshire petitioned the Supreme Court to resolve the matter, but, just prior to trial, New Hampshire and Maine agreed the lateral marine boundary separating the states between the mouth of Portsmouth Harbor and the entrance to Gosport Harbor in the Isles of Shoals. Accordingly, the two states proposed a joint consent decree based on a stipulated record.[642] It was agreed that the descriptive words 'Middle of the River' in the 1740 decree referred to the middle of the Piscataqua's main channel of navigation.[643] On the basis of this agreement, the two states were able to determine the northern terminus of the lateral maritime boundary.

The matter was referred to a Special Master, who objected to the filing of a consent decree on the ground, *inter alia*, that the language of the 1740 decree demonstrated that the intention was not to provide a *thalweg* or a main channel boundary but a line running along the geographic middle.[644] Accordingly, the *medium filum acquae* ought to be determined by reference to legal principles and not agreements of convenience (to which the Court was required to place its *imprimatur*).[645] A further fact was that the agreed boundaries were absolutely straight lines, and it was 'incredible that a line following the main or deepest channel would proceed on such an invariable course'.[646] The Supreme Court overruled the Special Master in *New Hampshire* v. *Maine* (1976). The logic was that the consent decree did nothing more than record the agreement regarding the precise location of the disputed points in the river and there was no prejudice to

[640] The dispute originated in a controversy over lobster fishing in the seabed: *New Hampshire* v. *Maine*, 414 US 810 (1973).

[641] Cf. the fact that, in theory and in law, the King in Council exercised his sovereign prerogative to determine the boundaries of royal provinces as opposed to individual proprietors whose disputes were judged by English courts: Brief for the United States as Amicus Curiae (note 497), pp. 10–12, especially note 5 on pp. 10–11 and note 3 on p. 3. Hence, where there was no agreement, the King acted not as a judge but as the sovereign acting on the advice of his council: *Rhode Island* v. *Massachusetts*, 37 US (12 Peters) 657, at pp. 739–40, p. 740 and p. 743; and Brief for the United States as Amicus Curiae (note 497), notes 5 and 7, pp. 11–12.

[642] 426 US 363, at p. 365 (1976).

[643] See Joint Dissenting Opinion, *ibid.*, pp. 369–71; and *New Hampshire* v. *Maine*, 532 US 742, at p. 747 (2001).

[644] 426 US 363, at p. 371 (1976); and Brief for the United States as Amicus Curiae (note 497), pp. 6–9.

[645] 426 US 363, at p. 371 (1976).

[646] *Ibid.*, p. 372.

the functions of the Supreme Court under Article III of the United States Constitution. The agreement invested imprecise terms with definitions which gave effect to a decree which permanently fixed the boundary between the states.[647] The consent decree was issued in 1977 in *New Hampshire* v. *Maine* (1977).[648]

However, the 1977 consent decree, which was, in effect, an interpretative agreement of the 1740 royal decree which in turn was an embodiment of an arbitral and adjudicative process, dealt with only the lateral seaward boundary; the landward side of the river remained outside the scope of the Court's decree of 1977. In *New Hampshire* v. *Maine* (2001), it was New Hampshire's position that the inland river boundary ran along the low water mark on the Maine shore and that, consequently, its title lay over the whole of the river and harbour, including the naval shipyard on Seavey Island.[649] The contention was that the term 'Middle of the River' used in the 1740 decree denoted the main branch of the river, and not a mid-channel alignment. Moreover, New Hampshire claimed that, even if the King's decree of 1740 once controlled, subsequent events had now placed the boundary along Maine's shore,[650] and to that extent it was argued that New Hampshire had exercised sole jurisdiction over shipping and military activities in Portsmouth Harbor during the decades before and after the 1740 decree.[651] Apart from asserting jurisdiction over the same harbour and shipyard on Seavey Island, Maine argued that the 1740 decree and the 1977 consent judgment divided the river along the *thalweg*, a division which placed Seavey Island within Maine's jurisdiction and control. 'Those earlier proceedings, according to Maine, bar New Hampshire's complaint under principles of claim and issue preclusion as well as judicial estoppel.'[652]

The Supreme Court decided unanimously to reject New Hampshire's complaint. It concluded that the doctrine of judicial estoppel applied, and that, under that doctrine, 'New Hampshire is equitably barred from asserting – contrary to its position in the 1970s litigation – that the inland Piscataqua River runs along the Maine shore'.[653] Nor was the Court persuaded by New Hampshire's argument that there was no searching historical enquiry into the meaning of the term 'Middle of the River', and hence the decree was based on imperfect knowledge. It was noted by the Court:

[647] *Ibid.*, p. 369. [648] 434 US 1 (1977). [649] 532 US 742, at p. 748 (2001).
[650] Brief for the United States as Amicus Curiae (note 497), p. 14.
[651] 532 US 742, at p. 748 (2001). [652] *Ibid.* [653] *Ibid.*, p. 749.

The pleadings in the lateral marine boundary case show that New Hampshire did engage in 'a searching historical inquiry' into the meaning of 'Middle of the River'. None of the historical evidence cited by New Hampshire remotely suggested that the Piscataqua River boundary runs along the Maine shore. In fact, in attempting to place the boundary at the geographic middle of the river, New Hampshire acknowledged that its agents in 1740 understood the King's order to 'adjudg[e] half of the river to' the portion of Massachusetts that is now Maine . . . In addition, this Court independently determined that 'there is nothing to suggest that the location of the 1740 boundary agreed upon by the States is wholly contrary to relevant evidence'.[654]

The Court went on to note Maine's objection, that, had New Hampshire's location of the frontier along the Maine shore been correct, it would have meant that the northern terminus would have been much closer to Maine, resulting in hundreds if not thousand of acres of Maine's territory falling to New Hampshire.[655] Tellingly, however, New Hampshire at the time understood the importance of placing the northern terminus as close to Maine as possible. However, it argued for a *medium filum acquae* by using the banks of the river and not low tide elevations therein as proposed by the Special Master, a methodology which would have placed the northern terminus 350 yards closer to the Maine shore.[656] The Court held:

In short, considerations of equity persuade us that application of judicial estoppel is appropriate in this case. Having convinced this Court to accept one interpretation of 'Middle of the River', and having benefited from that interpretation, New Hampshire now urges an inconsistent interpretation to gain an additional advantage at Maine's expense. Were we to accept New Hampshire's latest view, the 'risk of inconsistent court determinations' would become a reality. We cannot interpret 'Middle of the River' in the 1740 decree to mean two different things along the same boundary line without undermining the integrity of the judicial process.[657]

One very important element in these legal circumstances is the *facta* of concrete acts of State authority carried out on the ground. It is the case that tribunals have given the highest effect to such acts in various cases of acquiescence, including in the interpretation of decisions, provided of course all relevant criteria are also satisfied. A good example of this is to be found in *Dubai* v. *Sharjah*. In that case, the Court of Arbitration did not hesitate to give State acts full effect with a view to shedding light on the meaning and scope of the Tripp decisions. Although the Court here was dealing with decisions not of an arbitral character, and although its task was not that of interpretation *expressis verbis*, but that of, *inter alia*, identifying the places indicated in the Tripp decisions, it is nevertheless

[654] *Ibid.*, pp. 753–4. [655] *Ibid.*, p. 754. [656] *Ibid.* [657] *Ibid.*, p. 755.

interesting to note that the Court found that Sharjah had failed to protest the acts of authority performed by Dubai in the Al Mamzer peninsula, and *vice versa* with respect to the placing of the boundary in Nahada Amair.[658] 'The Court', it held, 'has thus arrived at the conclusion that the Government of Dubai must be taken to have acquiesced in this part [namely, the Nahada Amair segment] of the second decision of Mr Tripp.'[659] Accordingly, it went on to reject Dubai's contention that the boundary in this part passed through Gezirat al Hubab.[660] Thus, not only was the decision taken by Tripp given appropriate clarification, the Court by doing so effectively created rights in favour of the respective parties.

It is important to stress that acts of State authority are to be seen in conjunction with acts conveying acceptance. Where the losing State remains silent, the situation is that of acquiescence; where, however, positive acts on the ground convey acceptance, then those acts are more in the nature of recognition. In this context, it will also be useful to refer to *Virginia* v. *Maryland*, a case decided by the Supreme Court in 2003.[661] The question in issue involved ascertaining the nature and extent of the rights exercised by these two states with respect to the Potomac River.

A 400-year-old dispute over control of the river,[662] this case was in effect the latest milestone in the history of that controversy. In 1785, state commissioners from the two riparian states concluded an agreement, namely the Compact of 1785, which provided that the Potomac would be the common highway for the purposes of navigation and commerce and that all laws with respect to the river would be made with the mutual consent and approbation of both Maryland and Virginia. Jurisdiction over criminal offences was to be determined by reference to the citizenship of the offender. This agreement was subsequently ratified by the legislatures of the two states.

The Compact of 1785, however, did not decide the crucial issue of the boundary in and sovereignty over the Potomac, and thus in 1877 these issues were referred to arbitration. A decision returned by two eminent lawyers, the Black–Jenkins Award, allocated the entire river to Maryland and placed the boundary at the low-water mark on the Virginia (south) shore. However, Article Fourth of the Award also provided that Virginia was 'entitled not only to full dominion over the soil to the low-water mark on the south shore of the Potomac, but has a right to such use of the river beyond the low-water mark as may be necessary to the full enjoyment of

[658] 91 ILR 621–8. [659] *Ibid.*, p. 627. [660] *Ibid.*, p. 628.
[661] 540 US 56 (2003); 157 L Ed 2d 461. All references below are to 157 Law Ed.
[662] *Ibid.*, p. 470.

her riparian ownership, without impeding the navigation or otherwise interfering with the proper use of it by Maryland, agreeably to the compact of seventeen hundred and eighty-five'. Article Seventh granted the citizens of both states full property rights on the shores of the Potomac 'and the privilege of making and carrying out wharves and other improvements, so as not to obstruct or injure the navigation of the river'.[663]

The modern dispute crystallised when in 1996 Virginia applied for and was subsequently refused permits from Maryland for the construction of a water intake structure extending 725 feet from the Virginia shore. Although Virginia went through an administrative appeals process for two years, it continued to maintain that it was, in principle, entitled to build the disputed structure.[664] Before the Supreme Court the issue was whether Maryland was precluded from requiring Virginia to obtain a permit in order to construct improvements appurtenant to the Virginian side of the river.

To decide this and related questions, the Court was obliged to interpret the Black–Jenkins Award. One of the arguments put forward by Maryland was that, although Article Seventh did not expressly grant Maryland the sovereign authority to regulate the riparian rights of citizens of both states, this was because the issue of sovereignty over the river was well settled by the time the Award was issued. The Court held that such a claim was belied not only by the Compact of 1785 but also by the findings contained in the Award of 1877.[665] It also rejected the argument that the clause in Article Fourth, which made Virginia's riparian rights subject to non-interference with Maryland's 'proper use' of the Potomac, was evidence of its right to regulate water usage from the Virginian side.[666]

More importantly for present purposes, Maryland also argued that Virginia had lost her sovereign riparian rights by acquiescing in Maryland's regulation of water withdrawal and waterway construction activities. It was pointed out that Virginia had applied for such withdrawal permits in 1956 and that, between 1957 and 1996, Maryland had issued twenty-nine water withdrawal permits to Virginian entities.[667] Further, 'in the 125 years since the Black–Jenkins Award, Virginia ha[d] acquiesced in [Maryland's] pervasive exercise of police powers over activities occurring on piers and wharves beyond the low-water mark'.[668]

[663] *Ibid.*, pp. 471–2. [664] *Ibid.*, p. 473. [665] Generally, *ibid.*, pp. 475–80.
[666] *Ibid.*, pp. 479–80. [667] *Ibid.*, pp. 472–3 and 480–2. [668] *Ibid.*, p. 480.

The Court ruled against this contention by drawing a distinction between criminal jurisdiction and the narrower question of Maryland's alleged regulatory rights to the river. As regards the exercise of activities of the latter kind, the time period in question was just forty-three years at the most. This, it held, was too short a period for prescription. However, even if it were adequate in terms of time, there was no evidence of acquiescence by Virginia. It had vigorously protested Maryland's asserted authority during negotiations which led to the passage of section 181 of the federal Water Resources Development Act of 1976, and it had continued to resist Maryland's proposals at three Congressional hearings. Section 181 required the riparians to enter into an agreement with the Secretary of the US Army apportioning waters of the Potomac during times of low flow, and there was nothing in this agreement, namely, the Low Flow Allocation Agreement, which would suggest that Virginia had acknowledged that Maryland had a vested right to regulate Virginia's riparian rights.[669]

The observations made above demonstrate, in the first place, that, where a territorial regime, maintained steadfastly on the ground, is at variance with the award, then, in the event of sustained silence by the other party over a period of time, the tribunal's award will be understood as having been modified to the extent of the variance as compared to the delimitation provided by the tribunal. This was the essence of Maryland's assertion before both the Court, and earlier before the Special Master, an assertion not accepted by either body.

In the second place, the principle of acquiescence comes into play as an aid also to the interpretation of the award. Although it had not argued from acquiescence, had Maryland done so, it could also easily have been asserted that Articles Fourth and Seventh of the Black–Jenkins Award ought to be interpreted in light of the fact that Virginia had failed to protest the regulatory activities of Maryland and that Virginia had accepted Maryland's right to grant permits for withdrawal and construction activities in the Potomac. It would then have followed that any interpretation of the two relevant provisions not consistent with this legal and factual state of affairs could not be urged before the Court, that is to say, Virginia would be estopped from urging an interpretation which effectively contradicted the fact that Maryland had regulatory rights in the Potomac. This indeed was not the decision of the Court, but the application of the principles of acquiescence is clear.

[669] *Ibid.*, pp. 480–2.

Acts on the ground were also given legal significance in *Colombia* v. *Venezuela* (1922),[670] an arbitral proceeding in which a dispute concerning the Arbitral Sentence of the Crown of Spain of March 1891 was finally put to rest. In the latter arbitration, namely, *Colombia* v. *Venezuela* (1891),[671] a long-standing border dispute was settled and certain disputed territories in the possession of Venezuela were awarded to Colombia.[672] In April 1894, a treaty was agreed whereby Venezuela conceded some parts of the line for the purposes of rectification in a spirit of mutual convenience and common interest.[673]

In 1898, a treaty for the delimitation and demarcation of the frontier as defined by the 1891 line was concluded, and in 1899 a Mixed Commission was established to execute the award on the ground. Operating in two sectors, the Commission was able to decide the location of the line in some parts of the frontier; it failed, however, to find agreement with respect to other sectors. By 1901, further work on the boundary was suspended. Colombia argued that territory allocated to it by the line of 1891 and the partial demarcation carried out by the Commission ought to be transferred to it without further formalities, while 'Venezuela insisted on delays said to be necessitated by her internal law requiring the participation of her Legislature'.[674]

In 1916, the two States concluded a *compromis*,[675] Article 1 of which requested the Swiss Federal Council to determine whether the execution of the award could be carried out partially or integrally 'in order that the territories may be occupied which were recognised as belonging to each of the two Nations, and which were not occupied by them before the award of 1891'. It is, of course, the case that the matter before the Council was not one of interpretation of the award, for it was not requested to explain the *meaning* of certain passages therein, a task central to interpretation. Nevertheless, the decision is not altogether irrelevant for present purposes because the tribunal was indeed asked to clarify the precise legal *effects* of that decision, a task it could not have performed without looking at the award of 1891 and the legal context and circumstances thereof. To that extent, then, it was a different *kind* of interpretative exercise, that is, an *ad hoc* judicial remedy executed for the purpose of resolving a question arising from the exercise of arbitral authority.

Venezuela argued, *inter alia*, that insofar as it was an indivisible whole, the award could not be executed in some sectors of the frontier and not

670 1 *Annual Digest* 84. 671 83 BFSP 387. 672 1 *Annual Digest* 85.
673 Stuyt (note 136), p. 125. 674 Supra (note 670), p. 85. 675 110 BFSP 829.

others: it would amount to satisfying only some rights while others remained unsatisfied. Colombia's argument rested on the point that a partial execution of arbitral awards was admissible in both law and State practice; and that no formalities regarding the handing over of territory were required where the latter was judged indisputably to belong to the receiving State, particularly where the award was based on the principle of *uti possidetis*, a principle recognised by both disputant parties. Moreover, the principle of partial execution of the award involving the division of the frontier into various sectors was recognised by Colombia and Venezuela in the negotiations and agreements between them.[676]

The Swiss Federal Council decided in favour of Colombia. One of the arguments it upheld was that there was no absolute rule requiring a formal transfer of territory.[677] There were cases on record in which no formal delivery of territory had ever taken place in matters of cession. Moreover, by virtue of the principle of *uti possidetis*, cession had already taken place and either State was presumed to have possessed since 1810 sovereignty over the territories awarded to it by the arbitrator, the Spanish Crown.[678] For present purposes, it is more relevant to examine the argument from conduct. The Swiss Federal Council pointed out that, since the 1891 award, the two parties had by their acts acknowledged the principle of partial execution of the award, and both Colombia and Venezuela had occupied territory held respectively to belong to them. Further, it held:[679]

> When in 1907 Colombia ceded to Brazil part of these territories Venezuela did not protest against the cession; neither did she protest in 1900 against the Colombian occupation of the Orinoco basin. If the arbitrator were now to adopt the view that the parties ought to restore to one another territories which they occupied by virtue of the award of 1891, then that would mean to impose upon them the duty not only to refrain from occupying what has been recognised as belonging to them, but also to restore for an indefinite period their own territory to an irregular possessor. Thirty years have elapsed since the Spanish award was given; that award cannot indefinitely remain in the nature of a juridical abstraction.

Thus, it seems that, while it accepted the principle of acquiescence and estoppel, the Swiss Federal Council hesitated to apply it *eo nomine*. In effect, it stopped just short of holding that Venezuela had acquiesced in the partial execution of the decision of 1891, and that it was, therefore, estopped from arguing that Colombia ought to wait for the demarcation of the whole frontier before Venezuela formally transferred possession of

[676] Generally, see supra (note 670), p. 86. [677] *Ibid.*, pp. 87–8. [678] *Ibid.*, p. 86.
[679] *Ibid.*, pp. 88–9. Inverted commas from last sentence deleted.

the territory. Nor was Venezuela able to urge the Council to oblige the occupant to restore territory to the former possessor State.

The crucial issue here is that the conduct of the parties, particularly Venezuela's conduct, was such that it not only cast light on the scope and purport of the 1891 award, it also had a direct effect on the positions adopted by the parties where and to the extent that it was inconsistent with such conduct. Thus, the conduct, namely, occupation and cession of territory by the parties and a failure by them to register their protest at the appropriate occasions with a view to preserving their respective positions, had both substantive and procedural effects on the situation. Thus, in the first place, it clarified the full scope of the rights gained by Colombia and Venezuela on the basis of the Spanish arbitrator's award. In the second place, it prevented both parties from urging any contentions inconsistent with the position adopted earlier by them.

To be sure, the doctrine under consideration does not apply only to concrete acts of State authority carried out on the ground. Insofar as the main legal requirement is good evidence of some manifestations of State authority, only one kind of which is acts of sovereign authority, even documentation may be relevant to acquiescence. Reference in this regard may be made to *Request for Revision and Interpretation of the 1994 Judgment*. Although they were made in the context of the application of a request for revision of the award, the observations set out below are closely related to and connected with the interpretation of the decision of 1994 and hence warrant close attention here.

One of Chile's arguments was that the map of the Mixed Boundary Commission of 1991, the scale of which was 1:50,000, contained crucial errors, and that accordingly it ought not to have been taken into account by the Tribunal in the 1994 interpretative proceedings with respect to the award of 1902.[680] In the interpretative and revision proceedings of 1995, the Tribunal held that Chile had relied extensively on that map in 1994 and that it had never made any objections as to its cartographic accuracy. On the contrary, Chile had confirmed it.[681] Accordingly, 'Chile's conduct in the course of the arbitral proceedings with regard to the Map of the Mixed Boundary Commission . . . debars it from now alleging that that map contains errors that were never referred to in those proceedings'.[682]

In order to dissociate itself from the map, Chile had claimed that it was neither an official map nor a document of the Commission. 'To this', the Tribunal said, '[we] would point out that what counts is not whether the

[680] See, generally, 113 ILR 215–17. [681] *Ibid.*, pp. 220–2. [682] *Ibid.*, p. 222.

Map was an official document of the Commission, but whether Chile relied upon it without reservation, irrespective of the status – definitive, provisional or official – attributed to it by the Mixed Boundary Commission'.[683] In other words, when Chile relied on the Commission's map, it thereafter prejudiced its right to denounce the map on the ground of geographical inaccuracy. As such, Chile was effectively estopped from questioning its legal significance, and this meant that the Tribunal was within its powers to apply the map and clarify the matter.

Of course, the precise scope and effect of this doctrine of law will depend on the context and circumstances of the case, including the powers of the tribunal. Thus, in the *Palena* case, where it was required to determine the extent to which the frontier between Boundary Posts 16 and 17 had remained unsettled since the 1902 award and to interpret and fulfil that decision in the unsettled areas, if any, the Court of Arbitration had to respond to Chile's argument that Argentina, by way of diplomatic representations to Chile between 1913 and 1915 'regarding the course and source of the river whose mouth is opposite [Boundary] Post 16, was and still now is precluded from denying that the boundary follows the course of a channel which had its source in the vicinity of Cerro Herrero'.[684] Argentina had its own claim of estoppel against Chile. Argentina argued that Chile, by reason of a series of official maps published between 1913 and 1952, was precluded from claiming that the frontier should follow the channel which Argentina called Rio Falso Engano and that it should follow the Argentine Rio Encuentro.[685]

The point of concern here is that, after examining the correspondence between the parties and other documentation, including the cartography, the Court came to the conclusion that no claim of estoppel had been made out by either party against the other, and therefore both were free without preclusion of any kind to put forward their respective contentions as regards the course of the boundary.[686] The significance of this is, on the one hand, that the principles of acquiescence and estoppel were relevant in that their application could have affected the location of the frontier, and, in view of that, any finding of the Court based on estoppel would have had a direct effect on the interpretation and fulfilment of the boundary award of 1902. On the other hand, acquiescence is not to be lightly presumed, that is to say, there is in such matters a reasonably high threshold to cross before acquiescence can be established.

[683] *Ibid.* [684] 38 ILR 77. [685] *Ibid.* [686] *Ibid.*, pp. 77–9.

The dispute between the United States and Canada arising from the *Alaska Boundary Case* is illustrative of this high threshold rule. To support its contentions that the 1903 award created a proper maritime frontier, the Government of Canada has asserted that, in 1908, the United States ambassador to Great Britain asked for permission to lay a telegraph cable in Hecate Strait and the Dixon Entrance and admitted that, because both were 'British waters', permission from London would be desirable.[687] It also points to a statement issued in 1897 by a Mr Alexander, a fishery expert from the United States, who is reported to have observed in that statement that the best banks of halibut were in Canadian waters. 'The principal halibut grounds', the Canadian Committee of the Privy Council said, 'in the waters in question are, without dispute, in the Hecate Strait.'[688]

Furthermore, Canadian sources also point to a request submitted by the United States Government in 1952 for permission to erect certain installations in the Dixon Entrance, permission for which installations was granted.[689] In 1955, the United States ambassador requested the Canadian Government to allow one of its survey ships to make a reconnaissance survey in the Strait ahead of a cable-laying exercise by a US company, and assured the Canadian Government that the cable would not be within three miles of the Canadian coast. The Canadian position was that, under the Navigable Waters Protection Act, permission from the Governor in Council was needed. Eventually, however, the cable was not laid.[690] It has also been pointed out that the US–Canadian International Boundary Commission did not treat the line differently from other sectors of the Alaska boundary; and that the US Commissioner 'kept trying to persuade his Canadian counterpart to agree to request their governments to move the boundary line from Cape Muzon to the middle of Dixon Entrance'.[691]

In their analysis of the matter, Bourne and McRae observe that the rule of estoppel cannot be applied in cases where there has been no reliance on the assertion, which, in this case, was the statement made by the US ambassador to Great Britain in 1908. While their overall conclusions on the non-applicability of estoppel are correct, Bourne and McRae are perhaps relying on an unnecessarily strict test for estoppel based on domestic law analogy. There is no reason, in international law, to look for reliance by the other party; neither case law nor State practice requires

[687] Report of the Committee of the Canadian Privy Council, see Parry (note 560), p. 40; and Bourne and McRae (note 557), pp. 212 and 219–20.

[688] Report of the Committee of the Canadian Privy Council (note 560), p. 40.

[689] Bourne and McRae (note 557), p. 215. [690] *Ibid.*, p. 215. [691] *Ibid.*, p. 214.

considerations of this kind. The rule in international law is far simpler in operation, and it is this. A State may be estopped from claiming a territorial or boundary regime, situation or location which is inconsistent with a regime, situation or location to which it has either acquiesced or recognised, where the former is an implied state of affairs and the latter express. In effect, therefore, acquiescence has to be proved by reference to three considerations of law.

The first is the existence of manifestations or assertions of territorial sovereignty based on rights arising from treaty or a judicial or arbitral decision or other legally valid facts, provided they create a *risk of loss* to another claimant State; the second is the *consideration of response*, that is, the absence of any evidence to counter or resist these manifestations, including acts on the ground and the issuing of protests; and the third is *the result* emerging out of these facts, that is, gain for the dominant State, loss for the recessive State and its consequential estoppel as a procedural device. This is, of course, an abbreviated account of an extremely complex doctrine, and for present purposes it is necessary only to state that there is normally no real risk of loss in isolated statements. It is the predominant effect of statements and conduct of the losing State which ought strongly to suggest that the losing State had effectively agreed to the boundary line and to the effects thereof. Where the overall effect is not that of acquiescence, there can be no estoppel.

On the whole, then, while a self-prejudicial statement may, in all the appropriate circumstances, amount to an admission of the situation and constitute evidence of the position adopted by the relevant State and its government, the fact is that acquiescence and estoppel are not to be lightly construed or presumed. It follows that, if the dispute were referred to a tribunal for the purposes of interpretation of the award of 1903, the tribunal would be obliged to consider, in the first place, these and other matters in order to determine the true legal and judicial intentions of the previous tribunal. It would have to determine whether the position adopted by the United States over the years with respect to the findings of the award of 1903 was or is consistent with having acquiesced in the interpretation urged by Canada, that is, that the Dixon Entrance is under Canadian sovereignty. The facts do not, however, convey any overarching sense of agreement on the part of the United States as regards the existence of a maritime frontier in the Dixon Entrance. In fact, the position adopted by the United States Government was that of rejection of the thesis that the line of 1903 was a maritime frontier. The general point is that not only does the principle of acquiescence have to be seen and applied with restraint owing to the fact that issues of territory are not to be determined on grounds other than those resting on complete certainty. The fact is that all the legal and factual circumstances have to be brought to bear in deciding what a particular tribunal had meant to convey in its disputed judgment.

VII. General recapitulation

Providing a brief recapitulation on the salient aspects of interpretation as practised by international tribunals in the matter of territorial and boundary disputes is useful insofar as it provides overall perspective. Perhaps the more fundamental of observations in this context is the one which has gone largely unnoticed in the literature, namely, that the right to request an interpretation of a judgment *as an incidental proceeding* – best represented by Article 60 of the Statute of the International Court of Justice – is but one species of a larger judicial remedy. Indeed, interpretation cannot be fully appreciated without emphasising the other species, namely, main case interpretation, a category which is more in the nature of a new case involving interpretation of a decision by a tribunal other than the one issuing the operative decision. Dividing interpretation into these two categories not only enables a better understanding of a complex remedy: it puts into perspective the fact that, because a new *compromis* will have to be made out for a main case interpretation, the tribunal may have to assume an approach which reflects a broader range of options, as opposed to the relatively narrow focus of incidental interpretation.

Nonetheless, a basic rule for both categories is that interpretation can only be put into effect as a remedy once the threshold criteria have been strictly applied. These criteria include proving the existence of a dispute and focusing primarily on the operative part of the decision. Examining the meaning and scope of an award or judgment and applying the restrictions with reference to the temporal element are part of the other set of threshold criteria. A fundamental fact is that the remedy of interpretation exists only by way of mutual agreement or consent. The converse point is of central concern, namely, that interpretation cannot be considered an inherent right or remedy of a tribunal. Where the tribunal is a permanent court, the right to provide clarification may be vested in the constitutive instrument or statute of that tribunal, and it would follow that becoming a party to such a treaty constitutes agreeing to a standing right to clarify the decision without having to seek agreement for interpretation.

Furthermore, the purpose and scope of interpretation are also to be viewed restrictively. The case law demonstrates that there must be a *bona fide* need for interpretation. Of course, this would exclude frivolous claims for clarification, but an observation of this kind, although true in nature, does not do justice to the principle. The essence of the requirement is that the clarification sought by one of the parties must not relate to issues other than those directly related to the need for clarification of the judgment or a decision. For the fact is that interpretation is not a licence to rehear the case in appeal; nor can the remedy of interpretation be seen as another attempt to secure a more favourable boundary or greater territory. It follows that applications predicated on reconsideration of the boundary for the purposes of securing a readjustment are in principle ruled out.

However, it may also be that clarification of *bona fide* uncertainties in the decision may, in practice, result in the alteration of the boundary. This may appear to be contrary to the *res judicata* rule, but it is not impossible to reconcile the two conflicting doctrines. One technique of reconciliation is predicated on the view that, in *terms of law*, there is no modification to the frontier line even if there is modification in fact. The boundary described in the subsequent decision could arguably be seen as always being *the* frontier in law, that is to say, the adjusted boundary can be seen as reflecting not only the situation described in the decision, but also what the tribunal had said or had intended to say. It is also possible to reconcile these contradictory principles by reference to the fact that States parties are free to vest a greater range of powers in the interpreting tribunal, and this is especially the case where the remedy of interpretation is a main case one. In this way, it can be argued that, provided there exists an appropriate range of powers vested in the tribunal, either in express terms or by necessary implication, interpretation can and does entail modification and adjustment, albeit to varying degrees of magnitude and extent. *Aliter*, the whole purpose of the interpretative process would, in such cases, stand defeated. It is clear that this construction is based on the *effet utile* principle.

As far as the basic principles of interpretation are concerned, it needs to be noted that tribunals are guided by rules similar to those of treaty interpretation, and accordingly the ordinary meanings of words are to be given full weight. There is also, generally speaking, a rule enabling tribunals to interpret an award or decision on the general rebuttable presumption that the terms of the previous decisions were consistent with general principles of law. In other words, while interpreting such decisions, the tribunal will operate on a *presumptio juris* that the previous tribunal, or the same tribunal in an earlier set of proceedings, did not decide to locate the boundary or determine the status of territory in any way inconsistent with principles of international law. A tribunal will also take into consideration all appropriate materials, relevant circumstances and even the subsequent conduct of the parties. The *caveat* here is that that, on many occasions, the role of the subsequent conduct of the *parties* will be extremely limited insofar as such conduct sheds light on what the *tribunal* had purported to decide.

Closely related to this is the principle of acquiescence and estoppel, and, in these situations, the tribunal may, in all the appropriate circumstances, find that one of the parties has succeeded in demonstrating to the tribunal's satisfaction that an interpretation contrary to that put forward by the losing State is unacceptable inasmuch as the latter had acquiesced in the location of the line and/or the status of the territory and was accordingly estopped from putting forward that construction before the tribunal.

PART IV · JUDICIAL REMEDIES: REVISION

7 The revision of judgments and awards

I. Preliminary observations

A judicial remedy closely related to, but different from, the interpretation of judgments and awards is that of the revision of decisions, that is to say, the power of a tribunal to revise its judgment or award.[692] In view of the pre-eminent status of the International Court of Justice, perhaps the most authoritative provision on the matter is Article 61 of its Statute, paragraph 1 of which provides the basic rule. It stipulates:

An application for revision of a judgment may be made only when it is based upon the discovery of some fact of such a nature as to be a decisive factor, which fact was, when the judgment was given, unknown to the Court and also to the party claiming revision, always provided that such ignorance was not due to negligence.

[692] See, generally, Rosenne (note 226), pp. 1669–86; and Rosenne (note 269), pp. 201–2 and 205–7; Sandifer, *Evidence Before International Tribunals*, 2nd edn, Charlottesville, VA, 1975, Chapter IX; Simpson and Fox (note 136), pp. 242–5; Fox (note 185), p. 168; Collier and Lowe (note 226), pp. 179–80; Bos (note 226), pp. 339–44; Geiss, 'Revision Proceedings Before the International Court of Justice', 63 (2003) Zeitschrift für ausländisches öffentliches Recht und Völkerrecht 167; Carlston (note 181), pp. 224–43 (inclusive of rehearing); and Carlston (note 305), pp. 222–3; Scelle, Special Rapporteur, 'Report on Arbitral Procedure', 1957 *Yearbook ILC*, vol. II, p. 1, at p. 11; UN Secretariat's Commentary on Arbitral Procedure (note 226), pp. 99–104; Hudson (note 136), pp. 122–6; Thirlway (note 226), pp. 89–102; Plender (note 226), pp. 305–8; Bowett (note 226), pp. 589–91; Jenks (note 226), pp. 133–4; Cheng, *General Principles of Law as Applied by International Courts and Tribunals*, London, 1953 (Cambridge Reprint, 1994), pp. 364–74 and 358–61; Hyde, *International Law Chiefly as Interpreted and Applied by the United States*, Boston, 1947, vol. II, pp. 1633–42; Merrills (note 136), p. 135; Strupp (note 136), pp. 683–5; Verzijl (note 136), pp. 564–74; Stone (note 226), pp. 94–5; and Reisman (note 226), pp. 208–12; and see Reisman, 'Revision of the South West Africa Cases', 7 (1966) VJIL 1, at pp. 16–19 and 58–9; and Brower and Brueschke (note 414), pp. 242 *et seq.*

Paragraph 2 provides that the proceedings shall be opened by a judgment in which the Court expressly records the existence of the new fact, recognises that it has such a character as to lay the case open for revision and (accordingly) declares the application admissible on that ground. Paragraph 3 states that the Court may require compliance with the terms of the judgment before it admits proceedings in revision. Paragraphs 4 and 5 provide temporal limits. All applications are to be made within six months of the discovery of the new fact, and a final overall time limit is placed for applications for revision at ten years from the date of the judgment. The evolution of the rule of revision is described below. At this preliminary stage, it will suffice to observe that the rule was modelled on Article 83 of the 1907 Hague Convention on the Pacific Settlement of Disputes,[693] and was also preceded in time by Article 63 of the Rules of Procedure Annexed to the 1923 Convention for the Establishment of an International Central American Tribunal.[694] Article 61 of the Statute of the International Court of Justice was later echoed in Article 38 of the International Law Commission's 1958 Draft Rules on Arbitral Procedure.[695] The rules expressed therein are regarded as being declaratory of customary international law. However, this matter is not free from complications, an aspect discussed in Chapters 10 and 11 below. In any event, the power enabling tribunals to revise their judgments (a) upon application by a litigating State and (b) under strict criteria, was, as Plender observed, followed closely by clauses on revision in the Statutes of the Courts of the European Communities (namely, the Euratom, European Community and European Coal and Steel Community).[696] These

[693] For commentary, see Hudson (note 136), pp. 208–9; and Sandifer (note 692), pp. 446–7. See also Strupp on revision clauses in the rules of procedure of the mixed arbitral courts established under the Treaty of Versailles, (note 136), pp. 683–4.

[694] Annex B to the Central American Convention for the Establishment of an International Central American Tribunal: Habicht (note 304), p. 38, at p. 46. Cf. the 1907 Convention for the Establishment of a Central American Court of Justice, which has no provision on revision: 2 (1908) AJIL 231; but see the Draft Pan American Court of Justice: see note 695.

[695] Further, see Article 11 of the Statute of the UN Administrative Tribunal: General Assembly Resolution 351 (A) (IV), 24 November 1949, and amended subsequently, including on 15 December 1997. Further, see Article 40 of the Draft Statute of the Pan American Court of Justice (note 301), p. 379; and Draft Article 13 of the Costa Rica Plan for a Pan American Court of Justice: see Appendix to the Statute of the Pan American Court of Justice (note 301).

[696] Supra (note 226), pp. 305–6. See Article 42 of the Treaty Establishing the European Atomic Energy Community, in 5 (1959) EYB 454, at p. 571; Article 44 of the Protocol to the Treaty of Nice (2001) on the Statute of the Court of Justice of the European Communities, OJ C325, 24 December 2002; and see Articles 98–101 of the Rules of

powers were not replicated in the relatively more recent Statute of the International Tribunal for the Law of the Sea, or in Annex VII to the UN Convention on the Law of the Sea dealing with the arbitration of disputes.

II. Brief history of the evolution of the notion of revision

a. Early writers and the nineteenth century

It will be appropriate to preface this work with a brief enquiry into the evolution of the notion of revision. The observations made in section IV.d of Chapter 5 above will already have provided some insight into the matter. Even so, it may be reiterated that revision, as noted above, is simply the act of examining the judgment or award on the basis of the discovery of a hitherto unknown but decisive fact relevant to the decision, provided certain criteria are fulfilled. Importantly, the decision itself is not regarded as null and void. Early writers were more concerned with questions of the nullity of arbitral awards. Jurists such as Grotius,[697] Vattel, Bluntschli and Pufendorf discussed the legal principles relating to arbitration.[698] Vattel spoke of the invalidity of a decision arising from the corruption or partiality of the arbitrators.[699] Pufendorf remarked that no agreement, which prejudices the impartiality of the arbitrator, ought to exist between the latter and one of the parties. He observed that an award was final because no superior judge could revise the arbitrator's award.[700]

By the latter half of the nineteenth and the early twentieth centuries, the idea that decisions, although binding and not subject to appeal, were also governed by certain criteria in order to make them valid *and hence*

Procedure of the European Court of Justice as amended in April 2004, OJ L127, 29 April 2004; Article 38 of the Protocol to the Treaty of Paris on the European Coal and Steel Community (1951) on the Code of the Court of Justice in 1 *Peaslee* 358; 261 UNTS 140; and further Article 92 of the European Free Trade Area Court Rules of Procedure: www.eftacourt.lu/rulesprocedure.asp.

[697] See *De jure belli ac pacis libri tres*, 1646, Book II, Chapter XXIII, section 9; and Book III, Chapter XX, sections 46–8, in Grotius, *De jure belli ac pacis libri tres*, 1646, trans. F. W. Kelsey, in *The Classics of International Law* series, Carnegie Endowment for International Peace, Oxford, 1925, pp. 561–2 and 823–6, respectively.

[698] See the materials collected by Darby (ed.), *International Tribunals: A Collection of the Various Schemes Which Have Been Propounded; And of Instances in the Nineteenth Century*, 4th edn, London, 1904, pp. 122–45 and 188–92.

[699] *The Law of Nations or the Principles of Natural Law Applied to the Conduct and to the Affairs of Nations and of Sovereigns*, 1758, Book II, Chapter XVIII, section 329 (trans. C. G. Fenwick, Carnegie Institution, Washington, DC, 1915), pp. 223–4.

[700] *On the Way of Deciding Controversies in the Liberty of Nature*, as translated by Darby (note 698), p. 130, at p. 134.

binding, began to gain ground and to be reflected not only in the writings of jurists but also in the agreements between States. In his 1867 (Code on) Arbitration Proceedings, Bluntschli observed that the decision was invalid if the tribunal exceeded its powers; if there were any dishonesty on the part of the arbitrators; if the tribunal breached the *audi alteram partem* rule; or if the award was incompatible with either international law or human rights.[701] In 1874, Goldschmidt presented to the Institute of International Law a set of rules for international arbitration tribunals, and Article 32 thereof provided elaborate criteria for impugning and annulling the award.[702] The Institute adopted Draft Regulations for International Procedure on Arbitration in 1875, Article 24 of which provided for the correction of errors of writing or reckoning. Article 27 laid out criteria for nullity; this included *excès de pouvoir*.[703] Professor Corsi's Rules for International Arbitration are significant because they were relied on by the Hague Conference in 1899, discussed below, and also because he referred to revision, *inter alia*, for error of fact: 'provided that the award is founded expressly on the existence or on the want of a document or a fact, whose existence or want has not been observed before the Tribunal, or could not be proved, whereas after the publication of the award success has been attained in giving such proofs of it that all the parties must admit them as decisive.'[704] Fiore's 1897 code on arbitration distinguished between void and voidable decisions, with decisions founded on fraud and on error both falling in the latter category of decisions.[705]

Clearly, the notions of nullity and revision were still in need of some refinement. The same degree of interchangeability of terms was evident in the treaties concluded between States. These treaties were concerned

[701] 'Arbitration Proceedings', 1867, in Darby (note 698), p. 188, at p. 190.

[702] See 'International Arbitral Procedure: Original Project and Report of Mr Goldschmidt, 20 June 1874', in Scott (ed.), *Resolutions of the Institute of International Law Dealing with the Law of Nations with an Historical Introduction and Explanatory Notes*, New York, 1916, p. 205, at pp. 233–4, and commentary on *ibid.*, pp. 235–9; and 'Supplementary Observations by Mr Goldschmidt Relative to the Regulations for International Tribunals', *ibid.*, p. 239, at p. 240 and 242–3.

[703] See Scott (note 702), p. 1, at pp. 6–7.

[704] See Darby (note 698), p. 520, at p. 544. To be sure, there were many other arbitral and pacific settlement codes, rules and projects of international conferences and leading jurists of the times, including the Pan American Conference of 1890, Bentham, Hornby, and Leone Levi, on which see Darby (note 698), *passim*; Ralston (note 148), Chapters XI, XIII and XIV; and Wehberg (note 186), pp. 128–40, distinguishing the writers from the various societies, including the Universal Peace Congresses and the Institute of International Law.

[705] 'The Arbitration Tribunal', in Darby (note 698), p. 546, at pp. 570–1.

with both procedural as well as substantive nullity. The former, which is concerned with questions of the validity of decisions in situations where an arbiter has failed to fulfil certain procedural criteria, particularly those of time limits for the production of awards, requires little or no attention here.[706] More significantly, contracting States used the terms 'revision' or 'review' to confirm the treaty-based right to seek a remedy not only for substantive invalidity, as for example the exercise of excess powers, but also for the correction of errors, essential or otherwise. By contemporary international legal standards, the correction of errors does not fall into the category of revision. This usage reflected a certain lack of sophistication in the creation of categories, but this was understandable given the nascent status of the remedy. Thus the seminal Treaty of Arbitration of 1898 between Italy and Argentina stipulated in Article 13:[707]

> The revision of the Award before the same Tribunal which has pronounced it may be asked for before the execution of the sentence: First, if the judgment has been based upon a false or erroneous document; and, second, if the decision in whole or in part has resulted from an error of fact, positive or negative, resulting from the acts or documents of the trial.

Similarly, in June 1899, just a few weeks before the international conference at The Hague concluded its deliberations – on which more presently – Argentina and Uruguay concluded an arbitration treaty which allowed either party to ask for revision where the award was based on 'a document having been falsified or tampered with', or where the award was wholly or partly the consequence of an error of fact resulting from the arguments of the case or documents.[708]

[706] For example, Article II of the Treaty of Arbitration of All Boundary Disputes, concluded between Costa Rica and Colombia in 1880 required that, in order to be valid the award must be delivered within ten months reckoned from the date of acceptance of the task of arbitration by the umpire: 71 BFSP 215. These provisions were modified in 1886 by Article IV of the Supplementary Convention: the period was extended by a further ten months reckoned from the date of the expiration of the first ten-month term: 92 BFSP 1036. Different time limits (six months) ascertained from the expiry of the date agreed upon for the presentation of answers to either party's allegations are also to be found in the Nicaragua and Costa Rica boundary treaty arbitration agreement of 1886: 77 BFSP 476. The importance of this kind of validity ought not to be underestimated, for arbitrators in ancient Greece were time and again instructed to provide an award within the given time periods: see Tod (note 138), pp. 108–9.

[707] Darby (note 698), p. 400. The Anglo-American Arbitration Treaty of 1897 is also usually mentioned, but it did not provide for either revision or nullity or the correction of errors. It did allow a review of awards if they were not decided unanimously: see Article 5, in Darby (note 698), p. 390.

[708] Manning (ed.), *Arbitration Treaties Among the American Nations to the Close of the Year 1910*, New York, 1924, p. 262.

Before a detailed account is given of the development at the diplomatic level which culminated in the Hague Convention for the Peaceful Settlement of International Disputes, it is important to point out that revision as a remedy had begun to make its mark relatively early in judicial practice. In 1868, the United States and Mexico established the Mixed Claims Commission to resolve all outstanding claims of corporate bodies and private persons of the United States and Mexico against the Governments of Mexico and the United States respectively. In the famous *George Moore* case,[709] decided in 1871, the Commission adopted what in contemporary terms would be a fairly liberal approach. It held that, even in the absence of a term in the *compromis*, where the evidence produced for a rehearing showed conclusively that it would undoubtedly have produced a change in the minds of the Commissioners and would have convinced them of the petitioner's right to an award, then they would be disposed to grant the motion and the award according to public law, equity and justice. However, gross laches by the applicant party and injustice to the defending party constituted a bar to this remedy.[710]

It was the *Pelletier and Lazare* case[711] which brought the remedy of revision into sharper focus, and indeed controversy. Haiti and the United States agreed to arbitrate the claims for compensation arising out of acts of the Haitian authorities. After the award was delivered in 1885, Haiti petitioned for a rehearing on the basis of evidence discovered subsequent to the award, but the arbitrator refused on the ground that he was *functus officio*.[712] However, the United States Government accepted the basic veracity of the claim for revision, and eventually decided not to enforce the award.[713] Two things are clear. First, although the remedy had begun to be considered seriously by tribunals, there was no great consensus or clarity on the matter. Secondly, the remedy of revision had certainly got the stamp of approval within the United States, a fact of some significance at the multilateral diplomatic level.

b. The Hague Peace Conferences and other treaties

Thus, when the delegates to the International Peace Conference convened in 1899 at The Hague to discuss, among other things, a convention on the pacific settlement of international disputes, there was still a sense of

[709] Moore (note 136), pp. 1357 and 1749–805; and see Cheng (note 692), pp. 365–7.
[710] Moore (note 136), p. 1357.
[711] *Ibid.*, pp. 1749–805; and Cheng (note 692), pp. 369–70.
[712] Moore (note 136), p. 1793.
[713] *Ibid.*, p. 1805.

confusion, a lack of interest and even hostility with respect not only to the precise meaning and scope of this remedy but also to whether it ought to be incorporated into a multilateral treaty. Nonetheless, it is the case that revision did make its diplomatic debut in a multilateral setting in 1899 at that Conference.[714] Some detail is important here because at the end of the proceedings not only had it taken its first steps in being accepted as a right or remedy in international law, revision, *as formulated and clarified* in the resulting convention, began thereafter to serve as the template for other international instruments.

Inasmuch as the idea of revision was then a novel and controversial one, it faced vigorous opposition from the foremost authority on international arbitration at that time, Mr F. de Martens, the delegate from Russia. The Third Commission of the Conference, which was mandated to discuss the pacific settlement of international disputes, had before it a number of draft proposals, one of which was the Russian delegation's proposals for an arbitral code. While no provision on revision was included in the draft code, draft Article 26 thereof provided for nullity of decisions based on a void *compromis*, *excès de pouvoir* or corruption of one of the arbitrators.[715] The delegation of the United States submitted a Plan for an International Tribunal, draft Article 7 of which introduced the idea of revision.[716] It provided that every litigant shall have the right to a re-examination of its case before the same tribunal within three months of the notification of the decision if it declared itself able to invoke new evidence or questions of law not raised or settled the first time. The Third Commission's Committee of Examination first discussed the matter at its tenth meeting on 26 June 1899 when Mr F. W. Holls, the delegate from the United States, announced that he wondered whether 'the time has not come to discuss before entering into the examination of this article, the principle of the amendment which [I have] prepared regarding revision and appeal'.[717] While Mr T. M. C. Asser from The Netherlands gave the draft article his support,[718] the Russian delegate was and remained 'absolutely opposed' to revision. Accepting revision, he said, constituted tearing down with one hand what was constructed

[714] For an account of the Conference, see Scott (ed.), *The Proceedings of the Hague Peace Conferences: Translation of Official Texts: The Conference of 1899*, New York, 1920 (hereinafter referred to as *Proceedings, 1899*). For a select collection of the documents, see Rosenne (ed.), *The Hague Peace Conferences of 1899 and 1907 and International Arbitration Reports and Documents*, The Hague, 2001.

[715] Annex 1, B, Annexes to the Minutes of the Committee of Examination, in Scott, *Proceedings 1899* (note 714), p. 801.

[716] Annex 7, *ibid.*, p. 833.

[717] Committee of Examination, *ibid.*, p. 741.

[718] *Ibid.*

with the other; part of the strength of arbitration would be taken away from it and 'we shall perpetuate disputes which we would terminate'.[719]

The matter was reserved and discussed more thoroughly on 30 June 1899 at the eleventh meeting of the Committee. The arguments submitted by Holls in support of his proposals are not irrelevant to this study. He admitted that the award should be final and without appeal and that his amendment respected this principle. He wished, however, to provide for dissatisfaction based on the discovery of fact, and said:

> It cannot be admitted that this discovery should be considered as not having been made when it may completely modify the situation which was before the arbitrators. For example, if it happened that several days after the award an authentic map should be discovered which fixed exactly the boundaries regarding which they had previously had only indefinite data, it seems that, in that case, without resorting to the procedure for revision, strictly speaking, and without its being necessary to call upon new judges, it will be very natural for the arbitrators to be authorised to examine again the situation which they knew but imperfectly before.[720]

After an inconclusive debate, the matter was taken up again on 1 July 1899 at the twelfth meeting where, after first voting in favour of the general principle, the Committee began to discuss the precise text of the draft article, with de Martens steadfast in his opposition. Arguing that the principle of revision was contrary to the very nature of arbitration, he recalled that, in certain cases, the losing party had proclaimed that it had documents which had not been submitted to the arbitrator; and that, if the losing party were to be given three months, why, he asked, ought it not to be given six months.[721] 'As lawyers', he said, 'we are certainly conscientiously in favour of revision. But revision is a dangerous weapon which will shake the authority of arbitration.'[722]

Stressing that discovery of fact could also take place many years after the decision, the President, Mr Léon Bourgeois, intervened against the principle and observed that an additional three months would produce only inconvenience without any advantages.[723] Both Holls and Asser

[719] *Ibid.*, p. 742. See also de Martens' reflections similar to these in 'International Arbitration and the Peace Conference at The Hague', 169 (1899) *North American Review* 604, at p. 621. [720] Committee of Examination (note 715), p. 749. [721] *Ibid.*, p. 753.

[722] *Ibid.*, p. 754.

[723] *Ibid.*, p. 754. He also stressed the fact there was a distinction between the discovery of an error and the discovery of a new fact. In the former case, he said, the case could not be reopened because the conscience of the judges was at issue. The opposite was true for the latter case, because there was no question of conscience of the judges: *ibid.*, p. 753.

thought that a three-month period was sufficient and accepted the draft as formulated by the President.[724] The text of the Italo-Argentine Treaty of 1898 was rejected, and the Committee adopted by a small majority the Asser–Holls draft as amended by the President. It limited revision to the discovery of a fact exerting a decisive influence upon the award, provided that it was unknown to the tribunal and the parties. Revision could only be 'demanded' from the tribunal which had pronounced the original decision; it had to be preceded by an admissibility proceedings, and the demand had to be made within three months.[725]

It was at the fifth meeting of the Third Commission, held on 17 July 1899, that de Martens strived again to derail the revision principle, but of course the delegate from the United States was not inclined to abandon his proposal. The Russian delegate argued that it would be 'most unsatisfactory and unfortunate to have an arbitral award, duly pronounced by an international tribunal, subject to being reversed by a new judgment'. The point was that the award should 'terminate, finally and forever, the dispute between the litigating nations' and that revision would 'inflame the passions anew, and menace once more the peace of the world'. He observed, perhaps presciently, that the losing litigant party 'will make every effort imaginable to find new facts or documents'. Indeed, the 'idea of a rehearing is the most fatal blow which could be struck against the idea of arbitration'.[726]

Holls responded by saying, among other things, that it was extremely desirable and necessary to 'provide for the possibility of rectifying evident errors, in a regular and legal manner, without incurring the danger of having the decision repudiated by the aggrieved party'. Revision, then, was 'a golden mean between two extreme dangers, that of perpetuating an injustice, and that of leaving a difference unsettled'. Nor could new facts 'be forged or manufactured, at least not by civilised Governments'. The possibility that the new fact could be discovered one day after the judgment was an inconvenience, which would exist in equal measure if the period were six and not three months.[727]

[724] Generally, see *ibid.*, pp. 753–5.

[725] Generally, see *ibid.*, pp. 754–5. Views in favour were also expressed by Sir Julian Pauncefote from Great Britain, while Count Nigra, the Italian delegate, queried whether the tribunal was competent to declare fraud in cases where a litigating government produced a forged document: see *ibid.*, pp. 753–4. Asser pointed out that the tribunal would decide whether or not it was a false document: *ibid.*, p. 754.

[726] Third Commission, *ibid.*, pp. 618–19. A slightly different version of this translated speech is to be found in Holls, *The Peace Conference at The Hague and its Bearings on International Law and Policy*, New York, 1900, pp. 287–90. Excerpts from these speeches also appear in Wetter (note 95), vol. II, pp. 542–52. Further, see de Martens (note 719), p. 621.

[727] Third Commission (note 715), pp. 620–1.

Taking advantage of the fact that de Martens was then serving as President of the Arbitral Tribunal in the *British Guiana* v. *Venezuela* boundary case, and wanting to draw attention to the fact that a delay in execution was not an argument against revision, Holls observed that, in that case, 'the [hypothetical] delay of three months or six months could not truly be called anything but minimal, in view of the fact that this difference has existed . . . for three or four years, and, in a form more or less obscure, for more than eighty years'.[728] He added:

> Among other things this controversy implies the interpretation of treaties made more than two hundred and fifty years ago; it includes a great number of historical precedents, of questions about colonisation, of jurisdiction over barbarous tribes, as well as questions of the weight and authority to be given to different maps . . . Up to the moment of the decision of the tribunal it will be impossible to know what kind of facts and what argumentation have determined the award. Now the seeking of new facts is limited to that category. If that inquiry should be successful, for example, if a new map or a new document of incontestable and unquestioned authority should be found, it is evident that the interested party would refuse to submit to an award which could not be rectified in a legal and regular manner.[729]

While Chevalier Descamps, from Belgium, and Mr Seth Low, from the United States, spoke generally in favour of revision, it was, at any rate, not without a degree of apprehension,[730] even as the delegate from The Netherlands, Mr J. van Karnebeek, remained convinced that revision was dangerous.[731] In any event, it was the compromise drafted by Asser which finally produced a positive result. 'We must endeavour', he said, 'to save the principle, while meeting the wishes of those who do not want to weaken *a priori*, by means of a treaty provision, the moral force of arbitral awards. The wording . . . [proposed] does not imply a right of revision as a natural consequence in every arbitration case, but it allows the parties to reserve this right expressly and, if they do, it fixes the rules and procedure to be followed.'[732]

[728] Scott, *Proceedings 1899* (note 714), pp. 620–1.

[729] *Ibid.*, pp. 621–2. It must be noted that the arguments put forward here for revision would have been given short shrift had they been submitted in contemporary times, for it appears that Holls was attempting to use the discovery of facts as an *ex post facto* technique to get a better judgment. This would probably be seen as an abuse of right and would not be a strong platform upon which to seek support for a novel idea.

[730] *Ibid.*, pp. 623–4.

[731] *Ibid.*, p. 625. There were other points of view as well. Count Nigra suggested that Article 13 of the 1898 Italo-Argentine Treaty be adopted: *ibid.*, p. 619. Mr Corragioni d'Orelli, the Siamese delegate, emphasised the need for a six-month time period: *ibid.*, pp. 624–5.

[732] *Ibid.*, p. 618.

Echoing this general point, Descamps observed that revision must not be the rule but the exception.[733] In other words, revision could only take place by way of a specific agreement and not as of general right inherent in all arbitral proceedings. Holls agreed to this compromise, but added that disputing parties should determine in every case the precise time limits for submitting pleas for revision.[734] The Commission, then, adopted the draft article unanimously.[735] On 25 July 1899, at its seventh meeting, the Commission's draft articles were put to the Plenary Conference, which adopted them without discussion, and the principle of revision emerged definitively as Article 55 of the Convention for the Pacific Settlement of International Disputes.[736] It provided:

> The parties can reserve in the *compromis* the right to demand the revision of the award. In this case, and unless there be an agreement to the contrary, the demand must be addressed to the tribunal which pronounced the award. It can only be made on the ground of the discovery of some new fact which is of a nature to exercise a decisive influence upon the award and which, at the time the discussion was closed, was unknown to the tribunal and to the party demanding the revision.
>
> Proceedings for revision can only be instituted by a decision of the tribunal expressly recording the existence of the new fact, recognising in it the character described in the preceding paragraph, and declaring the demand admissible on this ground.
>
> The *compromis* fixes the period within which the demand for revision must be made.

The point of interest is that de Martens' proposals on the nullity of decisions were not adopted by the Committee of Examination, and were, therefore, not put to a vote at the Plenary Conference and hence failed completely.[737] In recapitulation, it is appropriate to point out that

733 *Ibid.*, p. 623. 734 *Ibid.*, p. 625. 735 *Ibid.*

736 Plenary Conference, *ibid.*, p. 91. For a brief account and commentary, see Annex to the Minutes of the Seventh Meeting, *ibid.*, p. 106, at pp. 150–1.

737 *Ibid.*, p. 151. It is perhaps ironic that the Russian delegation's proposals failed to be adopted. Ironic because arguably the most important (notorious?) case of alleged nullity of an award in a boundary dispute, namely, the *British Guiana* v. *Venezuela* arbitration of 1899, is linked to Mr de Martens who served as President of the Tribunal. It is the case that his draft article included corruption of an arbitrator as a basis for nullity, and, importantly, the Venezuelan allegation was that the British and Russian Governments had approached him to arrange, with other members of the tribunal, a compromise award, and that this indeed was done. See above, text to notes 213 and 219. In any event, no reasons were provided for the award, and this could, in contemporary terms, be seen as an argument for nullity. From de Martens' point of view, however, the question of a lack of reasons was not a ground for nullity. It was perhaps fortunate that he is formally on record as having spoken against the proposition that arbitrators should be obliged to provide reasons for an award: see

territorial and boundary award considerations were certainly not alien to the proposals submitted by the United States delegation with respect to revision. It is also safe to surmise that Holls was influenced in the need for such a provision by virtue of the fact that the United States Government was dissatisfied with and had rejected the award in the *Northeastern Boundary* case; and that the award in the *Aves Island* case was, on the face of it, a nullity. Nor were they so distant in time that these arbitrations could be ruled out as being irrelevant.

Despite this studied and careful formulation, the earlier notion of an appeal for revision persisted. Soon after The Hague Convention, Argentina concluded, in November 1899, a General Treaty of Arbitration with Paraguay which reproduced *verbatim* the provisions of Article 16 of the Uruguay–Argentina agreement of June 1899 referred to above.[738] This practice continued in 1902, when Argentina went on to agree similar treaties with identical provisions on revision with Chile and Bolivia.[739] Similarly, Article 16 of the International Treaty for the Arbitration of Pecuniary Claims, concluded between Bolivia, Chile, Colombia, Costa Rica, the Dominican Republic, Ecuador, Guatemala, Haiti, Honduras, Mexico, Nicaragua, Paraguay, Peru, El Salvador, the United States and Uruguay,[740] also provided for revision on grounds identical to the various bilateral treaties mentioned above.

Matters, however, did not stand still, and in 1907 the Second International Peace Conference began at The Hague.[741] While the remedy in question did not attract the same level of debate between the delegates, there was, to be sure, continued opposition by de Martens, who formally proposed that Article 55 of the Convention be omitted.[742] The International Bureau of the Permanent Court of Arbitration at The Hague had earlier echoed its opposition by asserting that, in practice, revision could be a source of grave inconvenience and that the smallest possible use ought to be made of the

Eleventh Meeting, 30 June 1899, *ibid.*, p. 748. Wehberg, who acknowledged the fact that M. de Martens was regarded 'as [being] the most distinguished representative of international arbitration in the whole world', (also described by (perhaps) the editor of the *North American Review* as the 'Lord Chief Justice of Christendom': see supra (note 719), p. 604) provides a clue to this, and writes: 'As was his wont, Martens allowed political reasons to figure largely in his arbitral decisions.' See supra (note 95), p. 26.

[738] Manning (note 708), p. 284.

[739] *Ibid.*, p. 327 (Article 13) and p. 316 (Article 16), respectively. However, the treaty of 1905 with Brazil provided for a 'rehearing' as opposed to 'revision' in Article 17 on similar grounds: *ibid.*, p. 357.

[740] *Ibid.*, p. 313.

[741] For an account of this Conference, see Scott, *Proceedings 1907*, vol. II (note 228), *passim*.

[742] Annex 11, *ibid.*, p. 869, at p. 870.

remedy accorded by Article 55.[743] At its eleventh meeting, on 13 August 1907, the First Subcommission of the First Commission heard de Martens' arguments to suppress Article 55, including the fact that The Hague 'arbitrators' had recommended the 'abolition of the recourse to revision'.[744]

There was, however, no support for his proposal, and several delegates spoke in favour of retaining it without change, the arguments being that justice was the sole object of arbitration and that it would be regrettable if a decision could not be revised;[745] that arbitrators were not infallible;[746] and that, as long as States were not formally forbidden to have recourse to revision, they were at liberty to provide for it in the *compromis*.[747] Committee of Examination C of the First Subcommission, which was mandated to study questions of procedure, decided, at its fifth meeting on 2 September 1907, to retain the provision.[748] At its ninth meeting, on 11 September 1907, the question of amending the provision was considered but rejected inasmuch as it was, according to Mr Lammasch, a compromise clause cobbled together from a large number of differing opinions.[749] Committee of Examination A of the First Subcommission, whose task it was to examine and record the decisions of Committee of Examination C, adopted without discussion the provision on revision, now Article 83, at its seventeenth meeting, on 1 October 1907.[750] The Plenary Conference adopted the draft convention unanimously at its ninth meeting, on 16 October 1907.[751] The definitive version is identical to the 1899 version noted above.

c. Developments since the Great War: the Statute of the Permanent Court of International Justice

The next major milestone for the principle of revision was the Statute of the Permanent Court of International Justice. As indicated in section II.c

743 International Bureau of the Permanent Court of Arbitration to the Dutch Foreign Minister, 14 October 1902: Annex 64, *ibid.*, p. 938, at p. 941.

744 *Ibid.*, p. 369. Of course, this was not strictly speaking an accurate assertion because the Bureau had not asked for its *abolition* but for a *minimum possible usage* of the remedy of revision. In fact, this was an adverse reaction to the very short revision period provided in the *compromis* agreed between the United States and Mexico which led eventually to the *Pious Fund* case (2 (1908) AJIL 898): see Hudson (note 136), pp. 122–3.

745 See the US delegate, Mr Choate, in Scott, *Proceedings 1907*, vol. II (note 228), p. 369.

746 See the Brazilian delegate, Mr Ruy Barbosa, *ibid.*, p. 370.

747 See the delegate from Romania, Mr Beldiman, *ibid.*, p. 371. It may be that the unanimity of views was influenced by Argentina's groundbreaking uniform arbitration treaties in which revision for nullity was provided: see Annex 63, *ibid.*, p. 920.

748 *Ibid.*, p. 731.

749 Meeting of 11 September 1907, *ibid.*, pp. 757–8.

750 *Ibid.*, pp. 588–9.

751 Scott, *Proceedings 1907*, vol. I (note 240), p. 330.

of Chapter 3 above, the Council of the League of Nations commissioned the Advisory Committee of Jurists to provide draft articles for adoption by the League. The Committee met at The Hague in June and July 1920 and had before it several sets of documents, including the two Hague Conventions and the Root–Phillimore Plan, the set of proposals drafted by the delegates from the United States and Great Britain.[752] While this working draft contained no provision on revision, the Five Power Draft, prepared by Denmark, Sweden, Norway, Switzerland and The Netherlands, contained a draft article modelled on Articles 55 and 83 of the 1899 and 1907 Conventions, respectively.[753] Not unlike the 1907 proceedings, the principle did not attract a great deal of debate. Nevertheless, discussions were held on the matter at several meetings between 20 and 24 July 1920,[754] and four significant modifications to the principle contained in Article 83 were introduced.

First, at the initiative of Lord Phillimore, the Committee sought to provide a standard against which the absence of knowledge of the newly discovered fact was to be judged. Hence, the lack of knowledge could not be defended if there existed any negligence on the part of the discovering State.[755] Secondly, it was considered inappropriate to leave the matter of time limits for revision to the parties. A six-month period was considered very short, but five years from the date of the 'sentence' were deemed adequate.[756] The third issue was concerned with compliance with the Court's judgment. Hence, the Court could refuse revision until the judgment was carried out. The objective was to frustrate attempts to delay compliance in the hope of discovering a decisive new fact.[757]

Lastly, and most significantly, the draft provision had, unlike Article 83, no clause which allowed the parties to reserve in the *compromis* the right to demand a revision. This meant that the proposed Court was expressly being granted the right to revise its judgments provided, of course, certain conditions were met. By deleting Asser's 1899 compromise clause, the Committee effectively decided that a permanent adjudicative body ought

[752] See, generally, *The Hague Advisory Committee Proceedings* (note 246).

[753] Annex 3 to Fifteenth Meeting, 3 July 1920, *ibid.*, p. 347; and see Synopsis, Annex 7 to the Second Meeting, 17 June 1920, *ibid.*, p. 51, at p. 93.

[754] Twenty-Eighth Meeting, 20 July 1920, *ibid.*, p. 587; Thirtieth Meeting, 21 July 1920, *ibid.*, p. 617; Thirty-First Meeting, 27 July 1920, *ibid.*, p. 645; Thirty-Second Meeting, 23 July 1920, *ibid.*, p. 671; and Thirty-Fourth Meeting, 24 July 1920, *ibid.*, p. 684.

[755] Twenty-Eighth Meeting; and see the discussions between Messrs Phillimore, Fernandes and de Lapradelle, *ibid.*, p. 592; Thirtieth Meeting, p. 621; Thirty-First Meeting, p. 669; Thirty-Second Meeting, p. 684; and Final Report, Annex 1, p. 693, at p. 744.

[756] Final Report, *ibid.*, p. 744. [757] *Ibid.*, pp. 744–5.

to have a right of revision as an inherent power, as opposed to being given this right by separate agreement. The Advisory Committee adopted the Draft Statute unanimously on 24 July 1920 at its thirty-fourth meeting. Draft Article 59, as revised, read as follows:

> An application for revision of a judgment can be made only when it is based upon the discovery of some new fact, of such a nature as to be a decisive factor, which fact was unknown to the Court and also to the party claiming revision, always provided that such ignorance was not due to negligence.
>
> The process for revision will be opened by a judgment of the Court expressly recording the existence of the new fact, recording that it has such a character as to lay the case open to revision, and declining the application admissible on this ground.
>
> The Court may require previous compliance with the terms of the judgment before it admits proceedings in revision.
>
> No application for revision may be made after the lapse of five years from the date of the sentence.

The Hague Committee's draft scheme was then forwarded to the Council of the League of Nations where, as noted earlier, the discussion was concerned only with the politically more significant issues, particularly the idea of compulsory jurisdiction; these issues are not relevant for present purposes.[758] In its deliberations at Brussels, the Council amended several provisions of the Hague Committee's draft scheme, but none of those amendments concerned the remedy of revision.[759] The amended draft Statute was then forwarded to the First Assembly, where the matter was allocated to a Subcommittee of the Third Committee on the Permanent Court of International Justice. The Subcommittee, of course, had before it various draft amendments proposed by different States, but only two are material here.

On the one hand, Argentina proposed suppressing the five-year limitation on the period for the application for revision.[760] On the other hand, Italy proposed that the five-year limitation be extended to a ten-year period. The reason given was that ten years 'are of the most practical periods of prescription in the laws of the different countries – the time during which an application for revision may be made'.[761] It also proposed

[758] Twentieth Plenary Meeting, 13 December 1920, *Records of the First Assembly, Plenary Meetings, 15 November–18 December 1920*, Geneva, 1920, p. 436, at p. 437.

[759] See Doc. 30, *Documents on Action Taken* (note 252), pp. 42 *et seq.*

[760] Doc. 36: Amendments Proposed by the Argentine Delegation to the Draft Statute of the Advisory Committee of Jurists for the Institution of a Permanent Court of International Justice, *ibid.*, p. 65, at p. 69.

[761] Doc. 25: Extracts from the Deliberations of the Council for Diplomatic Litigation Attached to the Italian Ministry of Foreign Affairs: *ibid.*, p. 28, at p. 30.

that the words 'or document' be added to 'new fact' in draft Article 59, thus making it clear that revision could take place when either a fact or a document were discovered.

These conflicting proposals were discussed at length by members of the Subcommittee at its sixth meeting, on 29 November 1920.[762] The Italian delegate, Mr Ricci Busatti, decided to withdraw its proposal with respect to adding the words 'any document' once the Greek representative, Mr Politis, had reassured him that the discovery of a document was deemed included in the discovery of a fact.[763]

However, Mr Ricci Busatti could not be made to yield on the matter of the extended period of time. The Swiss delegate, Mr Max Huber, supported the Argentine proposal, while Mr Doherty, the delegate from Canada, put forward a compromise solution. He suggested that the period be reduced, making it run from the date of the discovery of the new fact, as opposed to the date of the 'sentence'. He noted that, if a fixed period of time were adopted, it might be necessary to maintain a situation (between two States) which was manifestly unjust; even so, to dispense with the limitation (altogether) would also be an excessive measure. M. Fromageot, the French delegate, put forward a proposal which sought to meet the concern expressed by the Italian and Canadian delegates. He put forward two periods of time, the first of which dealt with the right to submit an application for revision reckoned from the *date of discovery* of the new fact; in the second, the time limit was reckoned from the *date of the judgment*. The first period lasted for six months and the second for ten years.[764] The upshot of this proposal was that a State had a right to request the Court to revise the judgment within six months of the discovery, but this right to request revision lasted only for ten years from the date of the judgment.

While the Subcommittee remained sharply divided on these issues, there was, nevertheless, unanimity with respect to the Argentine proposal suppressing time limits altogether: it was rejected by all the delegates. The Subcommittee took the view that difficulties might result from revision taking place at a time when a certain situation, based on the judgment, had become established and had existed for many years, and accordingly

[762] Minutes of Meetings of the Subcommittee of the Third Committee: *Procès-Verbaux* (I to VIII Meetings) of the First Assembly Meeting with Minutes of the Subcommittee on the Constitution of the Court with Annexes: Doc. 44, *ibid.*, p. 82, at p. 111; Sixth Meeting of the Subcommittee starts: p. 137.

[763] Over eighty years later, this matter became a source of controversy before a Chamber of the International Court of Justice, on which see section II.b of Chapter 10 below.

[764] Minutes of the Meetings of the Subcommittee: Doc. 44, *Documents on Action Taken* (note 252), p. 139.

it was unable to adopt the Argentine proposal.[765] The Italian ten-year proposal, however, was accepted by seven votes in favour to three against. Referring to the Doherty compromise, Mr Ricci Busatti and Brazil's Mr Fernandez signified their objection to a time limit based on discovery of the new fact on the ground that it was an 'indefinite point of departure'. Mr Fernandez said that the six-month period would nullify the ten-year limit.[766] In support of his proposal, M. Fromageot pointed out that it was in the interest of the party to bring an application for revision to the Court as soon as possible.

Notwithstanding clear support for the Italian proposals, M. Fromageot's draft was also put to a vote and was also accepted but with even less support, that is, with five votes in favour to four against, with the chairman abstaining.[767] Eventually, however, the Subcommittee decided against the Italian proposal, preferring to put forward the Fromageot compromise to the Third Committee.[768] Thus, while the Subcommittee agreed that the absolute period of limitation ought to be extended from five to ten years, it also felt that a very short period, that is, six months, was sufficient for a State to make an application to the Court after the discovery of the new fact.[769]

The Third Committee distributed the Subcommittee's report to all Member States, and subsequently the Main Committee adopted it, but not without some modifications.[770] These modifications are not relevant to the issues at hand. The plenary session of the Assembly of the League, at its twenty-first meeting on 13 December 1920, adopted the draft articles of the Statute without amendment, save draft Article 27.[771] The final version, Article 61, was identical to the Hague Committee's draft scheme, except that two paragraphs were added to the end of the article, as follows:

> The application for revision must be made at latest within six months of the discovery of the new fact.
>
> No application for revision may be made after the lapse of ten years from the date of the sentence.

[765] See Annex A, Annexes to the Twentieth Plenary Meeting (note 758), pp. 465–6.

[766] Minutes of the Meetings of the Subcommittee: Doc. 44, *Documents on Action Taken* (note 252), p. 139.

[767] *Ibid.*

[768] Report Submitted to the Third Committee by Mr Hagerup on Behalf of the Subcommittee, in Report and Draft Scheme Presented to the Assembly by the Third Committee: Doc. 48, *Documents on Action Taken* (note 252), p. 206, at p. 206; see p. 213.

[769] *Ibid.*

[770] Third Committee Report: Doc. 48, *Documents on Action Taken* (note 252), p. 206.

[771] Records of the First Assembly (note 758), p. 478, at p. 500; and see Annex B, *ibid.*, p. 468.

d. The inter-war years

The inter-war years provided not a little inspiration. In 1928, the League of Nations adopted the General Act for the Pacific Settlement of International Disputes of 1928,[772] and, while it failed to include the remedy directly, revision was provided for by way of default in Article 18: if the *compromis* were devoid of sufficient particulars as regards, *inter alia*, procedure, then the provisions of the Hague Convention of 1907 would be applicable. The General Act, however, did not come into force. Similar default incorporation is evident in the earlier Convention on Conciliation and Arbitration, concluded between Estonia, Finland, Latvia and Poland in 1925.[773] The several Locarno treaties on conciliation and arbitration between Germany, Czechoslovakia, Belgium, France and Poland did not provide for the revision of decisions.[774]

However, it was the experience of the mixed arbitral tribunals instituted on the basis of the various peace treaties which provided the most positive of developments, for, as Cheng noted, the rules of procedure of practically every tribunal provided for revision,[775] including the rules of procedure of the Franco-German, Franco-Bulgarian and Romania-Germany Mixed Arbitral Tribunals of 1920, 1921 and 1923, respectively. Equally significant is the fact that a number of applications requesting revision on grounds of discovery of facts and evidence were brought before some of these tribunals, a few of which are referred to in the appropriate place below.

e. Developments since 1945

In 1945, the rule of revision was reiterated and incorporated into the Statute of the International Court of Justice, an incorporation which is of the highest significance. However, insofar as the diplomatic history of such incorporation is identical with that of interpretation, discussed above,[776] that history need not be repeated here. Suffice it to say that the principle of revision was adopted without virtually any discussion and with only very minor textual changes to Article 61 of the Statute of the Permanent

[772] See Hudson (ed.), *International Legislation: A Collection of the Texts of Multipartite International Instruments of General Interest*, vol. IV, Washington, DC, 1931, p. 2529.

[773] See Hudson, *International Legislation* (note 772), vol. III, p. 1571.

[774] See Habicht (note 304), pp. 285–319.

[775] Supra (note 692), p. 364, and especially note 99; and Strupp (note 136), pp. 683–5.

[776] See section II.d of Chapter 3 above.

Court of International Justice, chief of which was that the paragraphs were (finally) numbered.[777] The important point is that, by 1945, the principle had not only begun firmly to take root in the international community of States. It also appears that the formulation of the remedy in 1920 was considered so satisfactory that it did not need any modification.

The reason, of course, for this is simple. While there was some limited practice in the inter-war years before certain Mixed Arbitral Tribunals,[778] and although, as will be seen in the following chapters, the Permanent Court of International Justice did make its contribution in this regard by way of advisory opinions, no major problems or questions with respect to revision as a remedy had actually materialised. The 1949 Revised General Act for the Pacific Settlement of International Disputes provided that, where the *compromis* failed to stipulate sufficient particulars, then the Hague Convention shall apply where necessary.[779] Similarly, when the International Law Commission began, as noted above, to consider arbitral procedure in 1950, it readily accepted the notion of revision and incorporated it in Article 38 of the final Draft Articles on Arbitral Procedure. These provisions were subsequently 'noted' by the General Assembly in 1958.[780] Some discussion of these articles appears at the appropriate places below, and hence it will be appropriate to note here that the general criteria of revision were incorporated in the Model Rules unchanged, including the time limits thereof.

As far as regional international courts and tribunals are concerned, the reception of the principle of revision was gradual but somewhat mixed, as could be expected. Thus, while the Convention for the Establishment of a Central American Court of Justice of 1907[781] did not include any provision on revision, as it is understood today, by 1923, when the five Central American States concluded the Treaty of Arbitration and established the

[777] The English language term 'sentence' was changed to 'judgment' at the suggestion of the representative of the United Kingdom, Mr Gerald Fitzmaurice, insofar as it accorded with correct usage: Seventh Meeting, Committee IV/1, 13 April 1945: G/30, Jurist 40, UNCIO, vol. 14, p. 162, at p. 174. The corresponding provisions in the 1978 Rules of the International Court of Justice are contained in Article 99, the commentary to which is to be found in Rosenne (note 269), p. 205. The earlier versions of this provision are to be found in Articles 78 and 83 of the 1946 and 1972 Rules of the Court.

[778] See subsection f of this section.

[779] See Article 26: 71 UNTS 101.

[780] Resolution 1262 (XIII), 14 November 1958. For a brief account and progress of the draft articles, see Watts, *The International Law Commission 1949–1998*, vol. III, Oxford, 1999, Chapter 18. It is the case, of course, that the draft articles were not adopted by the General Assembly as Model Rules on Arbitral Procedure as recommended by the Commission. Nevertheless, they serve as a stage in the development of the law on the matter. See *ibid.*, p. 1772.

[781] 2 (1908) AJIL 231.

International Central American Tribunal, they agreed to incorporate, *inter alia*, Article 83 of the 1907 Hague Convention with respect to arbitration cases. Indeed, Article XIX made revision inherent in the arbitral process, for it provided that 'the silence of the parties in the drafting of the protocol of arbitration does not imply the renunciation of the right of recourse to revision in the cases provided in this Convention'.[782] However, in 1929, when the General Treaty of Inter-American Arbitration was concluded, parties to the International Conference of American States on Conciliation and Arbitration decided to leave the remedy out.[783] Similarly, the 1995 Statute of the Central American Court of Justice eschewed the remedy of revision.[784]

The European experience is more consistent: the Court of Justice of the European Communities, the European Free Trade Area Court, the Euratom Court and the European Court of Human Rights all provide, as noted above, for revision, as did Article 24 of the 1957 European Convention for the Settlement of International Disputes by way of default incorporation of the Hague Convention of 1907.[785] There are, of course, bilateral treaties on boundary arbitration which contain provisions on revision, just as there are cases on revision. Some of them are examined below. For present purposes, it need only be noted that States accept that a tribunal has the right to revise its decisions but with one important caveat, namely, that the revision of a judgment or award can take place only on the basis of an agreement of the parties given *ad hoc* or *ante hoc*. The criteria and conditions of application with respect to territorial and boundary disputes are, of course, of central concern and are discussed below.

f. Judicial contribution to the development of the notion

As far as its judicial practice is concerned, only brief mention at this point will suffice given that this aspect constitutes the main part of the present work. While the Permanent Court of International Justice was asked early in its existence to give interpretative judgments and opinions to States Parties and to the League of Nations, the International Court of Justice had to wait until 1985 to give its first judgment on the matter of revision. This was done in response to an application by Tunisia for the revision and interpretation of the Court's judgment in the matter of the *Tunisia–Libya Continental Shelf* case, an application which had mixed results for the

[782] 130 BFSP 504. [783] Habicht (note 304), p. 958. [784] 34 (1995) ILM 923.
[785] 5 (1957) EYB 347.

requesting State. The seminal judgment for revision, the *Application for Revision and Interpretation of the 1982 Judgment* case, is discussed at the appropriate places below.

Mixed arbitral tribunals made important contributions in this respect. One of the earliest influential cases was *Heim and Chamant* v. *The German State*. In 1922, the Franco-German Mixed Arbitral Tribunal took the position that a restrictive approach to the notion of facts was justified 'so as not to injure the course of international justice, in which as a rule there exists only one instance and no possibility of appeal'.[786] Equally, the notion could not be so comprehensive that it was in disregard of the requirements of certainty and stability. Nor could facts be rigidly opposed to that of law insofar as they embrace all means of proof relating to questions of law.[787] The Tribunal rejected the request for revision insofar as the facts putatively discovered were in the form effectively of preparatory materials for the Paris Peace Conference, and as such little weight attached to them. At any rate, these materials were neither uniform nor accessible to courts in their entirety.[788]

In *Battus* v. *The Bulgarian State*,[789] the Franco-Bulgarian Mixed Arbitral Tribunal confirmed the proposition that facts for the purposes of revision must have existed before not after the close of pleadings, while in *Baron de Neuflize* v. *Germany and the Deutsche Bank*,[790] the Franco-German Mixed Arbitral Tribunal held that, in order to justify revision, it was not enough that there was an error on a point of law or in its appreciation of the facts or both. It was only a lack of knowledge on the part of the judge and one of the parties of a material and decisive fact which may in law give rise to the revision of a judgment.[791]

786 1 *Annual Digest* 379. 787 *Ibid.*, p. 380.
788 *Ibid.*, pp. 380–1. For discussion, see Strupp (note 136), p. 685. 789 5 *Annual Digest* 458.
790 4 *Annual Digest* 491. 791 *Ibid.*, p. 492.

8 General features of revision

I. Preliminary observations

In order better to understand the notion of revision, several core issues are examined below. Two preliminary matters, however, need to be considered. As with interpretation, the first involves scrutinising the threshold criterion, namely, the essential role of consent in revision proceedings. This scrutiny appears next below. The second preliminary matter involves a discussion regarding the basic scope of powers exercised by international tribunals. The rule that revision is a remedy to be exercised in exceptional circumstances suggests clearly that a cavalier or liberal approach to revision is laden with difficulties. Preliminary issues exhausted, the work turns to an examination of three relevant areas of the law. The first is concerned with classifying the two main branches of revision; the second investigates issues of admissibility; while the third analyses the salient substantive and procedural aspects of revision. The discussion follows below.

II. Revision as a remedy based in consent

Not unlike the notion of interpretation, the power of a tribunal to revise its decisions upon the discovery of a decisive fact is not an inherent power.[792] States must agree to vest an international tribunal with the power to revise

[792] See Simpson and Fox (note 136), p. 242; Rosenne (note 394), p. 103; but see his observations regarding the advisory opinion in the *Effect of Awards of Compensation* (ICJ Reports 1954, p. 47, at p. 55): see Rosenne (note 269), p. 269; and see further note 796 below; generally, see also Verzijl (note 136), pp. 567–8; Bowett (note 226), pp. 590–1 (cautiously denying an inherent power); Sandifer (note 692), pp. 454–5; and Habicht (note 304), p. 1054. Cf. Reisman (note 226), p. 210. For a review of the very restrictive approach adopted by the Iran–United States Claims Tribunal, see Brower and Brueschke (note 414), pp. 245–6.

its decisions, and Article 61 of the Statute of the International Court of Justice serves this purpose as a standing right for litigating parties. It is interesting that the opening clause of Article 83 of the 1907 Hague Convention provides: 'The parties can reserve in the "Compromis" the right to demand revision of the Award.' This indicates that, while they were not entirely averse to providing litigating parties the option to request the tribunal to revise its decision, State delegates to the Conference were also not fully prepared in 1907 or earlier in 1899 to provide it as a *standing right*. This was in contrast with what they had agreed to in Article 82 with respect to interpretation, that is, where the right to request interpretation could only be ousted by way of an agreement to the contrary.[793]

By contrast, it is interesting to note that Article 38 of the International Law Commission's 1958 Draft Rules on Arbitral Procedure eschews any reference to this permissive course of action, based as it is on 'the principle that the right of revision should be considered to be at all times such a part of the system of arbitration that no express reservation of the right in the *compromis* would be necessary'.[794] The fact, however, is that Article 38 is inspired directly by Article 61 of the Statute of the International Court of Justice, a provision predicated on the notion that revision is a remedy based in the consent of contracting States. Nor can it be ignored that the General Assembly finally adopted the Commission's draft articles not as binding compulsory rules but as model guidelines for States contemplating arbitration, leaving them the liberty of using all or some of the provisions at will. Accordingly, a provision such as Article 38 does still appear to suggest that if the *compromis* remains silent on the matter, then the rule of revision cannot apply.[795]

The general position is supported by the observations made by the Permanent Court of International Justice in the *Jaworzina Boundary* advisory opinion, where it took a cautious approach to both interpretation and revision. Although it accepted that there was assimilation between the duties of the Conference of Ambassadors and those of an arbitrator, it stated: 'But in the absence of an express agreement between the parties,

[793] The evolution of this clause and provision has been discussed in Chapter 7, section II, particularly subsections b and c, above. For an abbreviated account based on the reproduction of the materials of the proceedings of 1899, see Wetter (note 95), vol. II, pp. 542–52; refer further to Sandifer (note 692), pp. 444–6; Strupp (note 136), pp. 684–5; and Geiss (note 692), pp. 170–1.

[794] See Secretariat's Commentary on Arbitral Procedure (note 226), p. 102.

[795] Cf. the fact that, while the *competence de la competence* rule is mentioned in Article 9, there is no reference to the power to rectify material, non-essential errors in the award, a power fully recognised as being inherent in all tribunals.

the Arbitrator is not competent to interpret, much less to modify his award by revising it. The decision of July 28th, which was accepted by the Polish and Czechoslovak Governments, contains no mention of an agreement of this kind.'[796]

The question of consent for revision and the related issue of *functus officio* were at the centre of the problem in *Monastery of Saint-Naoum*. It is important to emphasise the fact that the request by the Council of the League for an advisory opinion from the Permanent Court of International Justice was in effect an adaptation of the Yugoslav request to the Conference for a revision of the decision allocating the monastery to Albania. The request to the Conference was made in May–June 1923, that is, five months after it had adopted its decision. This fact is noteworthy because the Conference did not rule out the request *in limine* on the ground that there was no agreement authorising it to revise its decision. On the contrary, following an exchange of notes between the Albanian and Yugoslav Governments, the Conference submitted the question to an *ad hoc* committee for further examination, and subsequently to the Drafting or Juridical Committee, and, in the words of the Court, '[a]s nevertheless divergent opinions with regard to the allocation of the Monastery of Saint-Naoum continued to prevail, the Conference then took a decision which was communicated to the Secretary-General of the League of Nations', with a recommendation that the Council of the League approach the Permanent Court of International Justice for an advisory opinion on the matter.[797]

While this plainly indicates that the Conference did examine the Yugoslav request for revision on its merits, the fact is that such examina-

[796] Supra (note 107), at p. 38. See further Sandifer (note 692), pp. 404–7, 448–9 and 455; Verzijl (note 136), pp. 567–70; and Ralston (note 136), pp. 207–10. Cf. the International Court's observations in *Effect of Awards of Compensation*: the rule of finality contained in former Article 10(2) of the Statute of the UN Administrative Tribunal (modified in 1955 by giving the power of review to the International Court of Justice, a power abolished subsequently in 1995) could not be considered as excluding the Tribunal from revising a judgment in the event of the discovery of new facts; see ICJ Reports 1954, p. 47, at p. 55, and the dissents of Judges Alvarez and Hackworth regarding the broad powers of review and revision, *ibid.*, pp. 73–4 and 90–1, on which aspect see Report of the Special Committee on Review of Administrative Tribunal Judgments, Doc. A/2909, June 1955: Agenda Item 49, Annexes, Tenth Session, 1955, *General Assembly Official Records*, p. 1, at pp. 9–10; and Strupp (note 136), pp. 683–4, especially note 33, p. 684. Cf. further Rosenne (note 226), pp. 1669–70; and Rosenne (note 269), where he writes: 'However, the possibility of the parties concluding a special agreement regarding proceedings for the revision of an earlier judgment cannot be excluded.' See *ibid.*, p. 206.

[797] Supra (note 296), p. 11.

tion was not without its problems. The concern was that, insofar as it had settled the boundary with final dispositive effects, the Conference of Ambassadors, and ultimately the Principal Allied Powers, had exhausted the task of delimitation vested in them, and consequently both bodies were *functus officio*. This concern was clearly reflected in the question put to the Court, that is, whether the Conference had 'exhausted, in regard to the Serbo-Albanian frontier at the Monastery of Saint-Naoum, the mission which was recognized as belonging to them [*sic*]'.[798] The Court held that it could not accept the case for revision of the boundary delimited by the Conference not only because the Yugoslav Government had failed to produce new facts, as opposed to documents, to support and justify its plea for revision.[799] The Court also relied on the fact that the Conference's decision was of a definitive character, and that it did 'not feel called upon to give an opinion on the question whether such decisions can – except when an express reservation to that effect has been made – be revised in the event of the existence of an essential error being proved, or new facts being relied on'.[800]

In other words, the Court effectively held that, in the absence of enabling provisions, the Conference (and indeed the Court) was, in principle, unable to consider revision. However, it added that, 'even if revision under such conditions were admissible, these conditions were not present in the case before the Court'.[801] The Court's opinion, thus, effectively precluded the Conference from entertaining the Yugoslav request for revision of the decision of 6 December 1922. It follows inevitably that, had it not exhausted its mission, the Conference would not have been *functus officio*, enabling it to continue to consider the Yugoslav request.[802] In any event, the Conference went on to accept the advisory opinion in April 1925 when it decided to fix definitively the frontier, leaving the monastery to Albania.[803]

798 *Ibid.*, pp. 11–12. It is also clear that a decision by the Conference on the matter was postponed by it until the opinion was forthcoming from the Court.

799 Issues of facts and documents are discussed in section II of Chapter 10 below.

800 Supra (note 296), pp. 21–2.

801 *Ibid.*, p. 22.

802 Importantly, the Conference had also recommended asking the Court, if it found that in fact the mission was not exhausted, to provide a solution in regard to the disputed frontier; but this part of the recommendation was not accepted by the Council of the League when it resolved to submit the matter to the Court; the second question referring to the Court's solution was deleted from the resolution forwarding the request. See *ibid.*, p. 12 and p. 7.

803 See Hudson, *World Court Reports*, vol. I, Washington, DC, 1934, p. 392. Eventually, in July 1925, the Albanian Government agreed to adjust the border, leaving the monastery to Yugoslavia: *ibid.*

In the *United Kingdom–France Continental Shelf Interpretive Decision* case, the question of the rectification of the award line was in issue with respect to the Channel Islands sector. The United Kingdom claimed that there were contradictions in the reasoning of the award and the *dispositif*, and that the Court of Arbitration was permitted under Article 10(2) of the *compromis* to provide a clarification of the matter leading to a rectification of that part of the alignment. The Court took special note of the fact that the United Kingdom had 'explicitly disclaimed any right to seek or obtain a "revision" of the Decision of 30 June 1977'.[804] It decided that the contradiction in the reasoning and the *dispositif* were in the nature of a material, non-essential error and that, as such, it could rectify the award boundary north and west of the Channel Islands. Importantly, however, it also observed: 'The power of the Court to rectify the resulting error remains, however, its inherent power to rectify a material error found to exist in its decision. The power to rectify need not, therefore, be stated in the compromissory clause; but equally the compromissory clause *does not enlarge the Court's power to rectify its decision, unless expressly so provided in the clause*.'[805] In other words, the power to interpret judgments could not be enlarged without express authorisation to carry out any changes to the boundary in excess of those required to rectify the material mistake in the boundary delimited by the decision.

Before closing this line of enquiry, two notes of caution are advised. In the first place, it is important to remember the fact that, although consent is the threshold criterion, any revision of a decision actually depends upon whether or not the application is admissible. As the Chamber of the International Court of Justice observed in *El Salvador* v. *Honduras*:

> Finally, the Chamber notes that, regardless of the parties' views on the admissibility of an application for revision, it is in any event for the Court, when seised of such an application, to ascertain whether the admissibility requirements laid down in Article 61 of the Statute have been met. Revision is not available simply by consent of the parties, but solely when the conditions of Article 61 are met.[806]

Although the Chamber espoused this position, which, of course, is correct in substance, the circumstances, including the demands of international justice, may be such that a tribunal may find itself commenting on issues going to the substance of the application while rejecting the revision claimed overall. Thus a modicum of flexibility is needed, as shown below.[807] In sum, then, while the power to revise judgments is based on

[804] 54 ILR 171. [805] *Ibid.*, p. 174 (emphasis added). [806] ICJ Reports 2003, p. 392, at p. 400.
[807] See the discussion of this case in sections II.a, II.b and II.c of Chapter 10 below.

mutual consent, and is not therefore inherent, as is, for example, the power of a tribunal to determine its own jurisdiction (*competence de la competence*), the substantive criteria on admissibility have also to be satisfied.

Secondly, it may be that, where the discovery of the fact constitutes discovery of the existence and submission of false evidence, the tribunal has an inherent right to revise its decision, the rationale being that a decision tainted by fraud and perjury is no decision in law and, accordingly, the right and indeed the duty to render a valid judgment or award must be seen to continue. The argument that, in such circumstances, the reopening of the case can hardly be described as revision in the normal understanding of the notion is clearly a strong one.[808] The matter of fabricated evidence and the right to revise judgments is examined in section II.c.2 of Chapter 10 below.

III. Revision as a remedy to be exercised in exceptional circumstances

This is consistent with the rule on interpretation, that is, revision, not unlike interpretation, is a judicial remedy which must be exercised restrictively and as such cannot lightly be provided. Rosenne described the power to interpret judgments and awards as 'an exceptional power', and accordingly the tribunal should exercise 'tight control' over it, 'although not to the point of allowing artificiality and formalism to play any significant role in that process'.[809] *A fortiori*, the power of revision is to be regarded even more cautiously where the avowed purpose of the application is to change all or part of the judgment or award, and, in the case of boundary delimitation, an application for revision will almost certainly have implications for the location of the boundary. These issues raise questions relating to *res judicata*, an aspect discussed in section II of Chapter 11 below. At this stage, it is important to note that, in practical terms, the adoption of a cautious approach to this remedy means that the relevant criteria for revision have to be examined and applied strictly. Thus, tribunals are obliged to apply a strict test in order to determine, first, whether the application ought to be admitted and, secondly, whether revision ought to be carried out as claimed by the applicant State.

Indeed, in *Application for Revision and Interpretation of the 1982 Judgment*, the International Court of Justice observed: 'Strictly speaking, once it is

[808] See section II.c.2 of Chapter 10 below, especially note 880.

[809] Supra (note 394), p. 103; Geiss (note 692), p. 172; and see Thirlway (note 226), p. 91.

established that the request for revision fails to meet one of the conditions of admissibility, the Court is not required to go further and investigate whether the other conditions are fulfilled.'[810] Further, in *El Salvador* v. *Honduras*, it was argued by the Government of Honduras that there was a good reason why, as a matter of judicial policy, the International Court of Justice, in line with other tribunals, exercised a great deal of restraint and caution on matters of revision, and that was because the principle of *res judicata* could only be overridden in exceptional circumstances.[811] At this point, it will be more appropriate to consider the observations made by Judge Ad Hoc Paolillo who, in his Dissenting Opinion, introduced an interesting qualification into the rule by arguing that, although revision, *as a judicial remedy*, ought to be seen as an exceptional process, the text of Article 61 *as a treaty provision* need not be seen in a restrictive light. In his own words, Judge Paolillo wrote:

> While it is true that an application for revision is by its very nature and object exceptional and hence that the conditions in which it is exercised are . . . necessarily limited . . . and that it is admissible only when all the – very strict – conditions of Article 61 of the Statute are satisfied, the restrictive nature of the conditions governing its exercise cannot be extended to the manner in which the language of those conditions is interpreted. To say that the admissibility of an application for revision is subject to strict conditions is one thing; to argue that the provisions governing the use of such an application must therefore be narrowly interpreted and applied is quite a different matter. There is no justification for applying a narrow interpretative criterion to the terms of Article 61 . . . by virtue of which documents are not to be regarded as facts within the meaning of Article 61. The Article should be interpreted in accordance with general rules of interpretation, which require that terms should be given their ordinary meaning. And there can be no doubt whatsoever that the ordinary meaning of the term 'facts' includes documents.[812]

By way of comment, the following observations will be useful. First, the Chamber did not rule that facts did not include documents; tacitly, it did agree that there was an identity between the two. Secondly, Judge Paolillo is correct that Article 61 ought to be interpreted in accordance with the normal rules of treaty interpretation, but that fact alone does not help him. The point is that the notions of strict and liberal interpretation of

[810] ICJ Reports 1985, p. 207. However, the Court went on to consider other criteria after it found that one of the conditions was found wanting in Tunisia's application, on which see sections II.c.2 and II.d of Chapter 10 below.

[811] Counsel for Honduras, Oral Argument, 12 September 2003, *Pleadings, Verbatim Record*, C6/CR 2003/5, p. 22. For the relation between revision and *res judicata*, see section II of Chapter 11 below.

[812] ICJ Reports 2003, p. 422.

treaties have reference to the way words and phrases in a treaty are interpreted in light of the facts and circumstances described in Articles 31 and 32 of the Vienna Convention on the Law of Treaties. It is in this context that the rule of strict interpretation must be viewed, for what is being urged is not that the normal meanings of words and phrases be sacrificed or compromised with a view to keeping the recourse to revision to minimum levels. The essence of the matter is that, if the words and phrases are, consistent with Articles 31 and 32 of the Vienna Convention, capable of being interpreted in a way which would not make revision a continuously available process for boundary modification, then that interpretation ought to be given serious consideration. The matter cannot be put any higher than that. An approach based on caution is advisable for the simple reason that, as a judicial remedy, revision can legally effect changes to the decision and the judgment boundary, and a relatively liberal approach would not only upset the juridical *status quo*, but also encourage other dissatisfied States to consider making applications for revision.

This approach, however, has also to be seen in the context of the fact that, on occasion, tribunals have examined arguments relating to revision even where the basic criteria of admissibility have failed to be fulfilled by the applicant State. This was the case in *Request for Revision and Interpretation of the Judgment of 1994*, when Chile's request for revision fell effectively at the first hurdle. Its request for the revision of the *Laguna del Desierto* judgment was grounded not in the discovery of a new decisive fact, but in the argument that the 1994 decision was wholly or partially attributable to errors of fact resulting from 'an act or document of the proceedings'.[813] These alleged errors included a disregard for established cartography, a disregard for the rule of the stability of boundaries, the alleged surrendering of the tribunal's powers to the Expert Geographer, and a failure to apply correctly the notion of a water-parting.[814] Argentina objected to Chile's application by arguing that it was inadmissible.[815]

Taking a strict view of Article 40 of the *Tratado de Paz y Amistad* of 1984, on which the request had to be grounded, the Tribunal held that, while claims of errors of fact could be entertained, as Chile had argued, it had

[813] Chile was obliged to pursue this route, for the only two grounds of revision provided in Article 40 of the 1984 *Tratado de Paz y Amistad* dealt with (a) judgments given on the basis of a forged or altered document and (b) errors of fact resulting from an act or document of the proceedings. Ground (a) was not relevant here. In a sense, therefore, the request was more in the nature of an application for judicial review, rather than revision properly so called. See 113 ILR 199.

[814] 113 ILR 201 and 203–5.

[815] *Ibid.*, p. 198.

no power to *correct under its revision procedure* any alleged errors of law. Nor could it re-examine the evidence or alter the reasoning on which the judgment was based. All that the Tribunal could do where revision was sought was to amend the judgment insofar as it was given in consequence of an error resulting from an act or document of the proceedings.[816] It noted that there were in international law either errors of law or errors of fact: *tertium non datur*.[817] It pointed out that Chile had recognised that its grounds were really those of errors of *law* as opposed to those of errors of *fact*, and that, had this ground been provided in Article 40, 'it would have been able to appeal against the Award'.[818] On this fact alone, the Tribunal observed, it was entitled to dismiss Chile's request for revision;[819] it proceeded, nevertheless, to examine the various alleged errors of fact in detail, and came to the conclusion that no errors of fact had actually been made by the Tribunal, and, accordingly, there were no grounds for revision.[820] The Tribunal decided against dismissing Chile's application *in limine litis*, probably because it felt a measure of duty in terms of dispensing international justice. The same deference to the administration of international justice was evident in the decision of the Permanent Court of International Justice to consider Yugoslavia's unfounded plea for revision in the *Monastery of Saint-Naoum* case. These and other matters are discussed below.[821]

[816] *Ibid.*, p. 200. [817] *Ibid.*, p. 202. [818] *Ibid.* [819] *Ibid.*
[820] *Ibid.*, p. 228. See also section I of Chapter 10 below. [821] See Chapter 12 below.

9 The classification of the notion of revision

I. Preliminary observations

In keeping with the classification offered in Chapter 4 above with respect to interpretation, revision can also be divided into two basic kinds, namely, revision which is incidental to the main proceedings, and revision which is not incidental but is in fact the main case before the tribunal. While the basic distinguishing criteria for the classification offered are the same, the two judicial remedies, on account of their legal nature, are in fact asymmetrical in their classification.

II. Revision incidental to the main case

Revision is incidental where it takes place in proceedings supplementary or ancillary to the main case. Such proceedings can come about either as a result of *ad hoc* arbitral proceedings, not unlike *Request for Revision and Interpretation of the 1994 Judgment*, or under Article 61 of the Statute of the International Court of Justice, for example, *Application for Revision and Interpretation of the 1982 Judgment* and *El Salvador* v. *Honduras*. They may also come about under Article 83 of the 1907 Hague Convention for the purposes of the Permanent Court of Arbitration.

The difference between *ad hoc* incidental revision, including applications under the Hague Convention, and incidental revision under the Statute of the International Court of Justice is that, while the criteria provided under the Statute cannot be varied – or, if they are, the varied provisions are in principle unenforceable where their application or interpretation is contested by one of the contracting parties – *ad hoc* arbitral agreements can empower tribunals to revise their judgments on the bases of varying criteria. Indeed, Article 51 of the Hague Convention provides:

'With a view to encouraging the development of arbitration the contracting powers have agreed on the following rules, which are applicable to arbitration procedure, unless other rules have been agreed on by the parties.' Not only is it relevant that Article 83 is to be found in Chapter III of Part IV of the Convention, it also expressly allows variation in terms of the tribunal to which the request can be addressed.

The criteria of admissibility are examined in Chapter 10 below, and it will be appropriate merely to note here that, where permitted, grounds and criteria for revision such as the discovery of a fact, standards of negligence in discovery, legal characteristics of discovered facts and restrictions *ratione temporis* may be different in different *compromis*. Thus revision under Article 40 of the 1984 *Tratado de Paz y Amistad* read with Article XVIII of the 1991 Special Arbitral Agreement which established the Argentina–Chile Arbitral Tribunal for the *Laguna del Desierto* case allowed revision on grounds wholly different from the 'standard' grounds of revision mentioned above, and identified forgery and alteration of a document, and error of fact affecting the whole judgment or part thereof, as grounds for revision.[822]

However, what is common to both kinds of incidental revision – and this is the crux of the matter – is the fact that the tribunal requested to provide a revised judgment is also the tribunal which provided the original decision, that is, the decision in need allegedly of revision. This, of course, applies especially to the International Court of Justice under Article 61 of the Statute. Importantly, the continuing identity of the tribunal, be it an *ad hoc* body, the International Court of Justice or the Permanent Court of Arbitration, is not to be confused with the identity of its members; thus changes to the membership of the tribunals can have no effect on the continuing identity thereof. Similarly, for either kind of incidental revision, no new *compromis* or special agreement is needed insofar as the original instrument is itself the legal basis for revision.

III. Main case revision

Main case revision is not wholly the exact counterpart of main case interpretation, but some features are nevertheless similar. The main similarity is that both are products of a new agreement, either to interpret or to revise the judgment boundary, or both. Accordingly, when an *ad hoc* arbitral agreement for revision is concluded, the tribunal established

[822] See 113 ILR 199; for the text of the agreement, see *ibid.*, p. 23.

pursuant to that agreement cannot be regarded as the same as that which heard the earlier case, even if all the members of the tribunal are the same. This view is grounded in the simple rule that, once the decision has been delivered and after it has become definitive (that is, once all restrictions *ratione materiae* or *ratione temporis* have passed), the tribunal is *functus officio*. However, where the first decision is a judgment of the International Court of Justice and where after the time period has passed and if the States agree to a new special agreement empowering the Court to revise, then obviously the tribunal will be the same, but the case and cause of action will be a different one, and consequently the case cannot be seen as being incidental to the main proceedings.

In this kind of revision, then, where consent to jurisdiction is given anew, States are free to agree any criteria for admissibility, and accordingly they need not restrict themselves to the criteria provided in Article 61 of the Statute or Article 83 of the Hague Convention. It follows that the new tribunal may not be concerned with restrictions *ratione temporis*, or with any of the other admissibility criteria discussed in section II of Chapter 10 below. Nor will it be necessary to show a provision allowing the revision of the judgment in the original *compromis*, which agreement will become, strictly speaking, legally irrelevant. In short, as a new case, the litigating States have the option of including or excluding any qualifications or criteria in their arbitral agreements.

The difficulty, however, is that, if all the accepted admissibility criteria of revision are ignored, and others are substituted, then the new process may not easily lend itself to being described as 'revision' in the accepted sense of the term. For it is persuasively arguable that the notion of revision properly so called will always need some commonality with respect to the key attributes of revision, namely, the discovery of a 'new' fact, the existence or otherwise of negligence in discovery and the decisive influence of that fact on the judgment boundary. The point is that, even if revision is main case revision, and even if it is not incidental revision under Article 61 and Article 83 of the Statute and the Convention respectively, some characteristics of revision are so central to the notion of revision that tribunals would in all probability seek them out as a matter of law.

Although it is only persuasive, the advisory opinion of the Permanent Court of International Justice in *Monastery of Saint-Naoum*, discussed below, would seem to suggest that, in the absence of any provision spelling out the grounds of revision in an enabling instrument, whenever a State requests the revision of a previous judgment boundary, it would be obliged to adduce some evidence regarding the existence of newly discovered facts, provided, of course, that other criteria are also present, including consent to jurisdiction for revision. If, however, various grounds for revision other than discovery of fact are provided in the *compromis*, then the tribunal would have to take all of them into consideration and it would appear that it cannot compel or require the production of evidence of newly discovered facts as the only criterion for revision.

10 Issues of admissibility

I. Preliminary observations

Where it invokes a vested right of revision under the Statute of the International Court of Justice, the applicant State must satisfy the criteria provided in Article 61. As stated above, paragraph 2 of this provision obliges the Court to decide by way of judgment whether or not a decisive new fact exists such as to lay the case open to revision. Thus it is for the applicant State first to establish the admissibility of the request, and, once this is established, the Court will give leave to proceed to the second stage for the purposes of examining the request on its merits. For purposes of admissibility, the State claiming revision will have to fulfil both substantive as well as procedural criteria. Indeed, it is essential to state here that all of the relevant criteria have to be established to the satisfaction of the Court; even if only one of the conditions remains fully to be established, the Court will refuse to admit the case. It was this point that the Chamber of the International Court of Justice emphasised in *El Salvador* v. *Honduras*,[823] discussed below in section II.

At any rate, this two-step procedure is also to be found in Article 38 of the International Law Commission's 1958 Draft Rules on Arbitral Procedure and in Articles 55 and 83 of the Hague Conventions of 1899 and 1907. While other bilateral, multilateral and legally binding instruments also provide a similar procedure, to wit, Article 11(3) of the Guinea and Guinea-Bissau arbitral agreement of 1983, Article 44 of the Statute of the Court of Justice of the European Communities, Article 42 of the Euratom Court and Articles 93 and 94 of the Rules of Procedure of the European

[823] ICJ Reports 2003, p. 392, at p. 399.

Free Trade Area Court, it is not the case that a two-step process is obligatory for tribunals in terms of customary international law.

For present purposes, it suffices to note that certain *compromis* provide for revision, but remain silent on the procedure to be followed, and, in that case, the *ad hoc* tribunal will decide how it wishes to proceed, that is, whether the proceedings at the merits stage are to be preceded by hearings on admissibility. In *Request for Revision and Interpretation of the 1994 Judgment*, the Argentina–Chile Arbitral Tribunal noted that, while its Rules of Procedure of 1992 prescribed a procedure for interpretation, there was nothing to cover a request for revision.[824] By way of a resolution, it decided simply to adopt an *ad hoc* process which began by forwarding the Chilean request for revision to the Government of Argentina, and, after an exchange of submissions and replies, the tribunal commenced an examination of the merits of the request, although it did examine the basic elements of the notion of revision in light of the *Tratado*.[825]

Significantly, in his Individual Opinion, Judge Galindo Pohl noted that the tribunal's *ad hoc* procedure and its forwarding of the Chilean document to the Argentine Government did not exclude a decision on admissibility, but recognised the issue and implicitly postponed a decision on it until the parties had presented their submissions.[826] 'Thus', he wrote, 'the question of admissibility was left pending, subject to a subsequent decision'. His main point, however, was that, '[f]rom the procedural point of view it would have been preferable if, before embarking on a discussion of the substance, the Tribunal had ruled on the application's admissibility, preferably in a separate decision'.[827] He added: 'It is not sufficient that the reader is left to infer that the application was admitted from the fact that the second Judgment ruled on the substance. Sometimes, it is the forms which underpin the substance and give it its full significance.'[828]

Form, however, is not the only reason why a two-step procedure is an appropriate one to adopt. On this point, it could be argued that it is fairer to both the parties and the tribunal. By keeping issues separate, the tribunal is obliged first to examine all the legal criteria relevant to the discovery of the new fact and then to follow it up where relevant with an examination of the merits of the request. It is fairer in terms generally of the administration of international justice and in terms of ruling out or minimising a confusion of issues. Some of the relevant issues are examined below.

[824] 113 ILR 194. [825] *Ibid.*, pp. 194–8. [826] *Ibid.*, p. 237. [827] *Ibid.*, p. 236.
[828] *Ibid.*, p. 237.

II. Substantive criteria

In general terms, and to the extent that Article 61 represents the stereotypical criteria of revision in terms of customary international law, the tribunal will have reference to the following elements: (i) the claim of *discovery* of (ii) a *fact existing* at the time of the judgment but *unknown to both the tribunal and the applicant State* at the time when the judgment was given and (iii) a fact or item of evidence which is *decisive in character* for the purposes of the judgment or award (iv) provided that ignorance of the newly discovered fact was not on account of *negligence* on the part of the State claiming revision. Although these elements have been examined individually below, there is substantial overlapping of notions and ideas and accordingly the itemised statement appearing below is one primarily of convenience for the purposes of organising materials and presenting the law on the matter.

a. Discovery of fact

Discovery, the first element, simply means acquiring knowledge of the existence of a fact after the decision has been made. There is of course no duty to discover or seek out the fact or facts, but, given the time limits of Article 61(5) of the Statute, any discovery after ten years from the date of the decision can have no effect for the purposes of revision. At the same time, as El Salvador argued in *El Salvador* v. *Honduras*, because there is no obligation actively to seek out fresh facts, there cannot be a question of laches for discovery, provided always that the eligibility criterion, discussed below, is fully satisfied.

Similarly, there is a difference between, on the one hand, the discovery of a fact by way of accident or simple perseverance, and, on the other hand, the acquisition of knowledge by a process of creation of 'facts' in terms of a commissioning of reports, surveys and a variety of instruments and documentation. This was the central plank of El Salvador's dispute with Honduras and is discussed below. Suffice it to say here that Honduras' reply was that El Salvador's application was artificial,[829] and that the great majority of the material had been generated by El Salvador itself by way of commission, and hence could not be regarded as having been 'discovered' in the proper sense of the word.[830]

[829] See Agent for Honduras, Oral Argument, 9 September 2003, *Pleadings, Verbatim Record*, C6/CR 2003/3, pp. 11 and 14. [830] See Counsel for Honduras, *ibid*., p. 15.

In this context, it is curious to note that the Permanent Court of International Justice in *Monastery of Saint-Naoum* appeared not to have put due emphasis on discovery in terms of the acquisition of knowledge of facts, that is, facts unbeknownst to Yugoslavia. It held that, as far as facts unknown were concerned, it was difficult to believe that members of the Conference of Ambassadors were unacquainted with the proposals of 1913, which, Yugoslavia argued, were important for the purposes of the interpretation of the London Protocol. The Court relied on the fact that these documents were not secret; and that the Conference had made the decision regarding the frontier 'with full knowledge of the facts', including those in the documents relating to the 1913 Protocol.[831]

On this view, however, the Court ought to have put greater emphasis on the fact that there was no discovery in the proper sense of the term of new facts *by the requesting State*, namely, the Serb-Croat-Slovene State; nor did it observe that, because the facts relating to the London Protocol of 1913 were firmly within the knowledge of Yugoslavia, there was no need to consider whether or not these facts were within the knowledge of the members of the Conference when the decision was taken to allocate the monastery to Albania. The short point here is that, in matters of revision, it is primarily for the *requesting State* not to have knowledge of certain decisive facts when the matter is being considered by the tribunal; the latter's lack of knowledge is normally a reflection or consequence of the requesting State's ignorance. It cannot, however, be right to rely *exclusively* on the lack of knowledge of the tribunal for the purposes of revision. Nor can it be right that, while it has full knowledge of the facts, the requesting State seeks to exploit, by way of a request for revision, the tribunal's ignorance of the relevant facts.

It follows, then, that, if there is knowledge of (i) the existence of the fact or (ii) the contents of the evidence or (iii) both, then there can be no discovery. This is very closely related to the requirement itemised in subsection b below, but it may be useful to examine here some of the relevant law and facts in *El Salvador* v. *Honduras*,[832] currently the leading case on the matter. The detail is examined presently in the context of newly discovered facts or evidence. It will suffice for present purposes to note that El Salvador requested that the Goascorán river sector boundary in the judgment of 1992 by the International Court of Justice be revised because El Salvador now had new proof that the river had abandoned its course owing to avulsion in the course of the seventeenth century; that,

[831] Supra (note 296), p. 22. [832] ICJ Reports 2003, p. 392.

according to the rules of river boundaries, the alignment in avulsion did not suffer any changes thereto; and that accordingly it continued to run along the old river bed of the Goascorán.

Apart from this new evidence, which was assimilated to new facts, El Salvador relied on certain facts which were admittedly within its knowledge and for which there was no actual discovery following the judgment. These facts included the Saco negotiations between 1880 and 1884, the geographical characteristics of the lower reaches of the Goascorán river and the eruption of Cosigüina volcano.[833] 'The Court', El Salvador pleaded in its Application, 'has to put the heretofore unknown or new facts into the balance, including secondary and circumstantial evidence. It must then compare these to the grounds upon which the Judgment was based. The Republic of El Salvador believes it has proven that the grounds upon which the Judgment was based are not as solid as the Chamber considered them to be at the time.'[834] It argued that, because 'the evidentiary value of the "Carta Esférica" and the report of the El Activo expedition is in question, the use of the Saco negotiations (1880–1884) for corroborative purposes becomes worthless, a problem compounded by what the Republic of El Salvador considers to be the Chamber's erroneous assessment of those negotiations'.[835]

A curious argument, it turned the issue of knowledge on its head, for it was based on a perceived need to reconsider *known facts* in light of *changed circumstances* arising from *unknown, newly discovered facts*. It was contented by El Salvador that the proper contextualisation of such new facts necessitated further consideration of 'other facts' insofar as they had been affected by the new facts. While it accepted that these other facts, while they had the character of evidence and proof, were not new facts (properly so called), El Salvador nevertheless urged that they be considered new for the purposes of revision insofar as the Chamber had not taken them up in 1992; they were indeed essential for the purposes of *supplementing* and *confirming* the new facts.

The Honduran defence claimed that, to allow El Salvador's application would be 'tantamount to expanding the restrictive list of elements in Article 61, paragraph 1, of the Court's Statute to unheard-of lengths,

833 *Ibid.*, pp. 410–11. Generally, see Counsel for El Salvador, Mr M. Mendelson, Oral Argument, 8 September 2003, *Pleadings, Verbatim Record*, C6/CR 2003/2, p. 19; and Mr Brotóns, Oral Argument, 10 September 2003, *Pleadings, Verbatim Record* (note 829), C6/CR 2003/4, pp. 31 and 33–4.

834 *Application for Revision of the Judgment of 11 September 1992*, p. 52; see also p. 59.

835 *Ibid.*, p. 70.

calculated to turn revision into a habitual method of appeal and to undermine the authority of *res judicata*'.[836] The Chamber agreed that, in order to determine whether the alleged new facts fell within the provisions of Article 61, it would have to put the new facts into context, and it went on to confirm that it had indeed done so in the course of its reasoning regarding the evidence-based 'new facts' as covered by the new documents. However, it held that it 'cannot find admissible an Application for revision on the basis of facts which El Salvador itself does not allege to be new facts within the meaning of Article 61'.[837]

Importantly, the essence of discovery lies in the *gaining of knowledge* on the strength of the evidence which, more often than not, will be in the shape of documents and other kinds of archival information, for example maps, governmental records and even ancient historical texts and instruments. However, it may be that, on occasion, revision will be justified even where the *existence* of the documents is known; what in these circumstances may be unknown, are the *contents* of the relevant documents. This, indeed, was the case in one recent proceedings before the European Court of Human Rights.

In *Pardo* v. *France*,[838] the Court was asked to decide a plea for revision with respect to a judgment of a Chamber of the Court. The essence of the grievance was that two relevant documents were not produced by the party before the Chamber of the Court despite being requested to do so by the tribunal, and accordingly the Chamber had returned a judgment without having had the opportunity of examining these documents. Thus, revision was not being claimed on the strength of the discovery of new facts, for there were in fact none: both parties and the Chamber were all aware of the *existence* of the two relevant documents. In other words,

[836] ICJ Reports 2003, pp. 410–11. See also, generally, Counsel for Honduras, Mr Dupuy, Oral Argument, 9 September 2003, *Pleadings, Verbatim Record* (note 829), pp. 14–30; Mr Piernas, Oral Argument, *ibid.*, pp. 30–9; Mr Meese, *ibid.*, pp. 39–43; and Sanchez Rodriguez, Oral Argument, *ibid.*, pp. 50–9.

[837] ICJ Reports 2003, p. 411. In *Application for Revision of the Judgment in the Genocide in Bosnia Case*, the Court held that paragraphs 1 and 2 of Article 61 both referred to a fact existing at the time when the judgment was given but which was discovered subsequently. A fact, it said, which occurred several years after a judgment was given was not a new fact within the meaning of Article 61; this, it went on, remained the case irrespective of the legal consequences which such a fact may produce. It also made clear that Article 99 of the Rules of Court makes express provision for proceedings on the merits if, in its first judgment, the Court has declared the application admissible. See ICJ Reports 2003, p. 7, at pp. 30 and 11.

[838] *Pardo* v. *France*, ECtHR, Judgment of 10 July 1996, *Reports of Judgments and Decisions*, vol. 11, 1996-III, p. 860; 22 ECHHR 563.

while the fact of the *existence* (at least at one stage of the dispute) of the documents in question was not controverted by either party, it was the absence of the *information contained in those documents* which was of crucial importance, a situation which, the Court held, could have been decisive for the outcome of the case. Accordingly, the Court admitted the request of the European Commission and referred it back to 'the Chamber which gave the original judgment to determine whether these documents actually cast doubt on the conclusions reached in 1993'.[839] In short, the crucial element for revision is the gaining of knowledge of some relevant crucial fact and *not necessarily the existence* of the document or documents as such, although, having said that, in most cases the existence of knowledge will be the direct result of a discovery of facts, particularly newly discovered documents.

b. The existence of newly discovered facts or evidence

This leads on to the second element, namely, the existence of newly discovered facts or evidence, a requirement which goes to the very essence of the matter.[840] Although Article 61 and most other instruments refer only to facts and not evidence, it is the case that the notion of evidence is related closely to fact and is in some sense only another aspect thereof. Thus, *allegations* and *claims* in the form of new documents and the like are not necessarily new facts which would justify revision of the boundary judgment. Clearly, where parties rely on the discovery of new documents, they must establish that the latter *proved* the existence of some new fact or facts. Hence, it is the information conveyed in the documents which is essential, and not the documents themselves, and it is this point which assimilates it to evidence.

[839] *Ibid.*, p. 870. Subsequently, the Chamber found that the documents were not decisive and dismissed the application: *Pardo* v. *France*, ECtHR, Judgment of 29 April 1997, *ibid.*, vol. 36, p. 735.

[840] See, generally, Strupp, who pointed out that facts, not legal principles, could be made the subject of new evidence: Strupp (note 136), p. 684; Simpson and Fox (note 136), p. 245; Reisman (note 226), pp. 210–11; and Geiss (note 692), pp. 174–81 and 185–9, especially p. 189. For French authorities on the matter, refer to those cited by Judge Ad Hoc Paolillo in his Dissenting Opinion in *El Salvador* v. *Honduras*, ICJ Reports 2003, p. 392, at pp. 421–2, note 7, especially Scerni, 'La procedure de la Cour permanente de Justice internationale', 65 (1938) *Hague Recueil* 672; Reuter, 'La motivation et la revision des sentences arbitrales a la conference de la paix de La Haye (1899) et la conflit frontialier entre le Royaume-Uni et la Venezuela', in Ibler (ed.), *Mélanges offerts a Juraj Andrassy*, The Hague, 1968, p. 243, at p. 245; and Zoller, 'Observations sur la revision et l'interpretation des sentences arbitrales', 24 (1978) *Annuaire francais de droit europeen* 331, at p. 351.

Although it was not a case brought by States under Article 61 of the Statute, the advisory opinion in the *Monastery of Saint-Naoum* is useful insofar as it underlines the approach adopted by the Permanent Court of International Justice in these kinds of situations and circumstances. Highly critical of the decision of 6 December 1922 on the basis of which the Principal Allied Powers had allocated the disputed monastery to Albania, the Serb-Croat-Slovene Government argued that either the decision was based on erroneous information, or it was adopted without regard to certain essential facts, and accordingly urged its reconsideration.

Rejecting Yugoslavia's arguments, the Court ruled that there were no *new* facts as such which would have led the Conference of Ambassadors to a different decision. It was noted that the Conference was admittedly unacquainted with a set of documents sent by the Serb-Croat-Slovene Government in June 1923, that is, after the decision had been adopted, to support its claim for revision, and accordingly the contents thereof would have been new to that body. 'But', the Court observed, 'in the opinion of the Court fresh documents do not in themselves amount to fresh facts. No new fact – properly so-called – has been alleged.'[841] It is easy to appreciate the logic and rationale behind this: to allow a realignment by way of revision of a frontier settled by an authoritative judicial or quasi-judicial award on the basis of the submission of a new document the contents of which are *not newly discovered* facts could, in many circumstances, constitute a recipe for uncertainty and friction between States.

It was in *El Salvador* v. *Honduras* that the significance of evidence as 'new facts' was fully played out. This issue is best discussed in two stages, but, as a preliminary to that discussion, it would be appropriate to provide some background for the purposes of perspective. The case was concerned with El Salvador's application for revision of the sixth sector of the land boundary delimited by the Chamber of the International Court of Justice in *Land, Island and Maritime Frontier Dispute* in 1992.[842] In the earlier proceedings, El Salvador had contended that the boundary river in that sector, the Goascorán river, had changed its course by way of avulsion at some point during the seventeenth century, and accordingly there could, in law, be no change to the *uti possidetis* boundary of 1821, which continued to run along the original bed of the Goascorán river, a river which debouched in the Gulf of Fonseca along the Estero La Cutú, opposite Isla Zacate Grande.

In 1992, the Chamber, however, found no record of an abrupt change in the course of the river; nor was any scientific evidence adduced to establish

[841] Supra (note 296), pp. 21–2. [842] ICJ Reports 1992, p. 351.

an earlier 'original' course. Even so, the Chamber was careful not to adopt a definitive position with respect to the existence or otherwise of any earlier course of the Goascorán which might have debouched into the Estero La Cutú or on any alleged avulsion of the river, nor, *a fortiori*, on the precise date of such alleged avulsion or its legal consequences. It restricted itself to defining the *framework* in which it could *possibly* have taken a position on these various points.[843] It held that any claim by El Salvador that the boundary followed an old course of the river abandoned at some time before 1821 must be rejected. It was a new claim and inconsistent with the previous history of the dispute.[844] Hence, the line of *uti possidetis* of 1821, and the boundary between El Salvador and Honduras was materially the same as it was at the time of the judgment (1992), and that the boundary river flowed into the Gulf northwest of the Islas Ramaditas in the Bay of La Unión.

In its application for revision, El Salvador relied on the existence of these alleged new facts which were in the form of evidence of three major kinds, that is, scientific, technical and historical facts, in order to demonstrate the existence of the old course of the Goascorán and of its abrupt alteration.[845] Although it accepted that it was for the Chamber to decide to accept or dismiss these alleged new facts, El Salvador insisted that this evidence had to be construed as a set of new facts, that is, new discoveries about past facts, and that there was no basis for excluding evidence on the ground that it was not a fact.[846] In effect, the argument was that El Salvador's evidence was based on and proved a fact and that accordingly it was admissible for the purposes of revision.

Honduras took the position that the new facts alleged by El Salvador were not to be confused with new evidence which, being commissioned, was in truth self-generated; nor could they be confused with intellectual constructions based on such facts. Similarly, *opinions* contained in scientific reports could not serve as *facts* for the purpose of revision even if they contained *scientific* evidence.[847] 'According to Honduras', the Chamber noted, 'a "fact" cannot "include evidentiary material in support of an argument, or an assertion, or an allegation". Accordingly, the evidence submitted by El Salvador cannot open a right to revision.'[848]

[843] Supra (note 842), pp. 404–6. [844] *Ibid.*, p. 406.

[845] El Salvador's Application for Revision (note 834), pp. 13 *et seq.*; and see Counsel for El Salvador, Oral Argument, 8 September 2003, *Pleadings, Verbatim Record* (note 833), pp. 42–51.

[846] See, generally, Counsel for El Salvador, Oral Argument, 8 September 2003, *Pleadings, Verbatim Record* (note 833), pp. 37–41; and 10 September, *Pleadings, Verbatim Record* (note 833), pp. 15–17; and see El Salvador's Application for Revision (note 834), p. 15.

[847] See, generally, Counsel for Honduras, Oral Argument, 12 September 2003, *Pleadings, Verbatim Record* (note 811), pp. 11–15. [848] ICJ Reports 2003, p. 403.

The Chamber, however, felt it unnecessary to decide this question insofar as El Salvador had misconceived the *ratio decidendi* of the case. It observed:

It is apparent from this discussion that, while the Chamber in 1992 rejected El Salvador's claims that the 1821 boundary did not follow the course of the river at that date, it did so on the basis of that State's conduct during the nineteenth century . . . In short, it does not matter whether or not there was an avulsion of the Goascorán. Even if avulsion were now proved, and even if its legal consequences were those inferred by El Salvador, findings to that effect would provide no basis for calling into question the decision taken by the Chamber in 1992 on wholly different grounds.[849]

For this reason, the Chamber did not, *at that stage*, find the need to decide the question of evidence as an aspect of new facts. It did, however, come back to the matter, albeit indirectly, when it discussed the second tier of arguments urged by El Salvador.

At this second stage, it claimed a different kind of 'new fact'.[850] It claimed to have discovered a copy of the report of the expedition of the *El Activo*, the ship which had sailed in 1794 to survey the Gulf of Fonseca, and a copy of the *Carta Esférica* prepared by the captain and navigators of the *El Activo*. Both documents were discovered by El Salvador in the Newberry Library in Chicago. It is important to note that copies of the same report and two copies of the chart had been submitted in the previous proceedings by Honduras having obtained them from the Madrid Naval Museum.

The position taken by El Salvador was that, in view of the alleged 'differences' and 'anachronisms' between these two sets of documents, the evidentiary value which the Chamber had attached to the documents submitted by Honduras, stood compromised. In other words, the documents discovered and produced by El Salvador highlighted the 'insubstantiality of the Madrid Naval Museum documents from which the Chamber inferred such significant geographical consequences'.[851] It was claimed that 'the discovery of hitherto unknown documents is a typical example of

[849] *Ibid*., pp. 406–7. Cf. the Dissenting Opinion of Judge Ad Hoc Paolillo, *ibid*., pp. 423–4. Cf. Thirlway who writes that it was open to El Salvador to present the existence, or the occurrence, of the avulsion, as a new fact for the purposes of revision on the ground that the occurrence or non-occurrence of avulsion was a question of fact: Thirlway (note 226), p. 96.

[850] See El Salvador's Application for Revision (note 834), pp. 31–67.

[851] ICJ Reports 2003, pp. 407–8 (quotation marks in the original deleted). See El Salvador's Application for Revision (note 834), pp. 31–40; also Counsel for El Salvador, Mr Brotóns, Oral Argument, 8 September 2003, *Pleadings, Verbatim Record* (note 833), pp. 55–71, especially pp. 66–70.

the type of fact which lays open a case to revision . . . either because they themselves constitute the *factum* or because they are the source of knowledge of them'.[852] El Salvador also alleged that the documents obtained from the Madrid Naval Museum and submitted by Honduras had no official status and accordingly their evidentiary value was 'doubtful'.[853]

The Honduran reply was that the production of the Newberry Library documents from Chicago could not be characterised as new facts because they were simply another copy of one and the same set of documents already submitted by Honduras and evaluated by the Chamber. Going to the substance of the documents, it argued that there were 'insignificant differences' between the charts, and that, in any case, they also showed the mouths of the river Goascorán in its present-day position, a finding on which the 1992 judgment was based. Accordingly, the documents, it argued, were inadmissible.[854] Nor had Honduras ever claimed that the Madrid documents were official in status.[855]

On this issue, the Chamber held in favour of Honduras. It did not specifically examine the question of evidence as a new fact; it proceeded to examine the evidence/facts for their probative weight. The test it applied was whether it would have come to a different conclusion in 1992 had it had for evaluation the documents from the library in Chicago in addition to those from the museum in Madrid. It discovered that the two sets of documents were different only in minor insignificant details, such as legends, handwriting and the placing of accents (on the relevant words); and that the 'new' chart submitted by El Salvador actually bore out the geographical location of the mouth of the Goascorán and the Estero La Cutú as contended by Honduras.[856] The Chamber concluded that 'the new facts alleged by El Salvador in respect of the "Carta Esférica" and the report of the *El Activo* expedition are not "decisive factors" in respect of the Judgment whose revision it seeks'.[857]

The following observations on the matter are noteworthy. By examining the contents, as opposed to the legal nature, of the Chicago documents,

[852] ICJ Reports 2003, pp. 407–8 (words deleted in original quotation).

[853] *Ibid.*, p. 407. See, generally, Counsel for El Salvador, Mr Brotóns, 8 September 2003, *Pleadings, Verbatim Record* (note 833), pp. 55–7; and Oral Argument, 10 September 2003, *Pleadings, Verbatim Record* (note 833), pp. 28–34.

[854] Counsel for Honduras, Oral Argument, 12 September 2003, *Pleadings, Verbatim Record* (note 811), pp. 14–15; and ICJ Reports 2003, p. 408.

[855] ICJ Reports 2003, p. 408. See, generally, Counsel for Honduras, Mr Piernas, Oral Argument, 9 September 2003, *Pleadings, Verbatim Record* (note 829), pp. 30–9.

[856] ICJ Reports 2003, pp. 409–10.

[857] *Ibid.*, p. 410. Cf. Judge Ad Hoc Paolillo's Dissenting Opinion, pp. 423–5.

the Chamber effectively accepted in principle that what is known as newly or 'after discovered' evidence might be a valid ground for admissibility for the purposes of revision or a rehearing.[858] In other words, it agreed with El Salvador that, in theory, a certain kind of evidence, *and not only facts properly so called*, could come within the purview of Article 61. The difficulty is that the Chamber accepted this without examining the basic question whether the notion of after discovered evidence was a valid ground for the purpose of revision under Article 61.

It is acknowledged, of course, that the International Court of Justice, and indeed all international tribunals, are quick to eschew theoretical exegeses on doctrinal matters, preferring to interpret and apply the law and facts in as concise and economical a manner as possible. Even so, the precise scope and effect of after discovered evidence for the purposes of revision was an issue which went to the heart of the matter; it was *the* main aspect of the dispute between the two parties. It is reasonable, therefore, to have expected the Chamber to spell out not only the fact that, in general principle, a newly discovered, but existing, fact could also be in the shape and form of an item which was more in the nature of evidence than fact. It fell to Judge Ad Hoc Paolillo to comment in some detail about the value of evidence in the shape of documents for the purpose of Article 61.

Observing that the Chamber did not ask itself whether or not this documentary evidence could be regarded as new facts within the meaning of Article 61, Judge Paolillo noted that it went on (nevertheless) to hold that the alleged new facts were not decisive in character, 'which is tantamount to an implicit acknowledgment of its status as "new facts". The Chamber thus confirms that the production of such documents may substantiate an application for revision provided that they meet the criteria laid down by Article 61 of the Statute.'[859] He went on to examine the thesis that documentary evidence may be put forward as 'new facts' and took into consideration the *travaux préparatoires* of Article 59 of the Statute of the Permanent Court of International Justice and the 'scant . . . corpus of international jurisprudence', including that of the International Court of

[858] See Cheng (note 692), pp. 364–70; Sandifer (note 692), pp. 407–56; Carlston (note 181), pp. 231–3; and Secretariat's Commentary on Arbitral Procedure (note 226), p. 102. For further commentary on this and related aspects, refer to the elaborate argumentation presented by (Sir) Elihu Lauterpacht in a petition for a rehearing in the *British Petroleum* v. *Libya* arbitration on the basis of fundamental errors of law having been made in the Award of 10 October 1973, reproduced in Wetter (note 95), vol. II, pp. 587–609.

[859] ICJ Reports 2003, p. 392, at p. 421.

Justice. His unequivocal conclusion was that documents constituted facts within the meaning of Article 61.[860]

This rule has a good legal pedigree. In *Heim and Chamant* v. *The German State*, the Franco-German Mixed Arbitral Tribunal confirmed that the notion of facts was elastic [in character] and that the relevant legal concept included all means of proof relating to questions of law.[861] In short, the objection, such as it is, is that it ought to have taken a more rigorous approach to admitting after discovered fact, and particularly evidence, not least because this was the first time that the matter was before the International Court of Justice or Chamber thereof.

In this context, it needs to be observed that the principles of revision with respect to after discovered evidence allow such evidence to be admitted if it can be established that the later evidence demonstrates that the contents and facts gleaned from the earlier set of documents or testimony and the like, are factually or legally incorrect or unreliable; that the conclusions arrived at by the tribunal are untenable in light of the evidence discovered after the decision was handed down by the tribunal; and that, to that extent, the new evidence is a corrective, for it demonstrates that the old evidence was unreliable, and hence this knowledge constituted a 'new fact'.

Evidence of this kind may go to questions of error of fact. As Cheng puts it: 'Error produced through lack of knowledge, at the time of the judgment, of facts which would have exercised a decisive influence upon the decision may be regarded as a particular form of error in fact.' He takes

860 *Ibid.*, p. 422.

861 1 *Annual Digest* 379, at p. 382. Eventually, however, the tribunal went on to reject Germany's application for revision. The question involved the discovery of documentary material in the form of minutes of the Alsace-Lorraine Conference held just prior to the Paris Peace Conference. These minutes, which allegedly showed that Alsace-Lorrainers had been regarded by the French as having German nationality during the Great War, had greatly influenced the Committee on Alsace-Lorraine at the Paris Peace Conference. The Committee's projects on the question of Alsace-Lorraine nationality were in turn adopted almost in their entirety by the Peace Conference in the Treaty of Versailles. The minutes also allegedly showed that the Alsace-Lorraine Conference had rejected the idea of any retroactive effect arising out the reintegration of Alsace-Lorraine with France and the bestowal of French nationality on the inhabitants of that region. These minutes, the German Government argued, constituted in effect preparatory materials for the Alsace-Lorraine Peace Conference Committee; and, to the extent that they belied the assumptions made by the lower tribunal regarding French nationality in Alsace-Lorraine, these minutes thus constituted new facts. While the Tribunal dismissed the legal effects and importance of these minutes for the purposes of revision, it did accept that the nature of the documents discovered was such that they did not warrant dismissal *in limine*: see pp. 380–1, and see Strupp (note 136), p. 685.

the view that it was to accommodate this kind of post-decisional evidence that Articles 55 and 83 of the 1899 and 1907 Hague Conventions were formulated by the respective delegations. 'The aim', he said, 'is to provide a remedy against possible injustice arising from errors of fact which have become demonstrable for the first time after the judgment.'[862] This line of enquiry is pursued in subsection d below.

c. Decisive character of newly discovered facts or evidence

For purposes of revision, a newly discovered fact must be of crucial significance to the judgment or award. A newly discovered fact is of crucial significance where it would have had a decisive effect on the decision, that is, for present purposes, where it would and could have exercised a decisive effect on the judgment boundary or status of territory. This is the decisive character test. To put the matter the other way round, new facts which have *no* direct bearing on, or facts which would *not* have influenced the decision one way or another, or which were merely tangential to the *dispositif* or the relevant part thereof, cannot fulfil legal conditions for the purposes of revision. Importantly, the general rule with respect to newly discovered facts applies *mutatis mutandis* to evidence. It follows that the terms of Article 61 are thus relevant for both fact and evidence. Both are examined separately below.

1. Decisive facts qua facts

The requirement that the facts discovered must be such that had they been known at the time of the judgment they would have exercised a decisive effect thereon is best seen in the context of *Application for Revision and Interpretation of the 1982 Judgment*. It was shown above that Tunisia objected to running the boundary line through the point 33° 55' North, 12° East on the ground that it would have allocated to Libya areas of continental shelf lying within the Tunisian petroleum concession line of 1966.[863] This, it said, was in fact contrary to the Court's decision which was based entirely on the idea of a perfect alignment between the Libyan and Tunisian petroleum concessions, and on the perceived absence of any overlapping claims of the parties up to 1974 in the nearest offshore areas, a maximum of fifty miles from the coast.[864]

[862] Supra (note 692), p. 364.

[863] This summary of Tunisia's views is based on the comments made by the Court in its judgment: see ICJ Reports 1985, pp. 198–204 and 206–11.

[864] *Ibid.*, p. 201.

The 'new' fact, which Tunisia relied on to justify its application for revision, was the discovery of the precise geographical co-ordinates of Libya's Concession No. 137 (subsequently No. NC 76), the north-western boundary of which was taken into consideration by the Court in its judgment of 1982. The Tunisian Government claimed that the precise co-ordinates had become known to it after the judgment was adopted, and that these co-ordinates differed from the various descriptions of the relevant boundary given by Libya during the proceedings before the Court. The Libyan position was consistent with objecting to the Tunisian application on legal and factual grounds, including the contention that the facts could have been discovered by due diligence and that they were not decisive in character.[865]

As obliged by the Statute, the Court first examined the request for admissibility. It decided that there was no 'new' fact which Tunisia could not have discovered with the usual diligence.[866] It then examined the Tunisian argument that the Court's perceived coincidence of Libyan and Tunisian petroleum concession boundaries was a fact decisive in character. It held, *inter alia*, that the Court's reasoning remained wholly unaffected by the discovery of the precise co-ordinates of Concession No. 137; and that, in relation to the Tunisian stepped boundary, a bearing of 26° from Ras Ajdir was adopted only for the purpose of expressing its general direction; it was with that general direction that the Libyan petroleum concession boundary was said by the Court to be aligned.[867] In view of this, the Court decided that that fact was not decisive in character and therefore the request was inadmissible.

Interestingly, the Court acknowledged that, had the co-ordinates of Libyan Concession No. 137 been more clearly indicated in 1982, the judgment would not have been worded identically. It added that the distinction between the bearing of the actual boundary of that concession (24° 57' 03") and the bearing of the boundary from Ras Ajdir, which was implied by the choice of the point 33° 55' North, 12° East (26°), might usefully have been included in the judgment. Even so, it held:

> But what is required for the admissibility of an application for revision is not that the new fact relied on might, had it been known, have made it possible for the Court to be more specific in its decision; it must also have been a 'fact of such a nature as to be a decisive factor'. So far from constituting such a fact, the details

[865] See Libya's Observations on the Application Submitted for Revision, *Pleadings, Application for Revision* (note 337), pp. 59–72; see also ICJ Reports 1985, pp. 202–3.

[866] ICJ Reports 1985, pp. 204–7.

[867] *Ibid.*, pp. 212 and 213. Cf. Judge Oda's Separate Opinion, *ibid.*, pp. 236–41.

of the correct co-ordinates of Concession No. 137 would not have changed the decision of the Court as to the first sector of the delimitation.[868]

In his Separate Opinion, Judge Oda stated that, no matter how forcefully the judgment were to be criticised, the *cause and motives* underlying the judgment are not matters subject to revision under Article 61. If any case for criticism of the judgment were to be made out, it could only be on the basis of its reasoning rather than on the discovery of new facts.[869]

Reference must also be made to *El Salvador* v. *Honduras*. A central feature of El Salvador's claim was that 'decisive' meant that, when placed in the chain of reasoning of the previous tribunal, it could make a difference to the outcome of the case, but that, at the admissibility stage, it was sufficient for the applicant to demonstrate that it could plausibly or reasonably have made such a difference.[870] El Salvador argued simply that the new facts/evidence established that the change in the location of the river had been by way of an avulsion and not accretion, and accordingly the decision as to the location of the boundary would have been radically different; and that the finding of fact was part of the *ratio decidendi* of the case.[871]

Honduras pointed out that the decisive character of the fact must be linked to the *dispositif*, and that the operative clause of the 1992 judgment was not (for this purpose) paragraph 308, but paragraphs 312 and 322. In order to be decisive, the allegedly new facts would have to undermine the Chamber's factual determination that, between 1880 and 1972, the applicant State had treated the boundary as being based on the 1821 course of the river and that, in that year, the river debouched at Ramaditas. According to Honduras, this finding remained unaffected by the 'new' facts produced by El Salvador.

Moreover, Honduras continued, even if El Salvador's arguments on the operative paragraph were accepted, there was still no evidence to demonstrate that avulsion had indeed taken place in the Spanish colonial period—or indeed at any point—with any degree of precision. In any event, the standard of proof was to be set high, for revision was inherently an exceptional judicial remedy.[872] The Chamber examined its own judgment

[868] *Ibid.*, p. 214. [869] *Ibid.*, p. 241. Further, see Thirlway (note 226), pp. 90–2 and 101–2.

[870] Counsel for El Salvador, Oral Argument, 8 September 2003, *Pleadings, Verbatim Record* (note 833), pp. 33–5; and El Salvador's Application for Revision (note 834), pp. 14–15.

[871] Counsel for El Salvador, Oral Argument, 8 September 2003, *Pleadings, Verbatim Record* (note 833), pp. 33–5. See also El Salvador's Application for Revision (note 834), pp. 5–12 and 30.

[872] Counsel for Honduras, Oral Argument, 12 September 2003, *Pleadings, Verbatim Record* (note 811), pp. 15–18. In fact, El Salvador relied on paragraphs 306–22 of the 1992 judgment as containing the underlying reasoning for the operative paragraph in the *dispositif*, namely, paragraph 430: see El Salvador's Application for Revision (note 834), p. 5.

in order to determine the *ratio decidendi*, and decided that it was indeed paragraph 312 which contained the essence of its decision with respect to the sector under consideration. As discussed above, the Chamber pointed out that, in 1992, it had rejected El Salvador's claims that the 1821 boundary did not follow the course of the river at that date, and it did so on the ground that El Salvador's conduct throughout the nineteenth century was consistent with accepting the fact that the boundary in 1821, the year of independence for the purposes of the *uti possidetis* rule, did follow the course of the Goascorán.[873] It held:

> The facts asserted in this connection by El Salvador are not 'decisive factors' in respect of the Judgment which it seeks to have revised. In light of the 1992 Judgment, the Chamber cannot but reach such a conclusion, independently of the positions taken by the parties on this point in the course of the present proceedings.[874]

Similarly, as was noted above, the Chamber ruled that the new evidence-based facts drawn from the newly discovered documentation from the Newberry Library in Chicago were also not decisive facts in respect of the judgment the revision of which El Salvador sought to obtain from the Chamber.[875]

2. Evidence as decisive fact

The rule regarding the discovery of decisive facts applies in equal measure to the discovery of decisive evidence, and indeed the two are, and can be, assimilated efficiently. For purposes of clarification, the close relation between fact and evidence can be viewed by examining facts relating to evidence of nationality or of the authenticity of evidence. Thus, (i) where the decision of the tribunal in terms of granting or failing to grant rights and obligations to a party exclusively (a) on grounds of nationality or the absence thereof, or (b) on account of a lack of authenticity of evidence, and (ii) where subsequently facts are discovered which appear to demonstrate the absence or presence of nationality[876] or the authenticity

[873] ICJ Reports 2003, pp. 404–6.

[874] *Ibid.*, p. 410. Cf. Judge Ad Hoc Paolillo's Dissenting Opinion, *ibid.*, pp. 423–5.

[875] *Ibid.*, p. 410, paragraph 55. For further commentary, see Thirlway (note 226), pp. 98–101.

[876] See, for example, the *Schreck* case, where the US–Mexico Claims Commission had mistakenly assumed that the claimant was a Mexican, and not a US citizen, on grounds of his birth in Mexico; but the United States 'produced the appropriate law of Mexico, by which it appeared that the assumption was clearly erroneous, and Sir Edward Thornton [the Umpire] made an award in favour of the claimant'. See Moore (note 136), vol. II, pp. 1357–8. See also Sandifer (note 692), pp. 451–2. On the Iran–United States Claims Tribunal, see Brower and Brueschke (note 414), pp. 245 *et seq.*

of evidence,[877] as the case may be, then that applicant may have made out a good case for revision or rehearing. In other words, where nationality or the authenticity of evidence are the decisive factors for the success or failure of an application for revision, the discovery of new evidence clearly showing that nationality or the authenticity of evidence did or did not exist (as the case may be) when the decision was made will constitute a ground for revision.

In the *George Moore* case, the United States–Mexican Claims Commission had initially dismissed the case for want of proof of citizenship, but subsequently allowed a rehearing on the ground that the Commission had observed that there was now conclusive evidence of Mr Moore's American citizenship, and that, if the evidence were such that it would have produced a change in the minds of the Commissioners, then justice, equity and public law allowed a rehearing.[878] In the case of evidence based on forgeries, false witness, faulty translation and the like, it can be argued strenuously that such evidence is devoid of probative weight and hence easily rejected, and that, if such evidence were crucial to the decision, then a case for revision or rehearing can successfully be made out without doing violence to the notion of revision in general, and Article 61 of the Statute in particular. The awards of the US–Germany Mixed Claims Commission in the *Sabotage Claims*[879] are an embodiment, as Sandifer

[877] The question whether revision was available for the purposes of rectifying a judgment rendered on the strength of fraudulent evidence exercised the minds of certain delegates during the Hague Conference on the Peaceful Settlement of Disputes of 1899 in the Committee of Examination, including Mr Holls, Sir Julian Pauncefote, Count Nigra and Leon Bourgeois, the President of the Committee: see, generally, Third Commission, *Proceedings 1899* (note 714), pp. 617–25; for commentaries, see Carlston (note 181), pp. 237–8; and Sandifer (note 692), pp. 427–30 and 444–7. This has ceased to be an issue consistent with some judicial practice, including the *Sabotage Claims* (see next footnote below) and the *Benjamin Weil* and *La Abra Silver Mining Company* cases. Although Sir Edward Thornton, the Umpire, had refused in 1876 to grant a rehearing in view of being debarred by the Claims Convention, various sums of money were eventually refunded to the Mexican Government by the United States on the ground that there was sufficient proof of fraudulent and exaggerated claims before the US–Mexican Claims Commission, but the cases were never revised at the international level; they were finally set aside under Acts of Congress and reviewing authority was vested in the Court of Claims; these acts were confirmed by the US Supreme Court. See Moore (note 136), pp. 1324–48; Ralston (note 136), pp. 118–19; Sandifer (note 692), pp. 435–9 and 430–3 respectively; and Hyde (note 692), pp. 1640–2.

[878] Supra (note 136), pp. 1357–8.

[879] It is important to note that, while the Umpire, Mr Justice Owen J. Roberts, held in his decision of 15 December 1933 (see below for a select synopsis of the complex series of cases) that the Commission could not grant a rehearing on the basis of after-discovered evidence insofar as sufficient time was given to the parties for the purposes of producing relevant evidence, a petition for revision based on the discovery of

asserts, of 'a clear finding of gross and wilful fraud and of the authority of the tribunal to reopen, modify, and reverse its prior decisions upon the production of satisfactory evidence to prove such fraud'.[880]

fraudulent and collusive evidence ought not to be disallowed. Every tribunal, he said, had inherent power to reopen and to revise a decision induced by fraud: 34 (1940) AJIL 154, at p. 164. Generally, with respect to these cases, see the decision of the US–German Mixed Arbitral Commission, 16 October 1930, dismissing US claims alleging sabotage by German agents of certain terminals on the New Jersey shore of New York harbour in 1917: 25 (1931) AJIL 147; the decision of 5 December 1932 refusing to reopen the case for the purposes of admitting newly found evidence which proved that the Commission had been misled by false German evidence: 27 (1933) AJIL 345; the decision of 15 December 1933 accepting the position that the Commission had the right to rehear a case where there were allegations of false evidence, followed by the granting of a new hearing on the basis of such allegations: see above; the decision of 15 June 1936 holding that Germany had indeed adduced false evidence on material issues: 33 (1939) AJIL 770; and the decision of 3 June 1936 setting aside the original decision of 16 October 1930: 33 (1939) AJIL 771; on which, see, generally, Woolsey, 'The Arbitration of the Sabotage Claims Against Germany', 33 (1939) AJIL 737; Woolsey, 'The Sabotage Claims Against Germany', 34 (1940) AJIL 23; and Woolsey, 'Litigation of the Sabotage Claims Against Germany', 35 (1941) AJIL 282; and Sandifer (note 692), pp. 435–9. There is some evidence to suggest that the Iran–United States Claims Tribunal accepted an inherent right to reopen and revise the case in proceedings tainted by perjury and fraud: see Brower and Brueschke (note 414), p. 259.

[880] Supra (note 692), p. 439. Claims of fabricated evidence and the like are no strangers to boundary and territorial dispute cases, although they have not led to revision. In *Qatar* v. *Bahrain*, the latter challenged the authenticity of eighty-two documents submitted by Qatar; and, after the International Court of Justice had ordered the two parties to produce definitive reports on these allegations, Qatar accepted that for the purposes of the case they should be discounted. The Court agreed to disregard the impugned documents: ICJ Reports 2001, p. 40, at pp. 46–7. In the *Palmas Island* case, the Sole Umpire observed that the authenticity of documents could not be questioned because they had been certified by the competent officials of the Dutch Government and accordingly the production of facsimiles of texts and seals was superfluous: 22 (1928) AJIL 867, at pp. 895–6; and see Sandifer (note 692), p. 275. In the *British Guiana* v. *Venezuela* dispute, the latter State chose to claim that maps decisive in character to the arbitration proceedings in 1899 were tampered with by the United Kingdom's Colonial Office: see section entitled Conclusions, *Report on the Boundary Question with British Guiana Submitted to the National Government by the Venezuelan Experts*, Venezuela Foreign Ministry, 1967, reprinted in Wetter (note 95), vol. III, pp. 140–41, at p. 141; and see UK Foreign Office Library memoranda of 1886 relied on by Venezuela to assert falsification of maps: reprinted, *ibid.*, pp. 1475–48. In *El Salvador* v. *Honduras*, one of the objections maintained by Honduras against the evidence produced by El Salvador was that certain photographs had been obtained illegally. El Salvador denied that any illegality was involved, but insisted that there was no settled rule in international law which precluded consideration of evidence illegally obtained. See the Oral Argument of the Counsel for Honduras, 9 September 2003, *Pleadings, Verbatim Record*, (note 829) pp. 52–3; and of Counsel for El Salvador, 10 September 2003, *ibid.*, (note 833) pp. 19–22, respectively. The Chamber, however, did not pass upon the matter. On illegally obtained evidence and the paucity of case law on the matter, see Kazazi, *Burden of Proof and Related Issues: A Study on Evidence Before International Tribunals*, The Hague, 1996, pp. 203–9.

It is true, of course, that the question of after discovered evidence or facts is not always as straightforward as described in the examples given above, and that there are, indeed, various kinds of such evidence. In *El Salvador* v. *Honduras*, the essential character of the alleged new fact was in the nature of knowledge of the fact of the alleged unreliability of the old evidence, that is knowledge which came only by way of a *comparison* of the old and new items of evidence. Hence, the new fact had an interpretative dimension to it: what the Chamber was in fact invited to do was to compare the new Chicago documents with the old Madrid report and charts, and then to decide whether or not the later evidence showed that the earlier evidence was so unreliable that the judgment of 1992 ought to be revised to the extent of the flaws exposed by the Chicago documents. It was this comparison between the two sets of documents which brought out the 'new fact' of *unreliability* of the earlier evidence. It follows that the 'new fact' did not exist on its own, in the sense that, without an exercise in comparison, the putative fact of unreliability of evidence could neither have arisen nor indeed have even existed.

It ought to be pointed that the Chamber, on this view, ought to have clarified the fact that, inasmuch as after discovered evidence is a valid ground for admissibility for the purposes of revision, the test provided in Article 61 has to be seen in a more nuanced light. This is predicated on the fact that up to now the 'decisive factor' test contained in Article 61 was applied primarily in the context of the merits of the judgment. It is the case that the decisive factor test of newly discovered facts properly so called is seen traditionally as going to the *ratio decidendi* of the judgment; if the newly discovered facts were so persuasive in character that they effectively upset the juridical basis of the judgment, then it stood to reason that they would have to relate to a matter which was crucial to the judgment. If this were not so, then their decisive characteristics would either be weak or non-existent.

However, following the Chamber's judgment in *El Salvador* v. *Honduras*, it can now be posited that the decisive factor test may take on rather a different hue when applied with respect to after discovered evidence. Not only does the substance of the new evidence have to relate to a fact which was crucial to the judgment, the party relying on the new evidence must demonstrate that the intrinsic character or probative weight of that evidence was such that its effect was crucial to the finding contained in the first judgment. This is predicated on the fact that the unreliability of the Madrid evidence was not of itself sufficient for the purposes of revision. Two related but distinct aspects of the decisive factor or influence test can readily be seen in the case under examination.

On the one hand, the Government of El Salvador had to satisfy the Chamber that the Chicago documentation was such that it related to a decisive aspect of the judgment in the sixth sector, which, in the contention of El Salvador, was the avulsion of the Goascorán. On the other hand, the Government of El Salvador also had to demonstrate the 'insubstantiality' of the Madrid documentation when compared with the maps and charts from Chicago. In effect, then, El Salvador was urging the Chamber to accept that the nature and scale of the discrepancies were of an order which precluded any reliance on the Madrid documentation, keeping also in mind the fact that the latter documentation bore no official status. This would mean that the discrepancies were crucial and decisive: had the Chamber been aware of them in 1992, it would *not* have decided the matter in the manner in which it did. In short, the decisive factor test is used not only for the general admissibility of the application for revision where the fact relates directly to the substance of the judgment; it could also be used to evaluate the evidence where the latter was discovered after the decision of 1992 was made. The point is that it was crucial for El Salvador to establish that this unreliability was such that it would have led the Chamber to the conclusion that the judgment of 1992 was flawed. It is this aspect of the matter which is crucial to this review of the judgment.

The basic difficulty, however, is that the Chamber failed to apply this decisive factor test in a satisfactory manner. For, when it observed that the irregularities and discrepancies in the two sets of documentation were minor and insignificant, and that accordingly they were 'not "decisive factors" in respect of the Judgment whose revision [El Salvador] seeks',[881] it was clearly saying that a comparison of the two sets of documents had led to the conclusion that, because the irregularities and discrepancies were of no consequence, the Chamber had decided not to admit El Salvador's application for the purposes of revision. By doing so, it linked the decisive factor test of Article 61 to the nature and quality of evidence submitted to it, whereas the decisive factor test ought, in fact, to have been applied in the context of the *decisive reason or reasons* for the judgment for that sector of the frontier.

It can, of course, be argued that the Chamber ought not to be criticised for applying the decisive factor test to the documents in terms of examining them and discovering only minor irregularities, for there is little or no sense in applying the test to the *ratio decidendi* of the case where the

[881] ICJ Reports 2003, p. 410.

documents themselves are unable to pass muster at that stage. There would be no point in investigating the question whether or not the facts emerging from a comparison of the documents can have any effect on the *ratio decidendi* of the case where the documents themselves are not of a kind which bear any legal significance in terms supplying a new fact. This argument has the merit of judicial economy, but it also has the demerit of giving the impression that there can be two hierarchical tests, the first of which is to evaluate the documents in order to see if there is any inherent probative weight to the evidence submitted and to see if any new facts eroding the reliability of the evidence have emerged; and the second of which is to investigate whether or not the newly discovered evidence/fact can have or has had a decisive effect on the reason for the decision. The fact is that Article 61 provides only one test.

Again, it could equally be argued that the Chamber's rejection of the application on the basis of an absence of any major irregularities and inconsistencies between the two sets of documents was consistent with the terms of Article 61 in that all that the Chamber was required to investigate was the question whether the irregularities and inconsistencies were such that they seriously affected the reliability of the judgment and to that extent had a decisive effect thereon; it did not need to go into questions of *ratio decidendi*.

Although attractive in its logic and simplicity, this argument cannot be sustained. For it gives the impression that the Chamber's comparison and analysis of the two sets of documents could have made a difference to its findings, and the fact is that it could have made no difference. It is the case that, had the irregularities and inconsistencies been significant enough to have seriously eroded the reliability of the Madrid documentation, then the Chamber, had it known of this unreliability in 1992, would have decided not to give any credence to the Madrid documents, but that would not have made any difference for the purposes of revision because the *ratio decidendi* would not have been affected; and, in this case, it was the *acquiescent conduct of El Salvador* which was the true *ratio* for the Chamber's decision with respect to the Goascorán sector of the boundary. In other words, it would still have made no difference to the overall decision because the latter did not turn on the veracity of the eighteenth-century charts and reports produced by the parties but on the conduct of El Salvador, which was effectively estopped from asserting that the boundary lay in a different bed of the river.

Indeed, viewed in this light, it could be argued strongly that the Chamber ought not to have even sought to compare the two sets of documents, for to do so was an exercise in futility. Arguably, had the documents in question gone to issues of conduct, and in particular to the absence of tacit recognition or acquiescence by El Salvador, then it would have been apposite to investigate thoroughly the evidence supporting such claims. Hence, either the test was not properly formulated, or, at worst, the Chamber was unable to state the nature, scope and effects of the test in a satisfactory manner. By way of abundant caution, it must be added that the judgment of the Chamber was limited to the admissibility of El Salvador's application. It would have to apply different tests had it decided to admit and judge the merits of El Salvador's application. It would be idle to speculate what those tests might have been, except to observe that the Chamber would have taken into account the requirement that any revision of the judgment must ultimately be equitable for *both* States, regardless of the discovery of any new fact. It follows that, as a general principle, the International Court of Justice ought to admit an application and to consider revising the location of its judgment boundary only where it is overwhelmingly equitable to do so in the circumstances of the case and in the interests of both parties.

Finally, in this context, it is extremely important to bear in mind that, by admitting the second category (as described above) of newly discovered evidence-based fact, that is one which partakes more of the character of evidence than a simple application of the fact to the case, the Chamber has potentially opened up for the International Court of Justice a predicament which, common juridical sense dictates, it must studiously seek to avoid in most cases. It can hardly be doubted that, if States were assured that newly discovered evidence may, in all the right circumstances, be assimilated to a new fact, and that the International Court of Justice could and might be persuaded to reconsider such evidence in the hope of gaining some revision of the decision and a relocation of the boundary, then parties to previous litigation might be tempted to employ the relatively abundant resources of their governments to search every conceivable location for more evidence. Conversely, satisfied States would naturally be exercised by the fact that, for ten years after the judgment, the losing party would, in principle, be free to scour around for such evidence in the hope of gaining a revision judgment in all the appropriate circumstances from the International Court of Justice.

Indeed, as early as 1899, when Article 55 of the Hague Convention was being debated at the International Peace Conference, the delegate from Russia, Mr F. de Martens, as noted in Chapter 7 above, held out against rehearings of arbitral awards, and observed, as presciently as ever:

A rehearing of the arbitral award, as provided in Article 55 [of the Asser draft], must necessarily have such a disastrous effect. There should not be left the slightest doubt on this point. The litigating Power against which the arbitral award has been pronounced will not execute it, certainly not during the three months, and it will make every effort imaginable to find new facts or documents. The litigation will not have been ended, but it will be left in suspense for three months with the serious aggravation that the Government and the nation which have been found guilty will be drawn still more into recrimination and dangerous reciprocal accusations.[882]

In the definitive version of Article 55 of the 1899 Convention, as seen earlier, the precise time limits were left to the discretion of the parties in the *compromis*. Clearly, however, under the ten-year period provided in the Statute of the International Court of Justice, opportunities will abound for the discovery of evidence, as opposed to the discovery of decisive facts properly so called, after the Court has delivered the judgment. Nor can it be ignored that resources available to a dissatisfied State tend to magnify where, as in this case, plans and prospects for regaining 'lost' territory constitute a perennial *agendum* in foreign policy for the government of that State. Clearly, this can create a degree of anxiety and uncertainty for that period of time. It is obvious, therefore, that, without clearer indications or limitations with respect to after discovered evidence, the Chamber's approach to the problem in *El Salvador* v. *Honduras* was less than satisfactory. On this view, it ought to have stressed with all the emphasis at its command that revision was a remedy to be viewed with a maximum degree of restraint.[883]

More disconcertingly for the International Court of Justice, this judgment may prove to be a disincentive to States currently considering

[882] Third Commission, *Proceedings 1899* (note 714), pp. 618–19. He expressed similar views subsequently: (note 719), p. 621. See also the statement of M. Chevalier Descamps, who observed that popular opinion would want them [i.e. dissatisfied governments] to invent new facts in order to reopen an arbitration case which had been decided against them; see *ibid.*, p. 623. Cf. the sanguine riposte of Mr F. W. Holls, the delegate from the United States, who said: 'New facts cannot be forged nor manufactured, at least not by civilised Governments. In fact, every Government will hesitate to expose its country to the humiliation which would undoubtedly attach to an unsuccessful attempt for a rehearing of the litigation upon a pretended discovery of new facts, the existence of which would be denied by the tribunal.' See *ibid.*, p. 621, and generally sections II.a and II.b of this chapter.

[883] In *Pardo* v. *France*, the European Court of Human Rights observed: 'Inasmuch as it calls into question the final character of judgments, the possibility of revision, which is not provided for in the Convention but was introduced by the Rules of Court, is an exceptional procedure. That is why the admissibility of any request for revision of a judgment of the Court under this procedure is subject to strict scrutiny.' See supra (note 838), pp. 869–70.

submitting land or maritime delimitation disputes to the Court. For, if they are apprehensive about possible reinvestigation and revision of judgments of the Court, disputing States may find it more convenient to opt for *ad hoc* arbitration. This probability is predicated on the fact that prospective litigant States will consider themselves more able to control the formulation of terms in the *compromis* for the revision and interpretation of the arbitral award, whereas, under the Statute of the Court, Articles 60 and 61 provide entrenched rights which cannot be enforced against the other party if they are challenged by one of the litigant States at the expense of the other.

Without going into this issue again, it may suffice to assert that, at least in theory, it could prove difficult, if not impossible, to be held to any term in a special agreement which is at variance with the above-mentioned articles in view of the provisions of Article 103 read with Article 92 of the United Nations Charter. It was seen above, in *Application for Revision and Interpretation of the 1982 Judgment* with respect to interpretation under Article 60, that the International Court of Justice adopted the position that whether or not a special agreement could validly derogate as between the parties from the Statute was a matter not to be lightly presumed in terms of renouncing or fettering its right of interpretation under that provision in the Statute.[884]

3. Decisiveness of fact and evidence at the admissibility and merits stages

The observations made above lead to an interesting doctrinal issue. Article 61(2) clearly states that the Court has to provide a judgment 'expressly recording the existence of the new fact, recognizing that it has such a character as to lay the case open for revision, and declaring the application admissible on this ground'. Once the application has been declared admissible, the parties can then expect to proceed to the merits of the case. If that is correct, and it is stressed that it is, then the problem which leaps to mind is an obvious one. It is a problem predicated on the fact that, if the application is to move forward to the merits stage, the Court will have to decide positively in favour of the view that the facts are 'of such a nature as to be a decisive factor' for the purposes of the previous judgment, to employ the terminology of the first paragraph of Article 61; and/or that the newly discovered fact 'has such a character as to lay the case open for revision', as stipulated in the second paragraph of Article 61.

[884] See the text to notes 337–42 above.

Thus, the difficulty appears to be two-fold. On the one hand, by the time the application is considered by the Court at the merits phase of the proceedings, it will have already made up its mind on the decisiveness or the crucial characteristics of the newly discovered fact, and, on the other hand, both the respondent State and the Court will have to contend with this prejudged fact at the merits stage.

This problem would not, of course, have arisen had Article 61 obliged the Court to provide an order, as opposed to a judgment, on the basis of a *prima facie* test applied to determine whether or not the alleged newly discovered fact was sufficiently decisive to warrant revision of the judgment. It is appropriate to contrast this provision with Article 41 of the Statute, which empowers the Court to indicate 'any provisional measures which ought to be taken to preserve the respective rights of either party'. These measures are adopted by way of an order of the Court on the basis of the so-called *prima facie* test developed by it in the context of the *Fisheries Jurisdiction* cases[885] and subsequent cases. Article 61, however, refers to a 'judgment' in which the Court has expressly to record the decisive nature of the alleged new fact. The Court, it may be noted, did not subscribe to the view maintained by El Salvador in *El Salvador* v. *Honduras* that the latter had only to make out a reasonable case for revision at the admissibility phase of the revision proceedings.[886] Although the Chamber did not rule directly on this point, it stated clearly that, under Article 61, there were five conditions, and, relying on its earlier judgment in *Application for Revision of the Judgment of 11 July 1996 in the Genocide in Bosnia Case*,[887] it held that 'an application for revision is admissible only if each of the conditions laid down in Article 61 is satisfied. If any one of [the conditions] is not met, the application must be dismissed.'[888] It examined the alleged decisiveness of El Salvador's newly discovered facts or evidence in careful detail on the basis of which it finally decided that the quality was absent in the documentation submitted.

[885] *United Kingdom* v. *Iceland (Interim Protection)* and *Germany* v. *Iceland (Interim Protection)*, Orders of 17 August 1972: ICJ Reports 1972, p. 12 and 30, respectively. On interim protection generally, see Elkind, *Interim Protection: A Functional Approach*, The Hague, 1981; Merrills, 'Interim Measures of Protection and the Substantive Jurisdiction of the International Court', 36 (1977) *Cambridge Law Journal* 86; Mendelson, 'Interim Protection of Protection in Cases of Contested Jurisdiction', 46 (1972–3) BYIL 259; and Kaikobad, 'The Court, the Council and Interim Protection: A Commentary on the Lockerbie Order of 14 April 1992', 17 (1996) *Australian Yearbook of International Law* 87.

[886] Counsel for El Salvador, Oral Argument, 8 September 2003, *Pleadings, Verbatim Record* (note 833), pp. 33–5; and El Salvador's Application for Revision (note 834), pp. 14–15.

[887] (*Yugoslavia* v. *Bosnia and Herzegovina*), Preliminary Objections, ICJ Reports 2003, p. 12, paragraph 17.

[888] ICJ Reports 2003, p. 392, at p. 399.

What is nevertheless clear is that, once it has decided in its judgment that the newly discovered facts are indeed decisive in character, the Court is not at liberty thereafter to re-examine the question of the decisive character of the newly discovered fact at the merits phase of the proceedings insofar as it would clearly be *res judicata*. Inevitably, then, the criticism which may sensibly be made is whether this restriction does not throw into doubt the whole purpose of the revision process. For, if a positive decision has already been made regarding the satisfactory existence of all four factual and legal criteria stipulated in Article 61(1), and, if the Court cannot re-examine them at the merits stage, then it could be argued that the whole matter stands more or less decided and the judgment boundary would need *perforce* to be revised at the merits stage in accordance with and in relation to the newly discovered fact. In other words, the merits stage is but a formality. If criticism of this kind were correct, then the process of Article 61 would indeed appear to be inconsistent with the administration of international justice.

Notwithstanding the above, it is not impossible to be relatively more sanguine regarding Article 61. This is based on two facts, the first of which turns on an interpretation of paragraphs 1 and 2 of Article 61. The difference between paragraphs 1 and 2 is that, while paragraph 1 is in effect a set of obligatory requirements which have to be proved by the applicant State to the satisfaction of the Court, paragraph 2 has relevance only for the Court and not the applicant State. Paragraph 1 is therefore simply a set of threshold criteria, while paragraph 2 sets out what the Court may do after or in the context of the facts alluded to and/or claimed by the applicant State. The short point therefore is that the true impact of Article 61 is to be found in paragraph 2 of that article, for it spells out what the Court can do in all the right circumstances: it can only, in the first place, recognise that the new fact 'has such a character as to lay the case open for revision', and, in the second place, 'declare the application admissible on this ground'.

Arguably, the expression 'lay the case open for revision' in paragraph 2 suggests simply that the claims and evidence adduced by the applicant party are such that they would justify revision. In other words, it is not *exclusively* what the paragraph *stipulates* which is important; it is also *what it does not provide* which is of central importance. The fact is that paragraph 2 does not state that, if the five substantive and procedural criteria are positively established to the satisfaction of the Court, then the Court, in its judgment, 'shall revise its previous judgment'. In other words, it seems clear that the use of the phrase 'lay the case open for revision' implies that the matter remains open for the Court to decide in its subsequent judgment whether or not the first judgment is actually to be revised and that, if it is, the extent to which the revision is to be carried out commensurate with the circumstances flowing from the newly discovered fact or facts and evidence.

It is this latter set of facts which provides the platform for the second level of discussion, and it is predicated on the trite fact that, when the Court decides that an application is admissible on the facts, it does not judge the matter on its merits in law. Clearly, the two stages in the revision process were instituted to keep the issue of the newly discovered crucial fact procedurally separate from the issue of the actual decision to revise the judgment for the simple reason that the latter question will primarily be an issue of law whereas the question of the newly discovered fact is primarily, but by no means exclusively, a matter of fact. It is evident that the gravity of the revision process was not lost on those who drafted the provision: they realised that an application to revise a previous judgment needs to be viewed with the utmost caution and circumspection, and, accordingly, even if the factual stage of the application process is made out, it is for the Court to decide at a subsequent stage in the proceedings a number of matters connected with the revision application. For the purposes of this study, the fact that a judgment boundary can be revised after several years of existence is not a matter which can be regarded without a degree of anxiety by the respondent party.

It follows that, at this stage of the proceedings, the Court will not be bereft of important issues to decide one way or the other, and the first major decision the Court will have to take is whether, despite the discovery of the crucial fact, the judgment cannot stand and must be revised. The decision to revise the judgment, and, in the context of territorial and boundary disputes, the decision to revise the location of the boundary and the status of the territory, will be governed by a variety of legal considerations. This aspect of the matter is discussed separately below in section III of Chapter 11 below.

d. Negligence in discovery

The element of negligence on the part of the requesting State was also in issue in *El Salvador* v. *Honduras*. Acknowledging the fact that, in 1992, it had not produced the evidence necessary for the purposes of revision, El Salvador showed that there were various reasons why it had failed so to do. As far as scientific evidence was concerned, it was something not available at that time. Some of the scientific evidence had been obtained only very recently. The technology was new, the relevant data, which was owned by the United States, had always been classified by it for reasons of security, and access was denied until the Internet made information much more readily available.[889]

As far as historical evidence was concerned, El Salvador pointed out that a savage civil war had drained the country's resources and that this had affected its ability to collect the relevant evidence. It did not have unlimited resources or the time to pursue every possibility to the very limit given that this matter was only one out of six sectors in dispute. Another difficulty was that it did not have access to the Honduran National Archives. Nor did its efforts enable them to locate such documents in the national archives of other States; in fact it had not even known at that time that such documentation existed in different libraries in different States.[890] The nub, of course, of the claim was that, in 1992, it had not been negligent in tracking down the evidence in the form of new facts.[891]

However, for Honduras, there was evidence that El Salvador had indeed been negligent in preparing arguments and providing proof; that the material produced in 2003 could have been submitted ten years ago; and that systematic and diligent research could have produced the evidence, including independent scientific evidence at the earlier hearing.[892] The Chamber, however, did not address these arguments. Having taken the decision that the facts alleged by El Salvador were neither new nor decisive, it observed that it was 'not necessary for the Chamber to ascertain whether the other conditions laid down in Article 61 of the Statute were satisfied in the present case'.[893] Once again, it was Judge Paolillo who commented upon the matter, not least, of course, because he dissented from the majority view. He held:[894]

> Any assessment of the terms 'diligence' and 'negligence' is likely to be highly subjective owing to their abstract content. It is thus generally not possible to determine *a priori* whether conduct has been diligent or negligent. The degree of diligence or negligence involved must be assessed on a case-by-case basis, having regard to the context. In examining an application for revision, each individual

[889] See Counsel for El Salvador, Oral Argument, 10 September, *Pleadings, Verbatim Record* (note 833), p. 23; and El Salvador's Application for Revision (note 834), p. 20.

[890] El Salvador's Application for Revision (note 834), p. 27.

[891] Counsel for El Salvador, Oral Argument, 8 September 2003, *Pleadings, Verbatim Record* (note 833), pp. 31–3; and Oral Argument, 10 September 2003, *Pleadings, Verbatim Record* (note 833), pp. 11–12.

[892] Counsel for Honduras, Oral Argument, 12 September 2003, *Pleadings, Verbatim Record* (note 811), pp. 19–20.

[893] ICJ Reports 2003, p. 411.

[894] *Ibid.*, p. 425.

situation must be considered, taking into account, in particular, the nature of the facts presented as 'new facts', the means of access to these 'facts' by the party applying for revision, and the conduct of the parties.

Applying these criteria, he decided that El Salvador's arguments were persuasive and gave due weight to the unstable social and political situation in that State and to the difficulties attending the gathering, consulting and analysis of the various items of evidence. In his view, the essential conditions of Article 61 were shown satisfactorily to exist and therefore the application was admissible.[895]

This approach is valid, but only up to a point. On the one hand, it is the case that the test for due diligence has been applied strictly in matters of international responsibility. In *Alabama Claims*, the Tribunal rejected the argument from *diligentia quam in suis* advocated by the British Government by stating that due diligence ought to be exercised by neutral governments in exact proportion to the risk to which either of the belligerents may be exposed, from a failure to fulfil the obligations of neutrality.[896] Applying this test, the standard of diligence required of El Salvador was that which would have preserved its claims; consequently, when it fell below that standard, there was a risk that it would lose its rights.

On the other hand, no forensic application of the law can be totally oblivious to the circumstances attending a legal problem. Writing in the context of national and international minimum standards, Brownlie observed that, where reasonable care and due diligence standards are applied, the *diligentia quam in suis* might well be employed. An advantage of this, he writes, is that it allows for variations in wealth and educational standards between the various States of the world without being a mechanical national standard tied to equality.[897]

A number of multilateral conventions refer in general terms to circumstances as a qualifying factor in carrying out certain obligations. Article 194(1) of the 1982 United Nations Convention on the Law of the Sea qualifies the duty on States Parties to take measures to prevent and reduce marine pollution by reference to 'the best practicable means at their disposal and in accordance with their capabilities'. Schwarzenberger pointed out that the *Alabama* Rules of Washington were subsequently watered down with respect to neutrality in Articles 8 and 25 of the Hague

[895] *Ibid.*

[896] 62 BFSP 233, at p. 234. On this, see Schwarzenberger, *International Law as Applied by International Courts and Tribunals*, vol. II, *The Law of Armed Conflict*, London, 1968, pp. 562–5; and Cheng (note 692), pp. 221–2.

[897] *Principles of Public International Law*, 6th edn, Oxford, 2003, p. 502.

Convention Concerning the Rights and Duties of Neutral Powers in Naval War[898] insofar as the obligations of a neutral power were limited to the employment of 'means at its disposal' to prevent the fitting out of any vessel within its jurisdiction and the prevention of a violation of the Convention in its ports.[899] As Cheng put it succinctly, the *Alabama* rule is only an elaboration of the adjective 'due' in the phrase 'due diligence' which requirement does not, as a whole, go beyond the capacity of the neutral State.[900]

These, of course, are matters related directly to questions of international State responsibility, and relevant by way of analogy to the question of gathering evidence for the purpose of litigation. The optimal solution to the problem here is that standards of diligence must be assessed by reference to those a State can *objectively* be expected to adopt with a view to preserving, fortifying and proving its claims. It follows that diligence and negligence in gathering evidence must be assessed by reference to objective standards of conduct expected of States where they have *agreed* to adjudication as a method of dispute settlement. Certainly, it would not be realistic to expect high standards of management, organisation and resourcefulness from a State devastated by internal warfare. Yet, to regard such warfare as a circumstance precluding negligence or justifying a failure to exercise due diligence would constitute granting a litigating State a way out of its difficulties only to place a consequential burden on the other party.

In matters of revision, it would be particularly burdensome on the respondent State to be faced with an item of evidence which could have been but was not placed before the International Court of Justice ten years earlier in the original proceedings. Thus, even if an efficient gathering of evidence were not possible during a civil war, the benefit granted the applicant State would be inequitable compared to the burden placed on the respondent State. Furthermore, problems posed by internal warfare, although real and serious, are also highly dynamic and are prone to subjective assessment. It may also be difficult to show precisely how a civil war frustrated the discovery of evidence as opposed to submitting generalisations about the war. Thus, in principle, an assessment of negligence and diligence cannot *exclusively* be 'highly subjective owing to their abstract content', *pace* Paolillo. To accept that would be to introduce considerable uncertainty and unpredictability into the relations between litigating States. While his views on the need to assess negligence and diligence on a

[898] 2 (1908) AJIL (Supp.) 202. [899] Supra (note 896), p. 564. [900] Supra (note 962), p. 222.

case-by-case basis are irreproachable, they fail fully to detract from the overall conclusion that the Chamber was correct in rejecting El Salvador's plea to be excused for failing to discover the relevant evidence in time for the original suit but just in time for the revision application.

In *Application for Revision and Interpretation of the 1982 Judgment*, the International Court of Justice clearly employed an objective test based on reasonable standards of conduct of States. Tunisia claimed that it had no information regarding the precise co-ordinates of Concession No. 137 insofar as Libya had failed to supply such information despite 'vainly requesting their Libyan counterparts to communicate this text to them during their meetings between the two sides ever since 1968'.[901] The Court held that, following Libyan non-co-operation, there was no reason why Tunisia could not seek out the information itself by employing lawful and proper means, including requests to private consultants who had obtained the information in 1976. '*Normal diligence*', the Court observed 'would require that, when sending a delegation to negotiate a continental shelf delimitation, following the grant by each side of neighbouring or conflicting concessions, a State should first try to learn the exact co-ordinates of the other party's concession'.[902] It went on to refer to the fact that:

> [I]t is to be expected that a State would not assert that such concession extended to its own area of continental shelf without knowing, *or making efforts* to discover, the exact limits of the concession. It is also to be expected that, in litigation, the ultimate purpose of which is the establishment of a continental shelf delimitation, and in the course of which a petroleum concession in the relevant area is described by one party without precision, the other party will not limit itself to commenting on the matter in its pleading, but itself seek out the information.[903]

It is safe to conclude that, despite the need at times to accommodate certain restrictions and the realities on the ground, the test of negligence in discovery ought primarily to be an objective appreciation of the facts based on the reasonable expectations of a State's conduct in the circumstances of the case.

Although not a case concerning negligence in the discovery of a fact, *Qatar–Bahrain Hawar Islands and Continental Shelf (Jurisdiction and*

901 ICJ Reports 1985, pp. 205–6. 902 *Ibid.*, p. 206 (emphasis added).
903 *Ibid.* (emphasis added). Cf. the Separate Opinion of Judge Oda who remarked: 'But it is *not* crucial whether Tunisia's unawareness of the precise co-ordinates of the Libyan concession was due to its negligence or whether Tunisia exercised normal diligence, because the validity of the respective concessions of the Parties was not at issue.' See *ibid.*, p. 239 (emphasis in original). For commentary, see Thirlway (note 226), pp. 97–8.

Admissibility First Phase)[904] did go some way forward in upholding objectively verifiable legal facts as opposed to the subjective intentions of the parties with a view to determining the existence of an agreement vesting jurisdiction in the International Court of Justice. Dismissing Bahrain's argument that its Foreign Minister had never signed the 1990 Minutes with the intention of creating a legally binding agreement, the Court held that it was not necessary to consider what the intentions of the Foreign Ministers of Qatar and Bahrain might have been: the two sides had in fact signed a text recording commitments accepted by their respective governments. Bahrain then tried again to establish a lack of intention regarding the creation of a legally binding instrument by showing that Qatar had delayed registering the alleged agreement with both the UN Secretariat and the Arab League. Rejecting these claims as well, the Court held: '[N]or could any such *intention*, even if shown to exist, prevail over the actual terms of the instrument in question.'[905] Thus, in both cases, the Court was willing to set aside any subjective claims, preferring to rely on the objective existence of the relevant instruments. The point here, which is based on analogy, is that the Court is known to eschew reliance on subjective criteria.

Finally, it could also be argued that the standard be set as high as possible in respect of all the criteria considered above, namely (i) the question of the facts allegedly discovered and of the circumstances of the actual discovery thereof; (ii) the requirement of negligence, if any, in the discovery; and (iii) the matter of the decisive nature of the fact for the purposes of the decision. In other words, revision, as stated above, cannot lightly be presumed because the very nature of the remedy is such that it commends great caution in its exercise, because, very simply, it can result in a change to the alignment. The prospect of revising judgment boundaries is politically and legally so controversial, indeed so delicate, an issue that it cannot lightly be entertained even at the stage of admissibility, and it is for this reason that the plausibility standard for admissibility, as urged by counsel for El Salvador[906] in the above-mentioned case, is flawed as a proposition of law. Indeed, the very fact that Article 61 of the Statute and Article 99 of the Rules of Court provide a two-step procedure demonstrates that all the preliminary issues must be settled definitively before the tribunal can begin the task of evaluating, interpreting and applying the facts of the case; and at times this task can be a complex one indeed.

904 ICJ Reports 1995, p. 112. 905 *Ibid.*, pp. 121–2 (emphasis added).

906 Counsel for El Salvador, Oral Argument, 8 September 2003, *Pleadings, Verbatim Record* (note 833), pp. 41–2.

Nor is there anything in the text of paragraph 2 of Article 61 to suggest that a preliminary or *prima facie* case needs only to be made out at the first stage. The argument that the Court would otherwise have nothing to do at the merits stage is equally untenable insofar as the tribunal would still have the task, not only of determining the *precise extent* of the revision warranted by the new facts as urged by the applicant State, but also of applying them in light of the law and arguments submitted by both States. This is examined in section III of Chapter 11 below.

III. Procedural criteria

Procedural criteria for the purposes of admissibility must also be met. It is not unusual for treaties allowing revision to include provisions which specify precise periods of time in which revision may be requested. In most cases, time begins to run from the date of the discovery of the fact, not unlike the position in Article 61(4) of the Statute of the International Court of Justice which gives the discovering State six months from the date of discovery in which to submit a request. This precludes laches. However, Article 61(5) also allows ten years from the date of the judgment for a State to discover a new fact, and hence there are double temporal criteria to meet before a request is admissible. It follows that, while the general *eligibility criterion* for revision is generous, the actual period of time in which the request must be submitted once a fact has been discovered is relatively short.

While Article 38 of the International Law Commission's 1958 Draft Rules on Arbitral Procedure has temporal limits identical to Article 61, it is generally the case that different treaties have different time limits.[907] Thus, while the general eligibility period was only five years with respect to the *Guinea–Guinea-Bissau Continental Shelf* award, the period of discovery of facts was fixed at six months. However, the time period for discovery and request was shorter still, and perhaps unrealistically so, in the matter of the *North Atlantic Coast Fisheries* arbitration where Article 10 limited it to five days from the date of the promulgation of the award.[908]

[907] Article 48 of the 1948 Pact of Bogotá restricts applications for revision to one year after the notification of the award; Article 65 of the 1923 Central American Court of Arbitration precluded, with respect to complaints, revision after ninety days from the date of the last notice of the final decision; and Article 92 of the EFTA Court Rules of Procedure allow requests to be made within three months of the date on which the facts on which the application is based came to the applicant's knowledge.

[908] Insofar as Article 10 of the *compromis* had expressly allowed either party to request revision, it became necessary to provide time limits: the last paragraph of Article 83 of

In this context, it is again interesting to consider *El Salvador* v. *Honduras*, where it was asserted by Honduras that El Salvador had shown bad faith by applying conveniently for revision on the eve of the expiry of the ten-year period.[909] Moreover, the applicant State, it was argued, had to submit proof that each and every fact was discovered within the six months prior to the submission of the application to the Court, and there was no evidence to that effect.[910] El Salvador emphatically maintained that it was within the temporal limits established by the Statute, and it was therefore exercising its rights under the Statute.[911]

Further, the legal requirement was that discovery had to have occurred *after* the judgment, and that the criticism that it had taken until 1992 to discover the material was misconceived: while there was no obligation to look for documents *after* the judgment, there had to be proof of due diligence in respect of that fact *before* the judgment.[912] The only requirement was that, if the fact were discovered by accident and the like, it had only six months to utilise this in the form of a revision application, and that both sets of criteria were fully satisfied. It was also urged that it was for Honduras to prove bad faith.[913] As noted above, once the Chamber had found that El Salvador's application was founded on a misconception in terms of the decisive nature of the alleged new facts, and that the applicant State had accepted that there were no new facts, as opposed to new interpretations of the submitted evidence, it became unnecessary to scrutinise the temporal aspects of the discovery of the evidence.[914]

Nonetheless, for the purposes of completeness, it must be stressed that Honduras was correct in asking for evidence for each and every new item of fact/evidence discovered. It is abundantly clear that the entire purpose of providing temporal limits would be defeated if the applicant State were

the Hague Convention of 1907 left it to the parties to decide these limits in their *compromis*: see section II.b of Chapter 7 above.

909 See Minister of Foreign Affairs, El Salvador, Oral Statement, 8 September 2003, *Pleadings, Verbatim Record*, (note 833), p. 12. Indeed, Honduras maintained that the application was filed a few hours short of the expiration of the ten-year limit: *ibid.*, p. 12; and see *ibid.*, pp. 22–3. Further, see Counsel for El Salvador, *ibid.*, pp. 27–8. Honduras did not, of course, deny El Salvador's right in principle to file the application: Agent of Honduras, Oral Statement, 9 September 2003, *Verbatim Record*, (note 829), pp. 8–9.

910 Counsel for Honduras, Oral Argument, 12 September 2003, *Pleadings, Verbatim Record* (note 811), pp. 20–1.

911 Foreign Minister of El Salvador, Oral Statement, 8 September 2003, *Pleadings, Verbatim Record* (note 833), p. 12 and p. 18.

912 Counsel for El Salvador, Oral Argument, 8 September 2003, *Pleadings, Verbatim Record* (note 833), pp. 27–8.

913 *Ibid.*, p. 27.

914 ICJ Reports 2003, p. 411.

to be given the benefit of a general presumption that the facts were within time but without evidence thereof. Nor can the scale of convenience and coincidence of facts, allegedly discovered within ten years and submitted within six months of the discovery, be underestimated. Perhaps the Chamber ought to have taken the opportunity to express in peremptory terms that it tends in general to shy away from procedural strategies which could on the surface be seen as an abuse of the process of the Chamber. To be seen indulging in such strategies is not compatible with the requirements of the administration of international justice.

The issue of time limits as a procedural obstacle also arose in the aftermath of the *Beagle Channel* arbitration. Thoroughly dissatisfied with the award handed down by the Court of Arbitration, Argentina issued a Declaration of Nullity in January 1978 in which a variety of arguments, including *non ultra petita partum*, distortion of the Argentine thesis, faulty interpretation and geographical and historical errors were marshalled by it in support of its claims.[915] In its communication of March 1978 to both parties, the Court advised Argentina that Article XIII of the General Treaty of Arbitration of 1902, which governed the *Compromiso* of 1971, allowed a 'recourse to revision' on certain grounds specified therein,[916] provided that such recourse to revision were taken within the time allowed for the execution of the award. It noted that, for the purposes of the *Beagle Channel* award, the time limit was nine months from the date the award was communicated to the parties by the Government of the United Kingdom.[917] 'This time limit', the Court observed, 'having now expired, the fulfilment of the Award is . . . left "to the honour" of the parties.'[918]

It is not difficult to fathom the reason why in general these limits exist, but it will be readily agreed that decisions dealing with territorial rights and boundary delimitation need special protection, not least because States abhor boundary modifications which involve loss of territory. An application for revision of a judgment boundary will almost never be

[915] See the post-award correspondence at 52 ILR 267; and the Declaration at *ibid.*, pp. 269–77, on which see Himmelreich, 'The Beagle Channel Affair: A Failure in Judicial Persuasion', 12 (1979) *Vanderbilt Journal of Transnational Law* 971; and Lauterpacht, 'Whatever Happened to the Beagle Channel Award?', in *Melanges Virally: Le droit international au service de la paix, de la justice et du developpement*, Paris, 1991, p. 359, at p. 359.

[916] 95 BFSP 759. The grounds were falsification of, or tampering with, documents and the consequence of an error of fact resulting from the arguments or documents of the case.

[917] 52 ILR 267, at pp. 283–5, especially p. 282, after ratification by the said government: see paragraph 2 of the *dispositif* of the award: *ibid.*, p. 227.

[918] *Ibid.*, p. 282.

welcome, bringing with it a degree of uncertainty, tension and possible friction. In 1958, while debating the issue of time limits for requests for revision for the purposes of the Draft Rules on Arbitral Procedure, certain members of the International Law Commission objected to extended periods of time in which revision requests were admissible. 'It was', Mr Amado observed, 'for instance, by virtue of an arbitral award that large areas had been adjudged part of the territory of Brazil. Yet, according to the [draft] article, so momentous a decision would be subject to revision as much as ten years after the award had been made.'[919]

Even so, members of the Commission were agreed that 'nothing was settled until it was settled right',[920] and that a provision on revision was indeed essential to the arbitral process in general. This would apply with equal emphasis to judgment boundaries as well. A fixed period of time for revision is thus merely a device for controlling and minimising friction. Conversely, the need to provide opportunities for the revision of decisions must be balanced by the need to provide an appropriate closure to all post-adjudicative proceedings in order to stabilise the situation between neighbouring States or States with conflicting territorial issues.

[919] 447th Meeting, 21 May 1958, Consideration of the Model Draft on Arbitral Procedure, 1958 *Yearbook ILC*, vol. I, p. 81. See also Mr Yokota (five years), *ibid.*, p. 78; Mr G. G. Fitzmaurice (between three and five years), *ibid.*, p. 79; and M. Tunkin, *ibid.*, p. 81; cf. Mr Matine-Daftary, *ibid.*, p. 79; and Mr Zourek (not too short, not too long), *ibid.*, p. 79.

[920] 191st Meeting, 11 June 1953, Arbitral Procedure, 1953 *Yearbook ILC*, p. 40, at p. 42.

11 Selected substantive and procedural aspects of revision

I. Preliminary observations

In this final chapter it is intended to examine three salient aspects of revision. The first is the very real problem of reconciling the legal effects and implications of two conflicting aspects of international law, namely, the basic rule of *res judicata* and the remedy of revision. While the former axiom refuses to countenance, in all the appropriate circumstances, a re-examination of an existing judgment or award, the latter, where admitted, could in many cases lead to re-examination. This issue was considered in the context of interpretation in Chapter 5 above. Here, in the context of revision, it will suffice to consider the matter in some detail with a view to clarifying and reconciling these conflicting positions.

The second issue discussed below seeks to explain the impact of what, for want of a better description, may be referred to as 'indirect delimitation', on the remedy of revision. However, in view of the fact that indirect delimitation is not the technique States normally choose to resolve their boundary disputes, it will be appropriate to consider an appreciation of the limits of revision in this kind of request for delimitation.

The third and final issue examined in this context is predicated on the view that it is necessary to seek an understanding of the scope of the precise task of the tribunal once it has determined that a newly discovered fact is clearly decisive in terms of being crucial to the judgment or award. Some clarification is necessary here inasmuch as the task of the tribunal at the merits phase may seem somewhat limited given that it will already have determined two crucial facts, namely, that the fact or facts in question are decisive and that they were newly discovered by the applicant State. It turns out, of course, that the scope of the tribunal's remit is not as limited as it would appear.

II. Revision and res judicata

As with the process of interpretation, there exists in this area of the law a measure, or at least a sense, of tension between two conflicting rules of law, and the tension, it would appear, is greater in this case than it is with respect to interpretation. There is, indeed, on the face of it, some contradiction in the law: if the judgment is final, binding and without appeal, then the dispute has reached its quietus, and all matters decided by the tribunal are *res judicata*. On the other hand, powers of revision allow the tribunal to vary or modify the judgment, albeit on very strict and narrow grounds; thus, the possibility of revision could, in principle, be seen as detracting from considerations of finality which are behind every judicial decision.[921] As Judge Ad Hoc Mme Bastid observed in *Application for Revision and Interpretation of the 1982 Judgment*:

> Whether in certain circumstances this form of challenge to *res judicata* had ever been contemplated and why, if it was, the idea was eventually dropped remain unknown. The Statute of the Court, while laying down the conditions of admissibility of an application for revision, is silent as to the effects of that application if deemed admissible. What would it imply to reopen the merits of a case, and to what extent should the case as a whole be reviewed? Such a situation would call for an examination of the very concept of revision in light of any existing practice of international tribunals and the, at times, conflicting practice of the various municipal judiciaries. But this question would not arise until after the delivery of a judgment declaring an application admissible.[922]

It is correct to state, as Rosenne did, that the provisions on revision and interpretation have been 'couched and placed in the Statute in such a way as to emphasise the exceptional nature of [such] proceedings, as possibly impairing the stability of the jural relations established by the *res judicata*'.[923] Similarly, Geiss wrote that the 'concept of revision adversely

[921] For a general discussion on this, see Bowett (note 226), pp. 577–9, 586–8 and 589–91; Cheng (note 692), Chapter 17; Stone (note 226), pp. 94–5; Reisman (note 692), pp. 59–61; Verzijl (note 136), pp. 565 *et seq.*; Scobbie, 'Res Judicata, Precedent and the International Court: A Preliminary Sketch', 20 (1999) *Australian Yearbook of International Law* 299; Geiss (note 692), pp. 172–4; and Lowe (note 489), pp. 38 *et seq.*

[922] ICJ Reports 1985, p. 247. In *Application for Revision of the Judgment in the Genocide in Bosnia Case*, Judge Koroma observed in his Separate Opinion that the revision procedure was about newly discovered facts and not a legal challenge to the conclusion reached earlier on the facts known, although the outcome of the challenge may have an effect on the judgment: ICJ Reports 2003, p. 34.

[923] Supra (note 269), p. 201. See, generally, section III of Chapter 8 above.

affects the principle of *res judicata*'.[924] It appears, however, that this is an unnecessarily restrictive position, and that the two rules can be harmonised by seeking points of reconciliation. In other words, there is no dichotomy which cannot be explained away by reference to certain propositions of law, four of which are discussed below.

First, although a decision is indeed final and dispositive of the issues, there is nothing sacrosanct about it. Like everything in law, an act is, in general terms, only creative of legal effects if it is legally valid. International law recognises that a decision may be flawed in terms of law and fact, and allows claims alleging the nullity of a decision. Thus States are not precluded from maintaining that a decision is null and void on a variety of grounds, including *excès de pouvoir, non ultra petita partum* and a failure to provide reasons for the decision, *provided, of course, that all allegations of nullity are established before, and accepted by, a tribunal*.[925] It follows that claims *ipsi dixit* carry no weight.[926] As Hyde put it:

> If the available facts are such as to sustain the contention of an aggrieved litigant that there has been a departure from [the terms of the agreement], it is not apparent why it should not be free to avail itself thereof, at least in the absence of arrangement providing for a remedy to cover such contingency. This does not signify that the aggrieved litigant assumes through such action on its part to be the sole judge of its cause, but rather that when the facts reveal the tribunal as having acted in excess of its powers, that litigant in availing itself thereof is merely taking a stand of which the correctness must be accepted by any judicial body which may later be empowered to pass on the validity of the award.[927]

[924] Supra (note 692), p. 172. The same sort of concern was evident when certain States responded to the 1953 draft rules on arbitral procedure prepared by the International Law Commission, especially Honduras, Chile and Yugoslavia. The Government of Honduras had submitted the draft for comments to its Commission on Territorial Questions and the response of the Commission was to reject the notion of revision: see Communication from the Honduran Delegation to the United Nations, 19 September 1955 in A/2899 and Add.1 and 2, *GAOR*, Annexes, Tenth Session, New York, 1955, p. 16, at p. 17; and see Chilean and Yugoslav letters of 18 February 1955 and 26 February 1955, *ibid*., p. 4 and p. 8, respectively.

[925] See, generally, Hyde (note 692), pp. 1636–40; Cheng (note 692), pp. 357–61; Kaikobad (note 223), p. 293, *passim*; Merrills, 'The International Court of Justice and the Adjudication of Territorial and Boundary Disputes', 13 (2000) *Leiden Journal of International Law* 873, at pp. 894–8; Sandifer (note 692), pp. 426–8 and 435–9; Oellers-Frahm, 'Judicial and Arbitral Decisions', 1 (1972) *Encyclopaedia of Public International Law* 118; Simpson and Fox (note 136), pp. 250–9; and Murty, 'Settlement of Disputes', in Sørensen (ed.), *Manual of Public International Law*, London, 1968, p. 673, at pp. 692–6.

[926] See Cheng (note 692), p. 372. Refer also to Stone (note 226), pp. 92–3; Collier and Lowe (note 226), pp. 257–61; and Lowe (note 489), p. 40.

[927] Supra (note 692), p. 1639.

Be that as it may, the theory here is that the very object and purpose behind adjudication and arbitration would be defeated if a flawed judgment were allowed to stand and create rights and obligations for the parties. Writing in the context of the discovery of fresh evidence and errors committed through a lack of knowledge and its implications for revision, Cheng observed: 'The aim [generally behind Article 61 of the Statute and Article 83 of the 1907 Convention for the Pacific Settlement of International Disputes] is to provide a remedy against possible injustice arising from errors of fact which have become demonstrable for the first time after the judgment.'[928] He concluded: 'What is otherwise a final judgment possessing the force of *res judicata* may be declared null or set aside by the tribunal for any of the [stated] reasons if it still has jurisdiction over the case.'[929] In other words, it can be argued strongly that a flawed decision based on incomplete knowledge with potentially adverse effects cannot create valid legal rights and hence the restrictive effects of *res judicata* cannot be seen to apply. Judge Koroma indicated to this effect in his Separate Opinion in *Application for Revision of the Judgment in the Genocide in Bosnia* case:

> In my view, when an application for revision is submitted under Article 61 and where fresh facts have emerged and are of such importance as to warrant revising the earlier decision or conclusion, the Court should be willing to carry out such a procedure. Such an application is not to be regarded as impugning the Court's earlier legal decision as such, as that decision was based on the facts as then known. I am of the view that the admission of the [Former Republic of Yugoslavia] to membership of the United Nations in November 2000 does have legal implications for the Judgment reached by the Court on this matter in July 1996.[930]

The logic of the reasoning is very simple. From an objective point of view, if a judgment is demonstrably flawed, for example by bribery or the prejudice of one or more members of the tribunal, or proved to be flawed by application of the *nemo judex in sua causa* maxim, then there would be little or no hesitation to accept, in principle, the notion of nullity of the decision. The applicant State would not feel inhibited by the *res judicata* rule. By the same token, although there is a difference between retrial on the ground of nullity of a decision, and revision on the basis of discovery of a

[928] Supra (note 692), p. 364. See also Shihata, *The Power of the International Court to Determine Its Own Jurisdiction*, The Hague, 1965, p. 78.

[929] Supra (note 692), p. 370. Murty wrote: 'The principle of finality of arbitral awards is subject to the qualification that under certain circumstances the awards may be null and void.' See supra (note 925), p. 692.

[930] ICJ Reports 2003, p. 7, at p. 38.

new fact affecting a *valid* decision, *res judicata* cannot be seen to inhibit the operation of a judicial process available against decisions which need to be remedied for one reason or another.

In short, while the rule of *res judicata* applies to all decisions and judgment boundaries, there is an implied qualification that a tribunal may revise a decision in all the appropriate circumstances, both procedural and substantive, provided always, of course, that the tribunal is authorised so to do by agreement between the parties. This does not of course mean that the decision is not *res judicata*, or that it is in abeyance or is suspended until such time that the decision can no longer be considered for revision owing to the operation of existing temporal restrictions. Such an interpretation is not warranted because it would introduce an element of inconclusiveness, an element hardly desirable in matters of objective territorial and boundary settlements. On the contrary, Article 94 of the Rules of Court stipulates that the judgment is binding on the parties as of the day of the reading. The basic position is simply that, not unlike all other notions and regimes of international law, *res judicata* is not immune from the relevant rules of international law which condition its operation and application.

Secondly – and this stems from the above – the objective of revision is simply to adjust the judgment (and the boundary) in light of the fact discovered after the decision was given by the tribunal, and the line of argument here is that, had the tribunal been aware of the newly discovered fact when the original decision was given, then the latter would have been different in substance and in law. Consequently, the modification envisaged by the request for revision, if admitted and upheld, would reflect, in a sense, the judgment which ought to have been given in the first place.

With respect to this, Scelle's observation in his final report to the International Law Commission on the Draft Rules on Arbitral Procedure in 1958 is useful. 'Furthermore', he reported, 'the authority of *res judicata* is not in question here, for there is no case for revision unless a "new fact" has come to light since the award was rendered and makes it appear that, had the judges known it, they would have made a different award'.[931] It

[931] See commentary to draft Article 38, Doc. A/CN.4/113, 1958: 1958 *Yearbook ILC*, vol. II, p. 1, at p. 12. See also Scelle, 'Report on Arbitral Procedure', Doc. A/CN.4/109, 1957: 1957 *Yearbook ILC*, vol. II, p. 1. He observed: 'We had occasion in 1950 . . . to stress that it was impossible to maintain the common assumption of the "irrefragable" force of *res judicata* which normally attaches to every court finding, because it had become a matter of common knowledge after the new fact had arisen that the arbitrator had been materially unable to render his judgment with full knowledge of the facts, since he was not in possession of the necessary elements on which to base his conclusions.'

was this consideration which was highlighted by the Permanent Court of International Justice in the *Monastery of Saint-Naoum* advisory opinion. The Court examined the question 'whether, as alleged by the Serb-Croat-Slovene State and Greece, the Conference of Ambassadors allocated the Monastery to Albania simply because it was unacquainted with new facts or unaware of facts already in existence, which, if taken into consideration, would have led to a contrary decision'.[932] It went on to find that there were no new facts, and hence ruled out revision.

Thirdly, insofar as a tribunal has no inherent power to revise its judgments, that is to say, it cannot act by way of revision in the absence of an express or implied power vested in it by way of a special or arbitral agreement, it could be argued that parties to such an agreement have agreed to accept, in principle, the likelihood that either State might, if so minded, submit a request for revision, provided that (a) it was within the stipulated time limits and (b) all the legal requirements of the plea were satisfied. The essence of this point is that, if States had wished to preclude the possibility of revision, then they would have withheld such powers from the tribunal.

Clearly, then, Guinea and Guinea-Bissau effectively waived the inherent right precluding revision by agreeing to the terms of Article 11 of the Arbitral Treaty of 1983 wherein either party was entitled to request revision within five years from the date of the award. A similar argument could be made out with respect to the Argentina–Chile situation resulting from Article XVII of the Special Arbitral Agreement of 1991 read with Article 40 of the *Tratado de Paz y Amistad* regarding the *Laguna del Desierto* case;[933] from Article XIV of the *Compromiso* of 1971 read with Article XIII of the 1902 General Treaty of Arbitration for the purposes of the *Beagle Channel* affair;[934] from Article 10 of the 1902 Bolivia–Peru *compromis* regarding their boundary dispute read with Articles 12 and 13 of the 1901 Treaty of General Arbitration;[935] and from Article VIII of the Norway–Sweden agreement regarding the *Grisbadarna* dispute which integrated, among

See p. 11; for commentary see Bowett (note 226), p. 589. Further, refer to Strupp, who observes that in these cases the criterion is that the new fact would have in law and justice caused a decision more favourable to the applicant State: supra (note 136), p. 684.

[932] Supra (note 296), p. 22.

[933] Note that in the latter article the right of revision is not based on the orthodox criterion, namely, the discovery of a fact of a certain kind, but in the existence of forged documents and error of fact: 113 ILR 199; see 24 (1985) ILM 11 for the text of the *Tratado*. Cf. the Secretariat's Memorandum on Arbitral Procedure (note 226), p. 102.

[934] Article XIII of the 1902 Treaty (95 BFSP 759) is similar to Article 40 of the *Tratado* with respect to the unorthodox notion of and grounds for revision.

[935] 3 (1909) AJIL 383 and 378; and Manning (note 708), pp. 334 and 297, respectively.

other provisions, Article 83 of the 1907 Hague Convention into the arbitral process.[936] It is also possible that Argentina and Chile were impliedly allowing for revision in Article IX of the 1965 Treaty of Arbitration in the matter of the *Palena* dispute.[937]

By the same token, the absence of provisions allowing revision strengthens the view that, in some cases, parties to *compromis* dealing with the resolution of territorial and boundary disputes prefer the certainty flowing immediately from the full effect of the judgment to the uncertainty emerging from a possible reopening of the issues and potential modification of judgment boundaries. Indeed, a good number of twentieth-century arbitration agreements dealing with such disputes provide for the interpretation, but not the revision, of awards.

These include the agreement between the United States and the Netherlands (1925) for the *Palmas Island* case;[938] the agreement between Guatemala and Honduras (1930) in the matter of the *Honduras–Guatemala Borders* case;[939] the agreement between Israel and Egypt (1986) in the matter of the *Taba* award; the agreement between India and Pakistan (1965) regarding the *Rann of Kutch* dispute; the 'fall-back' arbitration agreement between Canada and the United States in the *Gulf of Maine* dispute;[940] the Libya–Tunisia Special Agreement of 1978; and the continental shelf disputes *compromis* between the United Kingdom and France (1975), France and Canada (1989) and Eritrea and Yemen (1996). None of these agreements provided for the revision of the tribunals' decisions. Moreover, the Guinea-Bissau and Senegal continental shelf arbitral agreement of 1983 refers to neither interpretation nor revision.

The fact that these treaties contain no provisions on revision must mean that the contracting parties decided to rule out any chance of subsequent modifications to the judgment boundary. *A contrario*, the inclusion of clauses authorising the submission of revision applications means that parties have accepted that the judgment boundary may undergo

[936] 4 (1910) AJIL 226. See also Article 10 of the *North Atlantic Coast Fisheries* arbitral treaty of 1909 between the United Kingdom and the United States: 3 (1909) AJIL 168.

[937] Simpson and Fox point to the *Monastery of Saint-Naoum* advisory opinion as an example of implied agreement for revision: Simpson and Fox (note 136), p. 242; and also see Bowett (note 226), pp. 590–1. On implied consent to interpretation, see the text to notes 332–6 above.

[938] 2 UNRIAA 829.

[939] 9 UNRIAA 1309.

[940] Annex II to the 1979 Maritime Boundary Settlement Treaty; Annex I was the Special Agreement: see Article XII regarding interpretation. However, Article VI incorporates the Rules of Procedure of the International Court to the extent that the Permanent Court of Arbitration deems them appropriate. The summary text is at 1979 *Digest of US Practise in International Law* 1001.

modification in all the appropriate circumstances. Of course, as shown above, interpretation may also lead to revision in terms of adjustments, but the former remedy can be distinguished by reference to the argument that the core object and purpose of interpretation is not normally the changing of the judgment boundary, whereas revision is avowedly dedicated to that very purpose.

Similarly, when States agree to vest jurisdiction in the International Court of Justice, they can also be assumed to be aware of and to have accepted the fact that the Court may in principle be approached by either party to consider applications for revision and, where admitted, to revise its judgment under Article 61 of the Statute, and, by virtue of this provision, the power of revision is exercisable with respect to every judgment without the need of a specific agreement to that effect by the litigating States. Thus, by agreeing in 1986 to submit their six boundary disputes to the International Court of Justice, Honduras and El Salvador could be assumed to have taken into consideration and agreed that the judgment in *Land, Island and Maritime Frontier* would remain open for revision for ten years from the date of the judgment pursuant to Article 61 of the Statute, and indeed this was one of the arguments advanced by El Salvador to counter the Honduran objection that the application was 'in disregard of the authority of *res judicata* of the 1992 Judgment'.[941] El Salvador's argument in *El Salvador* v. *Honduras* ran as follows:

> El Salvador recognised, recognises and will always recognise the legal validity of the Court's judgment and its authority as *res judicata*. Filing a request for revision – in this case, one that concerns just one sector of the land border – does not constitute disrespect for the authority of a judgment; it is the exercise of a right that the Statute and Rules of Court recognise and give to the parties. El Salvador and Honduras both signed the Convention that created the Statute. We have no knowledge of any Honduran reservation that would exempt it from the legally binding force that the Statute of the International Court of Justice gives to requests for revision and interpretation of judgments.[942]

Notwithstanding the fact that El Salvador's application invited speculation in that it was submitted on the last day of the ten-year period the fact remains, in short, that to accept the jurisdiction of the Court is to accept its jurisdiction to revise. As Reisman observed:

> Moreover, the Court's important ruling in the *Corfu Channel* case is authority for the proposition that consent to jurisdiction for a case is a grant for all aspects of

[941] Oral Statement, Agent for Honduras, 9 September 2003, *Pleadings, Verbatim Record* (note 829), p. 10.

[942] Oral Statement, Minister for Foreign Affairs, El Salvador, 8 September 2003, *Pleadings, Verbatim Record* (note 833), p. 17; see also *ibid.*, p. 21.

that case. It follows that consent to jurisdiction includes consent to a revision hearing, if the Court deems it proper, as well as to new hearings and a new judgment if the Court should determine factors which vitiate the original decision.[943]

It is also appropriate to be reminded of the fact that, in *Application for Revision and Interpretation of the 1982 Judgment*, the International Court of Justice held that it was not lightly to be presumed that a State would renounce or fetter its right under Article 60 of the Statute dealing with the right to request the Court to interpret its judgment.[944] The same rule would apply with respect to revision under Article 61.

Fourthly and finally, it is not unheard of for States to resubmit the dispute to the same or another judicial or arbitral forum once it has become clear that the vexed decision, although fully valid in all respects, is unacceptable to one party and is threatening to create a prolonged destabilisation of relations between them.[945] In other words, acting in a spirit of reconciliation, the two (or more) disputant States may decide to approach another tribunal or to request mediation by any other body or person. The Papal Mediation in the Argentina–Chile *Beagle Channel* arbitral award impasse illustrates this point. Two years after Argentina had purported to reject the award of 1977 on the ground of nullity, the disputing States agreed in January 1979 to invite Pope John Paul II to act as mediator in 'their search for a solution to the dispute . . . with a view to contributing to a peaceful settlement, acceptable to both parties'.[946]

In December 1980, the Pope submitted a 'Proposal' which provided a delimitation of the maritime areas from the terminal point of the 1977 award line beyond the Beagle Channel as far as Cape Horn to the south.[947] In 1984, continuing with the general principles laid down in the Papal mediation, the parties concluded the *Tratado de Paz y Amistad*, Article 7 of which provided a maritime delimitation which greatly reduced the

[943] Supra (note 692), pp. 15–16.

[944] ICJ Reports 1985, p. 216. The Court made this observation in the context of Libya's argument regarding the effect of Article 3 of the Special Agreement which empowered the two States to request the Court to provide 'explanations and clarifications' of the judgment; that the procedural requirements of that stipulation had not been followed; and, hence, Tunisia had no right to make a request unilaterally to the Court: *ibid.*, pp. 214–16.

[945] Grzybowski (note 226), p. 486. In the *Corfu Channel* case, the Court ruled that the Albanian Government could not object to the exercise of jurisdiction by the Court regarding the assessment of damages. The jurisdiction of the Court was established by the judgment of 9 April 1949 and that, in accordance with Article 60, this was a decision final and binding on the Albanian Government. Accordingly, the matter was *res judicata*. See ICJ Reports 1949, p. 244, at p. 248; and see Reisman (note 692), p. 63.

[946] 82 ILR 671, at pp. 678–9. [947] *Ibid.*, pp. 680–3.

maritime areas to which Chile was entitled under the 1977 award.[948] However, the islands attributed to Chile remained unaffected. The short point is that, despite the *res judicata* element in all decisions, States may agree to provide other, more consensus-based legal foundations for their land and/or maritime boundaries, and choose to forsake areas they may be entitled to on the basis of the original arbitration in a spirit of compromise and friendship.

III. Revision and indirect delimitation

There are two salient points to be made in this section. First, it is a cardinal rule of international and domestic arbitration and adjudication that, in the process of entering a decision on a matter before it, a tribunal cannot exceed the jurisdiction vested in it by the parties. *A fortiori*, when it is in the process of revising its decision, the tribunal cannot lose sight of the original decision, and, more particularly, the scope of the jurisdiction vested in it by the parties with respect to the matter at hand. Putting the matter in a different way, the precise scope, nature and effect of a decision revising a previous judgment of a tribunal must reflect, and be contained by, the scope of authority given by the States Parties to the tribunal in the matter of the dispute leading to the previous judgment. It follows that, where a tribunal is concerned only indirectly with maritime delimitation, as indeed the International Court of Justice was in *Tunisia* v. *Libya*, the judgment revising the first decision can only deal with the relevant issues in exactly that very context, and nothing else.

Accordingly, the Court in *Application for Revision and Interpretation of the 1982 Judgment* would not have been able to revise the 1982 judgment by providing a delimitation *eo nomine*, for that function had not lain within the remit of the Court in *Tunisia* v. *Libya* in 1982. The Court in the former case refused to agree to Tunisia's request for an expert survey for the purposes of ascertaining the exact co-ordinates of the most westerly point of the Gulf of Gabes. The reason offered for this rejection was that to have acceded to Tunisia's request would have been appropriate only if the determination of the exact co-ordinates were required to enable the Court to give a judgment on the matters submitted to it, and which, in this case,

[948] See, generally, Oellers-Frahm, 'Beagle Channel Arbitration', 1 (1972) *Encyclopedia of Public International Law* 33, at p. 36; and Lankosz, 'Beagle Channel', 12 (1972) *Encyclopaedia of Public International Law* 53, at pp. 54–5; and Lauterpacht (note 915), pp. 361 *et seq*. For Argentina, the core issue was recognition of the 'Oceanic Principle', which made the latter State an Atlantic power, and Chile a Pacific one: see Lauterpacht (note 915), p. 366.

as the Court noted, was 'a request for interpretation of a previous judgment'.[949] The Court could also have added, but did not, that the need for an expert survey would have been more acutely felt had the tribunal been requested to establish a boundary with technical accuracy, but this was not one of Court's tasks in *Tunisia* v. *Libya*. The task in that case was simply to identify the principles and rules of international law for the delimitation of the continental shelf and to clarify the practical method for the application of those principles and rules: *vide* Article 1 of the Special Agreement).[950]

The same rules would apply in the matter of revision; and, although the Court did not state as much, Tunisia's request could have been accommodated had the determination by the expert survey been of crucial importance, as it would have been in a case of direct delimitation. The Court did note that it could have determined the most westerly point in 1982, and also that the geographical point was indeed a necessary element in its decision regarding the practical method of delimitation. Yet, it went on, the Court preferred to leave this task to the experts of the two parties.[951] It is almost as if the Court were saying that the very nature of its task, namely, indirect delimitation so to speak, precluded it from contemplating the ordering of an expert survey. Arguably, a determination of the precise co-ordinates of the most westerly point of the Gulf was out of place in a revision proceeding dealing with the principles and methods of delimitation, as opposed to delimitation properly so called of the maritime areas between the States. In general principle, then, it follows that, even if an application for revision is admitted, the revising judgment can hardly proceed to actual delimitation where the original decision was confined to (a) identifying the relevant principles and rules; and/or (b) indicating the practical method for the application of those principles, provided, nevertheless, that the combination of (a) and (b) may at times produce a delimitation of sorts.

Conversely, in the second place, and continuing in the context of *Application for Revision and Interpretation of the 1982 Judgment*, if the Court had admitted the request for revision submitted by Tunisia; and if the Court had subsequently accepted Tunisia's claims for a judgment revising the co-ordinates as requested by that State, then, in principle, the Court would have revised, albeit indirectly, or at least once again would have substantively influenced, the limits of the continental shelf between Libya

[949] ICJ Reports 1985, p. 228. See sections IV.f and V.a of Chapter 5 above.

[950] Libyan version of translation: supra (note 337), p. 26.

[951] ICJ Reports 1985, p. 228.

and Tunisia. This, of course, did not happen, because the request for revision was not admitted. It is almost certain, however, that, even if the application for revision had been admitted, the Court would still not have proceeded to revise its first judgment. This view is predicated on the basis of the fact that Tunisia's substantive arguments for revision were very clearly based on a misunderstanding of the Court's findings in the 1982 judgment. The fact remains, however, that, in terms of maritime delimitation effected by the Court, whether by way of direct, quasi-direct or indirect delimitation (depending upon the precise task given to the Court), judgments, and consequently the boundary line *eo nomine*, or the very principles relevant to maritime delimitation and the practical methods for the application of those principles, also remain subject to revision, provided, of course, that the criteria of Article 61 are met.

IV. Revision at the merits stage

At this stage it is appropriate to dwell briefly on the legal situation arising from a judgment of the International Court of Justice admitting an application for revision under Article 61. The problem, which was adverted to in section II.d of Chapter 10, is that, once the Court has accepted the applicant State's contentions (i) that the fact was newly discovered, (ii) that the newly discovered fact was decisive in character, (iii) that there was no negligence on the part of the applicant State with respect to its discovery, and (iv) that all conditions *ratione temporis* are fully met, then the role of the Court at the merits stage is effectively limited to modifying the judgment boundary: the implication being that the merits phase thus becomes one of legal formality as opposed to substance. The Court, then, would only have to apply the facts to the case and thereafter alter the boundary accordingly. Logical though this proposition would appear to be, this is not an entirely accurate statement of the law.

Of course, the Court would need to apply the newly discovered facts and modify the boundary consistent with such facts, but that is not necessarily what it will be bound to do in all cases which come before it. The point is that the Court is bound neither by law nor by Article 61 to modify the judgment boundary consistent with the newly discovered fact, nor, indeed, even to modify it at all. Although it has not had the opportunity of admitting and then revising a judgment boundary, it is safe to suggest that the Court will apply equitable considerations to determine at least two distinct questions, namely, (i) whether the judgment boundary ought indeed to be disturbed despite the discovery of the newly discovered fact, and (ii) the extent to which the judgment boundary ought to be revised once the Court has decided in principle to modify it.

In general terms, there can be absolutely no doubt that equitable considerations play an important part in the delimitation of boundaries, both land and maritime. Although the notion of equitable principles and considerations, and the formula of 'equitable solution', gained enormous currency in the context of maritime delimitation, a notion which then crystallised in Articles 75 and 83 of the 1982 United Nations Convention on the Law of the Sea, it needs to be emphasised that equity and equitable considerations generally constitute the bedrock of the law of title to territory and boundary delimitation.[952] The principles of acquiescence and estoppel, as the Chamber of the International Court of Justice observed in the *Gulf of Maine* case, 'follow from the fundamental principles of good faith and equity'.[953] Similarly rooted are the rules relating to ancient original title, recognition, boundary delimitation in navigable rivers, particularly the *thalweg*, accretion and avulsion rules and the doctrines of *uti possidetis* and the finality and continuity of recognised international boundaries.

These general observations, importantly, are not to be confused with the application of the rules of equity as, for example, rules relating to equity *infra legum* as applied in the *Land, Island and Maritime Boundary*[954] and *Burkina Faso* v. *Mali*[955] cases, but they, nevertheless, show how deeply intertwined all these rules are with the general notion of equity. The contention here is that the Court will, either *suo motu* or at the behest of the applicant or respondent State, begin its judicial examination by considering whether or not the judgment boundary ought to be modified in light of such newly discovered facts.

In order to answer this question, it is reasonable to suggest that the International Court of Justice or any other international tribunal will

[952] See, generally, the excellent survey by Miyoshi, *Considerations of Equity in the Settlement of Territorial and Boundary Disputes*, Dordrecht, 1993; and further see Nelson, 'The Role of Equity in the Delimitation of Maritime Boundaries', 84 (1990) AJIL 837; Rossi, *Equity and International Law: A Legal Realist Approach to International Decisionmaking*, Irvington, NY, 1993, Chapters VIII and IX; Thirlway, 'The Law and Procedure of the International Court of Justice 1960–1989', 60 (1989) BYIL 1, at pp. 29–62; and Brownlie (note 1), pp. 165–80; and, more generally, see Akehurst, 'Equity and General Principles of Law', 25 (1976) ICLQ 801; and Cheng (note 692), pp. 20 and 48–9.

[953] ICJ Reports 1984, p. 246, at p. 304; and see Thirlway (note 952), pp. 29–30.

[954] ICJ Reports 1992, p. 351, at pp. 514–15, with respect to a small part of the fourth sector on the basis of unratified delimitation negotiations in 1869.

[955] ICJ Reports 1986, p. 554, at pp. 632–3, with respect to the frontier pool at Soum which the Chamber divided into half on the basis of the unratified 1956 Voltan–Malian agreement which had drawn the boundary along the midpoints of the pool.

have reference to the doctrine of finality and continuity of international boundaries. There is ample State practice to show that international boundaries enjoy a degree of permanence, a characteristic clearly evident in Article 62(2) of the Vienna Convention on the Law of Treaties[956] and Article 11 of the Vienna Convention on Succession of States in Respect of Treaties,[957] among other treaties. Similarly, when confronted with pleas urging modification to long-standing alignments, most international tribunals, including the International Court of Justice, will view the matter with great caution and take into account all countervailing considerations. One such consideration is the *quieta non mouvre* principle which, as noted above,[958] precludes the unsettling of a state of affairs which has long been settled, a principle applied by the Permanent Court of Arbitration in the *Grisbadarna* case.[959]

The *Temple of Preah Vihear* case between Cambodia and Thailand is effectively predicated on this principle. Although the Franco-Siamese Treaty of 1904 established the boundary line along the Dangrek watershed range and allocated the Temple of Preah Vihear to Thailand, the International Court of Justice had to take into account certain counter vailing considerations. One such consideration was the Annex I map which showed the Temple to be in Cambodia. Although, strictly speaking, an unofficial document, the Annex I map had virtually acquired treaty status inasmuch as Siam/Thailand, by failing to protest, had implied that it had accepted the map as representing the work of the Mixed Delimitation Commission.[960] Taking the position that one of the primary objects of establishing a frontier was to achieve stability and finality, the Court observed that this would be impossible if the line so established could at any moment, on the basis of a continuously available process, be called into question and its rectification claimed.[961] The Court held that Thailand was now precluded from denying the depiction contained therein.[962]

The same deference to continuity and stability was evident in the *Rann of Kutch* case, in which Pakistan argued that the vertical line, which delineated part of the western sector, was an invalid alignment insofar as it had been demarcated in excess of the powers vested in the boundary demarcation commission pursuant to the frontier agreement of 1914 between the State of Kutch, an autonomous entity under the paramountcy of the British Government, and the British Indian Province of Sindh. While the Tribunal accepted that the vertical line was indeed not encompassed by

956 Supra, note 89. 957 17 (1978) ILM 1488. 958 Section VI of Chapter 6 above.
959 4 (1910) AJIL 226, at p. 233. 960 ICJ Reports 1962, p. 6, at p. 32.
961 *Ibid.*, p. 34. 962 *Ibid.*, pp. 33–4.

the 1914 agreement, it ruled that the Sindh Government and higher authorities had accepted the line without censure and challenge, and that it was now 'not open to the Tribunal to disturb a boundary settled in this manner by the British Administration and accepted and acted upon by it, as well as the State of Kutch, for nearly quarter of a century'.[963]

Similarly, in *Guatemala* v. *Honduras*,[964] the Special Boundary Tribunal pointed out that the *de facto* line of possession in the sector between Cerro Oscuro and Angostura on the Managua River was inconsistent with the *uti possidetis* of 1821: either party was in possession of territory which pertained to the other according to the *uti possidetis*. 'But', the Tribunal observed, 'the evidence furnishes no means of measuring the respective equities of either party with respect to these apparent encroachments of the other or to determine the balance of advantage which either party may thereby have derived. It is also evident that the Tribunal has no sufficient basis for an attempt to rectify the line of present possession so as to secure a more equitable division of the territory in dispute.'[965] The Tribunal, therefore, continued the definitive boundary along the line of possession and control.[966] It appears therefore that, where there is a lack of sufficient evidence for the purposes of balancing the relevant *de facto* equities on either side, the tribunal will exercise caution and resist claims for modification.

Before addressing the second issue, three important points must be noted by way of abundant caution. First, it is accepted, of course, that the category of cases scrutinised above deals with questions of acquiescence and estoppel, a category quite distinct from the judicial remedy of revision. There is, however, a common denominator here, which is that a tribunal, including the International Court of Justice, when faced with the prospect of changing a boundary which has had a degree of consolidation, in terms of time, law and other circumstances, will be minded to balance the plea for modification based on a technically correct application of the law against the need to continue the boundary on the strength of the circumstances attending the consolidation of that alignment. There is sufficient evidence to support the view that the tribunal will decide in favour of the latter in all the appropriate circumstances.

Secondly, it is not being argued here that, in every application for revision on its merits, the tribunal *will* or *ought to* reject the plea for modification based on the newly discovered fact. The simple thrust of the matter is that the tribunal will consider the entire range of arguments with a view to balancing the plea for modification based on the newly

[963] 50 ILR 1, at p. 475. [964] 2 UNRIAA 1307. [965] *Ibid.*, p. 1357. [966] *Ibid.*

discovered fact, and that it would be incorrect to assume that to establish the newly discovered fact is effectively to procure the modification.

Thirdly, it has not been forgotten that the maximum period of time available for revision under Article 61 is ten years and this span of time is not normally a sufficiently long period of time in which formidable equities could realistically have formed. The point, however, is that time is but one factor out of many, and that all of these factors have to be examined collectively. Other factors in question include the nature and extent of State control, the strength of the links displayed by local inhabitants with the territory in question, especially claims of ancient original title, and the nature, extent and control of private activities by public authorities in the disputed areas. A tribunal will be constrained to keep these and other considerations in mind when requested to revise a judgment boundary.

The second issue is concerned with the *actual modification* by way of revision of the judgment boundary once the International Court of Justice or other tribunal has decided to admit the application for revision. There is no gainsaying that the tribunal will, first and foremost, be guided by the newly discovered fact and may be able uncontroversially to apply the new fact and simply adjust the alignment appropriately. However, account must also be taken of facts and circumstances which could in principle militate against a simplistic application of the newly discovered fact. These facts could then prevent the newly discovered fact from having its full effect on the judgment boundary. This is predicated on the proposition that it is one thing to admit an application for revision; it is quite another to revise the judgment boundary in complete accordance with the newly discovered fact. If such considerations do present themselves, then it appears that a tribunal will in all probability turn once again to equitable considerations to help it determine the precise extent of the projected modification to the judgment boundary.

The reason why it is important to be aware of such an eventuality is because boundary delimitation, whether by way of diplomacy or by a process of adjudication and/or *ad hoc* arbitration, is normally never a mechanical process carried out without reference to a whole range of factors having a bearing on the matter. Importantly, international tribunals, including the International Court of Justice, have developed a rich vein of jurisprudence on the matter of equitable considerations and solutions, and, although there is evidence of their application to land frontier matters, the foremost developments come in the context of maritime delimitation. Thus, a tribunal will take into consideration, for the purposes of effecting such a delimitation, a number of relevant circumstances with a view to providing an equitable solution to the boundary dispute. In the *Gulf of Maine* case, the Chamber of the International Court of Justice formulated an important equitable rule of delimitation when it said that it regarded as a legitimate scruple the concern that the overall result of the delimitation, 'even though achieved through the application of equitable criteria . . . should unexpectedly be revealed as radically inequitable, that is to say, as likely to entail catastrophic repercussions for the livelihood and economic well-being of the population of the countries concerned'.[967]

Although not a maritime delimitation question, it is relevant that, in the *Rann of Kutch* arbitration, the Tribunal attributed two deep inlets on either side of Nagar Parkar to Pakistan on the grounds that 'it would be inequitable to recognise these inlets as foreign [Indian] territory. It would be conducive to friction and conflict. The paramount consideration of promoting peace and stability in this region compels the recognition and confirmation that this territory, which is wholly surrounded by Pakistan territory, also be regarded as such.'[968] In the *United Kingdom–France Continental Shelf Delimitation (First Decision)* case, the Tribunal gave half effect to the Scilly Isles on account of their position *vis-à-vis* their opposite number, the Isle d'Ouessant,[969] as did the International Court of Justice in *Tunisia* v. *Libya* with respect to the Kerkennah Islands,[970] while the Arbitration Tribunal in *Newfoundland and Labrador* v. *Nova Scotia (Second Phase)*,[971] gave no effect to Sable Island on account of its small size, its lack of population and its remoteness.[972] Similarly, while in *Jan Mayen* it accorded a lot of weight to capelin fishery resources in determining the continental shelf and the exclusive economic zone boundary between Norway and Denmark,[973] the Court in the *North Sea Continental Shelf* cases gave due deference to the unity of mineral deposits as a factor in negotiations between Germany, the Netherlands and Denmark.[974]

Given that equitable considerations dominate the law of maritime delimitation, there is no reason to belabour the point beyond stating that international tribunals have, since at least 1969, paid great heed to these considerations in carrying out their tasks. Again, *ex abudenti cautela*, it needs to be noted that it is not being suggested that equitable considerations will have to be taken into account whenever an application for revision of a judgment boundary is admitted by the tribunal, for that will

967 ICJ Reports 1984, at p. 342. 968 50 ILR 1, at p. 520.
969 54 ILR 6, at p. 124 (known as Ushant in English). 970 ICJ Reports 1982, p. 18, at p. 89.
971 www.boundary-dispute.ca/index.html. 972 *Ibid.*, paragraphs 5.13–5.15.
973 ICJ Reports 1993, p. 38. 974 ICJ Reports 1969, p. 3, at p. 52.

depend on the precise facts of a particular case. Moreover, and this is an important qualification, only those equitable considerations which are directly related to the newly discovered facts may be examined by the tribunal; it is indeed not a licence to re-examine equitable and relevant circumstances which have already been examined by the tribunal in the main judgment or award. Furthermore, it is true that, barring *Rann of Kutch*, which concerned the delimitation of a hybrid land/maritime feature, the principles and propositions described above relate to maritime territory delimitation. Even so, there is no reason to ignore variants of such considerations and rules in the context of land frontier cases provided, of course, that such considerations do present themselves.

Finally, it needs also to be noted that a tribunal will be called upon by the parties to examine evidence of all kinds on both sides, including the facts showing the precise effects of the newly discovered facts on the ground and evidence by the respondent party seeking to challenge the alleged effects of the newly discovered facts. It follows that revision at the merits stage will not be a legal formality; nor will it necessarily be an uncontroversial application of the newly discovered fact, especially where the law and facts of the case are complex in nature.

VI. General recapitulation

Revision, like interpretation, is a judicial remedy which can be exercised only where there is evidence of agreement between the parties to the effect that the same or some other tribunal has jurisdiction to revise the previous judgment. Insofar as it is a power provided in the Statute, the remedy of revision is inherent in the International Court of Justice. Hence, agreeing to vest the Court with jurisdiction to decide the dispute between the parties constitutes agreeing also to the possibility that the Court may be asked by either party or both parties to revise the judgment provided the qualifying criteria contained in Article 61 are met. It follows that, while no new agreement between the parties is needed in order to apply to the Court for revision, in *ad hoc* arbitration, if the arbitral agreement were silent, a new agreement would have to be concluded and a new tribunal established in order to carry out the task of revision.

Before the application for revision is admitted, it is usual to require the tribunal to examine whether the substantive and procedural criteria are satisfied. For the International Court of Justice, a finding to the effect that the case for revision has been made out is not an option but an obligation under Article 61(2). The qualifying criteria are provided in this article of the Statute, and are generally regarded as reflecting the position in customary international law. As far as substantive criteria are concerned, the party claiming revision must prove that the newly discovered fact was indeed discovered after the judgment was handed down, and that the newly discovered fact is crucial to the operative part of the decision. The applicant State must also demonstrate that there was no negligence in failing to discover the new fact earlier. The law expects all litigating parties to carry out a full and thorough investigation and review of the law, facts and evidence of the case before the proceedings are brought to a close. In *ad hoc* arbitration, the parties are free, in principle, to provide a regime for revision based on criteria of their own choosing, but usually these criteria are those mentioned above. While the liberty to vary is also available to parties before the International Court of Justice, such changes would have to come by way of additional terms in the special agreement. They would then supplement but not supersede the qualifying criteria provided in Article 61. Even so, it is important to note that, for the purposes of revision by either the Court or an *ad hoc* arbitral tribunal, the legal notion of facts includes certain kinds of evidence, especially new evidence which affects, or, more precisely, negates, the essential factual basis of the operative part of the decision and which necessitates thereby a fresh look.

As far as procedural criteria are concerned, parties in *ad hoc* arbitration are free to determine the temporal limits for revision, ranging from six months to five or ten years. In contemporary times, it is not usual to provide a lengthy period of years, especially in cases where the tribunal is called upon to decide a territorial issue or a boundary problem. The reason, of course, is obvious. Given the need for finality and stability of territorial regimes and boundary locations, the possibility of a judicial revision of a frontier line raises all manner of problems for disputing parties. The Statute of the International Court of Justice gives litigating parties a general right to request revision for up to, but not more than, ten years calculated from the date of the judgment. Nonetheless, once the fact or evidence is discovered, the party claiming discovery has only six months in which to submit an application.

Given the potentially serious nature of the difficulties caused by the revision of decisions, many disputing States in *ad hoc* arbitrations do not include such a right in the *compromis*, with the result that, once the decision is made, there is no inherent means of remedying the judgment even if a new fact or new evidence is discovered. While this may appear inequitable, the fact is that the need for quietus, especially in territorial and boundary problems, far outweighs the need to readjust the boundary or territorial allocation every time a crucial fact is discovered. It is for this reason that revision is a remedy which needs to be exercised sparingly and in exceptional circumstances. The point, then, is that revision is not a remedy for the party which has fallen below the required standards of vigilance. It is not even another chance to obtain the location of the frontier or the allocation of territory it had failed to secure in the first proceedings. Nor is it a reward for painstaking research and careful investigation carried out *after* the original decision is made by the tribunal with a view to discovering facts and evidence justifying a re-examination of the whole or part of the question.

Not unlike interpretation, revision has to be reconciled with the fundamental rule of *res judicata*, and this is best done in such a way that both principles are given full effect. Thus a judgment or award has effects *res judicata* only where the decision is not defective in one or more ways. If there is a demonstrable flaw arising from the discovery of a new fact or item of evidence, then the rule of *res judicata* ought not to be seen as stifling revision for the simple reason that a flawed decision, in whole or in part, is not one which has any value in terms of law. It can also be argued that the judgment boundary line, if and when revised, was the line which had actually been decided. In other words, there is no conflict with *res judicata* because the revised decision has retrospective effects going back to the date the decision was rendered to the parties. Furthermore, inasmuch as revision is a remedy based on consent, it could be argued that the litigating parties accepted the possibility that the judgment or award would in certain strict circumstances be revised and to that extent the parties could be seen as having waived the right to preclude re-examination of the decision until revision is legally ruled out owing to considerations *ratione materiae* or *ratione temporis*.

Finally, once an application for revision is admitted, a new set of proceedings dedicated to examining the effect and implementation of the newly discovered fact will have to be undertaken by the tribunal. The law and facts of boundary delimitation are such that it appears that the tribunal will be constrained to consider whether it is appropriate to reopen the settled boundary despite the existence of the newly discovered fact. Once it has decided to redraw the judgment boundary, the tribunal, either *suo motu* or otherwise, may seek to examine, in all the appropriate circumstances, whether and to what extent the judgment boundary needs to be redrawn in light of all the facts and circumstances of the case, including equitable considerations relating directly to the newly discovered fact.

PART V · CONCLUSIONS

12 Conclusions

By way of concluding remarks, it will be interesting to consider a few salient features of these two judicial remedies. In the first place, the remedies of interpretation and revision have a basic, practical usefulness when seen at the immediate, bilateral level. It can hardly be doubted that, for litigating States, these two processes are invaluable insofar as they provide opportunities for remedying difficulties which may have crept into the decision. An examination of the cases showed that the difficulties which can bedevil a State after the decision has been rendered are many and varied, and that their manifestations can range from simple, uncontroversial, typographical errors in the judgment or award, to the admission of hitherto undiscovered facts of crucial importance, with disputes, including the choice of a boundary watershed or the location of a branch or source of a frontier river, intermingling between them.

The sources of these difficulties are equally manifold, and include the lack of a proper geographical survey and the existence of an ambiguous passage or passages in the decision; difficulties may also arise as a consequence of technical miscalculations in the *dispositif*. Apart from the mundane political and procedural worries they may bring in their train, applications for interpretation and revision will nearly always involve issues associated with the *loss* of territory. These problems are in some ways compounded by the fact that, although the underlying common aim in all interpretation and revision applications is to secure from the tribunal a delimitation or a decision on title more favourable to the applicant State, many of the difficulties arising from unclear texts in judgments and/or newly discovered facts are in fact genuine ones.

There is no gainsaying, however, that, in their anxiety to avoid what they would normally perceive as 'losing territory', States are tempted, from time to time, to submit applications which lack *bona fide* bases for either interpretation or revision or both, that is, where the application for interpretation is grounded in the simple motivation to obtain an advantageous modification to the location of the award line or the judgment on title. These instances of abuse of a right or privilege, or indeed opportunity, are not altogether typical of the general phenomenon, and accordingly there is little reason, generally speaking, to adopt a cynical approach to the question concerning the utility of these remedies.

Thus, to the extent that these difficulties are genuine problems relating to the meaning, scope and effect of the decision and/or the discovery of a critical fact, the remedies of interpretation and revision have a very significant role to play, for they enable litigating States to resolve outstanding problems without having to revert to the antagonism or stalemate of what is, in effect, a new boundary or territorial dispute, with the potential for an escalation in tension between them.

This is, of course, particularly true of incidental interpretation and revision, but less true for what has been characterised as main case interpretation. The reason for this is that, in the latter situation, the reference, if any, by disputing States to a different tribunal after years of mutual intransigence will hinge in most cases on a thawing of relations on the issues and/or a sense of goodwill between them, and the like, whereas incidental interpretation is a right exercised by one of the parties as a result of the interpretation clause provided in the *compromis*. If the relevant tribunal is the International Court of Justice, then, even if there is no reference to it in the special agreement, the remedies of interpretation and revision remain unaffected, for the Court, by virtue of Articles 60 and 61, has inherent powers in this regard. For purposes of the latter article, the legal criteria provided therein are essential.

An advantage States gain from referring their cases to the International Court of Justice is that there is no temporal restriction on applying to the Court for a judgment under Article 60. While most provisions on interpretation in *ad hoc* arbitral agreements provide strict time limits, the right to apply to the International Court of Justice to construe its judgment is in fact open-ended in terms of time. The same is true for proceedings brought under the auspices of the Permanent Court of Arbitration, provided that the parties incorporate at least Article 82 of the Hague Convention of 1907 in the *compromis* and do not provide time restrictions therein. Revision, on the other hand, under the Statute has a ten-year time limit from the date of the judgment and a six-month time limit from the discovery of the fact, whereas the Hague Convention simply invites parties to include temporal restrictions in the *compromis*. Be that as it may, the short point here is that, by utilising these remedies, litigating States are able to resolve uncertainties and ambiguities deriving from the impugned decision, and they are therefore processes the importance of which cannot be underestimated.

In the second place, the abiding significance of these remedies lies in the sheer flexibility available to States and international tribunals at various levels of interaction. The ability to provide relief in different situations without being restricted by excess formalism is perhaps the real hallmark of interpretation and revision, especially the former. There are several aspects to this flexibility. The first is concerned with the fact that States may utilise the interpretative process to rectify a mistake or mistakes in the previous judgment. The theory is that tribunals are able to rectify material errors by way of the interpretative process on the basis that, in some cases, to rectify is also to clarify the problem in terms of confirming the existence of the error and then providing correctives which, in many cases, could constitute modifying the boundary line.

The fact, however, is that, if there is evidence of typographical or other material errors in the decision, then in principle the remedy of interpretation is, strictly speaking, not necessary because the power to rectify non-essential errors in the judgment or award is an inherent power of the tribunal which is not dependent on specific permissive provisions in the *compromis*. Yet, it is the case that States have relied on the inherent power of tribunals to construe decisions in order to rectify the mistake. Of course, it may be, and this was the case in *United Kingdom–France Continental Shelf Interpretive Decision*, that the applicant State will wish to keep its options open in terms of the pleas it decides to put forward, and to that effect it might decide to pursue the remedy of interpretation, and by doing so retain a degree of flexibility in its litigation, and, as such, this proves precisely the point being made, namely, that this remedy is anything but constrictive in scope and effect.

Notwithstanding the *United Kingdom–France Continental Shelf Interpretive Decision* case, it has also been seen above that some States resort to the remedy of interpretation in order to obtain corrections of mistakes and uncertainties of a more serious kind existent in the first decision. This was seen to full effect in the *Palena* case, and subsequently in the *Laguna del Desierto* arbitration. It is clear that the process can also be used where it is less a question of clarifying the meaning and scope of the decision, as for example in the alleged confusion with respect to the geographical co-ordinates of the most westerly point of the Gulf of Gabes in *Application for Revision and Interpretation of the 1982 Judgment*, and more a question of deciding the alignment in the light of more accurate geographical knowledge of the border region, without, of course, abandoning the basic textual delimitation decided by the first tribunal and the drawing of a boundary *de novo*.

The second aspect of this flexibility lies in the fact that tribunals are not averse to interpreting decisions which are not always straightforward arbitral awards or judgments, provided always, of course, that they are either legally binding decisions or carry great juridical weight. The latter two types of decision are exemplified by administrative decisions and advisory opinions, respectively. Thus, at times, international tribunals will have occasion to interpret not only arbitral awards or judgment boundaries but also administrative decisions made by a single State or a group of States which delimit the frontier between, and on behalf of, other States or component entities of States. Thus, despite its finding that the Tripp decisions were not arbitral awards, as Sharjah had claimed, the Tribunal in *Dubai* v. *Sharjah* nevertheless proceeded to interpret them as administrative decisions on the basis of international law. The Permanent Court of International Justice was relatively more liberal in the *Jaworzina* and *Monastery of Saint-Naoum* cases, when it held that the decisions of the Conference of Ambassadors were not unlike arbitral awards, but it is relevant that, in both cases, the Court was not called upon to decide whether these decisions were arbitral awards but to give a judicial advisory opinion on the final dispositive status of these decisions. It goes without saying that the International Court of Justice may be asked effectively to construe its own advisory opinion, as indeed it did in *South-West Africa Voting Procedure* with respect to one of its passages in the *Status of South West Africa* advisory opinion.

It is this which leads on to the third aspect of flexibility, and this is derived from the experience of the Permanent Court of International Justice's advisory opinions mentioned above, namely, that interpretative decisions do not necessarily have to be effected in contentious cases; they may also materialise in advisory proceedings; but, having said that, it is also important immediately to note that this observation is primarily one aspect of the functioning of the International Court of Justice which, in its advisory capacity, can in principle provide opinions capable directly of affecting title, provided of course that the Court does not feel that there are any compelling reasons why it should not supply an opinion. Thus, in *Status of Eastern Carelia*, the Permanent Court of International Justice rejected the request of the Council of the League of Nations to provide an advisory opinion on the dispute regarding the status of Eastern Carelia.

Fourthly, the very nature of interpretation is such that a tribunal may refuse, on the one hand, to admit the application on the ground, *inter alia*, that the request is not a *bona fide* one for clarification but a guise in fact for the revision and modification of the boundary, and yet, on the other hand, proceed to provide a clarification of the controversy. Clarifications of this kind may take place in the course of providing reasons for its rejection of the request for interpretation, or in the course of deciding the adjoined request for revision. Certainly, it is the case that a lot depends on the precise nature of the controversy and/or the attendant circumstances, but the central fact is inescapable, namely, that, in principle, the tribunal may, by accident or design, provide a measure of explanation of the vexed passage or passages, and by so doing satisfy the applicant State. This was partly what happened in *Application for Revision and Interpretation of the 1982 Judgment*, and it is clear that the Court accepted that some sort of indirect interpretation had indeed occurred.

Finally, with respect to its flexible characteristics, it appears that the remedy of interpretation is flexible enough to allow the tribunal dealing with the request to change the delimitation decided by the first tribunal to such an extent that there is in fact less interpretation and more modification of the alignment and a re-evaluation of the merits of the case. At least one case, namely, *Costa Rica* v. *Panama*, reflects this proposition of law. The underlying premise of this case was apparently that the interpretation provided by the second arbitrator was in fact consistent with what the first arbitrator would indeed have decided had the latter not gone beyond his jurisdiction and awarded territory in excess of what he was legally authorised to award and allocate.

The ultimate justification for this position is based on the consent of the parties, but consent which is best described as either indirect or oblique. Here, the contention was that the terms of the second arbitration were not confined to requiring the second arbitrator to provide a simple interpretation of the first award, because that would not have resolved the underlying problems; and that the true position was that the second arbitrator was in fact effectively authorised by the *compromis* to reinterpret the arguments made by the parties in the first proceedings. If this constitutes a correct interpretation of the terms of the second arbitral agreement, then it would of course reveal that the powers given to the second arbitrator were more than obvious from a simple reading of the *compromis*. The point here is that, in the right circumstances, the judicial remedy of interpretation is flexible enough to accommodate proceedings which could ultimately lead to a *de novo* delimitation, and yet remain strictly within the notion of interpretation.

The third significant feature of these two remedies is its relation to one of the more fundamental maxims of law, that is to say, *res judicata*. The relation between the maxim and the two judicial remedies is characterised by perceived tension between them, predicated as it is on the proposition that the notion of finality of decisions is critically ruptured when a tribunal decides to redraw a judgment boundary pursuant to an application for interpretation and revision. The importance of the *res judicata* rule to domestic legal systems and to the international community need not be rehearsed here, nor indeed can it be exaggerated. Suffice it to say that legal systems, municipal and international, would be in considerable chaos if this rule did not exist. For present purposes, however, it is important simply to highlight the fact that, in principle, there is no tension between these two aspects of international justice.

Not unlike many other rules of both international and domestic law, *res judicata* cannot be seen *in vacuo*: it has to be read and applied in the context not only of a variety of principles of law, but with respect to the facts applicable to a particular situation. Thus, in quite simple terms, while the *doctrine* of *res judicata* will apply when a judgment or award is handed down to the parties, a number of other *rules and principles* will serve also to inform and indicate its precise nature, scope, application and effect. It follows then that the rules of law attending the remedies of interpretation and revision are simply part of a set of principles which govern *res judicata* as a general doctrine of law.

Accordingly, neither revision nor interpretation is in any way antagonistic to *res judicata*; indeed, as important principles, they all hail from the same stable, as it were. A crucial consideration is the fact that *res judicata* can hardly be seen as an obstacle to change where the litigating parties have agreed in advance that revision is permitted, conditions *ratione materiae* and *ratione temporis* permitting, or where they agree *subsequently* to allow interpretation or revision or both. It is important to recall the fact that, in the absence of such an agreement, the two judicial remedies are not available to either litigating State.

One of the more fundamental of assumptions underlying these considerations is that there is no reason to resolve the matter by reference to a perceived hierarchy between the two norms, that is, on the one hand, the norm of finality, and, on the other, the permissive rule allowing matters decided by a tribunal to be reopened in appropriate circumstances. Insofar as both norms can exist side by side when applied to the same situation, the preferred route is to seek to harmonise any conflict rather than to set up doctrinal and/or intellectual barriers, that is, barriers which can only be surmounted by reference to hierarchical propositions, where one rule supersedes another, or by reference to the *lex generalis/lex specialis* rules of interpretation. On this view of the matter, not only does it accord with doctrinal reality, a process of reconciliation is also preferable because it obviates the problems which emerge from trying to establish a ranking of norms in this context.

Nor is it impossible to so reconcile. Thus, while a boundary established by way of a decision of the International Court of Justice is *res judicata* for the States on both sides of the judgment boundary, either one of them may apply for revision if it can prove the discovery of a crucial fact. While *prima facie* it would appear that the right of revision supersedes the rule which forbids the reopening and tinkering with a judgment on the same matter between the same parties, including their successor States, that is not necessarily so. For both rules can be harmonised if the position taken is that the revised boundary would have been the original boundary had the existent but unknown fact been taken into account and applied at the time of the original proceedings. Of course, all the relevant criteria regarding revision would have to be satisfied before the requested modification to the judgment boundary is accepted, including the rule on negligence with respect to the discovery of the crucial fact, and the two temporal limits provided in Article 61 of the Statute of the International Court of Justice.

This approach is even more apposite in the matter of applications dealing with the rectification of material errors where it can be easily established that the tribunal had not intended in law, if not in fact, to draw the alignment as indicated in the *dispositif*. In view of these considerations, it is clear that modifications to the award boundary in the Channel Islands sector following an interpretation of the award of the Court of Arbitration in the *United Kingdom–France Continental Shelf Interpretive Decision* case can easily be defended by taking the position that the *res judicata* rule was not an obstacle because the original alignment was flawed in terms of the true representation of the will of the tribunal. It is equally easy to reconcile *res judicata* with the modifications made to the alignment in the *Palena* case. Not only is there room for the view that the restrictions of the *res judicata* rule do not apply inasmuch as there was neither in law nor in fact ever an award boundary which could have been seen as a clear and effective delimitation in the disputed sector, that is, between Boundary Posts 16 and 17. It is also the case that the task of interpretation and fulfilment of the award of 1962 was eagerly vested in the Tribunal by the parties. The significance of this is that *res judicata* cannot arrest the progress of a solution arrived at mutually between States. They are free to change any judgment boundary with which they are unhappy. The same is true for *Laguna del Desierto*. In addition, there is, in any event, the factor of mutual consent with respect to both cases.

If the impression gained from the above interaction of rules is that somehow *res judicata* does not play as central a role in the international judicial process as it ought perhaps to play, then that impression is not warranted, because precisely the opposite is true. Indeed, it needs to be emphasised that *res judicata is* the dominant rule, for it applies *equally* to judgments given in the matter of interpretation and revision. Accordingly, once all judgment clarifications and factual applications have been secured under Articles 60 and 61 of the Statute, then all controversies over the judgment must be understood to have ended, and hence subsequent and repeated requests for interpretation or revision, especially where they entail modifications to the judgment boundaries, cannot readily be admitted. The fundamental point here is that an approach predicated on harmonisation cannot be utilised to give priority to interpretation and revision requests. Apart from the *res judicata* rule, this would be dangerous because it offends at least four principles of international law.

First, and quite simply, Article 60 is not a licence for either perpetual or periodic modification, notwithstanding the fact that the remedy does not come with temporal limits. It can hardly be doubted that repeated requests for further and better particulars from the Court with respect to the judgment would qualify as an abuse of right, and, accordingly, such requests would contravene a basic principle of international law.

Secondly, attempts of the above kind would also breach standards of treaty interpretation. A treaty, it is agreed, must be interpreted consistent with the closure of adjudication; an interpretation which permits States to return time and again to the court cannot be accepted.[975] 'The Court', wrote Sir Hersch Lauterpacht, 'has, in general, acted upon the view that treaties embodying territorial and cognate settlements, by way of provision for adjudication or otherwise, are intended to settle a difference of legal views – or a conflict of interests – and not to perpetuate them.'[976] *Interest rei publicae ut sit finis litium.*

[975] Lauterpacht, *The Development of International Law by the International Court*, 2nd edn, London, 1958, pp. 231–42; and Lauterpacht, 'Restrictive Interpretation and the Principle of Effectiveness in the Interpretation of Treaties', 26 (1949) BYIL 48, at p. 70. For him, this was primarily a reflection of the principle of effectiveness.

[976] Lauterpacht, *The Development of International Law by the International Court*, 2nd edn, London, 1958, p. 231. See also Zimmermann (note 226), p. 6.

It was this, among other factors, which prompted Judge Weeramantry to disagree with the majority in *Arbitral Award of 31 July 1989*. In his Dissenting Opinion, he held that the parties did not contemplate a partial resolution of the dispute. 'The determination', he wrote, 'of *the dispute* was thus the basis on which the Tribunal was entrusted with its heavy responsibilities. It was called upon to render certain a boundary obscured by the opposing contentions of [the] parties and to provide a firm basis on which they could henceforth order their affairs.'[977] A return to arbitration was thus not an option which could have galvanised the litigant States, and hence his observation: '[B]oth parties were entitled to expect a final resolution of the dispute between them rather than to have to face a second prolonged arbitral process.'[978]

Closely associated with this principle is the third consideration for shying away from repeated requests for interpretation and revision. These are the legal difficulties which Judge Weeramantry also alluded to in his magisterial Dissenting Opinion in *Arbitral Award of 31 July 1989*. They relate to problems of nullity and severability of the decision, but have relevance here by way of analogy. He pointed out[979] that there were good reasons why the integrity of the award of 31 July 1989 ought to be preserved, one of them being the fact that the decision determines at least *some* contentious issues, clearing the decks, as it were, for the future determination of outstanding issues. He observed that, where different segments in a boundary dispute could be decided as separate and discrete problems, the answers could stand independently of each other, as for example the different segments of boundaries in the 1902 *Argentina* v. *Chile* arbitration and the subsequent *Palena* case. However, all boundary disputes could not be compartmentalised into discrete segments, and hence there was an overriding principle which ought to have prevented the International Court of Justice from sustaining the 1989 award. His point was that a piecemeal approach to the settlement of different boundary segments could be counterproductive in terms of hindering a just and equitable solution to the problems.

Thus, where different component elements of the subject-matter were 'inextricably interlinked', any *one* award which did not take into account all those factors would be difficult to uphold. Although the essence of his argument was predicated in rejecting an award which failed to address all legally relevant issues in one composite whole and which was therefore

977 ICJ Reports 1991, p. 146 (emphasis added). See, generally, *ibid*., pp. 143–51, especially pp. 148–9. 978 *Ibid*., p. 149.

979 This is a paraphrasing of the original dissent: *ibid*., pp. 167–73.

unable to produce a boundary line which reflected those issues, Judge Weeramantry's general argument is relevant here, namely, that the task of delimitation of maritime boundaries was a delicately balanced one involving a plethora of factors, including geological, geomorphological, ecological and economic aspects thereof, which had be taken into account, along with law and equity. A tribunal would be somewhat strait-jacketed if it were faced with, on the one hand, a definitive delimitation, and hence an untouchable line, for some parts of maritime territory, as for example the territorial sea and the continental shelf, and, on the other, a request to provide a delimitation for the coastal States' fishery or exclusive economic zones. It could not be contended with any degree of assurance that the interests of both parties to the proceedings would not be prejudiced if such a piecemeal process were to take place instead of the composite process both parties originally had in mind.

Analogous situations exist with respect to revision and interpretation. The logic of Judge Weeramantry's argument is equally persuasive when applied to these two remedies. Any approach which seeks time and again to exploit to advantage the two remedies in question, namely, revision and interpretation, may result in a situation in which the tribunal is asked to take into consideration one new decisive fact which, when viewed in the light of *current* circumstances, produces one answer, but which, when viewed in the light of the gamut of facts and arguments considered holistically and historically, would provide a different delimitation in whole or in part. As Judge Weeramantry eventually put it:

> Needless to say, the compartmentalized enquiry can thus lead to vastly different results from the consolidated one. The result which is equitable in the context of any one or more boundaries viewed by themselves may well be inequitable in the context of a total determination.[980]

In short, the interests of both parties, and indeed the administration of international justice itself, would be better served if a dispute were examined judicially in one set of proceedings, leaving recourse to the remedies of revision and interpretation to be utilised in exceptional circumstances and in circumstances of studied restrictive control.

The third rule offended by a liberal approach to interpretation is associated with the doctrine of finality and stability of boundaries, a cardinal maxim in the law of title to territory. International law abhors a continuously available process whereby the location of frontiers is constantly subject to change, a rule confirmed by the International Court of Justice

[980] *Ibid.*, p. 172.

in the *Temple of Preah Vihear* case.[981] The problem, of course, is that, where *bona fide* difficulties in the text of the original or subsequent judgment persist, and there is no evidence of *abus de droit*, then in those cases the Court can be expected to provide the clarification needed, but not without emphasising the importance of seeking to suppress further disputes.

Problems for *res judicata* can also arise with respect to temporal limits to requests for revision and interpretation in arbitral agreements. Most contemporary arbitral agreements provide a period of time in which the remedies of interpretation and revision may be utilised by the parties acting jointly or individually: under the Statute of the International Court of Justice, revision, as has been noted, has two sets of time limits. The main problem is whether it is arguable that, until the time limits provided for the submission of applications for interpretation and/or revision have passed, *res judicata* remains suspended or in abeyance. By this reasoning, *res judicata* comes into play only after the relevant time limits have expired, the point being that it is only after the expiry of such a period of time that re-examination or modification by way of these remedies is finally precluded.

To accept this proposition, however, is to forget that the remedies of revision and interpretation are exceptional remedies. They are not remedies akin to appeal, and the conditions for revision are stringent, with the result that the remedy cannot lightly be provided. It is also to forget that Article 60 of the Statute provides that the judgment is final and without appeal, and, it may be noted in passing, that Article 94(2) of the Rules of Court makes it clear that the judgment is binding from the date it is read out in the Court. Moreover, it does not seem appropriate to consider a cardinal maxim of adjudication as being suspended or held in abeyance on the strength of a contingency which may not ever arise, but which is essentially an exceptional remedy to be exercised restrictively. Lastly, to argue that *res judicata* remains suspended until the relevant time limits have expired is to misunderstand the very nature of this axiom and its relations with the remedies of revision and interpretation. These judicial remedies are predicated in reconciling two opposing dynamics of law, namely, the doctrine of stability and finality of boundary regimes and the need in certain circumstances to realign frontiers and reallocate territorial possessions. In other words, *res judicata* does not have to be suspended in order to apply these judicial remedies; indeed, these remedies can and do co-exist with *res judicata*.

[981] ICJ Reports 1962, p. 6.

Finally, a few comments regarding some broader perspectives, particularly those concerned with the administration of international justice, are necessary. Generally speaking, dispute settlement by adjudication and arbitration has been a steadily growing phenomenon since the early part of the twentieth century. Of course, the history of arbitration stretches back, in one form or another, many centuries, as shown in Chapter 2, but this observation has a reduced role to play in light of the fact that international law needs and relies on modern, scientific arbitration and adjudication based on the interpretation and application of essential principles of the law relating to territory and boundaries, among other rules of international law. It is also the case that the genus of dispute which has the greatest potential for longevity and continuity is the dispute dealing with territorial and boundary issues. Given the fact that the fundamental building blocks of the international politico-legal order are States, and the fact that the State is essentially a legal notion hypostasised in a territorial unit, the *concern* with losing and the *predisposition* for gaining territory is always of central importance to governments. For that reason, States seek to avoid, postpone or delay settlement by arbitration or adjudication if the legal facts do not favour that State, or to consider ways and means of keeping the dispute alive after an unfavourable award is handed down.

Despite this predilection, the overall record of judicial and arbitral settlements is certainly an encouraging one. For present purposes, it suffices to take note of the fact that a significant number of territorial and boundary disputes have been settled by such pacific methods, and, even more encouragingly, that resort to such settlements began to take root well before the start of the Second World War. Before 1939, it was arbitration, as compared to adjudication, which dominated the peaceful dispute settlement process for the purposes of resolving problems of title to territory and international boundaries, with the Permanent Court of Arbitration playing a modest, but significant, role in terms of providing awards in three boundary and territorial disputes including servitudes, namely, the *North Atlantic Coast Fisheries*, *Island of Palmas (or Miangas)*, *Grisbadarna* and *Island of East Timor* cases. The Permanent Court of International Justice was called upon by States only once to give a judgment in contentious proceedings on a question of title to territory. Apart from the *Legal Status of Eastern Greenland* case,[982] the Permanent Court of International Justice gave three advisory opinions directly or indirectly affecting, by way of confirmation, the status

[982] PCIJ Reports, Series A/B, No. 53 (1933), p. 22.

of territory and the boundary line, namely, the *Jaworzina*, the *Monastery of Saint-Naoum* and, to a lesser extent, the *Interpretation of Article 3 of the Treaty of Lausanne*[983] cases. The Court, of course, rejected the request for an advisory opinion in the *Status of Eastern Carelia* case.

However, after 1945, the International Court of Justice and a good number of *ad hoc* arbitral tribunals, with the Permanent Court of Arbitration playing a marginal role, have settled many territorial and boundary problems referred to them by disputing parties. In this context, it is interesting to note that, in the vast majority of cases, litigating States have been content with the decisions handed down by the tribunals, and accordingly have decided not to refer matters back to either the original or subsequent tribunals for the purposes of either interpretation or revision of the judgment or award. It is certainly arguable that the relatively small number of requests for interpretation and revision is in fact a measure of the success generally of international judicial and arbitral processes, not least because it is a reflection of the quality of justice provided by international tribunals in the matter of territorial and boundary disputes.

This is certainly true of the International Court of Justice, insofar as the right to interpret judgments is contingent only on the need for clarification, a contingency relatively easier to satisfy than the admissibility criteria of revision. The latter is a remedy over which the International Court of Justice or other international tribunals have relatively little control; nor is the proven need for revision an adverse reflection on the first judgment or award of the tribunal. Equally importantly, the fact that few decisions, relatively speaking, have gone back either for revision or interpretation has to be viewed in the light of the observation that not all *ad hoc* arbitrations allow for such remedies to be exercised by arbitral tribunals, or by the Permanent Court of Arbitration with respect to revision, under the 1907 Hague Convention.

The conclusion therefore must be that small numbers of revision and interpretation applications can only be a very general *indicium* of the overall performance of the judicial and arbitral process seen collectively. In view of the above, the cautious observer would be content to note – and this is a matter of central significance to the administration of international justice – that, by and large, the international judicial and arbitral processes have justified the confidence placed in them by litigating parties by handing down judgments of the highest standards; that, despite exemplary standards, where difficulties are apparent in awards

[983] PCIJ Reports, Series B, No. 12 (1925), p. 6.

and judgments, the international legal system has not failed fully to provide judicial remedies, including those of interpretation and revision, for the resolution of problems of obfuscation in decisions and the consideration and application of decisive newly discovered facts; that, from time to time, States have approached international tribunals for further assistance in this regard; and that it has been so provided; but that, in the vast majority of cases, there has been no resort to either of these two remedies.

Interestingly, on occasion, clarifications have been supplied even where the request was not admitted; this is an aspect of the flexibility adverted to above. In any event, it was so in *Application for Revision and Interpretation of the 1982 Judgment*, where the International Court of Justice rejected the application for interpretation but noted that some clarification by way of its reasoning had indeed been supplied. This positive approach is also evident in other cases, for example the advisory opinion in the matter of the *Monastery of Saint-Naoum*. Despite the fact that the Serb-Croat-Slovene State could produce no evidence before the Permanent Court of International Justice of an agreement allowing for revision, that Court did, nevertheless, examine the basic arguments relative thereto, and then went on to rule them out. In more recent times, a willingness guardedly to accommodate *prima facie* untenable pleas has also been in evidence.

In *Request for Revision and Interpretation of the 1994 Judgment*, the Argentina–Chile Arbitral Tribunal accommodated Chile's application for revision, despite the fact that Chile had failed fully to satisfy either of the two grounds for revision. Further, the significance of this positive approach is readily discernible in the fact that, in *El Salvador* v. *Honduras*, the Chamber of the International Court of Justice was requested to, and did, provide a judgment on a request for revision submitted just one day short of ten years from the date of the original judgment, even if the Chamber eventually rejected the request and thus did not provide the revision sought by El Salvador.

The key point then is that the significance of the service provided by international tribunals cannot be underestimated. A positive, yet restrictive, approach to these judicial remedies strengthens the dispute settlement process at the general and global level. It is also clear that, if tribunals were generally to adopt an unhelpful approach, and were to reject the prospect of a re-examination of genuinely ambiguous, confused and/or flawed judgments, or were to refuse to revise decisions where there was a good case for revision, then such refusals would ultimately prove to be counter-productive.

For one thing, an unco-operative approach would tend to defeat the very object and purpose of international adjudication and arbitration as perceived by litigating States: the dispute would continue to fester and would jeopardise the relations between the disputing parties. The longer a judgment remains unimplemented, in whole or in part, the greater the sense of frustration and anxiety for the affected States. For another, disputing States, in the long term, would most probably become chary of referring their problems to international tribunals. Thus, by providing clarification and by considering requests for revision wherever appropriate and valid, international tribunals will continue to succeed in imbuing litigating States with confidence in these methods of dispute settlement, and, by so doing, tribunals will help to promote and protect an important component of the administration of international justice. This point has particular force where matters of title to territory are concerned. In sum, it is by strengthening the confidence States have in the adjudication and arbitration of disputes that tribunals will be able to continue to play a key role in the international legal order, especially where tensions arising out of boundary and territorial disputes are a perennial feature thereof.

Select bibliography

Ahmad, N., 'The Indo-Pakistan Boundary Disputes Tribunal, 1949–1950', 43 (1953) *Geographical Review* 329

Aitchison, C. U., *A Collection of Treaties, Engagements and Sanads Relating to India and Neighbouring Countries*, Delhi, 1933

Akehurst, M., 'Equity and General Principles of Law', 25 (1976) ICLQ 801

Al-Baharna, H., *The Arabian Gulf States Their Legal and Political Status and Their International Problems*, 2nd edn, Beirut, 1975

Al-Izzi, K., *The Shatt al Arab River Dispute in Terms of International Law*, Baghdad, 1972

Amin, S. H., 'The Iran–Iraq Conflict', 31 (1982) ICLQ 167

Anderson, C. P., 'The Costa Rica–Panama Boundary Dispute', 15 (1921) AJIL 236

Anderson, M., *Frontiers Territory and State Formation in the Modern World*, Cambridge, 1996

Andrews, J. A., 'The Concept of Statehood and the Acquisition of Territory in the Nineteenth Century', 94 (1978) LQR 408

Anon, *A General Collection of Treatys, Declarations of War, Manifestos and Other Publick Papers*, London, 1710

Anyangwe, C., 'African Border Disputes and Their Settlements by International Judicial Process', 28 (2003) *South African Yearbook of International Law* 29

Bishop, C. M., *International Arbitral Procedure*, Washington, DC, 1931

Blake, G. (ed.), *Maritime Boundaries*, vol. 5 of Blake, G. (general editor), *World Boundaries*, 5 vols., London, 1994

Bos, M., 'The International Law Commission's Draft Convention on Arbitral Procedure in the General Assembly of the United Nations', 3 (1956) *Nederlands Tijdschrift voor Internationaal Recht* 234

A Methodology of International Law, Amsterdam, 1984

Bourne, C. B., and McRae, D. M., 'Maritime Jurisdiction in the Dixon Entrance: The Alaska Boundary Re-examined', 14 (1976) CYIL 175

Bourne, E. G., 'The Demarcation Line of Pope Alexander VI', in Bourne, E. G., *Essays in Historical Criticism*, New York, 1901, p. 193

Bowett, D. W., 'The Dubai/Sharjah Boundary Arbitration of 1981', 65 (1994) BYIL 103

'Res Judicata and the Limits of Decisions by International Tribunals', 8 (1996) *African Journal of International and Comparative Law* 577

Brower, C. N., and Brueschke, J. D., *The Iran–United States Claims Tribunal*, The Hague, 1998

Brownlie, I., *African Boundaries: A Legal and Diplomatic Encyclopaedia*, London, 1979

Principles of Public International Law, 4th edn, Oxford, 1990

'International Law at the Fiftieth Anniversary of the United Nations General Course of Public International Law', 255 (1995) *Hague Recueil* 9

Principles of Public International Law, 6th edn, Oxford, 2003

Bustamante, A. S. de, *The World Court*, trans. E. Read, New York, 1926

'Arbitration in the Western Hemisphere', 7 (1929) *Foreign Affairs* 282

Caldwell, R. G., 'The Settlement of Inter-State Disputes', 14 (1920) AJIL 38

Calendar of State Papers Colonial Series, vol. V, *America and the West Indies 1661–1668*, HMSO, London, 1880; Kraus Reprint, Vaduz, 1964

Calic, M.-J., 'Kosovo in the Twentieth Century: A Historical Account', in Schnabel, A., and Thakur, R. (eds.), *Kosovo and the Challenge of Humanitarian Intervention: Selective Indignation, Collective Action, and International Citizenship*, Tokyo, 2000

Calvert, P. (ed.), *Border and Territorial Disputes of the World*, 4th edn, London, 2004

Camilleri, J. A., *Chinese Foreign Policy: The Maoist Era and Its Aftermath*, Oxford, 1980

Carlson, A., 'Constructing the Dragon's Scales: China's Approach to Territorial Sovereignty and Border Relations in the 1980s and 1990s', 12 (2003) *Journal of Contemporary China* 677

Carlston, K. S., *The Process of International Arbitration*, New York, 1946

'Codification of International Arbitral Procedure', 47 (1953) AJIL 203

Cassese, A., *International Law in a Divided World*, Oxford, 1986

Chen, L., and Reisman, M., 'Who Owns Taiwan: A Search for International Title', 81 (1971–2) *Yale Law Journal* 599

Chen, T., 'Some Legal Problems in Sino-US Relations', 22 (1983) *Columbia Journal of Transnational Law* 41

Cheng, B., *General Principles of Law as Applied by International Courts and Tribunals*, London, 1953; Cambridge Reprint, 1994

Child, C. J., 'The Venezuela–British Guiana Boundary Arbitration of 1899', 44 (1950) AJIL 682

Chiu, H. (ed.), *Normalising Relations with the People's Republic of China: Problems, Analysis and Documents*, Baltimore, 1978

'Normalisation and Some Practical and Legal Problems Concerning Taiwan', in Chiu, H. (ed.), *Normalising Relations with the People's Republic of China: Problems, Analysis and Documents*, Baltimore, 1978, p. 51

Collier, J., and Lowe, V., *The Settlement of Disputes in International Law*, Oxford, 1999

Colombos, C. J., *The International Law of the Sea*, 6th edn, London, 1967

Colson, D. A., 'The United Kingdom–France Continental Shelf Arbitration: Interpretative Decision of March 1978', 73 (1979) AJIL 112

Commager, H. S. (ed.), *Documents of American History*, New York, 1949

Corbett, P. E., *The Settlement of Canadian–American Disputes: A Critical Study of Methods and Results*, New Haven, 1937

Crawford, J., *The Creation of States in International Law*, Oxford, 1977

Cukwurah, A. O., *The Settlement of Boundary Disputes in International Law*, Manchester, 1967

Darby, W. E. (ed.), *International Tribunals: A Collection of the Various Schemes which Have been Propounded; And of Instances in the Nineteenth Century*, 4th edn, London, 1904

Darm, D., 'US–Canada Flag State Enforcement Arrangements: Dixon Entrance', in *Digest of United States Practice in International Law*, 1981–8, vol. II, p. 1928

Davies, C., *The Problem of the North-West Frontier 1890–1908: With a Survey of Policy Since 1849*, 2nd edn, London, 1975

De Visscher, C., *Theory and Reality in Public International Law*, trans. P. E. Corbett, Princeton, 1968

Dennis, W. C., 'Compromise – The Great Defect of Arbitration', 11 (1911) *Columbia Law Review* 493

Documents of the United Nations Conference on International Organisation, London, 1945

Editorial Comment, 'The Arbitral Award in the Peru–Bolivia Boundary Controversy', 3 (1909) AJIL 1029

Editorial Comment, 'The Chamizal Arbitration Award', 5 (1911) AJIL 709

Edmonds, C. J., 'The Iraqi–Persian Frontier: 1638–1938', 62 (1975) *Asian Affairs* 147

El-Hakim, A. A., *The Middle Eastern States and the Law of the Sea*, Manchester, 1979

Elkind, J. B., *Interim Protection: A Functional Approach*, The Hague, 1981

Evans, M. D. (ed.), *Remedies in International Law: The International Dilemma*, Oxford, 1998

Fitzmaurice, G. G., 'The Law and Practice of the International Court of Justice, 1951–4: Questions of Jurisdiction, Competence and Procedure', 34 (1958) BYIL 1

Fox, H., 'Arbitration', in Luard, E. (ed.), *The International Regulation of Frontier Disputes*, London, 1970, p. 168

'Arbitration', in Waldock, C. H. M. (ed.), *International Disputes: The Legal Aspects: Report of a Study Group of the David Davies Memorial Institute of International Studies*, London, 1972, p. 101

Francalanci, G., and Scovazzi, T., *Lines in the Sea*, Dordrecht, 1994

Frankfurter, F., and Landis, J. M., 'The Compact Clause of the Constitution – A Study in Interstate Adjustments', 34 (1925) *Yale Law Journal* 685

Fraser, H. S., 'A Sketch of the History of International Arbitration', 11 (1926) *Cornell Law Quarterly* 179

Garver, J. W., 'The Sino-Soviet Territorial Dispute in the Pamir Mountains Region', 85 (1981) *China Quarterly* 107

Geiss, R., 'Revision Proceedings before the International Court of Justice', 63 (2003) *Zeitschrift für ausländisches öffentliches Recht und Völkerrecht* 167
Glenn, J., 'Central Asian Republics', in Calvert, P. (ed.), *Border and Territorial Disputes of the World*, 4th edn, London, 2004, p. 143
Glenny, M., *The Balkans 1804–1999: Nationalism, War and the Great Powers*, London, 2000
Goldschmidt, 'International Arbitral Procedure: Original Project and Report of Mr Goldschmidt, 20 June 1874', in Scott, J. B. (ed.), *Resolutions of the Institute of International Law Dealing with the Law of Nations with an Historical Introduction and Explanatory Notes*, New York, 1916, p. 205
Gonzalo de Quesada, *Arbitration in Latin America*, Rotterdam, 1907
Government Printer, China, *The Sino-Indian Boundary Question*, enlarged edn, Peking, 1962
Government Printer, India, *Reports of the Officials of the Governments of India and the People's Republic of China on the Boundary Question*, Ministry of External Affairs, Government of India, New Delhi, 1961
Government Printing Office, *Foreign Relations of the United States of America: Diplomatic Papers*, Washington, DC, 1899, 1914, 1915 and 1921
Gray, C., and Kingsbury, B., 'Developments in Dispute Settlement: Inter-State Arbitration Since 1945', 63 (1992) BYIL 97
Green, L. C., and Dickason, O. P., *The Law of Nations and the New World*, Edmonton, Alberta, 1989
Greig, D. W., 'Sovereignty, Territory and the International Lawyer's Dilemma', 26 (1988) *Osgoode Hall Law Journal* 127
Grenville, J. A. S., and Wasserstein, B., *The Major International Treaties of the Twentieth Century*, London, 2001
Gross, L., 'The Peace of Westphalia', 42 (1948) AJIL 20
Grotius, H., *De jure belli ac pacis libri tres*, 1646, trans. F. W. Kelsey, in *The Classics of International Law* series, Carnegie Endowment for International Peace, Oxford, 1925
Grzybowski, K., 'Interpretation of Decisions of International Tribunals', 35 (1941) AJIL 482
Habicht, M., *Post-War Treaties for the Pacific Settlement of International Disputes*, Cambridge, 1931
Hazard, E., *Historical Collections; Consisting of State Papers, and Other Authentic Documents; Intended as Materials for an History of the United States of America*, Philadelphia, 1792
Hershey, A. S., *Essentials of International Public Law and Organisation*, 2nd edn, New York, 1930
Hertslet, G. E. P., *Hertslet's China Treaties: Treaties &c, Between Great Britain and China; And Between China and Foreign Powers*, London, 1908
Heuser, R., 'Taiwan', 12 (1972) *Encyclopaedia of Public International Law* 367
Hill, N. L., 'The Interpretation of the Decisions of the International Court', 22 (1933–4) *Georgia Law Journal* 535

Claims to Territory in International Law and Relations, Westport Reprint, Oxford, 1945

Himmelreich, D. M., 'The Beagle Channel Affair: A Failure in Judicial Persuasion', 12 (1979) *Vanderbilt Journal of Transnational Law* 971

Hoadly, C. J., *Records of the Colony and Plantation of New Haven from 1638–1649*, Hartford, 1857

Hoffman, G. W., *The Balkans in Transition*, Princeton, 1963

Holls, F. W., *The Peace Conference at The Hague and Its Bearings on International Law and Policy*, New York, 1900

Hudson, M. O., *International Legislation: A Collection of the Texts of Multipartite International Instruments of General Interest*, Washington, DC, 1931

World Court Reports, Washington, DC, 1934

The Permanent Court of International Justice 1920–1942: A Treatise, New York, 1943

International Tribunals Past and Future, Washington, DC, 1944

Hyde, C. C., *International Law Chiefly as Interpreted and Applied by the United States*, Boston, 1947

Ibler, V. (ed.), *Mélanges offerts a Juraj Andrassy: Essays in Honour of Juraj Andrassy*, The Hague, 1968

Independent Commission on Kosovo, *The Kosovo Conflict: International Response: Lessons to be Learnt*, Oxford, 2000

Ireland, G., *Boundaries, Possessions, and Conflicts in Central and North America and the Caribbean*, Cambridge, MA, 1941

Iwashita, A., *A 4000 Kilometer Journey Along the Sino-Russian Border*, Slavic Eurasian Studies No. 3, Sapporo, 2004

Jain, J. P., 'The Legal Status of Formosa: A Study of British, Chinese and Indian Views', 57 (1963) AJIL 25

Jenks, W. C., *The Prospects of International Adjudication*, London, 1964

Jennings, R. Y., 'The Progress of International Law', 54 (1950) BYIL 334

The Acquisition of Territory in International Law, Manchester, 1963

Journals of the Continental Congress, 1774–1789, Washington, DC, 1904–37

Kaikobad, K. H., 'Some Observations on the Doctrine of Continuity and Finality of Boundaries', 54 (1984) BYIL 119

The Shatt al Arab Question: A Legal Reappraisal, Oxford, 1988

'The Court, the Council and Interim Protection: A Commentary on the Lockerbie Order of 14 April 1992', 17 (1996) *Australian Yearbook of International Law* 87

'The Quality of Justice: Excès de Pouvoir in the Adjudication and Arbitration of Territorial and Boundary Disputes', in Goodwin-Gill, G., and Talmon, S. (eds.), *Reality of International Law: Essays in Honour of Ian Brownlie*, Oxford, 1999, p. 293

'Problems of Adjudication and Arbitration in Maritime Boundary Disputes', 1 (2002) *Law and Practice of International Courts and Tribunals* 257

Kazazi, M., *Burden of Proof and Related Issues: A Study on Evidence Before International Tribunals*, The Hague, 1996

Kellor, F., and Hatvany, A., *Security Against War*, vol. II, *Arbitration, Disarmament, Outlawry*, New York, 1924

Kelly, A. H., and Harbison, W. A., *The American Constitution: Its Origins and Development*, New York, 1963

Kelly, J. B., *Eastern Arabian Frontiers*, London, 1964

King, L. W., and Hall, H. R. H., *Egypt and Western Asia in the Light of Recent Discoveries*, London, 1907

Kirkham, D. B., 'The International Legal Status of Formosa', 6 (1968) CYIL 144

Krishna Rao, K., 'The Sino-Indian Boundary Question and International Law', 11 (1962) ICLQ 375

Lachs, M., 'Arbitration and International Adjudication', in Soons, A. H. A. (ed.), *International Arbitration: Past and Prospects*, Dordrecht, 1990, p. 37

Lamb, A., *The China–India Border: The Origins of the Disputed Boundaries*, London and Oxford, 1964

'The Sino-Pakistani Boundary Agreement of 2 March 1963', 18 (1964) *Australian Outlook* 299

The McMahon Line, London, 1966

Asian Frontiers: Studies in a Continuing Problem, London, 1968

Lankosz, K., 'Beagle Channel', 12 (1972) *Encyclopaedia of Public International Law* 53

Latham Brown, D. J., 'The Ethiopia–Somaliland Frontier Dispute', 5 (1956) ICLQ 245

Lauterpacht, E., 'River Boundaries: Legal Aspects of the Shatt al Arab Frontier', 9 (1960) ICLQ 208

'Whatever Happened to the Beagle Channel Award?', in *Melanges Virally: Le droit international au service de la paix, de la justice et du developpement*, Paris, 1991, p. 359, p. 359

Lauterpacht, H., 'Restrictive Interpretation and the Principle of Effectiveness in the Interpretation of Treaties', 26 (1949) BYIL 48

The Development of International Law by the International Court, 2nd edn, London, 1958

Lawrence, T. J., and Winfield, P. H., *The Principles of International Law*, 7th edn by P. H. Winfield, London, 1928

League of Nations, *Procès-Verbaux of the Proceedings of the Advisory Committee of Jurists, June 16th–July 24th, 1920 with Annexes*, The Hague, 1920

The Records of the First Assembly, Plenary Meetings, Geneva, 1920

'Minutes of the Twenty-Seventh and Twenty-Eighth Sessions of the Council of the League of Nations, 1923–1924', 5 (1924) *League of Nations Official Journal*

League of Nations, Permanent Court of International Justice, *Documents Concerning the Action Taken by the Council of the League of Nations under Article 14 of the Covenant and the Adoption by the Assembly of the Statute of the Permanent Court (Not Including Material Collected for, or the Minutes of, the Advisory Committee of Jurists)*, Geneva, 1921

Lester, A. P., 'State Succession to Treaties in the Commonwealth', 12 (1963) ICLQ 475
Li, T. T., 'The Legal Position of Tibet', 50 (1956) AJIL 394
Lindley, M. F., *The Acquisition and Government of Backward Territory in International Law*, New York, 1926
Liu, X., *The Sino-Indian Border Dispute and Sino-Indian Relations*, Lanham, MD, 1994
Lowe, V., 'Res Judicata and the Rule of Law in International Arbitration', 8 (1996) *African Journal of International and Comparative* Law 38
Lowe V., and Fitzmaurice, M. (eds.), *Fifty Years of the International Court of Justice: Essays in Honour of Sir Robert Jennings*, Cambridge, 1996
Luard, E. (ed.), *The International Regulation of Frontier Disputes*, London, 1970
Malcolm, N., *Kosovo: A Short History*, London, 1998
Manning, W. R. (ed.), *Arbitration Treaties Among the American Nations to the Close of the Year 1910*, New York, 1924
Marston, G., 'The Stability of Land and Sea Boundary Delimitations in International Law', in Blake, G. (ed.), *Maritime Boundaries*, vol. 5 of Blake, G. (general editor), *World Boundaries*, 5 vols., London, 1994, p. 144
Martens, F. de, 'International Arbitration and the Peace Conference at The Hague', 169 (1899) *North American Review* 604
McEwen, I., *The International Boundaries of East Africa*, Oxford, 1971
McLaughlin, A. C., *A Constitutional History of the United States*, New York, 1935
McNair, A. D., *The Law of Treaties*, Oxford, 1961
McWhinney, E., 'The International Court as Constitutional Court and the Blurring of the Arbitral/Judicial Processes', in Muller, S., and Mijs, W. (eds.), *The Flame Rekindled: New Hopes for International Arbitration*, Dordrecht, 1994, p. 81
Mendelson, M. H., 'Interim Measures of Protection in Cases of Contested Jurisdiction', 46 (1972–3) BYIL 259
Mendelson, M. H., and Hulton, S. C., 'The Iraq–Kuwait Boundary', 64 (1993) BYIL 135
Menon, P. K., 'Guyana–Venezuela Boundary Dispute', 6 (1972) *Encyclopaedia of Public International Law* 212
Merrills, J. G., 'Interim Measures of Protection and the Substantive Jurisdiction of the International Court', 36 (1977) *Cambridge Law Journal* 86
International Dispute Settlement, 3rd edn, London, 1998
'Reflections on the Incidental Jurisdiction of the International Court of Justice', in Evans, M. D. (ed.), *Remedies in International Law: The Institutional Dilemma*, Oxford, 1998, p. 51
'The International Court of Justice and the Adjudication of Territorial and Boundary Disputes', 13 (2000) *Leiden Journal of International Law* 873
Miasnikov, V. S., *The Ch'ing Empire and the Russian State in the 17th Century*, trans. Vic Schneirson, Moscow, 1980
Miner, C., *History of Wyoming in a Series of Letters*, Philadelphia, 1845
Miyoshi, M., *Considerations of Equity in the Settlement of Territorial and Boundary Disputes*, Dordrecht, 1993

Moore, J. B., *History and Digest of the International Arbitrations to Which the United States Has Been a Party*, Washington, DC, 1898

'Application of the Principle of International Arbitration on the American Continents', in Moore, J. B., *Collected Papers of John Bassett Moore in Seven Volumes*, vol. III, New Haven, 1944, p. 58

'Brazil and Peru Boundary Question: The Acre (Aquiry) Territory', in Moore, J. B., *Collected Papers of John Bassett Moore in Seven Volumes*, vol. III, New Haven, 1944, p. 120

'Memorandum on Uti Possidetis: Costa Rica–Panama Arbitration, 1911', in Moore, J. B., *The Collected Papers of John Bassett Moore in Seven Volumes*, vol. III, New Haven, 1944, p. 328

Moore, J. N. (ed.), *The Arab–Israeli Conflict*, Princeton, 1974

Morin, Y.-J., 'Les eaux territoriales du Canada au regard du droit international', 1 (1963) CYIL 82

'La zone de pêche exclusive du Canada', 2 (1964) CYIL 77

'Le progrès technique, la pollution et l'évolution récente du droit de la mer au Canada, particulièrement a l'égard de l'Arctique', 8 (1970) CYIL 158

Muir, R., 'The Iraq–Kuwait Border Dispute: Still a Factor for Instability?', 35 (2004) *Asian Affairs* 147

Muller, S., and Mijs, W. (eds.), *The Flame Rekindled: New Hopes for International Arbitration*, Dordrecht, 1994

Munkman, A. C. W., 'Adjudication and Adjustments – International Judicial Decision and the Settlement of Territorial and Boundary Disputes', 46 (1972–3) BYIL 1

Murty, B. S., 'Settlement of Disputes', in Sørensen, M. (ed.), *Manual of Public International Law*, London, 1968, p. 673

Murty, T. S., *India–China Boundary: India's Options*, New Delhi, 1987

Nelson, L. D. M., 'The Arbitration of Boundary Disputes in Latin America', 20 (1973) *Netherlands International Law Review* 267

'The Role of Equity in the Delimitation of Maritime Boundaries', 84 (1990) AJIL 837

Nussbaum, A., *A Concise History of the Law of Nations*, New York, 1947

Nyrop, R. F., and Smith, H. H., *Area Handbook for the Persian Gulf States*, Washington, DC, 1977

O'Connell, D. P., 'The Status of Formosa and the Chinese Recognition Problem', 50 (1956) AJIL 405

State Succession in Municipal and International Law, Cambridge, 1967

International Law, 2nd edn, London, 1970

Oellers-Frahm, K., 'Beagle Channel Arbitration', 1 (1972) *Encyclopaedia of Public International Law* 33

'Judicial and Arbitral Decisions', 1 (1972) *Encyclopaedia of Public International Law* 118

Olivier, M., 'Aspects of the Establishment of Sovereignty and the Transfer of

Government Authority', 14 (1988) *South African Yearbook of International Law* 85

Oppenheim, L., *Oppenheim's International Law*, 7th edn by H. Lauterpacht, London, 1955

Parry, C. (ed.), *A British Digest of International Law Compiled Principally from the Archives of the Foreign Office*, Part III, *Territory International Waterways Rights in Foreign Territory*, vol. 2b, London, 1967

Consolidated Treaty Series, Dobbs Ferry, NY, 1969

Permanent Court of International Justice, Advisory Committee of Jurists, *Documents Presented to the Committee Relating to Existing Plans for the Establishment of a Permanent Court of International Justice*, London, 1920

Pettisford, L., 'Guyana–Venezuela', in Calvert, P. (ed.), *Border and Territorial Disputes*, 4th edn, London, p. 117

Phillipson, C., *The International Law and Custom of Ancient Greece and Rome*, London, 1911

Pinto, M. C. W., 'The Prospects for International Arbitration: Inter-State Disputes', in Soons, A. H. A. (ed.), *International Arbitration: Past and Prospects*, Dordrecht, 1990, p. 63

'Structure, Process, Outcome: Thoughts on the Essence of International Arbitration', in Muller, S., and Mijs, W. (eds.), *A Flame Rekindled: New Hope for International Arbitration*, Dordrecht, 1994, p. 43

Plender, R., 'Procedure in the European Courts: Comparisons and Proposals', 267 (1997) *Hague Recueil* 9

Post, H., 'Adjudication as a Mode of Acquisition of Title to Territory: Some Observations on the Iraq–Kuwait Boundary Demarcation in Light of the Jurisprudence of the International Court of Justice', in Lowe V., and Fitzmaurice, M. (eds.), *Fifty Years of the International Court of Justice Essays in Honour of Sir Robert Jennings*, Cambridge, 1996, p. 237

Potter, L. G., and Sick, G. G. (eds.), *Iran, Iraq and the Legacies of War*, New York, 2004

Ralston, J. H., *The Law and Procedure of International Tribunals*, 2nd edn, Stanford, 1926

International Arbitration from Athens to Locarno, Stanford, 1929

Razvi, M., *The Frontiers of Pakistan*, Karachi, 1971

Reed, M. W., *Shore and Sea Boundaries*, Washington, DC, 2000

Reisman, 'Revision of the South West Africa Cases', 7 (1966) VJIL 1

Nullity and Revision, New Haven, 1971

Reuter, P., 'La motivation et la révision des sentences arbitrales à la Conference de la paix de La Haye (1899) et la conflit frontialier entre le Royaume-Uni et le Vénézuéla', in Ibler, V. (ed.), *Mélanges offerts a Juraj Andrassy: Essays in International Law in Honour of Juraj Andrassy*, The Hague, 1968, p. 237

Rosenne, S., *The International Court of Justice: An Essay in Political and Legal Theory*, Leyden, 1961

'Some Procedural Aspects of the English Channel Continental Shelf Arbitration', in *Essays in Honour of Erik Castren* (Finnish Branch of the International Law Association), Helsinki, 1979, p. 96

Procedure in the International Court: A Commentary on the 1978 Rules of the International Court of Justice, The Hague, 1983

'The International Court of Justice and International Arbitration', in Muller, S., and Mijs, W. (eds.), *A Flame Rekindled: New Hope for International Arbitration*, Dordrecht, 1994, p. 99

The Law and Practice of the International Court 1920–1996, vol. III, *Procedure*, The Hague, 1997

(ed.), *The Hague Peace Conferences of 1899 and 1907 and International Arbitration Reports and Documents*, The Hague, 2001

Rossi, C. R., *Equity and International Law: A Legal Realist Approach to International Decisionmaking*, Irvington, NY, 1993

Rubin, A. P., 'The Sino-Indian Border Dispute', 9 (1960) ICLQ 96

Sørensen, M. (ed.), *Manual of Public International Law*, London, 1968

Sadullah, M. M., *et al.* (eds.), *The Partition of the Punjab 1947: A Compilation of Official Documents*, Lahore, 1983

Sanders, P. (ed.), *International Arbitration: Liber Amicorum for Martin Domke*, The Hague, 1967

Sandifer, D., *Evidence Before International Tribunals*, 2nd edn, Charlottesville, VA, 1975

Savelle, M., *The Diplomatic History of the Canadian Boundary 1749–1763*, New Haven, 1940

Scelle, G., 'Report on Arbitral Procedure', UN Doc. A/CN.4/109, 1957, *Yearbook ILC*, 1957, vol. II, p. 1

'Final Report on Draft Articles on Arbitral Procedure', UN Doc. A/CN. 4/113, 1958, in *Yearbook ILC*, 1958, vol. II, p. 1

Scerni, M., 'La Procedure de la Cour permanente de Justice internationale', 65 (1938) *Hague Recueil* 672

Scheuner, U., 'Decisions Ex Aequo et Bono by International Courts and Arbitral Tribunals', in Sanders, P. (ed.), *International Arbitration: Liber Amicorum for Martin Domke*, The Hague, 1967, p. 275

Schindler, D., 'The Administration of Justice in the Swiss Federal Court in Intercantonal Disputes', 15 (1921) AJIL 149

Schlochauer, H. J., 'Arbitration', 1 (1972) *Encyclopaedia of Public International Law* 13

'The International Court of Justice', 2 (1972) *Encyclopaedia of Public International Law* 1084

Schnabel, A., and Thakur, R. (eds.), *Kosovo and the Challenge of Humanitarian Intervention: Selective Indignation, Collective Action and International Citizenship*, Tokyo, 2000

Schoenrich, O., 'The Venezuela–British Guiana Boundary Dispute', 43 (1949) AJIL 523

Schofield, R., 'Position, Function and Symbol: The Shatt al-Arab Dispute in Perspective', in Potter, L. G., and Sick, G. G. (eds.), *Iran, Iraq and the Legacies of War*, New York, 2004, p. 29

Schofield, R., and Blake, G., *Arabian Boundaries: Primary Documents 1853–1957*, vol. XIV, *Trucial Coast: Internal Boundaries, Archive Editions*, Farnham Common, 1988

Schreuer, C. H., 'The Brcko Award of 14 February 1997', 11 (1997) *Leiden Journal of International Law* 71

'The Brcko Final Award of 5 March 1999', 12 (1999) *Leiden Journal of International Law* 575

Schwarzenberger, G., *International Law* as *Applied by International Courts and Tribunals*, vol. II, *The Law of Armed Conflict*, London, 1968

Schwebel, S., *International Arbitration: Three Salient Problems*, Cambridge, 1987

'Concluding Observations', in Muller, S., and Mijs, W. (eds.), *A Flame Rekindled: New Hope for International Arbitration*, Dordrecht, 1994, p. 177

'The Majority Vote of an International Arbitral Tribunal', in Schwebel, S., *Justice in International Law: Selected Writings of Stephen M. Schwebel, Judge of the International Court of Justice*, Cambridge, 1994, p. 213

Schweisfurth, T., 'Boundary Disputes Between China and the USSR', 1 (1972) *Encyclopaedia of Public International Law* 49

Schwiesow, N., 'Mediation', in Luard, E. (ed.), *The International Regulation of Frontier Disputes*, London, 1970, p. 141

Scobbie, I., 'Res Judicata, Precedent and the International Court: A Preliminary Sketch', 20 (1999) *Australian Yearbook of International Law* 299

Scott, J. B. (ed.), *Resolutions of the Institute of International Law Dealing with the Law of Nations with an Historical Introduction and Explanatory Notes*, New York, 1916

(ed.), *The Proceedings of the Hague Peace Conferences: Translation of Official Texts: The Conference of 1899*, New York, 1920

The Project of a Permanent Court of International Justice and Resolutions of the Advisory Committee of Jurists, Washington, DC, 1920

(ed.), *The Proceedings of the Hague Peace Conferences: The Conference of 1907: Translation of the Official Texts*, New York, 1921

Sharma, S. P., 'The China–India Border Dispute: An Indian Perspective', 59 (1965) AJIL 16

Shaw, M., 'Territory in International Law', 13 (1982) NYIL 61

Title to Territory in Africa: International Legal Issues, Oxford, 1986

'The Heritage of States: The Principle of Uti Possidetis Juris Today', 67 (1996) BYIL 81

'Peoples, Territorialism and Boundaries', 3 (1997) EJIL 478

(ed.), *Title to Territory*, Dartmouth, 2005

Shihata, I. F. I., *The Power of the International Court to Determine Its Own Jurisdiction*, The Hague, 1965

Simpson, J. L., and Fox, H., *International Arbitration*, London, 1959

Smith, F., and Phillipson, C., *International Law*, 5th edn by Coleman Phillipson, London, 1918

Smith, M., 'China–Russia (Soviet Union)', in Calvert, P. (ed.), *Border and Territorial Disputes of the World*, 4th edn, London, 2004, p. 157

Sohn, L. B., 'Arbitration of International Disputes Ex Aequo et Bono', in Sanders, P., *International Arbitration: Liber Amicorum for Martin Domke*, The Hague, 1967, p. 330

'Settlement of Disputes Relating to the Interpretation and Application of Treaties', 150 (1976-II) *Hague Recueil* 195

Soons, A. H. A. (ed.), *International Arbitration: Past and Prospects*, Dordrecht, 1990

Spain, J. W., *The Way of the Pathans*, Oxford, 1962

Spate, O. H. K., 'The Partition of India and the Prospects of Pakistan', 38 (1948) *Geographical Review* 5

Stanczyk, J., 'Application for Interpretation of a Judgment Delivered by the International Court of Justice', 17 (1988) *Polish Yearbook of International Law* 193

Stone, J., *Legal Controls of International Conflict: A Treatise on the Dynamics of Disputes – and War – Law*, Sydney, 1959

'Peace and the Palestinians', in Moore, J. N. (ed.), *The Arab–Israeli Conflict*, Princeton, 1974, p. 581

Strupp, K., 'The Competence of the Mixed Arbitral Courts of the Treaty of Versailles', 17 (1923) AJIL 661

Strydom, H., 'Self-Determination: Its Use and Abuse', 17 (1991–2) *South African Yearbook of International Law* 90

Stuyt, A. M., *Survey of International Arbitrations 1794–1989*, 3rd edn, The Hague and Dordrecht, 1990

Tai Sung An, *The Sino-Soviet Territorial Dispute*, Philadelphia, 1973

Thirlway, H., 'The Law and Procedure of the International Court of Justice 1960–1989', 60 (1989) BYIL 1

'The Law and Procedure of the International Court of Justice 1960–1989 (Part Thirteen)', 74 (2003) BYIL 7

Tod, M. N., *International Arbitration Among the Greeks*, Oxford, 1913

Tyranowski, J., 'State Succession and Boundaries and Boundary Treaties', 10 (1979–80) *Polish Yearbook of International Law* 115

United Nations Secretariat, 'Commentary on the Draft Convention on Arbitral Procedure Adopted by the International Law Commission at its Fifth Session', UN Doc. A/CN.4/92, New York, 1955

Vallat, F. A., 'The Peaceful Settlement of Disputes', in *Cambridge Essays in International Law: Essays in Honour of Lord McNair*, London, 1965, p. 115

Van Eekelen, W. F., *India Foreign Policy and the Border Dispute with China*, The Hague, 1967

Vander Linden, H., 'Alexander VI. and the Demarcation of the Maritime and

Colonial Domains of Spain and Portugal, 1493–1494', 22 (1916) *American Historical Review* 1

Vattel, E. de, *The Law of Nations or the Principles of Natural Law Applied to the Conduct and to the Affairs of Nations and of Sovereigns*, 1758, trans. C. G. Fenwick, Carnegie Institution, Washington, DC, 1915

Vertzberger, Y. Y. I., *Misperceptions in Foreign Policymaking the Sino-Indian Conflict, 1959–1962*, Boulder, CO, 1984

China's Southwestern Strategy: Encirclement and Counterencirclement, New York, 1985

Verzijl, J. H. W., *International Law in Historical Perspective*, Part VIII, *Inter-State Disputes and their Settlement*, Leyden, 1976

Von der Heydte, F. A. F., 'Discovery, Symbolic Annexation and the Virtual Effectiveness of International Law', 29 (1935) AJIL 448

Wainhouse, D. W., *et al.*, *International Peace Observation: A History and Forecast*, Baltimore, 1966

Waldock, C. H. M. (ed.), *International Disputes: The Legal Aspects: Report of a Study Group of the David Davies Memorial Institute of International Studies*, London, 1972

Warbrick, C. J., 'The Boundary Between England and Scotland in the Solway Firth', 51 (1980) BYIL 163

Watts, A., *The International Law Commission 1949–1998*, Oxford, 1999

Wehberg, H., *The Problem of an International Court of Justice*, trans. C. G. Fenwick, Oxford, 1918

Westermann, W. L., 'Interstate Arbitration in Antiquity', 2 (1906–7) *Classical Journal* 197

Wetter, J. G., 'Analysis and Conclusion: Arbitration Itself is on Trial Here', in Wetter, J. G. (ed.), *The International Arbitral Process: Public and Private*, New York, 1979, p. 333

The International Arbitral Process: Public and Private, New York, 1979

Whiteman, M., *Digest of International Law*, Washington, DC, 1964

Wickham Legg, L. G., *British Diplomatic Instructions 1689–1789*, vol. VII, *France, Part IV, 1745–1789*, London, 1934

Williams, J. F., 'The Permanence of Treaties', 22 (1928) AJIL 89

Woolsey, L. H., 'Boundary Disputes in Latin America', 25 (1931) AJIL 324

'The Arbitration of the Sabotage Claims Against Germany', 33 (1939) AJIL 737

'The Sabotage Claims against Germany', 34 (1940) AJIL 23

'Litigation of the Sabotage Claims Against Germany', 35 (1941) AJIL 282

Wright, Q., 'The Chinese Recognition Problem', 49 (1955) AJIL 320

Zimmermann, A., *Interpretation of Judgments of the International Court of Justice under Article 60 of the Statute*, Tübingen, 1989

Zipp, K. E., 'Original Jurisdiction of the United States Supreme Court in Suits Between States', 68 L Ed 2d 969

Zoller, E., 'Observations sur la revision et l'interpretation des sentences arbitrales', 24 (1978) *Annuaire francais de droit europeen* 331

Index

CAMBRIDGE STUDIES IN INTERNATIONAL AND COMPARATIVE LAW

Books in the series

The Protection of Cultural Property in Armed Conflict
Roger O'Keefe

Interpretation and Revision of International Boundary Decisions
Kaiyan Homi Kaikobad

Multinationals and Corporate Social Responsibility
Limitations and Opportunities in International Law
Jennifer A. Zerk

Judiciaries within Europe
A Comparative Review
John Bell

Law in Times of Crisis
Emergency Powers in Theory and Practice
Oren Gross and Fionnuala Ní Aoláin

Vessel-Source Marine Pollution
The Law and Politics of International Regulation
Alan Tan

Enforcing Obligations Erga Omnes *in International Law*
Christian J. Tams

Non-Governmental Organisations in International Law
Anna-Karin Lindblom

Democracy, Minorities and International Law
Steven Wheatley

Prosecuting International Crimes
Selectivity and the International Law Regime
Robert Cryer

Compensation for Personal Injury in English, German and Italian Law
A Comparative Outline
Basil Markesinis, Michael Coester, Guido Alpa, Augustus Ullstein

Dispute Settlement in the UN Convention on the Law of the Sea
Natalie Klein

The International Protection of Internally Displaced Persons
Catherine Phuong

Imperialism, Sovereignty and the Making of International Law
Anthony Anghie

Necessity, Proportionality and the Use of Force by States
Judith Gardam

International Legal Argument in the Permanent Court of International Justice
The Rise of the International Judiciary
Ole Spiermann

Great Powers and Outlaw States
Unequal Sovereigns in the International Legal Order
Gerry Simpson

Local Remedies in International Law
C. F. Amerasinghe

Reading Humanitarian Intervention
Human Rights and the Use of Force in International Law
Anne Orford

Conflict of Norms in Public International Law
How WTO Law Relates to Other Rules of Law
Joost Pauwelyn

Transboundary Damage in International Law
Hanqin Xue

European Criminal Procedures
Edited by Mireille Delmas-Marty and John Spencer

The Accountability of Armed Opposition Groups in International Law
Leisbeth Zegveld

Sharing Transboundary Resources
International Law and Optimal Resource Use
Eyal Benvenisti

International Human Rights and Humanitarian Law
René Provost

Remedies Against International Organisations
Karel Wellens

Diversity and Self-Determination in International Law
Karen Knop

The Law of Internal Armed Conflict
Lindsay Moir

International Commercial Arbitration and African States
Practice, Participation and Institutional Development
Amazu A. Asouzu

The Enforceability of Promises in European Contract Law
James Gordley

International Law in Antiquity
David J. Bederman

Money Laundering
A New International Law Enforcement Model
Guy Stessens

Good Faith in European Contract Law
Reinhard Zimmermann and Simon Whittaker

On Civil Procedure
J. A. Jolowicz

Trusts
A Comparative Study
Maurizio Lupoi

The Right to Property in Commonwealth Constitutions
Tom Allen

International Organizations Before National Courts
August Reinisch

The Changing International Law of High Seas Fisheries
Francisco Orrego Vicuña

Trade and the Environment
A Comparative Study of EC and US Law
Damien Geradin

Unjust Enrichment
A Study of Private Law and Public Values
Hanoch Dagan

Religious Liberty and International Law in Europe
Malcolm D. Evans

Ethics and Authority in International Law
Alfred P. Rubin

Sovereignty Over Natural Resources
Balancing Rights and Duties
Nico Schrijver

The Polar Regions and the Development of International Law
Donald R. Rothwell

Fragmentation and the International Relations of Micro-States
Self-determination and Statehood
Jorri Duursma

Principles of the Institutional Law of International Organizations
C. F. Amerasinghe